MW01223209

GIANGALEAZZO VISCONTI

GIANGALEAZZO VISCONTI

From a drawing by Pisanello *in the* Louvre

Photo Giraudon

Giangaleazzo Visconti

DUKE OF MILAN
(1351–1402)

*A study in the political career
of an Italian despot*

BY

D. M. BUENO DE MESQUITA, M.A., Ph.D.

*Fellow of Corpus Christi College
Cambridge*

CAMBRIDGE
AT THE UNIVERSITY PRESS
1941

To

MY GODMOTHER

MRS DANIEL FINZI

IN GRATITUDE

CAMBRIDGE UNIVERSITY PRESS
Cambridge, New York, Melbourne, Madrid, Cape Town,
Singapore, São Paulo, Delhi, Tokyo, Mexico City

Cambridge University Press
The Edinburgh Building, Cambridge CB2 8RU, UK

Published in the United States of America by Cambridge University Press, New York

www.cambridge.org
Information on this title: www.cambridge.org/9780521234559

© Cambridge University Press 1941

This publication is in copyright. Subject to statutory exception
and to the provisions of relevant collective licensing agreements,
no reproduction of any part may take place without the written
permission of Cambridge University Press.

First published 1941
First paperback edition 2011

A catalogue record for this publication is available from the British Library

ISBN 978-0-521-23455-9 Paperback

Cambridge University Press has no responsibility for the persistence or
accuracy of URLs for external or third-party internet websites referred to in
this publication, and does not guarantee that any content on such websites is,
or will remain, accurate or appropriate.

CONTENTS

ILLUSTRATIONS

PLATE

PREFACE

The name of Giangaleazzo Visconti pervades the story of Italy at the end of the *Trecento*. The sphere of his activities and intrigues spread far beyond the peninsula. Italy was the centre of civilization, and Rome once again the focal point of the Western Church. The Moors still had a foothold in Spain, and the Turks, turning the flanks of Constantinople, were hammering at the doors of Hungary. When the Papacy was split in twain, the Emperor-elect a hopeless drunkard and the King of France a madman, the ruler of the rich and fertile plain of Lombardy held a key to the situation of a continent. He guarded the passes between Italy and the north.

Giangaleazzo Visconti, the wealthiest prince and most subtle politician in Europe, was not unequal to his opportunities. There was scarcely a chronicler in Europe who failed to record his fame. His ambitions shaped the destiny of every part of Italy. His name can hardly fail to appear in the records of European diplomacy. Yet no full account of his life has yet been published.

This record of Giangaleazzo's political career is intended to fill the gap. The carefully accumulated documents of his Chanceries were lost when the *Castello* of Milan was razed to the ground, in the first enthusiasm of liberty which ushered in the short-lived Ambrosian Republic. This misfortune at once explains the lack of a biography, and presents the main difficulty of the task. The walls of the palace buried in their fall the secrets of that mind, the guiding purpose which directed the threads of his policy. We must resort to indirect evidence, to pick up those threads. We must rely on the documents of other governments, making allowance for their different points of view, their inevitable bias.

The material of this kind already published would form the basis of a bulky volume; but it deals unevenly with the various aspects of Giangaleazzo Visconti's policy and the different periods of his life. I have supplemented it, wherever possible, from the unpublished sources which I was able to find within the limits of the time at my disposal in Italy.

I cannot claim to have done more than skim the surface of the available material. My account of Giangaleazzo's administrative system is no more than a brief summary based on the researches and conclusions of other writers. The Archives of Lombardy and of the other regions of Italy afford a wide scope for further investigation.

My object has been twofold: to set the life of Giangaleazzo Visconti within the political framework of his time, and to read his character and ambitions in the light of the evidence that is available. The old strictures, based on the hostile propaganda of Florence, stand discredited, and a new interpretation of the forces at work during the period has brought a reversal of judgment; but this is largely a revaluation of the old evidence. I have tried to present him neither as a monster who delighted in every form of treachery and vice, nor as a single-minded patriot deliberately seeking to anticipate the work of centuries. He was a man with human faults, ambitious, full of double-dealing, liable to error and miscalculation. He must bear his share of responsibility for the chaos and conflicts of his age. But he did not create them. And he was not without virtues—a sense of duty towards his subjects, a capacity for affection, and perhaps a more fundamental understanding of the needs of his country than any of his contemporaries. His world was not entirely dominated by the omnipresence of violence and brute force; it is possible to trace in his reign a stable idea of government, an emphasis on juridical rights, and the steady working of economic forces. Much remains to be learnt of these and other fields. But if I have succeeded in offering a sane and justly balanced picture of the man and his political achievement, derived without preconceptions from the sources at my disposal, I shall have attained my purpose. And it is in the hope that such a framework may be not without its value, both to those who would know something of the greatest of the Italian despots and to those who will open up the new fields, that I offer this book, with all its faults, to the reader.

My attention was first drawn to the absence of any monograph on Giangaleazzo Visconti, by Professor C. W. Previté-Orton. Since that day, nearly six years ago, I have been privileged to enjoy his constant interest and help, and to have the benefit of his suggestions on many points. While the opinions expressed are always my own, I hope that the standards of scholarship may not be found too unworthy of the master to whom this book and its author owe so great a debt.

My thanks are also due to Miss C. M. Ady and to Professor E. R. P. Vincent for some helpful criticisms offered when the book was in an early stage. I am deeply grateful to those Italian scholars who did me the honour of discussing my work with me while I was in Italy, and pre-eminently to the late Professor Romolo Caggese of Milan. The unfailing courtesy of the directors and officials of the State Archives in Milan, Florence, Siena, Venice and Mantua, and of the *Bibliothèque Nationale* in Paris, considerably lightened the task of my researches. I am indebted to Mr S. Breglia for his assistance in interpreting some difficult passages of fourteenth-century Italian in the documents.

Without the encouragement and assistance of the Master and Fellows of Corpus Christi College, Cambridge, this book could never have been written; to them, finally, I must record a profound and lasting obligation.

D. M. B. de M.

April 1940

I have been unable to attend fully to the final stages of publication of this book. I should like to express my gratitude to those members of the staff of the University Press on whose assistance I have depended, and whose minute care has eliminated many slips and inaccuracies.

Birmingham, September 1940

LIST OF ABBREVIATIONS
used in the footnotes and bibliography

ARCHIVES:

ASF.	Florence, Regio Archivio di Stato.
ASMa.	Mantua, Regio Archivio di Stato: Archivio Gonzaga.
ASS.	Siena, Regio Archivio di Stato.
ASV.	Venice, Regio Archivio di Stato.

PERIODICALS AND COLLECTIONS OF WORKS:

AAA.	Atti della Imperiale Reale Accademia di scienze lettere ed arti degli Agiati in Rovereto.
AAT.	Atti della Reale Accademia di scienze lettere ed arti di Torino.
AIV.	Atti del Reale Istituto Veneto di scienze lettere ed arti.
AMM.	Atti e memorie della Reale Deputazione di storia patria per le provincie Modonesi e Parmensi.
AMR.	Atti e memorie della Reale Deputazione di storia patria per le provincie di Romagna.
ASI.	Archivio Storico Italiano (Florence).
ASL.	Archivio Storico Lombardo (Milan).
ASN.	Archivio Storico per le provincie Napolitane.
BEC.	Bibliothèque de l'École des Chartes (Paris).
BSBS.	Bollettino Storico-bibliografico Subalpino (Pinerolo).
BSCr.	Bollettino Storico Cremonese.
BSP.	Bollettino della Società Pavese di storia patria.
BSSP.	Bollettino Senese di storia patria.
DET.	Delizie degli eruditi Toscani (ed. Ildefonso di San Luigi).
MAH.	Mélanges d'Archéologie et d'Histoire (École française à Rome).
MAT.	Memorie della Reale Accademia di scienze lettere ed arti di Torino.
MSF.	Memorie storiche Forogiulesi (Bullettino del R. Museo di Cividale).
MSI.	Miscellanea di Storia Italiana (Turin, Deputazione di storia patria).
NAV.	Nuovo Archivio Veneto.
NRS.	Nuova Rivista Storica (Milan).
(NS.	Nuova serie.)
RIS.	Rerum Italicarum Scriptores (ed. Muratori; *RIS,* NS refers to the new edition in process of publication).
RQH.	Revue des questions historiques (Paris).
RSAT.	Rivista Storica degli Archivi Toscani (Florence).
RSI.	Rivista Storica Italiana.
RTA.	Deutsche Reichstagsakten (ed. Julius Weizsäcker).
SS.	Studi Storici (Pisa and Pavia).

"Galeas, seigneur de Milan, qui ailleurs nommé vous ay, noble chevalier et bel et sagez et malicieuz."

TOMMASO III, Marquis of Saluzzo, *Le livre du Chevalier errant*

> "Of Melan grete Barnabo Viscounte,
> God of delyt, and scourge of Lumbardie,
> Why sholde I nat thyn infortune acounte
> Sith in estaat thow clombe were so hye?
> Thy brother sone, that was thy double allye,
> For he thy nevew was, and sone-in-lawe,
> With-inne his prisoun made thee to dye;
> But why, ne how, noot I that thou were slawe."

GEOFFREY CHAUCER, *The Monk's Tale*

"Jehan Galiace, le premier de ce nom en la maison de Milan, ung grant et mauvais tirant, mais honourable toutesfoiz....Et un natif de Bourge le m'appella sainct, et je luy demanday pourquoy...il me respondit bas: 'nous appellons, en ce pais icy, sainctz tous ceulx qui nous font du bien.'"

PHILIPPE DE COMMYNES, *Mémoires sub anno* 1494

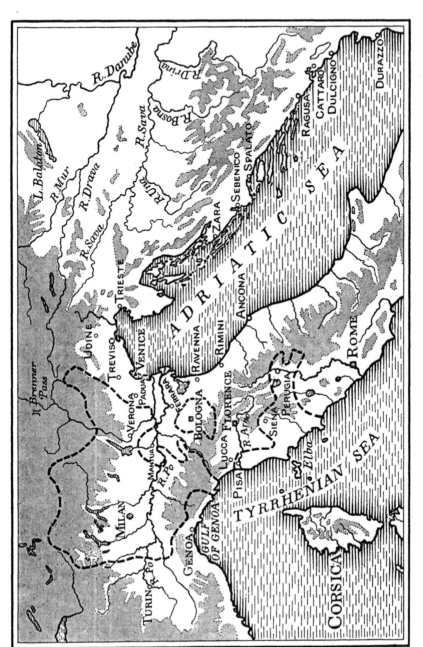

MAP I. Northern and Central Italy, showing the territories of Giangaleazzo in 1402
Land over 3000 feet is shaded

CHAPTER I

ITALY IN THE FOURTEENTH CENTURY.
THE GROWTH OF THE VISCONTI STATE

The fourteenth century marked the close of the great epoch of the Italian Communes: the passing of communal independence in Lombardy, its decline in Tuscany. The proud cities which had boldly defied and bravely resisted the might of the Empire, the wrath of Barbarossa and the swift hand of Frederick II, fell victims to a lesser but more insidious prey. An internal cancer killed the spirit of liberty which had defied the power of Germany.

Institutions and traditions were disintegrating throughout Europe. Italy was no longer the battlefield for the conflict of supra-national principles of government based on the doctrines of the medieval Church. The last of the Hohenstaufen had met his death in the public square of Naples, at the hands of the executioner. The Popes dwelt far away in Avignon, entangled in the struggles and ambitions of the French monarchs, their self-appointed hosts. The great conflict had played itself out, and neither Empire nor Papacy, neither Germans nor Italians, reaped the harvest. The ideas of Frederick II and of Innocent III left a legacy in the teaching of jurists, in the literature of the last schoolmen and the first humanists. But they had lost the power of practical application; beneath the sanction of time-worn phrases, the ferment of political experiment prepared the way for a new order. In France and England, national unity was advancing slowly under the stress of war; while Italy, relieved of her burden, turned to face the future with the abundant vitality of her own political life.

That future depended on the development of northern Italy. In the south, the power of the Angevin rulers of Naples—titular kings "of Sicily and Jerusalem"—was limited by the feudal system which, firmly implanted by the Normans two centuries before, survived to guarantee the immunities of the baronage;

and the Angevins aggravated their own weakness by consistently lavishing the resources of the "Regno", as their Neapolitan dominion was called, in vain efforts to recover Sicily from their Aragonese rivals, who had held the island since the Sicilian Vespers. Chaos reigned in central Italy in the absence of the Popes. The States of the Church fell a prey to the turbulent greed of the local nobility; and those Communes which were strong enough to defy the lawlessness of the nobles asserted their independence even of Papal authority. Rome, stripped of her glory, declined into poverty and desolation; and the Patrimony of St Peter became a desert and a refuge for brigands.

Even in the north, the future was clouded and uncertain. The independent city Republics were bitterly divided in and among themselves. The rapidly expanding commercial organizations required to free themselves from the shackles of a proud feudal order; but issues of local jealousy and of party tradition hampered their efforts. The struggles of conflicting interests and classes, the survival of old family feuds, the bitter names of Guelf and Ghibelline, the elements of personal ambition and greed, composed the incredibly intricate kaleidoscope of everyday life in a Lombard city. Often these interests cut across one another; and in the confusion that ensued, the party symbols, which were retained as old familiar things are retained, lost their early significance. The process will be found at work in Milan, where the leading Ghibelline family took upon itself the task of safeguarding the interests and promoting the development of the city's industrial and commercial middle class.

The Republic of Milan dominated the wide plain of Lombardy between the Alps and the Apennines. The city had grown rich in the fertility of its well-irrigated lands. It stood at the natural meeting-place of great trade routes—up and down the valley of the Po, over the Alps to Germany and across the Apennines to the port of Genoa—and in a strategical position between the mountains and the Po, between Ticino and Adda. It inherited the glories of an ancient past—as capital of the western Empire in the dichotomy introduced by Diocletian, as guardian of the traditions of St Ambrose and challenger of the ecclesiastical authority of Rome in the Dark Ages. The Commune defied Barbarossa, and outlived his vengeance to lead the allies of the Papacy in their resistance to Frederick II. Milan, in fact, played a leading part in the political and economic life of Italy. Her industries were flourishing, her manufactures of armour and cloth far-famed; her merchants and bankers were making a place for themselves in the commerce and finance of western Europe. But the clash of fully developed organizations within the city retarded the growth of prosperity. The quarrels of the great Ghibelline and Guelf families, the "Motta" of the lesser nobility and the wealthier citizens, the "Credenza" of the gilds, held the city in terror and uncertainty. The citizens of Milan who lived by the arts of peace sought a leader and protector. Only the class whose pretensions they were determined to fight could help them; and the price they had to pay was not small. Gradually, under the della Torre and the Visconti, the protector became a master.

Ottone Visconti, Archbishop of Milan at the end of the thirteenth century, may be called the architect of Milanese despotism. Having driven out the rival family of della Torre, he consolidated his authority by a revival of the old archiepiscopal rights; and, by establishing his nephew, Matteo the Great, as Captain of the People within the framework of municipal institutions, he was able to transmit that authority to his own heir.[1] Matteo, after an exile of ten years during which the della Torre ruled in Milan, renewed the fortunes of his house. Henceforth he held the joint office of Captain General for life, and of Imperial Vicar. This dual authority formed the juridical basis upon which the Visconti built their power, growing steadily more absolute throughout the fourteenth century. In 1317, while Habsburg and Wittelsbach fought to assert their rival claims to the Empire, Matteo temporarily surrendered the office of Imperial Vicar, and assumed the title of Lord of Milan; and after a further eclipse of the fortunes of the Visconti, Azzone who restored and Luchino who extended the tumbled edifice of Visconti power, enjoyed the fuller authority

[1] Visconti, *Storia di Milano*, 237–9.

represented in their title of "Dominus". There was now a "dominium", a "signoria", a "lordship"; and in 1349 the General Council of Milan conferred the title on the heirs of Matteo the Great as a perpetual hereditary right.

The Roman Emperor, in so far as his policy in Italy did not conflict with theirs, habitually confirmed the authority of the Visconti. The Peace of Constance reserved certain rights and privileges to the nominal overlord of the Italian Communes; the Emperors transferred the exercise of these rights, with the title of Imperial Vicar, to the despots who established themselves in northern Italy, and who in practice admitted no limitations to their power. But the office could be, and was on more than one occasion, revoked. The Visconti, while they ruled with the constitutional consent of their subjects, were also officials of the Emperor; and they did not relish the uncertainty which bound them, in so far as they valued that form of legitimation, to the Italian ambitions of a German prince. The fundamental weakness of the despots, however, lay in the absence of an incontrovertible claim to authority; and it was typical of the Visconti, so long as their practical interests were not in danger, to ensure for themselves every possible juridical title.[1]

The roots of their power lay deeper in the economic and political needs of their dominions. Matteo I identified his policy with the interests of the "borghesia", the wealthy middle class of Milan.[2] He offered them the assurance of internal harmony, to safeguard their industries and secure their profits. The expansion of his state afforded protection for their commerce along the trade routes of Italy, and commanded the respect of unscrupulous barons and arbitrary princes who might be tempted to prey on their helplessness.[3] These two principles represent the administrative and political aspects of the government of the Visconti.

[1] For the juridical authority of the Visconti, *v.* Sickel, "Vicariat der Visconti", in *Sitzungsberichte der Kaiserlichen Akademie der Wissenschaften*: Philosophisch-Historische Classe, vol. xxx (Vienna, 1859). More briefly in Salzer, "Anfänge der Signorie", 117–20.
[2] Cognasso, "Note e Documenti sulla formazione dello Stato Visconteo", *BSP* xxiii 23–31.
[3] Romano, "Guerra tra i Visconti e la Chiesa", *BSP* iii 420–1.

Amid the most bizarre episodes of personal pride and ferocity, they are never entirely obscured. Authority, dominion and renown steadily accumulated on the basis of this domestic alliance.

Other factors besides the impulse of Milanese trade favoured the elimination of the smaller city-states. The Communes, impoverished by the burdens implicit in their particularism, could scarcely carry on the business of government; competition and the policy of protection in England and France had checked the tide of economic prosperity, and the "Contado", the rural dominions of the Commune and foundation of the Commune's welfare, was exhausted by unscrupulous financial exploitation.[1] The deadly feuds of party and class, with the appendant system of wholesale proscription, and the riotous instincts of the nobility in town and countryside, hastened the degeneration of Communal government. Political exiles were prepared to sell their city's freedom as the price of revenge. Many citizens who stood outside these feuds were not unwilling to submit to a lord who had the power and the interest to reconcile, outwardly at least, the contending factions.[2] As early as 1317, Lombard clerics were openly expressing the opinion that Lombardy would never find peace "nisi habuerint regem unum proprium et naturalem dominum qui non sit barbare nationis et regnum eius continuet naturalis posteritas successiva". The country needed a natural lord, and one whose heirs could succeed him unchallenged. The power of the Visconti lay not so much in their dynastic strength as in the sentiments expressed in this comment.[3] Driven forward by the need for trade outlets and markets, welcomed as the

---

[1] Cognasso, "Note e Documenti", *BSP* XXIII 37 *sqq.* For the exhaustion of the Contado at the beginning of the Trecento, *v.* Caggese, *Classi e Comuni Rurali*, II 365–82. Even under the more unified system of the Quattrocento, the extravagance of political particularism prevented Italy from gaining the full benefit of her rich economic opportunities; Pieri, *Crisi militare italiana nel Rinascimento*, 103.

[2] By reconciling the divisions of a newly acquired city, the conqueror would free himself from too great a dependence on the party by whose aid he gained power: Salzer, *op. cit.* 212–13. The Visconti regularly adopted this policy: Cognasso, "Note e Documenti", *BSP* XXIII 68 *sqq.*

[3] *Ibid.* 25–6; Romano, "Niccolò Spinelli", *ASN* XXVI 495 note 2.

heralds of internal peace, the Visconti fulfilled the dynastic ambitions of their house in the creation of a Lombard state: retaining by the interested wisdom of their administration what they gained by a skilful and unscrupulous diplomacy.

By the middle of the fourteenth century, the rulers of Milan dominated the politics of northern Italy. They had helped to frustrate the attempts of every prince or adventurer who sought to turn the lingering traditions of Italian unity to his own advantage: the Imperial schemes of Henry VII and John of Bohemia; the Guelf alliance of Robert of Naples and Pope John XXII; the ambitions of the native ruler of Verona, Mastino della Scala, who acquired a strip of territory, strategically too long and too narrow, from the Mark of Treviso to the Tuscan coast. And with every step they added to their own dominions. Their territories formed a square block, firmly wedged between the Alps and the Apennines. From Como, they controlled the most important passes of the Alps west of the Brenner: the Gotthard and Lukmanier, the Splügen and Septimer. Their lands in the lower valley of the Ossola approached the foot of the Simplon pass. Luchino in 1347-8 cut deeply into the south-western corner of Piedmont as far as Cuneo, along the northern slope of the Ligurian Alps. The surrender of Bobbio unlocked a door into Liguria, and Pontremoli commanded the road through the Lunigiana to Tuscany. They ruled as far east as Parma and Cremona in the valley of the Po, and the Brescian shore of the Lake of Garda beneath the shadow of the Alps.[1]

Giovanni Visconti, Archbishop of Milan, transformed the Visconti state in five years from a Lombard into an Italian power.[2] He bought Bologna from the sons of Taddeo Pepoli, and defied the outraged anger of the Pope, the nominal overlord of the city.

---

[1] Azzone (1329–1339) and Luchino (1339–1349) gradually recovered the ground that had been lost during the eclipse of the family fortunes in the years 1322–1328. The accompanying Map, which shows the inheritance of Bernabò and Galeazzo Visconti in 1355, gives the dates at which the cities were reacquired.

[2] 1349–1354. He had held joint authority since 1339 with his brother Luchino, who appears, however, to have been mainly responsible for the direction of policy during his lifetime.

MAP II. The inheritance of Bernabò and Galeazzo Visconti in 1355

The dates in brackets indicate the year in which the cities were acquired
or recovered by Azzo, Luchino and Giovanni Visconti

Milan and Genoa were held jointly

He accepted the lordship of Genoa, and helped the Ligurian port, exhausted by exceptionally virulent internal feuds, to avenge a recent defeat at the hands of Venice. He married one of his nephews to a daughter of Mastino della Scala, another to a sister of the Count of Savoy; and when he died in 1354, his lands were divided between them in such a way as to afford the greatest possible scope for each to utilize his dynastic connections.[1]

Galeazzo Visconti, who had married Blanche of Savoy, inherited that part of his uncle's dominions which lay westwards from the Adda. In the reaction which followed Archbishop Giovanni's death, Genoa recovered her independence; and Cardinal Albornoz, who succeeded in restoring some semblance of order and unity to the States of the Church, brought Bologna once more under the dominion of the Pope. The Visconti never reconciled themselves to the loss of these cities, which were of such immense strategic and commercial importance to their dominions; and we shall find the themes of Genoa and Bologna constantly recurring throughout the story of this period. So it fell to Galeazzo to restore the position of his family in Piedmont and to reassert their authority in Genoa, while his brother Bernabò, who had married Regina della Scala, devoted his boundless energy to the recovery of Bologna.

Galeazzo's first step was to subdue Pavia, whose lands cut the main road from Milan to Genoa and formed a deep wedge driven into Visconti territory towards Milan. The city surrendered in 1359, after an heroic resistance inspired by the friar Jacopo Bussolari; and Galeazzo soon established his court at Pavia, leaving Bernabò in practical possession of Milan. The two brothers never allowed any grave breach to appear between them; but their temperaments were so different that the separation probably saved them from embarrassment. Different traditions began to appear at the courts of Pavia and Milan; and Galeazzo, turning away from the brutal necessities of the Middle Ages, laid

---

[1] I refer directly to the re-division of lands between Bernabò and Galeazzo after the death of their brother Matteo II in 1355: *v.* Map. Matteo's portion had been in the south-east—Bologna, Lodi, Piacenza, Bobbio and Pontremoli.

the foundations of a more graceful court, a prototype of Renaissance life.

The coalitions of this period were directed against the Visconti. The lesser despots of eastern Lombardy had learnt to fear this mighty neighbour. Neither the Popes nor the Florentine Republic wished to see Bologna fall again under Milanese dominion. While Bernabò met the danger from this side as best he could, Galeazzo alternated between rapid success and startling reverses in the west. His brother-in-law Amadeus VI, Count of Savoy, held the key of Piedmontese politics. His ambitions were ultimately bound to bring him into conflict with the Visconti; but between them lay the little state of Montferrat, curving away to the southwest from its apex on the Po at Valenza and Casale; and both hoped to profit from the weakness of Montferrat. Amadeus was prepared to use diplomacy to attain his object, if the occasion permitted; but he was not prepared to stand aside and watch the collapse of Montferrat under Galeazzo's attacks. In 1370, Galeazzo captured the Montferrine towns of Valenza and Casale. Giovanni II of Montferrat, who had struggled gallantly for thirty years against the Visconti on one side and Savoy on the other, died early in 1372. He named his old enemy Amadeus co-regent with a German adventurer, Otto of Brunswick, for his four young sons. Amadeus saw the chance of gaining control of Montferrat, and at the same time of driving the Visconti out of Piedmont. He accepted the regency, and joined forces with Bernabò's enemies in the south and east, to destroy the power of the Visconti.

In 1373, the Visconti survived one of the gravest crises of their history. The Emperor deprived them of their Vicariate. Amadeus marched to the gates of Pavia, ravaged the territory of Milan, and routed Galeazzo's army. A Papal force with Florentine support entered Bernabò's lands from Bologna. The Guelf nobles of the *Parmense*, the *Piacentino* and the *Pavese* rebelled under the protection of the invading army. The revolt spread to the *Bergamasco*, the *Novarese* and the Valtellina. The Bishop of Vercelli proclaimed his independent authority over his diocese.

The position was certainly serious, but not as serious as it might appear. The allies had made a supreme effort and gained no comparable reward. As winter approached, as the campaign ended and the invading armies spent their force, the moment for negotiation arrived. Amadeus had forced Galeazzo back and saved Montferrat; his own designs in Montferrat might now be furthered by making his peace with the Visconti. Galeazzo concluded a treaty of peace and alliance with him in June 1374, and at the same time made a truce with the Pope. The truce was renewed in the following year, while Galeazzo reduced to submission the rebellious Guelfs of his territory; and it was converted into a lasting peace in July 1376, with provision for an arbitration of Galeazzo's disputes with Montferrat.

Galeazzo was sinking into a premature and painful old age. Suspicion and avarice dominated his last years; he no longer had the vitality to follow Bernabò in further adventures. While Florence, bulwark of the Guelf cause and most faithful servant of the Popes, plunged into the war of the Eight Saints in alliance with the excommunicate Ghibelline Bernabò Visconti to defend the cities revolted against the excesses of their Papal governors, Galeazzo made his peace with the Pope. The work of pacification was sealed in 1377 by the marriage of Galeazzo's daughter Violante to Secondotto, Marquis of Montferrat.

It was practically the last public act for which Galeazzo was responsible. He died a year later, on 4 August 1378, unregretted by his subjects, and was succeeded by his only son, Giangaleazzo Visconti, Count of Vertus.

CHAPTER II

GIANGALEAZZO'S EARLY YEARS: THE COUNT OF VERTUS IN PIEDMONTESE POLITICS (1378–1385)

THE marriage of Galeazzo Visconti and Blanche of Savoy was celebrated at Rivoli on 28 September 1350. A son was born to them in Milan a year later, on 15 October 1351.[1] He was named, after his uncle the Archbishop and after his father, Giovanni Galeazzo. His earliest years were spent in his father's palace in Milan, and there, at the age of nine, he received his royal bride Isabella of Valois. King John of France had been unable to raise from his own impoverished kingdom the ransom demanded by his English captors; Galeazzo Visconti, eager to enhance his own dignity and the splendour of his family, "bought the daughter of King John for 600,000 francs".[2] The house of Savoy acted as intermediary in the transaction. The bridegroom, after some alternative proposals had fallen through, eventually received the County of Vertus in Champagne. This isolated possession in France will play no part in our story;[3] but Giangaleazzo derived from it the title "Conte di Virtù" by which he was universally known, and with which so much play was made in the polemics which centred around his character and his career.

Hardly a trace of the young prince's boyhood has survived. At the tender age of four years, he received the order of knighthood at the hands of the Emperor Charles IV;[4] and there is a famous, but possibly quite legendary story that, at one of his father's banquets, being asked to name the wisest man present,

[1] The debated questions of the date and place of Giangaleazzo's birth were finally solved by the discovery of the letter of notification, indexed in *Repertorio Diplomatico Visconteo*, I 55, no. 497.

[2] Froissart, *Chroniques*, xv 257.

[3] For the acquisition of Vertus, v. Romano, "Origine della Contea di Vertus", in *Rendiconti del R. Istituto Lombardo* 2, xxx 222–9; Cochin, "Jean Galéaz Visconti et le Comté de Vertus", *ASL* xxxii, 1, 281–96.

[4] Cibrario, *Economia Politica*, 261.

the boy singled out Petrarch without hesitation. Paolo Giovio tells us that he proved at an early age to be quick of intellect and unusually studious, with a predilection for the political studies which, in his case, supplemented the normal academic teaching of the day.[1]

By the year 1365, Galeazzo had left Milan and taken up his residence, with his son and his daughter Violante, in the newly constructed "Castello" of Pavia. This great palace of red brick, built in a perfect square around a magnificent courtyard, was to be Giangaleazzo's home until the day of his death. It was set into the northern wall of the town, near the head of the main street, now known as the Corso Vittorio Emanuele, which slopes down through the city to the Porta Ticino and the covered bridge over the river. At the back lay the broad gardens, where the court could be at ease in the warm weather; and beyond stretched the great park, where Galeazzo rode and hawked, and which Giangaleazzo was to extend until the circuit of the walls measured as much as twenty miles.[2]

The castle itself was defended by a deep moat, and presented a battlemented front to the world; but within, it was designed less as a fortress than as a palace. Each of the two storeys contained forty rooms; in the cellars beneath were ample storehouses, accommodation for horses, and a large court constructed by Galeazzo for the ball game of "pallone". On the upper floor, facing the gardens, was a great hall with a wide balcony, where the prince could dine in the open air on warm summer evenings. Within, spacious loggias looked out on to the courtyard, large enough for the splendid jousts and tournaments which marked special celebrations. A richly decorated chapel occupied a part of the western wing. One of the towers was used as an arsenal, another housed the precious library to which Galeazzo and his family devoted so much care. The rooms of the palace were lighted by wide windows, and decorated with paintings of landscapes and animal motifs, with historical and legendary scenes, and illustrations of the greatness of the Visconti.[3] Here Giangaleazzo grew

---

[1] Giovio, *Vite duodecim Vicecomitum*, 165.
[2] Magenta, *Visconti e Sforza nel Castello di Pavia*, I 234.   [3] *Ibid.* 76–9.

to manhood, and breathed the spirit of the Renaissance which was already faintly stirring in Italy.

The young Count's first son was born in March 1366. Isabella gave him a daughter and two more sons; but she died in 1372, when she was only twenty-three years old, in giving birth to her fourth child. The first Countess of Vertus has left no mark in history; but if anything of her character was reflected in the personality of her daughter Valentina Visconti, who charmed the court of Paris as the bride of Louis of Valois in 1389, we may imagine that her death was a source of bitter grief to her husband.[1] His loss was aggravated by the tragedy which continued to oppress his family. His youngest son died soon after birth, and the eldest not long afterwards. Azzone, the second son, attained his thirteenth year, but he too died in 1381.[2] Only Valentina survived, a last frail link between the families of Valois and Visconti.

These misfortunes cannot have been without their effect on the character of a young man who was only twenty-one years old at the time of his wife's death. No pictorial representation of Giangaleazzo in his youth has survived; but we are told that he was tall, well built, and strikingly handsome. He had the reddish hair of the Visconti, and he probably already wore the short, pointed beard which is made familiar to us in later representations. But the emphasis is always on his intellectual rather than on his physical qualities; and we may fairly surmise that the death of his wife, followed by that of his sons, increased that devotion to solitude and meditation on which many of his contemporaries remarked.

Giangaleazzo was present at the brilliant festivities which attended the wedding of his sister Violante to Lionel, Duke of Clarence, who died a few months after his marriage. In the following year he received a letter from his wife's brother, Charles V of France, appealing for his help in the ransom of the

---

[1] There is an unusually warm tribute to her in "Chronicon Placentinum", *RIS* xvi 512 E.

[2] *Ibid.* 512–13; Muratore, "Nascita e Battesimo del Primogenito di Giangaleazzo", *ASL* xxxii, 2, 257–84.

Count of Bar.[1] But he took no active part in public affairs until 1372. In that year, when the forces of northern Italy were combining against the Visconti, he sent the gage of battle to his uncle, Amadeus of Savoy.[2]

When Amadeus invaded the territory of the Visconti in 1372-3, Giangaleazzo went with his father's army to meet the attack. But he was surrounded by the precautions which his parents' affection inspired, and his experiences ended with a disastrous defeat and flight.[3] It was his first and last recorded appearance on a field of battle; but in the following year he was sent on a diplomatic mission more suited to his temperament. Galeazzo, was was suffering from an attack of gout, empowered his son to conclude the negotiations which he had begun with Amadeus of Savoy. The Count of Vertus went to Casale, and in a meadow by the banks of the Po he signed the treaty of peace and alliance with his uncle in June 1374.[4] His mother was with him. Blanche of Savoy had received as her dowry a small nucleus of lands within the territory of Savoy; and Giangaleazzo's mission to Casale underlined for him the importance of his Savoyard blood. So long as the Visconti heritage was split into two parts, the destiny of the house of Pavia lay in the west.

Galeazzo accepted this limitation. On 8 January 1375, he delegated to Giangaleazzo, now twenty-three years old, "the rule, governance and administration in full right" of Novara, Vercelli, Tortona, Alessandria, Valenza and Casale; he could appoint officials, control fortifications, annul bans, and with his father's consent make peace, war or alliance with Savoy. But it was not intended that the Count should have any claim to the title of "generalis dominus".[5] He was to have practical experi-

---

[1] Cochin, *op. cit. ASL* xxxii, 1, 290 note 4.
[2] Cibrario, *Economia Politica*, 102 note 1.
[3] "Chronicon Placentinum", *RIS* xvi 514 and 518.
[4] Galeazzo's procuration, 9 March 1374: *Repertorio Visconteo*, ii 236, no. 2007. The treaty of 6 June: *ibid.* 239, no. 2031. For the dowry of Blanche of Savoy, *v.* Romano, "Regesto degli Atti Notarili di C. Cristiani", *ASL* xxi, 2, 27 note 2; Muratore, "Bianca di Savoia e le sue nozze", *ASL* xxxiv, 1, 67-70.
[5] Published by Volta, "Età emancipazione e patria di Giangaleazzo", *ASL* xvi 595-8.

ence of government; Bernabò similarly sent each of his sons to rule over one or two cities, while at the same time he instructed his officials that no order of theirs should be valid against the principles of government laid down by himself.[1] So, too, Galeazzo retained supreme authority over all his dominions; but he deputed the control of a large district to his son, as lieutenant with extensive powers. Governor of the cities which defended Milan and Pavia from the west, Giangaleazzo could gain the experience necessary to teach him to hold his own against the attacks of Montferrat and the subtler penetration of Savoy. From this time until his death, Galeazzo gradually resigned much of the direction of political affairs to his son, who was associated with him in all the treaties and alliances of the period.

In 1378, Giangaleazzo's personal influence on political affairs becomes prominent for the first time. His sister, Violante, had married Secondotto, the weak and violent young Marquis of Montferrat; and the Count had probably established a powerful ascendancy over his brother-in-law. Asti, the city which had been an object of contention between Montferrat and the Visconti for forty years, had finally been awarded to the Marquis; and since it was occupied by a German soldier who refused to surrender it, Secondotto appealed to his wife's family for help. Giangaleazzo saw his opportunity. He entered Asti with his troops in February 1378, persuaded Secondotto to appoint him as governor, took the official oath to the Marquis, and swore a pact of eternal brotherhood. The Count was now the real master of the city, and Secondotto gradually recognized that he had been excluded from all practical authority. The Visconti had recovered, "without loss and under the guise of friendship", as Corio says, the keystone of their defence and communications in Piedmont; they had no intention of abandoning it again to Montferrat.[2]

[1] Letter of 17 February 1377: Cognasso, "Ricerche per la Storia dello Stato Visconteo", *BSP* XXII 174, Doc. 37. For the status of Bernabò's sons in the cities assigned to them, *v.* especially Verga, "Condanna a morte contro Carlo Visconti", *ASL* XXIX, 1, 393–4; Comani, "Dominî di Regina della Scala", *ASL* XXIX, 2, 214–26; Visconti, in a review in *ASL* XLIX, 187–8.

[2] Corio, *Storia di Milano*, II 279–80; Benvenuto di San Giorgio, "Historia Montisferrati", *RIS* XXIII 596–7; Gabotto, "Età del Conte Verde", *MSI* XXXIII 243.

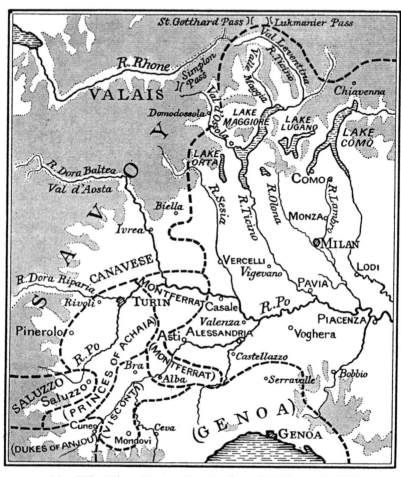

MAP III. Milan, Western Lombardy and Piedmont in 1378

Land over 3000 feet is shaded

This episode is worthy of notice, because it marks Giangale-azzo's personal entry on the political stage. Here for the first time we find what might be called, in modern phraseology, the technique of aggression which was peculiarly his own. The whole incident bears the hallmark of his particular genius. It is cha-racterized by those qualities which made him great—the sim-plicity of conception, the quiet ease and certainty of execution. He showed an utter lack of scruple, a contempt for ethical standards in political relations remarkable even in that age.

Secondotto protested throughout Italy, loudly but in vain, against the deceit of which he had been the victim. The Italian powers had troubles enough of their own to occupy them during the summer of 1378. The people of Florence were in revolt against their rulers. After the stormy election of Pope Urban VI, a majority of the Cardinals withdrew from Rome to Anagni, where they made a new election of Robert of Geneva, calling himself Clement VII, and inaugurated the great schism of the Church. The rivalry of Venice and Genoa had led to another war, in which most of Lombardy was involved. Galeazzo's death passed almost unnoticed amidst these upheavals; and Giangale-azzo quietly succeeded to his share of the Visconti dominions.

The new lord of Pavia proceeded to consolidate his authority in Piedmont. He needed the friendship of Savoy, to strengthen his position in Asti. Within a month of his father's death, he signed a treaty with Amadeus VI, to whom he resigned all claims in the lands acquired by Savoy in the districts of Vercelli and Ivrea.[1] He accepted the office of arbitrator in certain territorial disputes between Montferrat and Savoy, and gave his award in favour of Amadeus. A fortnight later Secondotto died, violently as he had lived.

Amadeus now had to fulfil his share of the understanding. Otto of Brunswick, regent for the new Marquis, was determined to enforce his ward's claims on Asti; other means failing, he pre-pared for war. Giangaleazzo ordered the evacuation of the district

---

[1] 29 August 1378, with additions and confirmations of 31 August and 21 November: Gabotto, *op. cit.* 246–7; Guichenon, *Histoire généalogique de la Maison de Savoye,* IV 211 13.

of Voghera in November 1378;[1] but a greater power intervened
before they could come to blows. Robert of Geneva needed the
help of his cousin Amadeus of Savoy, and of Otto of Brunswick,
in the struggle against his rival Urban VI. He imposed a two-year
truce, during which he himself and Amadeus were to be arbitrators between Montferrat and Pavia; the question of Asti was
not mentioned. According to the Montferrine chronicler, Giangaleazzo deceitfully prevented the presentation of Brunswick's
carefully prepared defence of his ward's claim to the disputed
city.[2] Amadeus, as an arbitrator, was no doubt able in this way
to repay his debt. In March 1379, Asti finally accepted the lordship of Giangaleazzo, who was confirmed in his possession by the
King of the Romans in the following year.[3]

Thus Giangaleazzo accepted his position as a Piedmontese
power. His uncle Bernabò still ruled in Milan—the most dreaded
figure in Italy, proud, brutal and violent; his five sons were
growing up, demanding scope for their ambitions. Giangaleazzo
was young, without much experience, without achievements to
command fear and respect. His cousins looked with envy on the
wide dominions which fell to him as an only son. Cautious by
nature, he understood the limits which were placed upon his
activities. He accepted the political tutelage of Bernabò, but
he was determined to avoid any intervention in his own affairs
and to preserve the integrity of his state.

Bernabò, not content to leave the care of Visconti designs on
Genoa to his nephew, had made an alliance with Venice in the
war which has taken its name from the central episode of the
struggle, the siege of Chioggia. Giangaleazzo, slower and subtler
by nature, would have preferred to gain his ends by negotiation
with the Ligurian Republic; but Bernabò pressed him, and the
Genoese showed no anxiety to meet his demands. The situation
in Piedmont was still uppermost in his mind; and when he joined
the Venetian alliance in April 1380, he stipulated that Venice

---

[1] Manfredi, *Storia di Voghera*, 187.
[2] Benvenuto di San Giorgio, *op. cit. RIS* XXIII 604 E.
[3] Gabotto, "Età del Conte Verde", *MSI* XXXIII 249–51. Wenceslaus'
diploma, in *RIS* XVI 789 c; he confirmed Giangaleazzo in the possession of
Asti in 1382: Gabotto, *op. cit. MSI* XXXIII 265.

should aid him in the event of a war with Montferrat.[1] He contributed his share to two inglorious expeditions against the Genoese Riviera, and took precautions to prevent the passage through his lands of Charles of Durazzo, claimant of the Neapolitan throne and nephew of the great enemy of Venice, Lewis of Hungary.[2] But his main resources were concentrated upon the southern corner of Piedmont. A treaty with the lords of Dogliani reveals the full extent of his ambitions;[3] he hoped to restore the glory of Archbishop Giovanni's day, when Visconti power in Piedmont had been at its height. Bernabò asked the Count of Savoy to guarantee the fullest interpretation of their nephew's rights, and Giangaleazzo made a new accord with Amadeus, whom he expected to bear the brunt of the fighting. He was preparing for a war against Montferrat at the end of 1380.[4]

Otto of Brunswick had gone to Naples, taking the young Marquis of Montferrat with him, to fight for his wife, Queen Joanna I, against Charles of Durazzo. Giangaleazzo was reported to be negotiating with Charles for a marriage alliance and for the purchase of all the Angevin rights in Piedmont.[5] Everything seemed to favour the Count of Vertus. In April 1381, he announced his intention of avenging a raid from Montferrat on his own lands.[6] In July, the Marquis fell on the field of Castelnuovo, where Otto

---

[1] 23 April 1380: Dumont, *Corps universel diplomatique du droit des gens*, ii, part 1, 149–51, no. 109. For Giangaleazzo's own account of his negotiations with Genoa in 1379, *v.* Scaramella, *Visconti nella guerra di Chioggia*, 9–10 and Doc. 3.

[2] Osio, *Documenti diplomatici tratti dagli Archivi Milanesi*, i 208, no. 141. For the Ligurian campaigns of 1380–1, *v.* Stella, "Annales Genuenses", *RIS* xvii 1111 B–C, 1112 E, 1117 B–1118 E.

[3] Della Chiesa, "Cronaca di Saluzzo", in *Monumenta Historie Patrie: Scriptores*, iii 1027–8.

[4] Gabotto, "Età del Conte Verde", *MSI* xxxiii 256–9. Giangaleazzo's accord with Amadeus, 5 September: *Repertorio Visconteo*, ii 318–19, nos. 2685, 2696. Bernabò to Amadeus, 29 September: Mugnier, "Lettres des Visconti aux Comtes de Savoie", 410–11, no. 12.

[5] Collino, "Politica Fiorentino-Bolognese", *MAT* 2, liv 115–16, and 153, Doc. 19, from the minutes of the Florentine Council. A despatch from Bologna: Lucca, *Regesti*, ii, part 2, 458, no. 2070.

[6] Giangaleazzo to Venice, 17 April 1381: *Repertorio Visconteo*, ii 329, no. 2774; and Predelli, "Libri Commemoriali della Repubblica di Venezia", iii 147, no. 84. In July, Giangaleazzo demanded 25 "uomini d'arme" from the Scotti family of Piacenza: Boselli, *Storie Piacentine*, ii 132, note 3.

of Brunswick was taken prisoner and Joanna's star eclipsed. In August, the Visconti at last began to make headway in Liguria, where the surrender of Novi and Serravalle gave them control of an important pass through the Alps to Genoa.[1]

At the last moment, however, the offensive against Montferrat was foiled by the desertion of Savoy. Amadeus had undertaken to make peace between Venice and Genoa, and summoned a conference at Turin. He regarded Giangaleazzo's plans to revive the authority of the Visconti with misgiving, and decided that they should be the scapegoats of the peace. The Venetians accepted this treatment of their allies, and with unfailing opportunism accused Giangaleazzo of undermining the pacific work of the conference. Bernabò sent his chancellor, and even his son, to protest against this treatment.[2] But Venice accepted a settlement with her enemies and signed the Peace of Turin on 8 August 1381, leaving her allies to fend for themselves. A month later, Amadeus made an alliance with Genoa against the Visconti.[3]

While Bernabò stormed, Giangaleazzo maintained a greater reserve; but his first act was to conclude a truce with the Marquis of Montferrat.[4] His task was made easy by the fact that the new Marquis Teodoro II had been brought up at the court of Pavia with Giangaleazzo's own son. Giangaleazzo and Teodoro, in a treaty of perpetual friendship signed in January 1382, agreed to maintain their existing borders; Montferrat thereby abandoned Asti, as the price of peace and friendship with the Visconti.[5]

It has been suggested that Amadeus, content to see his neighbours at peace, renounced the threatening attitude implicit in his

---

[1] Corio, *op. cit.* II 291. Novi surrendered on 8 August: letter of Giangaleazzo to Amadeus, published by Magenta, *op. cit.* II 46–7, no. 63.

[2] Accounts of Savoy, expenses for receiving Lodovico Visconti in Rivoli and Ivrea: Segre, "Dispacci di Cristoforo da Piacenza", *ASI* 5, XLIV 294, note 1.

[3] On 7 September: Scaramella, *Visconti nella guerra di Chioggia*, Doc. 4. Amadeus tried to bring the King of Cyprus, who had married a daughter of Bernabò, into the alliance: St Pierre, "Cenno storico intorno ad Amedeo VI", *AAT* XXXVI 435–7.

[4] Cognasso, "Aneddoti di Storia Viscontea", *BSP* XXV 8–13; Mugnier, *op. cit.* 412–17, nos. 13–18. Giàngaleazzo notified Amadeus of his truce with Montferrat on 12 August: Magenta, *op. cit.* II 46–7, no. 63.

[5] 22 January: Dumont, *op. cit.* II, 1, 161–8, no. 120.

alliance with Genoa.[1] But the evidence of Giangaleazzo's activities in Piedmont shows the incompatibility of Visconti interests with those of Savoy. Giangaleazzo pacified the lower valley of the Ossola in 1378, and three years later he received the submission of Domodossola and the upper valley, at the foot of the Simplon pass.[2] The acquisition of Asti and the *Astigiano*, the capture of Novi, his relations with the powerful nobility of the Ligurian Alps,[3] all showed in Giangaleazzo a determination to resist the trend of political development in Piedmont towards the supremacy of Savoy. A new field of rivalry now appeared to be opening in Genoa, the traditional goal of Visconti ambitions. Amadeus, not content with the close contact which he had established with the existing government of the Republic, had begun to intrigue with the exiled Guelf faction of the Fieschi.[4] In February 1382, observers in Avignon predicted a joint attack on Milan by Savoy and Genoa.[5] The rebel nobility of the *Astigiano*, still unreconciled to the new lord of the district, proclaimed their allegiance to Amadeus. Giangaleazzo on his side began to intrigue in the valleys of the Canavese, north of Turin, where the feuds and outrages of party faction had survived every effort at pacification or suppression.[6] But the crisis was averted by the sudden prospect of greater triumphs, which drew the attention of Amadeus to another quarter of Italy.

Joanna of Naples, having no children of her own, had adopted the French Duke Louis of Anjou, uncle of Charles VI of France, as her heir. After Charles of Durazzo's victory in Naples, Louis planned an expedition, first to rescue the captive Joanna, and later to avenge her death in prison and secure his promised throne. Amadeus agreed to join forces with him, in return for the surrender of nearly all the Angevin claims to territory in Pied-

---

[1] Scaramella, *Visconti nella guerra di Chioggia*, 17–18.
[2] Bianchetti, *Ossola Inferiore*, I 269–304.
[3] Especially the family of Ceva: Gabotto, "Età del Conte Verde", *MSI* XXXIII 262.
[4] *Ibid.* 266; Gabotto, *Ultimi Principi d'Acaia*, 9–10; Jarry, *Origines de la domination française à Gênes*, 22–4.
[5] From the diary of the Duke of Anjou's Chancellor: le Fèvre, *Journal*, 18.
[6] Gabotto, "Età del Conte Verde", *MSI* XXXIII 264–7.

mont. The ecclesiastical aspect of the proposed expedition offered an equally strong incentive to the Count of Savoy. Joanna had supported the claims of his cousin, Clement VII, while Charles of Durazzo enjoyed the blessing of the rival Pope, Urban VI. Clement had been driven out of Italy, and had established his court at Avignon; the support of the French monarchy was the backbone of his cause, and Louis of Anjou was his most active propagandist. The French expedition therefore took on something of the nature of a Clementist crusade; and the triumph of Anjou in Naples and of Clement in Rome would have given an irresistible impetus to the authority of Amadeus in the north-west of Italy. But the first need of the allies was a free and unhindered passage through Lombardy. Bernabò Visconti was prepared to grant this, in return for a marriage alliance with the Angevins; and in August 1382, Amadeus and Louis with their armies received a festive welcome from the Visconti on their journey southwards. Six months later, the Count of Savoy died in Neapolitan territory.

The departure, and later the death of Amadeus VI relieved Giangaleazzo of a dangerous neighbour. His position, however, was no longer as favourable as it had been before the Peace of Turin. The alliance of Montferrat against Savoy was a poor exchange for that of Savoy against Montferrat. His policy was confined to a series of petty aggravations which produced no noticeable results. Rid of an experienced and formidable rival, he continued the game of formal courtesy combined with secret intrigue against the new Count Amadeus VII. Giangaleazzo's representatives attended the funeral of the old Count;[1] his troops, in accordance with the obligations of their alliance, helped to subdue the rebels of the Valais and the Canavese, among whom the name of Vertus was a watchword and a battlecry.[2] Roving mercenary bands attacked Cervere and withdrew into Visconti

<hr/>

[1] Accounts of Savoy, 28 April 1383; Cordero de Pamperato, "Dernière campagne d'Amédée VI", in *Revue Savoisienne*, XLIII 275, no. 250.

[2] Segre, "Conti di Savoia e lo Scisma d'Occidente", *AAT* XLII 581. The Ossola valley was Giangaleazzo's centre for intrigues in the Valais, Vercelli for the Canavese: Gabotto, "Età del Conte Verde", *MSI* XXXIII 267–8; Id. *Ultimi Principi d'Acaia*, 16–19, 24–5.

territory for protection; Savoy negotiated with traitors in Vercelli.[1] Giangaleazzo's captain and counsellor, Antonio Porro, secured the county of Pollenzo, which formed a centre for Milanese interests in Piedmont without involving too closely the Visconti themselves.[2] Teodoro of Montferrat lost no opportunity of troubling Savoy; the resistance offered by the little Marquisate of Saluzzo to the Savoyard claim of suzerainty aroused suspicions of encouragement from Pavia. These constant irritations threatened to develop into a crisis in February 1385; but the moment had come when, as we shall see, Giangaleazzo could not afford to make enemies for himself. He accepted an offer of mediation, and resumed friendly relations with the Count of Savoy.[3]

The situation in Piedmont had not changed perceptibly since Galeazzo's death; Giangaleazzo had made no great progress in seven years. His policy was seriously hampered by the weakness and uncertainty of his own position at Pavia. While his interests were apparently centred in Piedmont, he had gradually reduced his commitments in that quarter, in order to concentrate his resources on a secret, immensely difficult, but vital task: the preparation for a day of reckoning with Bernabò.

[1] Gabotto, *Ultimi Principi*, 10, 12–14.
[2] Pollenzo was in the jurisdiction of the Bishop of Bra: *ibid.* 31–2.
[3] *Ibid.* 32–4.

CHAPTER III

GIANGALEAZZO AND BERNABÒ: THE HERMIT OF PAVIA (1378–1385)

AFTER the death of Galeazzo Visconti, the relations between the courts of Milan and Pavia suffered an imperceptible but definite deterioration. The causes which contributed to this deterioration may be found in the chronicles of the time, which refer to the growing ambitions of Bernabò's sons, and to the domineering attitude which Bernabò himself adopted towards his young nephew. Such assertions were made when Bernabò was no longer able to state his own case; Giangaleazzo's position was so insecure in these early years, and any activities directed against Bernabò were necessarily so shrouded in secrecy, that it is impossible to assess accurately the Count's share of responsibility for the differences which arose between him and his uncle. Bernabò himself was apparently unaware that Giangaleazzo was quietly nourishing his grievances—grievances of which only a one-sided account has survived. Only one or two glimpses are afforded of the private relations between the two princes; but we can still trace, beneath the apparent accord which they presented to the world, a gradual divergence of aims and of policy.

The serious limitations which Bernabò's tutelage imposed on the Count were brought home to him by the episode of the Sicilian marriage. When Frederick III of Sicily died in 1377, several princes sought the hand of his fifteen-year-old heiress Maria. While the other rivals disputed among themselves, Giangaleazzo quietly approached Maria's guardian, the Sicilian Grand Justiciar, and arranged his own marriage with the Queen.[1] The bargain was struck with that secrecy and efficiency which Giangaleazzo already knew how to command; but its execution was a less easy,

---

[1] Romano, "Visconti e la Sicilia", *ASL* xxiii, 1, 13–15 and 17–20.

although no less important matter. For according to the terms of the contract, the marriage would be automatically dissolved if it were not consummated within a year; and when the news of it was made public, it brought an outcry from many quarters. Giangaleazzo's envoys in Rome, Paris and Aragon, and no doubt elsewhere too, were kept busy, seeking to calm the fears aroused by the proposed union of Sicily with a Lombard power.[1] It was indeed an ambitious scheme to take shape in the mind of the mild and studious prince of Pavia. With a foothold in Sicily as well as in the north, he would no longer be a little lordling, uncomfortably sheltered in the protection of his uncle's authority and power. He would bestride the peninsula, he would bear the title of a king, he would be the heir of the Hohenstaufen.

It was a brilliant and youthful dream, but it failed. Giangaleazzo could count on no help, for it touched the interests of every power in Italy; and his own resources were very small. The fleet of the King of Aragon, who had his own designs on Sicily, destroyed the ships gathered at Pisa to fetch the bride and bring her to Pavia. The Aragonese party abducted the hapless Maria, and the year passed without the consummation of the marriage.[2] The watchful powers of Italy breathed a sigh of relief. Giangaleazzo had prematurely shown his hand in a bold venture in which he lacked the material resources necessary for success; his failure made him all the more dependent on his uncle's support.

No one realized better than Bernabò the possibilities of the proposed match. He made stringent demands, with which the Count had to comply. Giangaleazzo's Lombard territories were to be inherited by his surviving son Azzone, who was at once betrothed to one of Bernabò's daughters; in Sicily, on the other hand, he was to be succeeded by the offspring of his marriage with Maria. If the kingdom were to become a permanent appanage

---

[1] Pisa to Siena, 22 May 1379: Silva, "Governo di Pietro Gambacorta in Pisa", 317–18, Doc. 12. Report of the Mantuan envoy in Rome, 16 July 1379, published by Segre, "Dispacci di Cristoforo da Piacenza", *ASI* 5, XLIV 290–1, no. 35.

[2] Romano, "Visconti e la Sicilia", *ASL* XXIII, 1, 21 3. Pisa to Siena, 11 May: Silva, "Governo di Pietro Gambacorta in Pisa", 203 note 3.

of the ruler of Pavia, Bernabò's share of the Visconti dominions would be cast into the shade.[1] Even when the Sicilian project failed, Bernabò determined to prevent his nephew from increasing his influence by a successful matrimonial policy such as he himself had steadily pursued. Giangaleazzo, his twice widowed sister Violante, his son and his daughter were all betrothed to children of Bernabò. The marriages of Giangaleazzo to Caterina and of Violante to Lodovico were celebrated in 1380.[2] Valentina's betrothal was probably never formally completed, and Azzone died in 1381, leaving the Count without a male heir.

Giangaleazzo's compliance is the measure of his fear; he would never have accepted Bernabò's proposals if any other course had been open to him. Henceforward he understood that Lombardy could not hold them both; and his single asset lay in Bernabò's failure to appreciate his nephew's character—his readiness to embark on so obviously unequal a struggle. The death of Azzone in 1381 increased the expectations and the impatience of Bernabò's sons. But Bernabò himself was prepared to leave the Count alone so long as he confined his attention to Piedmont; for the moment, therefore, he dutifully followed his uncle's lead in all other political questions. The passage of the Angevin army in 1382 produced a demonstration of his affection for his Valois relatives. Valentina went out to greet her uncle, Louis of Anjou, when he encamped near Pavia, at Stradella on the Po; Giangaleazzo showered gifts upon him, and visited the camp each day until the Angevin army resumed its march.[3] But if he saw the strength which he might derive from his connection with the French court, the betrothal of Lucia Visconti to Louis' son threatened to rob him of the advantage which he expected to

---

[1] Romano, "Visconti e la Sicilia", *ASL* xxiii, 1, 15–17, 21–3. The complicated marriage proposals of 1380 and 1382 are set out in Table III at the end of the book.

[2] The dispensation for Giangaleazzo's marriage was granted by Urban VI: Achery, *Spicilegium*, iii 751–3. For the betrothal of Valentina to Carlo Visconti, *v.* Appendix II.

[3] The account of an observer at the Visconti court, published by Mirot, "Document inédit", *BSBS* xvii 93–6. A report from Piacenza, 25 July 1382: Lucca, *Regesti*, 180, nos. 1056–7. A letter of Louis to Marseilles: Valois, *France et le grand Schisme*, ii 40 note 3.

gain thereby.[1] Bernabò had united himself, by the ramifications of his dynastic policy, to some of the most powerful families in Europe. His daughters had married into the ruling houses of Austria, Bavaria and Wurtemberg, of Cyprus and Mantua. His son Carlo married a daughter of the Count of Armagnac, a powerful prince of Languedoc. The Angevin match would bring him into close contact with the French court.

Giangaleazzo began to set his own house in order. The mildness of his government gave relief to his subjects, but it was not solely a bid for popular support. He knew that a depopulated country-side was too heavy a price to pay for a full treasury; and he could afford to be generous, because the savage and often arbitrary onslaughts of Bernabò and Galeazzo had broken the resistance of Communal particularism.[2] Moreover, Bernabò in Milan completely overshadowed the little court of Pavia, which played the part of a diplomatic satellite; Giangaleazzo could therefore limit his expenses. He reduced the ordinary tribute paid every month by the cities.[3] Rather than place too great a strain on his subjects, he tried to borrow 10,000 florins in 1382, to meet the cost of Bernabò's Angevin alliance of which he had to pay his share.[4] Provisions for compensation or the restoration of property unjustly extorted by Galeazzo are in keeping with the character of pious simplicity which he assumed.[5] He reformed the local administration of the Milanese Contado,[6] and revised the regulations which governed the treasurers and tax-collectors of the Commune, in order to eradicate abuses and extortion.[7] In the

---

[1] Romano, "Primo Matrimonio di Lucia Visconti", *ASL* xx 603–6.

[2] Tagliabue, "Politica finanziaria nel governo di Giangaleazzo", *BSP* xv 35–7. And *v.* pp. 54–5, *infra*.

[3] The "salarium" paid by Pavia was reduced from 3500 to 3000 florins, 14 August 1378: Magenta, *Visconti e Sforza*, ii 43–4, no. 57. On 17 August, Giangaleazzo confirmed all pardons, etc., granted by Galeazzo: Pancotti, *Paratici Piacentini* ii 27–8.

[4] Credentials of the envoy of Mantua, 4 August 1382: Osio, *Documenti diplomatici*, i 230, no. 167.

[5] For the remission of Galeazzo's soul, 2 September 1383: Corio, *Storia di Milano*, ii 298. For the impartial judgment of claims to property extorted by Galeazzo, 24 December: *Antiqua Decreta*, 55–6.

[6] 1381–1384: *ibid.* 49–51, 54–5, 56–8, 72–5.

[7] *Ibid.* 59–63, 66–9; Giulini, *Memorie di Milano*, xi 358.

retirement of Pavia, he entered into his part of "ingesuato e cattolico uomo", of a solitary, pious and timid hermit. Wrapped in the observance of religious rites and inspired by a real or simulated fear, he guarded himself well from attack, and lulled his uncle to a sense of security and contempt.[1]

While he emphasized his timidity by an exaggerated withdrawal from personal contacts, Giangaleazzo lost no opportunity of winning friends outside Lombardy. The Emperor Charles IV died in 1378, and was succeeded as King of the Romans by his son Wenceslaus. In 1380 Giangaleazzo secured from Wenceslaus the revocation of all Imperial sentences against his father, and the restoration of the office of Imperial Vicar which had been forfeited by the Visconti in 1372; thus he ensured his juridical position in contrast to Bernabò, whose rights were not prejudiced by the new diploma, but who felt sufficiently confident of his own strength to disdain the favours of Charles IV's successor.[2]

The Swiss lords of the Grisons, in the upper reaches of the Rhine valley, formed an important link in the strategical and commercial relations of Lombardy with the north. Bernabò did not despise their friendship;[3] but Giangaleazzo as lord of Como was in closer contact with them. He secured the promise of the lord of Sargans to close the Alpine passes under his control against Giangaleazzo's enemies, and to come as far south as Locarno to fight for him in case of need.[4]

Giangaleazzo never lost sight of the possibilities which lay in his connection with the Valois. He bought the services of an

---

[1] Minerbetti, "Cronica", *RIS* NS xxvii, 2, 281. Most of the chroniclers refer to Giangaleazzo's "vita hipocritica": e.g. Gatari, "Cronaca Carrarese", *RIS* NS xvii, 1, 232; Froissart, *Chroniques*, x 324–7, and xv 258; Corio, *op. cit.* ii 321–2.

[2] Lünig, *Codex Italie Diplomaticus*, iii 305–14, nos. 27–8. Also in *RIS* xvi 788–94 (18 and 17 January).

[3] Bernabò had a claim on the Bishop of Chur: Romano, "Guerra tra i Visconti e la Chiesa", *BSP* iii 419 note 1. He was allied with Rudolf of Werdenberg-Sargans: Motta, "Relazioni dei Conti di Werdenberg-Sargans coi Duchi di Milano", in *Bollettino Storico della Svizzera Italiana*, ix 183–5.

[4] Pacts of 29 September 1380: *ibid.* 185–6, and indexed in *Inventari e Regesti del R. Archivio di Stato in Milano*, i 131; Reg. 16, no. 36.

observer at the French court in 1382, probably in connection with the Angevin negotiations of that year.[1] He made special efforts two years later to secure the release of a party of Angevin knights held captive at Ragusa.[2]

None of this offered Bernabò any ground for suspicion. Giangaleazzo took care to avoid measures which might give offence. Documents which he himself produced at a later date show—if they are genuine—the caution which he had to use; one of his officials aroused Bernabò's anger in a trivial incident over a stolen hawk, and when the Count refused to hand the offender over to his uncle's mercy, Bernabò expressed himself in violent terms which implied his readiness to visit his wrath on Giangaleazzo in person.[3] Bernabò's position in Milan seemed unassailable; after nearly thirty years' rule, his name was feared throughout Italy, a byword for ruthless tyranny. Giangaleazzo, in the shelter of his palace at Pavia to whose adornment he devoted so much care, watched and was not idle. Here and there he bought an ally and secured a friend. The first rumour of his intentions to reach Milan would seal his doom; but with the merest outline of a hint he began to instil suspicion of Bernabò and win sympathy and understanding for himself. He was ready to strike at the first sign of weakness.

The first symptoms of a divergence in the policy of the two Visconti appeared in their relations with the Tuscan cities. Bernabò, in spite of his great reputation, no longer had the vitality of his younger days. His wife's death, in June 1384, deprived him of a steady support. Nevertheless he chose this moment to embark on fresh projects in Tuscany. The suspicions of Florence had been momentarily lulled by the help which he had given to the Republic in the war of the Eight Saints. During the war of Chioggia he attempted to promote a general league, nominally directed against the foreign mercenary companies, but actually designed to help him in the war. The proposals fell to

<hr />

[1] La Trémoille, *Livre des Comptes*, 168–71, Doc. 11.
[2] Voinovitch, "Angevins à Raguse", *RQH* xciv 6–7, 13, 25.
[3] Ferrai, "Politica di Giangaleazzo", *ASI* 5, xxii 65–7; Novati, "Cattura di Bernabò", *ASL* xxxiii, 1, 139–41.

the ground after the Peace of Turin;[1] but relations with Tuscany continued to be friendly, and the Florentines were glad enough to have the help of Visconti troops to protect their lands from bands of wandering soldiers in 1382.[2]

The affairs of Naples were responsible for a change in the relations between Bernabò and Florence. The expedition of Louis of Anjou was dissolving under the stress of disease and inadequate resources. Enguerrand VII, Sieur de Coucy, reached Lombardy in July 1384, with a French army marching to the relief of Louis. He received a cordial welcome in Milan; but Florence, hostile to the Angevins, appealed to her neighbours to unite in the defence of Tuscany against Coucy. From one quarter she could expect no aid; the Florentine government, which came to power after the collapse of the democratic experiment of 1378–1382, looked with disfavour upon the popular regime of Siena, and at this time the relations between the two cities were strained. Sienese envoys came very secretly to Milan at the moment when Coucy arrived; and the ambassador of Lucca announced to his government on 23 July the likelihood that "these troops may pass into Tuscany by way of Pontremoli to help the Sienese, at Bernabò's request". A fortnight later, he wrote that "the Sieur de Coucy is as much at messer Bernabò's disposition, as I am at yours". And Coucy's army did indeed take the road, not through Romagna as Louis of Anjou had done, but over the Apennines into Tuscany.[3]

Giangaleazzo seemed at first disposed to welcome Coucy and his army.[4] But Coucy did not go to Pavia, in spite of the Count's preparations to receive him.[5] Bernabò had probably intervened

---

[1] Seregni, "Disegno federale di Bernabò", *ASL* XXXVIII, 2, 162–82; Professione, *Siena e le Compagne di Ventura*, 87–90; Landogna, *Politica dei Visconti in Toscana*, 44–8, and xi–xix, Docs. 11–17.

[2] Collino, "Politica Fiorentino-Bolognese", *MAT* 2, LIV 117–18.

[3] Details of Coucy's passage through Lombardy may be found in Lucca, *Regesti*, 225–35, nos. 1233, 1240–70, especially nos. 1233, 1240–2. Nos. 1230–2, 1234–9 refer to the Duke of Anjou's expedition, and should be dated 1382. For Florentine policy, v. Collino, "Politica Fiorentino-Bolognese", *MAT* 2, LIV 121–2.

[4] He sent his doctor to Coucy, who was ill in Piedmont: Lucca, *Regesti*, 226, no. 1240.

[5] *Ibid.* 470, nos. 2121–2. (Another report on the same day as this last still spoke of his coming: *ibid.* 227, no. 1242.)

to exclude his nephew from the demonstrations of Franco-Milanese friendship. When therefore the Florentines, with growing suspicions of an understanding between Bernabò, Coucy and the Sienese, appealed to Giangaleazzo for help, he made it known to them that he was not unfavourably disposed to their cause.[1] It was by no means an open defiance of Bernabò, but it was a significant private divergence from his policy. He did not join the defensive League of five Tuscan Communes in October—that would have unnecessarily irritated not only Bernabò but also Coucy and the French, against whom the League was directed. But he won the friendship of the government of Lucca by an offer of intervention with Coucy on their behalf; and he quietly hinted to the Tuscan Communes that his was not the inveterate enmity of Bernabò, and that he was prepared to be of service to them, if they would do as much for him.[2]

Fortune favoured Giangaleazzo's tentative assertion of a diplomatic individuality of his own. Coucy took possession of Arezzo, in defiance of Florence; but the Duke of Anjou was already dead in the *Regno*. Having nothing further to achieve in Italy, Coucy sold Arezzo to Florence and turned back to France, leaving Bernabò and the Sienese to fend for themselves.[3] Bernabò had discredited himself alike with the Sienese, whom he had failed to help, and with the Florentines, who were once more on their guard against him. Giangaleazzo, on the other hand, had strengthened his position. "He showed great friendship for those with whom Messer Bernabò was on hostile terms, and especially for the Florentines", records a Florentine chronicler.[4] The Commune of Lucca offered to send a garrison to Pavia while Coucy passed through Lombardy on his way back to France; and the Count also began negotiations with Florence and Bologna for a League against the marauding Companies of Venture.[5] He had

---

[1] *Ibid.* 222, no. 1219; Collino, "Politica Fiorentino-Bolognese", *MAT* 2, LIV 157, Docs. 33–4. Romano, "Niccolò Spinelli", *ASN* XXVI 417 note 1.

[2] Seregni, "Disegno federale di Bernabò", *ASL* XXXVIII, 2, 180–1.

[3] Durrieu, "Prise d'Arezzo", *BEC* XLI 161–94.

[4] Giovanni Morelli, *Cronica*, 292.

[5] Collino, "Politica Fiorentino-Bolognese", *MAT* 2, LIV 125–7, and 161–2, Docs. 13 8. Decision of the Council of Lucca, 8 January 1385: Seregni, "Disegno federale di Bernabò", *ASL* XXXVIII, 2, 181.

unobtrusively supplanted his uncle in Tuscan councils, for Bernabò had no part in these proposals.[1]

The veteran ruler of Milan did not, however, allow this setback to quench his ambitions. If the Republican institutions which survived in Tuscany did not allow him to pursue his favourite dynastic policy, he could still find scope for it elsewhere. He was in constant touch with the widowed Duchess of Anjou through the winter 1384–5, offering to send his daughter Lucia to Avignon for her marriage with the young Duke Louis II, and to support a united French expedition to set Louis on the throne of Naples.[2] After his wife's death, Bernabò liquidated certain claims which she had on the Scaliger dominions of Verona and Vicenza; the betrothal of his youngest son Mastino to Antonio della Scala's daughter sealed the agreement between them in February 1385,[3] but the last had not been heard of the Visconti claims to these dominions.

Giangaleazzo, mute and apparently helpless in Pavia, watched every step. Six years had passed since the failure of the Sicilian scheme. Under the cloak of fear, he had gathered a strong body-guard of troops to accompany him everywhere; we find his representatives in Tuscany enlisting troops at the end of 1383, when there was no threat of war.[4] Jacopo dal Verme and Antonio Porro, who remained in his service until his death, were already by his side to advise him and lead his armies. He had retained the services of his father's secretaries, Andreolo Arese and Pasquino Capelli, and of other tried counsellors. He had begun to attract followers from neighbouring states; Niccolò Diversi had come from Lucca and entered Giangaleazzo's " Camera " or financial depart-

---

[1] Giangaleazzo had also obtained a footing in Umbria and Romagna. He acted as arbitrator between Galeotto Malatesta and Antonio Montefeltro, lord of Urbino, in November 1384: Franceschini, "Giangaleazzo arbitro di pace", *ASL* NS III 292.

[2] Romano, "Primo Matrimonio di Lucia Visconti", *ASL* xx 594–601.

[3] Corio, *op. cit.* II 321. Evidence of Bernabò's designs on Verona between 1379–1384, in spite of the agreement made with the Scaligers in 1379, can be found in Corio, *op. cit.* II 296; in a letter of Francesco Gonzaga, indexed in *Repertorio Visconteo*, II 358, no. 3020; and in Collino, "Politica Fiorentino-Bolognese", *MAT* 2, LIV 157, Doc. 34.

[4] Lucca, *Regesti*, 199, no. 1139, and 212, no. 1179; a letter from Siena, in Seregni, "Documenti Viscontei", *ASL* xxvi, 1, 249–50.

ment, and two exiles from Verona, Spinetta Malaspina and
Guglielmo Bevilacqua, held positions of trust at his court.[1]
Pavia was already becoming the centre for that group of men who,
under his able direction, were to reorganize the government of
Lombardy and win for themselves a reputation as the most
astute body of politicians in Italy.

Giangaleazzo's mild government kept his dominions at peace,
and encouraged Bernabò's subjects, heavily oppressed by taxation and fear, to regard him with approval and hope. He had
made his peace with Savoy, and could count on the sympathy of
Florence and Bologna. He hoped for support from the enemies of
Bernabò's latest ally, Antonio della Scala, in eastern Lombardy.
But if he waited longer, Bernabò might entrench himself in-
vulnerably behind the formidable alliance of the Valois. It was
decided in an Angevin council on 29 April 1385 to summon Lucia
Visconti to Avignon; already, according to the account given in a
contemporary poem, the preparations for the marriage ceremony
were well advanced in Milan. It was necessary for Giangaleazzo
to act before Lucia set out for France.[2]

He left Pavia on 5 May 1385, on a pilgrimage to the Madonna
del Monte at Varese. The absurdly large bodyguard to which the
world had grown accustomed went with him. Verme and Porro
and Bevilacqua rode by his side. He relied on secrecy and the
impression created by long years of playing a part; for the rest,
simplicity of conception was once again the keynote of his plan.
The large bodyguard, the expressed fear of entering the walls of
Milan, were accepted by Bernabò not with suspicion but with
contempt. The Count wished to pay his respects to his uncle and
cousins—outside the city; Bernabò agreed. Giangaleazzo spent
the night at Binasco, midway on the road between Milan and
Pavia. On the following morning he set out with his troops for

[1] Diversi, Porro, and two old counsellors of Galeazzo, were specially mentioned by the government of Lucca as valuable friends at court: Lucca,
Regesti, 199, no. 1144.
[2] Romano, "Primo Matrimonio di Lucia Visconti", *ASL* xx 604-10.
The preparations in Milan were probably more important in forcing Giangaleazzo's hand, than the Angevin decision of 29 April. It is unlikely that
the Count learnt of this decision in time to make all his plans ready by 5 May.

Milan. No one can tell us of his demeanour or of his private thoughts at the most crucial moment of his career, as he rode past the rich fields of the Lombard plain in the morning of a spring day. But the ordeal was brief, for the plot worked without hitch or flaw. Within a few hours he was undisputed master of Milan, while Bernabò and two of his sons, riding out unprotected to greet him, were prisoners in his hands.[1]

[1] The chroniclers agree in the main in their treatment of the episode, although there are differences of detail. Bernabò, according to some accounts, was warned that his nephew's bodyguard was too large for a pilgrimage, and that mischief was afoot: Levi, "Medesina da Desio", *ASL* xxxiv, 2, 475–6. Can some inkling of the Count's intention have leaked out? There are two references whose precise bearing on these events remains obscure; unless they can both be ascribed to scribal errors, they would seem to confirm the idea that some rumour of Giangaleazzo's purpose was abroad. A messenger was despatched from Santhià, according to a record in the accounts of Savoy, on "die quinta[!] mensis maii", "pro sciendo veritatem de capcione domini Barnabonis captum [*sic*] per dominum Comitem Virtutum": "Eporediensia", 502, no. 202. The government of Pisa, according to its records, decided to congratulate Giangaleazzo on 6 May: Silva, "Governo di Pietro Gambacorta in Pisa", 222 and note 2; it is almost incredible that authentic news could have reached Pisa in time for this decision to be taken on the very day of Bernabò's downfall.

CHAPTER IV

NORTHERN ITALY AND THE FALL OF BERNABÒ (1385). THE NEW LORD OF MILAN

WESTERN Europe learnt with astonishment, but with little regret, of Bernabò's sudden and total eclipse.

> Of Melan grete Barnabo Viscounte,
> God of delyt, and scourge of Lumbardie,

the embodiment of tyrannical despotism, had seemed unassailable in his strength. The amazement of his contemporaries is the measure of Giangaleazzo's boldness; but he had not miscalculated the forces favourable to his enterprise. When his triumph was known, the people of Milan ran through the streets, burned the official records of the city, and acclaimed him as a liberator, crying: "Long live the Count, and down with the taxes." Giangaleazzo, secure in his father's old residence, the Castello di Porta Giovia, allowed this gust of emotional relief, born of the hope that a better time had come, to take its own course. On the following day, he summoned the Great Council of 900, the solemn deliberative body of the Commune, and formally received from them the dominion of the city with all the rights enjoyed by his predecessors. The Council in addition empowered him to choose his own successor from among his heirs—absolute power slowly receiving recognition.[1]

The other cities of Bernabò's dominions followed the example of the capital with hardly a struggle. There was no discussion of terms. Each city, having admitted Giangaleazzo's troops and formally accepted his authority, presented a petition; and Giangaleazzo, in possession of a fortune of several hundred thousand florins which had been found in Bernabò's Castello di Porta Romana, was able to bestow gracious favours, flatter local

---

[1] Sickel, "Vicariat der Visconti", 44–5.

wishes and grant financial relief to ensure the loyalty of his new subjects.[1]

Bernabò was transferred to the fortress of Trezzo on the Adda, where he died in December. The brief captivity of the fallen Prince was a congenial subject, from which contemporary poets soon built up a romantic story of barely foiled efforts to escape, of feminine devotion and of the ultimate and inevitable end by poison. Certainly he must have been a dangerous prisoner, safer out of the way. But there is no proof of any other cause of death than the rage and restlessness in his own heart.

Two of his sons remained at liberty; but in their adversity they found no friends powerful enough to espouse their cause. The careful diplomacy of seven years kept Italy passive. Giangaleazzo appealed to his allies for troops to defend his state, more perhaps as a test of friendship than from any pressing threat of danger. The official attitude of the Florentine government was one of reserve, and the Council was still discussing the question of sending troops six weeks later. "There was rejoicing in Florence, because messer Bernabò was our enemy; but certain wise men said: 'We rejoice at our own misfortune, because that which was ruled by two men is now ruled by one, and both are our enemies.'"[2] They already believed that the master of Milan must be the enemy of Florence, and feared the greater unity which Giangaleazzo had given to the Visconti state. But the Commune of Lucca, whose resources were small, placed 25 lances at the Count's disposal, and Pisa sent 200 knights.[3] The Count of Savoy sent 50 lances,[4]

---

[1] Corio, *Storia di Milano*, II 322–5; Giulini, *Memorie di Milano*, XI 279–82, 296–8. The petitions of Brescia: Lonati, *Stato Totalitario alla fine del secolo XIV*, 22–8, and 48–62, nos. 2–3; of Salò, answered on 14 June: Bettoni, *Storia della Riviera di Salò*, III 192–4; of Soncino, 18 June: Galantino, *Storia di Soncino*, I 138 note.

[2] Giovanni Morelli, *Cronica*, 292; and similarly Sozomeno, "Specimen Historie", *RIS* XVI 1128 B. For the documents relative to the Florentine attitude: Collino, "Politica Fiorentino-Bolognese", *MAT* 2, LIV 162–4, Docs. 49–56; Rado, *Maso degli Albizi*, 123 and note 1; Novati, "Cattura di Bernabò", *ASL* XXXIII, 1, 129–37.

[3] Novati, *ibid.* 136 and note 1.

[4] Accounts of Savoy: Camus, "Maison de Savoie et le mariage de Valentine Visconti", *BSBS* IV 120; Id. "Venue en France de Valentine Visconti", *MSI* XXXVI 49, Docs. 2–4; "Eporediensia", 502–3, no. 203.

and the Venetian government, which had not been in close touch
with the Visconti since the Peace of Turin, sent an embassy to
congratulate Giangaleazzo on his success—"factum quod est
magnum et arduum".[1]
Francesco Gonzaga of Mantua, Bernabò's son-in-law, did not
commit himself openly; but he kept Giangaleazzo informed of
the movements of Carlo Visconti, the elder of Bernabò's sons still
at liberty; and he showed no desire to receive the exile in
Mantua.[2] The means by which Giangaleazzo attached Gonzaga
to his cause are by no means clear, but the clue to them probably
lies in the six consecutive journeys to Mantua made by one of the
Count's agents in the earlier half of 1383,[3] at the moment when
Gonzaga was obtaining the Imperial revocation of the oath of
homage and allegiance which his father had been forced to swear
to Bernabò. The issue was certainly favourable to the Count, for
Gonzaga was devoted to his cause in the years which followed
1385.
Antonio della Scala alone remained faithful to Bernabò and
his family. Bernabò's youngest son Mastino, still a boy, was
besieged with his friends in Brescia by Giangaleazzo's troops.
Della Scala received Carlo Visconti in Verona, and mobilized a
force on the Brescian border for the relief of Mastino. But against
the superior forces of the Count, he could do nothing without the
help of the Venetians, who were not disposed to support him for
that purpose.[4] Carlo therefore set out for Germany, to look for
help at the court of his brother-in-law, Stephen of Bavaria, at
Munich.[5] Mastino, after a two months' siege, agreed to surrender

[1] Ferrai, "Politica di Giangaleazzo", *ASI* 5, xxii 39 note 2.
[2] Giangaleazzo to Gonzaga, 17 May, and a letter from Gonzaga: Romano,
"Giangaleazzo Visconti e gli Eredi di Bernabò", *ASL* xviii 309–310, Docs.
1, 3.
[3] Credentials to Giovanni Ferrante, the Count's "famigliare": *Repertorio
Visconteo*, ii 359–67, nos. 3028, 3036, 3045, 3051, 3067, 3096.
[4] "Annales Mediolanenses", *RIS* xvi 785; Conforto da Costoza, "Frammenti di Storia Vicentina", *RIS* NS xiii, 1, 34. Letter to Gonzaga: Romano,
"Giangaleazzo Visconti", *ASL* xviii 309, Doc. 1.
[5] Corio, *op. cit.* ii 323. Letter of Carlo from Ingoldstadt, 3 August:
Simonsfeld, "Beiträge zur Bayerischen und Münchener Geschichte", in
Sitzungsberichte der Königlich-Bayerischen Akademie der Wissenschaften, for
1896, 302, Doc. 12.

all rights in his father's dominions, in return for a monthly pension of 1000 ducats to be paid to him in Venice; "but if, and for how long, this agreement was kept, no one can say".[1]

Thus the Count of Vertus, secured from the danger of immediate attack, could devote himself to the task of consolidating the position which he had gained.

Giangaleazzo did not stay longer than a month in the bustling and noisy city which had witnessed his triumph in May 1385. He was back at Pavia early in June, in the palace which he knew and loved so well. He felt more at home here, where the river breezes alleviated the intensity of the summer heat, where he could stroll through his garden or ride in the quiet solitude of the great, wooded park. But any one who dreamed that Lombardy could look forward to an era of peaceful development for her fertile lands and prosperous industries, under the care of a mild and enlightened prince, was quickly to be disillusioned.

Little enough was known of the man who, at the age of thirty-three, became the master of the greatest state in Italy. He had hidden himself as far as possible from the eyes of the world for five years. But now he threw off his disguise, and stepped forward to assume the leading part in Italian politics which was rightly his.

The part which he had played during these years at Pavia was not entirely false to his nature. The verdict of his contemporaries was inevitably tinged by the political controversies of which he was the centre; but the account of a chronicler who wrote a century later, and had no reason for bias, is borne out by what we know of Giangaleazzo's character. He portrays for us a man of great intellect, cultured, patient and flattering, slow to anger and never heedlessly cruel; one who never acted without deeply considering the consequences; a philosopher with a taste for solitude; physically well endowed, but moderate in his personal needs. "Of deep intellect, gentle, mild, and without cruelty, rarely or never angered; of persuasive speech, flattering and honouring all; restraining himself when affronted, slow and

---

[1] Brunetti, "Nuovi Documenti dall' Archivio di Venezia", *ASL* xxxvi, 2, 8 note 3; Romano, "Giangaleazzo Visconti", *ASL* xviii 12.

prudent in action....He greatly loved solitude, was a late riser, and spent much time in the contemplation of the affairs of this world."[1] Corio records that he was "timid in adversity, but most bold when fortune favoured him".[2] He was never rash, but he could not always hide his feelings when his plans were crossed or disappointed.[3] His intellectual interests and his contemplative nature are recorded by Giovio.· "He was wont to give himself up to meditation during solitary walks, to hold discussions with those who were most experienced in every branch of affairs, to quote instances from the annals of the past, and to conform carefully to the institutions of his ancestors which had been established by the test of war....He found relaxation for his mind in the conversation of scholars and in constant reading." Giovio tells us, too, of his devotion to the business of the state, from which "neither the delights of hunting and hawking, nor games of dice, nor the allurements of women, nor the tales of buffoons and jesters could draw him away". He did not in fact renounce these pleasures entirely, but they played a far less conspicuous part at his court than at that of Bernabò. He had none of his uncle's crude vitality and abounding physical energy. "He exercised his body moderately, for the purpose of preserving his health."[4] When he hunted, he preferred the milder forms of sport with hawk or falcon.[5] But stag-hunting was also among his pleasures. The Mantuan envoy Filippo della Molza reports that, arriving in Pavia one day in the height of the summer, "I found that my lord Count had gone to hunt deer, which he hunts with the bow and on horseback; and when he returned home,. it was already the first hour of the night, and he sent messer Giacomo della Croce to tell me that he did not know how I felt for the heat, but that he had got very hot, and thought that I might be even hotter than he, so that for that day he wished to rest".[6] This was one occasion on which matters of state were postponed on account of the pleasures of the chase.

[1] "Annales Forolivienses", *RIS* NS xxii, 2, 79.
[2] Corio, *op. cit.* ii 438.   [3] E.g. in Doc. 6.
[4] Giovio, *Vite duodecim Vicecomitum*, 166.
[5] "La caccia più dilettosa e pittoresca": Dorsa, *Caccia nel Milanese*, 128.
[6] Despatch of 15 July 1392: *ASMa*, E. xlix. 3.

The exaggerated piety of Giangaleazzo's early years was not altogether assumed. He was always profoundly attached to the forms of religious observance, and showed special devotion to the Virgin and to St Anthony, in whose Church at Vienne he wished to be represented in the robe of an Antonine friar;[1] he had granted certain exemptions to the order in his younger days, in 1368 and 1379.[2] He was regular in his worship and, in accordance with the princely custom of his times, charitable in his endowments to religious institutions. But superstition went hand in hand with religion at the court of an Italian prince, and Giangaleazzo was as devoted to the cult of astrology as any of his contemporaries. Powerful and methodical as his intellect was, he could not free himself from the preconceptions of the age in which he lived; he surpassed his contemporaries in the degree of his abilities, but unlike the great Frederick II, his life and thought and policies were entirely moulded by the accepted conventions of his own times. Gusberto Maltraversi of Cremona,[3] the court physician and astrologer, and a Master Gabriel of whom very little trace has survived, were important personages at Pavia. Giangaleazzo himself admitted his belief in the influence of the stars to Filippo della Molza, whose intimate despatches to Francesco Gonzaga provide some of the most personal glimpses of the Count's court: "The reason why I do not wish to speak to you about it at present, is that I observe astrology in all my affairs. The moon is 'in combustion',[4] so that what I want to tell you I will not tell you at the moment, but tomorrow or the next day perhaps, I will certainly send for you, when the moment is favourable, and will tell you of a thing which will please my son [Gonzaga]."[5] In

---

[1] From his last will: Corio, *op. cit.* II 437, and the comments of Beltrami, "Storia documentata della Certosa di Pavia", 101 note 1. There is a figure of him in the Duomo of Milan "col tonaca dei frati antoniani": Sant' Ambrogio, "Colonna votiva", *ASL* XIX 677–8.

[2] *Repertorio Visconteo*, II 178, no. 1548; and 307, no. 2599.

[3] *V.* Romano, "Regesto degli Atti Notarili", *ASL* XXI, 2, 41 note 1. Master Gabriel may have been the court astrologer of Francesco Gonzaga.

[4] This expression refers to the position of the moon in relation to the sun. I am indebted to Signor S. Breglia for drawing my attention to the use of it in Milton's *Areopagitica* (ed. Hales, p. 134, where the term is explained).

[5] Despatch of 24 May 1389 (marked 1392): *ASMa*, E. XLIX. 3.

another interview with della Molza twelve days later, discussing the proposed assumption by Gonzaga of the Visconti arms, Giangaleazzo is reported as saying: " If any suitable day can be chosen, on which Master Gabriel and Master Usberto are agreed, he can take these arms in secret "; and again, " it seems to me that I have understood from Master Usberto that the 22nd of this month would be a suitable day; but I will tell Pasquino to get Master Usberto to give him in writing all those days which seem suitable to him and are favourable, and to take them to Master Gabriel, who can go through them, so that when my son comes here, an arrangement can be made and he can take my arms secretly ".[1] Master Gusberto, however, displayed a pleasant vein of scepticism towards the more extreme manifestations of his art. Galeazzo Busoni, another Mantuan agent, wrote in one of his despatches: " Regarding the Jews who announce that the end of the world is near, nothing is so far known here....The idea was laughed at by Master Usberto, who would be one of the most likely to hear of such matters; for he said that he wished to live as long as he might, and that unless the world is flooded entirely, it cannot be destroyed or brought to an end."[2]

Giangaleazzo was not unfortunate in his family relations. Blanche of Savoy commanded his dutiful respect and affection.[3] Caterina Visconti, the wife whom Bernabò imposed on him, always received the honours due to her position.[4] As Bernabò's daughter, her task cannot have been an easy one; there is no reason to doubt that they lived in harmony, but she probably never filled the place at Giangaleazzo's side as Isabella of Valois might have done. A curious incident, in which Caterina exceeded her powers in the appointment of an officer of the Commune of Milan, and Giangaleazzo cancelled the appointment, suggests that she may have had something of the imperious character which

[1] Despatch of 4 June 1389: *ibid.*
[2] Despatch of 28 October 1391: *ibid.*
[3] Magenta, *Visconti e Sforza*, I 176–80.
[4] The lands which Giangaleazzo gave to her are listed by Corio, *op. cit.* II 324, 328. She nominated a number of the lesser officials in the Communal administration of Milan, and many such appointments are recorded in Santoro, "Registri", *passim: v.* Valeri, "Eredità di Giangaleazzo", 26.

had marked both her parents.[1] She presided over the feminine
side of the court, sometimes joined with her ladies in the hunting
parties which were organized in the country residences of the
Visconti, looked after the interests of her younger and unmarried
sisters, and was consulted by her husband in matters which
concerned them.[2] But Giangaleazzo turned for softer consolation to Agnese Mantegazza, a Milanese lady on whom he bestowed
many honours; a square in Pavia bore her name, and she owned
the Castello of Sant' Angelo; when she travelled, she moved as a
princess, "with great company".[3] Other traces of Giangaleazzo's
infidelity are rare and obscure. The account books of Savoy
record gifts in 1390 to "the attendants and trumpeters of the
lady Lusotta mistress of the lord Count of Vertus"; and two
children, Antonio and Daniele, perhaps the offspring of Lusotta,
were living in the same year.[4] But apart from his affection for
Agnese Mantegazza and her son, Gabriele Maria Visconti, who
played an undistinguished part in the years which followed his
father's death, Giangaleazzo's private life left little impression on
the records of his time.

Dearest of all to him was his daughter Valentina. She spent
her youth in the happy and graceful atmosphere of Pavia, under
the guidance of Blanche of Savoy and surrounded by her father's
loving care; a tragic contrast to the bitterness of her later life
in France as Duchess of Orleans. Eustache Deschamps, one of
the writers who enjoyed her esteem, has paid tribute to her:

> Qui gent corps a, juene, fresche, joly,
> De hault atour, de lignie royal.
> Celle n'a pas a maniere failly;
> A bon droit n'est d'elle un cuer plus loyal.
>
> Elle aime Dieu, elle est de tous amée,
> Car plesir fait a toute creature,
> De son pais'est forment regretée,
> Et ou elle est se maintient nette et pure.[5]

---

[1] Santoro, "Registri", 18–22, nos. 69, 77, 79, 85–6. These documents give
merely a skeleton of what must have been an interesting dispute.

[2] Cf. the reference to Giangaleazzo's "concilium muliebrem", in Doc. 6.

[3] Manfredi, *Storia di Voghera*, 214; Magenta, *op. cit.* I 196; Giulini,
Memorie, XII 78.   [4] "Eporediensia", 505, nos. 212 and 214.

[5] Collas, *Valentine de Milan*, 18–23; Champion, *Vie de Charles d'Orléans*,
10–16.

Praises of her grace and her winning manner abound; and though these qualities could not save her from the consequences of a political intrigue which brought misery, persecution and strife in its train, she retained her dignity until the day of her death. Giangaleazzo sacrificed her to the inexorable demands of politics; it was the natural fate of a prince's daughter, and there is no doubt that he loved her. When Milan was given over to a week of festivities in honour of her departure for France, he shut himself up in the country, his heart too heavy for the celebrations which he had commanded as her due. " For my lord of Milan left Pavia without speaking to his daughter, and this he did because he could not take leave of her without weeping." Valentina herself must have related this to the advocate who defended the honour of her husband after his assassination; and it is confirmed by the Sienese ambassadors, who wrote from Milan while the celebrations were in progress: " the lord Count has not come here, nor does he wish to be at Pavia when she leaves. It is generally said that he is now at Pandino; and when she has departed, he will return to Pavia."[1]

Valentina shared with Giangaleazzo his love of beautiful things. The " Castello " of Pavia was a fair treasure-house, whose gaiety enchanted even the courtiers of Paris. Eustache Deschamps, who accompanied Louis of Orleans to Pavia in 1391, wrote:

> Il fait tresbeau demourer
> En doulz chastel de Pavie,
> Où l'en seult dames trouver
> Qui mainent joieuse vie.
> Car c'est noble compaignie
> Et qui dance voluntiers.[2]

The inventory of Valentina's dowry, the dresses and ornaments, the products of the goldsmiths and silversmiths of Lombardy, reveals the splendour and luxury of the court.[3] With Giangale-

---

[1] Despatch of 16 June 1389: *ASS*, Concistoro 1825, no. 50. The passage from Cousinot's *Justification* is quoted, from Monstrelet, by Collas, *op. cit.* 48.

[2] *Ibid.* 141–2.

[3] The list is published in *RIS* xvi 807 A–813 c. A French inventory, not completely identical, was published by Camus, " Venue en France ", *MSI* xxxvi 34–48.

azzo's patronage, and under the impetus of the great architectural foundations of his day, a new school of art and sculpture developed in Milan and Pavia in the last decade of the fourteenth century. The great library, commenced by Archbishop Giovanni and by Galeazzo, continued to expand. Giangaleazzo's love of learning in fact never deserted him; he brought scholars from all over Italy to teach in the University of Pavia, which owed its revival to his father and its great activity and fame to his own encouragement.[1]

Those who came into contact with him spoke of his great charm, of his "fluent eloquence". He seldom made great state appearances, although he could organize a most splendid display when the occasion arose—to celebrate his Ducal coronation in 1395, to name the most celebrated instance. Our rare personal glimpses of him usually have a more intimate setting. We see him exerting his charm on the representative of a useful but wavering ally. "When the lord Count saw me, he rose to his feet and came forward to meet me, and seized my hand and made me sit down, whether I would or no", wrote Filippo della Molza in one of his despatches; and he goes on to comment on the unwonted cordiality of his reception by the court, at a time when Gonzaga's allegiance was known to be wavering.[2] On another occasion, Filippo found the Count quietly reading. "Yesterday, at about the 22nd hour, I came into the presence of the lord Count, whom I found seated in a very small room; he had before him a book which he was reading, and which he told me was the bible."[3] But at times Giangaleazzo is in a different temper, hurrying across the courtyard of the palace with barely a nod and a word, preoccupied with other business. "While I was with Franceschino Barbavara", wrote Busoni, "wishing to arrange with him for an audience with his master, the lord Count himself came upon us. He did not seem in a good mood, but he took me by the hand and asked after your lordship, and I made suitable reply, paying your

[1] Magenta, *op. cit.* I 245–56; and *v. infra*, Chapter XIII.
[2] Despatch of 15 July 1392: *ASMa*, E. XLIX. 3.
[3] Despatch of 14 August 1390: Rambaldi, "Stefano III, Duca di Baviera", *ASL* XXVIII, 1, 324, Doc. 2.

respects to him and commending you to him, and he passed on to where his leopards are kept, nor could I have further speech with him."[1] When he took a holiday in the hunting districts, he moved from place to place with complete informality, so that none could say for certain where he would be found on the following night. Filippo della Molza, arriving at Belgioioso one morning, found there Gasparino Visconti and Antonio Balestraccio, "who told me that the lord Count had arrived there at Belgioioso yesterday in the second hour of the night, that no one knew anything about it, that he had left to go fowling,[2] as he could no longer fowl so well here. Messer Gasparino told me he knew for certain that the lord Count had said that he would come to Pavia without fail"; and the Mantuan was recommended to go there.[3]

The Sienese envoys at Giangaleazzo's court in 1392 have given a vivid picture of an audience held for them in a glade of the woods during an interval in a day's hunting. Giangaleazzo listened to them with sympathy and understanding, but with some abstraction, from which he roused himself at last, with a sigh, to give them their answer.[4] Here we have the prince, quick of intellect, reflective by nature, simple in his personal tastes, ready to give audience in a rustic and informal scene. Behind the remoteness of a despot in his court, and the greatness of a politician shaping the course of European events, there is always this strain of personal simplicity to be found in Giangaleazzo's character.

What then were the qualities which made him hated, feared, and admired throughout Italy and beyond? The halls of his palace housed more than courtiers and scholars and artists. They were crossed and recrossed by envoys and statesmen, by clerks and soldiers, moving to the command of a keen and restless

---

[1] Despatch of Galeazzo Busoni, 2 November 1391: *ASMa*, E. xlix. 3.

[2] The precise transcription of this phrase is difficult to obtain, owing to the haste with which the letter was written.

[3] Despatch of 4 September 1392: *ibid.* In 1388, during an outbreak of the plague, "sì celatamente andava tramutando luogo, che spesse volte avvenia, che dov' elli si fosse, non si potea sapere": Minerbetti, "Cronica", *RIS* NS xxvii, 2, 72.

[4] *V.* Doc. 8. A not unsimilar interview, with representatives of the committee for the construction of the Cathedral of Milan, took place on the road between Cusago and Biaggio: Boito, *Duomo di Milano*, 164–5.

mind. Giangaleazzo was a prince of the Renaissance not only in his private tastes but in his political ambitions. His keen and logical intelligence gave him a claim to be regarded as the founder of a state; and his ambition drove him on to conquest after conquest, in the unending political rivalry for security and power.

CHAPTER V

THE VISCONTI STATE: THE GOVERNMENT OF LOMBARDY AND GIANGALEAZZO'S ADMINISTRATIVE REFORMS (1385–1389)[1]

THE lands over which Giangaleazzo ruled in 1385 were marked by a diversity of characteristics and a diversity of needs. The great industrial centre of Milan and the other prosperous cities of Lombardy, the fertile agricultural districts of the valley of the Po, the more primitive Alpine valleys behind Como, Bergamo and Brescia, and the semi-feudal society of Piedmont—each had its own traditions, and presented its own individual problems to the ruler.

The Visconti never willingly set themselves to oppose the intense local patriotisms which had survived from the Communal age in northern Italy, or to break the continuity of local traditions. But as their dominions expanded, they were compelled, in their own interests and in those of their subjects, to impose a more unitary system of administration. The union of the two branches of the Visconti state under Giangaleazzo in 1385 created at once an imperative need to revise the instruments of government, in order to secure a greater efficiency and economy in the conduct of administrative business.

No one was better fitted than Giangaleazzo to undertake this task. The long studies, from which he acquired an intimate knowledge of the political ideas of the past as well as of the world in which he lived, had also given him something of the outlook of a lawyer.[2] His logical mind was repelled by the inconsistencies

---

[1] In this chapter I am concerned only to illustrate the process by which Giangaleazzo reorganized the government of his state and set it on a more permanent footing. Reasons of space and of proportion prevent me from giving here a more detailed survey of the dominions of the Visconti, and the methods by which they were governed.

[2] That the years of his retirement in Pavia had been well spent in the study of political problems, is the suggestion of Ferrai, " Politica di Giangaleazzo ", ASI 5, XXII 27–8.

which hampered the work of government, and his own temperament is reflected in the thoroughness of his administrative reforms. Unity was the keynote of his policy in every sphere, although he did not always achieve complete success. He could claim against Bernabò that his uncle had ignored this essential need of the Visconti state. Bernabò had foreshadowed in 1379 the division of his territory into equal shares among his five sons after his death.[1] Thus Giangaleazzo could represent himself, in contrast, not only as the champion of one united Lombard state, but as preventing by anticipation a further dismemberment of the Visconti dominions which could only have led to disaster. Union had been achieved; and the principle of unity can be observed in all the measures which Giangaleazzo proposed for the better government of the state.

The first weakness which Giangaleazzo had to overcome arose from the method which he had employed in the deposition of Bernabò. The reactionary nobility were always eager to revive the lost age of privilege, the Communes to restore the proud memories of their freedom; and it was natural that the forces of disorder should see in a revolution so sudden and startling an invitation to their own lawlessness. But Giangaleazzo acted with vigour and promptness, and enforced the principles of public order with a firm hand. A series of edicts restricted the carrying of arms, the gathering of crowds in public places, the construction of fortifications without permission, and the formation of leagues and conspiracies.[2] A month after his entry into Milan, the city administration prohibited unlicensed meetings of the trade gilds.[3] A confused popular riot which broke out in Parma was quickly suppressed; Giangaleazzo had won the support of the respectable

---

[1] 16 November 1379: *Repertorio Visconteo*, II 309, no. 2615; and Romano, "Visconti e la Sicilia", *ASL* XXIII, 1, 21–2.

[2] Decrees published in: *Antiqua Decreta*, 90, 90–1, 93, 93–4, 95–6, 98–9, 109, 111–12, 123–4; Valentini, "Statuti di Brescia", *NAV* XV 87; Comani, "Usi Cancellereschi Viscontei", *ASL* XXVII, 1, 391; Cognasso, "Ricerche", *BSP* XXII 182–4, Doc. 49; Grimaldi, *Signoria di Barnabò Visconti*, 122. And v. Giulini, *Memorie*, XI 406–7.

[3] 6 June 1385: Osio, *Documenti diplomatici*, I 247–8, no. 184. Giangaleazzo secured absolute control of the gilds in the city of Milan: Barbieri, *Economia e politica nel ducato di Milano*, 37–40.

citizen element of the towns, the traditional allies of the Visconti, and they helped to subdue the revolt.[1]

Thus the ground was prepared for a revision of the administrative and judicial system of the state. The four years which followed the deposition of Bernabò marked the peak of Giangaleazzo's administrative activity. The internal government of the Visconti dominions had grown gradually out of Communal institutions in the course of a century, and had been adapted by a process of trial and error to meet the needs of the moment. Giangaleazzo did not alter the main lines of this development; he attempted to systematize it, to co-ordinate the administration of his dominions according to the principles evolved by previous experience.[2] Thus a comparison between the government of Lombardy at his accession and at his death reveals not a revolution but a work of completion, the confirmation of existing tendencies and the rooting out of inconsistencies.

The administrative systems introduced by the despots of northern Italy in the fourteenth century bore in many cases a marked similarity to one another. They succeeded to the same traditions, were shaped by the same circumstances and conditioned by the same needs. The suppression of domestic feuds, impartial justice, financial reorganization, encouragement of agricultural production—these features constantly recur in the story of Italian despotism.[3] But the internal government of the Visconti was remarkable for the extent of the territory over which their system was applied, and for the thoroughness with which it was carried out.

A special interest attaches to Giangaleazzo's contribution to this work. He was able to give a logical shape and a real political significance to the system which had developed from force of circumstances and from the native temperament of his predecessors. It was this clear-sightedness, combined with a methodical nature, which evolved a real system from the tentative and haphazard innovations of his predecessors, who

[1] Corio, *Storia di Milano*, II 324-6.
[2] Cf. Tagliabue, "Politica finanziaria di Giangaleazzo", *BSP* xv 22.
[3] Anzilotti, "Per la Storia delle Signorie", *SS* xxii 82-93.

had yielded to the pressure of forces which they scarcely understood.

Despotic government had found no clear place in the political thought of the day. Bartolo had tried to adapt to the political conditions of Italy the recent nationalist trend of French thought, but his theories were not applicable to the institution of despotism. Discarding the outworn doctrine of a universal Imperio-Papal supremacy, he had reverted to the Aristotelian idea of the city-state as the perfect form of government, and had introduced the concept of the " civitas superiorem non cognoscens et sibi princeps " as a parallel to the French doctrine that "Rex in regno suo est Imperator regni sui ". The Visconti, with the other Italian despots, reverted in theory to the idea of Imperial authority in Italy, and accepted the title of Imperial Vicar; but in practice they upheld the new doctrine that any state, whether " civitas " or "regnum ", which exercised *de facto* the essential rights of sovereignty, was in itself an "Imperium" entitled to treat with every other such state on a footing of equality.[1] They were not concerned with the evolution of a coherent political doctrine; they preferred to safeguard their position by taking account of every possible theory which might be used against them. If they recognized the right of the Emperor to concede authority to them, they were scrupulously careful to respect the independent right of the people to choose their own ruler. In every city which came into their dominions, the authority of the Visconti was confirmed by the "free election" of the Commune.[2]

Thus they acquired the absolute power which, without reference to its origin, Giangaleazzo was determined in practice to enforce. On the one hand, he would never have permitted the Emperor to exercise any influence on the government or, save as an ally, on the external policy of his state. On the other, the cities over which he ruled had transferred to him all the powers which had formerly been vested in the people. A theoretical

[1] Ercole, *Dal Comune al Principato*, 248–80; Cusin, "Impero e la successione degli Sforza", *ASL* NS I 23–31.
[2] Ercole, "Comuni e Signori", *NAV* NS xix 302–13; Silva, "Ordinamento interno in Pisa", *SS* xxi 5–8.

dyarchy remained, because, the transference being in theory a free act of will, the people retained the right to revoke it.[1] But in fact it could not be revoked until the ruler's sword had grown too weak to support his commands; till then, Giangaleazzo's authority was absolute in respect of his subjects.

The declarations of the government during Giangaleazzo's reign reveal a tendency to regard this absolute power as an innate and stable quality invested in the person of the ruler. The Prince was the centre and life-blood of the state—the maker and unmaker of laws, the last resort of the oppressed, the source of all privilege, the arbitrary director of policy. The "Dominus" had acquired a new dignity, a new personality more sacrosanct and more remote from intimate association with his subjects. The person of the Prince required special protection; his state and his honour had grown peculiarly susceptible, not only to the attacks of his enemies, but to the verbal onslaughts of his detractors.[2] As early as October 1385, when perhaps discussion of Bernabò's fate was still rife, he issued decrees against those who criticized his actions or spoke against his state.[3] "Status domini", "honor domini" gained a new value; and it was to the state and the honour, as much as to the person of the Prince, that the new administration was attached. Bernabò once declared that "it is not compatible with our honour to write one day one thing, and the next day the opposite".[4] The Prince himself intended to abide by the principles of justice on which his rule was based; and he expected his officials to observe the same firm impartiality.[5]

[1] "Giuridicamente i Signori non possiedono ma solo temporaneamente detengono l'autorità": Silva, "Ordinamento Interno in Pisa", *SS* xxi 8. Ercole, "Comuni e Signori", *NAV* NS xix 317: "L'autorità che il popolo conferiva...era fuor di dubbio assoluta, piena, illimitata"; but "il Comune aveva mantenuta integra la sua autonoma personalità giuridica e politica": *ibid.* 335.

[2] Against the drawing of arms where the Duke is in residence, 1 December 1398: *Antiqua Decreta*, 224-5.

[3] 8 and 15 October 1385: *ibid.* 85-6, 88-9. A year earlier, a decree that "contra Dominum obloquentes condemnentur aeris et persona": *Repertorio Visconteo*, ii 391, no. 3294. Treason, naturally, was the gravest of crimes: *Antiqua Decreta*, 187-8, 204, 228.

[4] In 1355: Cognasso, "Ricerché", *BSP* xxii 155, Doc. 8.

[5] *Ibid.* 124-6, 133-4. Cf. Lonati, *Stato Totalitario alla fine del secolo XIV*, 45-6.

These principles accord well with Giangaleazzo's retiring nature, with his logical and rather legalistic mind; but they were never fully put into practice. Many modifications had to be made; for the Visconti were faced at once with a dead weight of inertia, and with positive forces of opposition and disintegration. The effort to construct an ordered system of government in Lombardy had brought the Visconti into direct conflict, not only with the ordinary criminal element of the population, but with the established privileges of the nobles, and with the jealous particularism of the Communes which cherished the right to conduct their local affairs in their own grossly incompetent way. In the first years of his reign, before the abnormal demands of a European policy distracted his attention and used up his resources, Giangaleazzo set himself to overcome these sources of resistance.

The ordinary routine of administration was conducted on lines closely resembling those of the Communal epoch. But the underlying spirit was changed, for all the major officials were now appointed by the Prince and owed allegiance exclusively to him. The Podestà had lost most of his authority, and the functions which he exercised under the Visconti were mainly judicial.[1] He enforced justice in accordance with the Signorial decrees. The Great Councils held rare formal meetings. The general administrative business of each city was under the control of a local short-term governing committee, such as the Office of Provisions at Milan. Upon this lesser Council, generally of twelve members appointed at intervals of two months by the Prince or his representative, lay the responsibility for the observance of the law and the suppression of disorder, for all the details of local government, and for the manifold routine of economic supervision imposed in the interests of justice and to ensure an adequate supply of food and the other necessities of life. It worked under the direction and close supervision of the officials sent to control the government of the cities in the interests of their ruler.[2]

---

[1] Lonati, *op. cit.* 28–31.

[2] The activities of the Office of Provisions in Milan are illustrated in its Registers of letters, of which the Index hâs been published by Santoro. Cf. Visconti, *Storia di Milano*, 240.

One of the major problems of the preservation of order was the absence of an efficient police system. The records of the criminal court of the Podestà in Milan have survived for the period from 1385 to 1429.[1] They show remarkably few examples of serious crime; but while about a sixth of the accused were acquitted, more than two-thirds were condemned in contumacy; and we may assume that the proportion of unsolved crimes was equally large. The Visconti never really struck at the roots of this problem. Unapprehended criminals were placed under the ban of outlawry, and their property was confiscated by the Treasury;[2] an outlaw who brought one of his own fellows to justice secured a reversal of his own condemnation.[3] But these measures were only palliatives, and Giangaleazzo did little more than repeat the edicts of his predecessors, tightening up the execution of the laws and making the punishments more severe.[4] The danger of the "banniti" is shown by the preoccupation of the government, and the lengths to which it was prepared to go against them; but the effort to disarm the populace could not achieve success until an adequate police force protected the interests of the peaceful citizen.

The main problem of civil legislation was to adapt the code of procedure to the needs of the age. Each successive stage was carefully regulated by the statutes of the Communes. The litigious spirit of medieval communities required a strict limit to be imposed on the duration of trial. In 1384, Giangaleazzo introduced in Pavia the experiment of arbitration in civil cases by untrained citizens, in order to relieve the pressure on lawyers and judges. He applied the new system to his expanded dominions

[1] Verga, "Sentenze criminali dei Podestà Milanesi", *ASL* xxviii, 2, 96–142; summarized by Muir, *Milan under the Visconti*, 179–84.

[2] The decrees in *Antiqua Decreta*, 87–8, 160, 164–8, 188, 188–9. A special judge presided over matters connected with the outlaws in Verona: Galli, "Dominazione Viscontea a Verona", *ASL* liv 507.

[3] Edicts of Bernabò and Galeazzo: Cognasso, "Ricerche", *BSP* xxii 142, no. 35; 147, nos. 72 and 75; 168–9, Doc. 24. Under Giangaleazzo: *Antiqua Decreta*, 182–4, 214; the latter document shows that such pardons were claimed and granted. A pardon, in Santoro, "Registri", 41, no. 209.

[4] A decree from Pavia, 1381: Cognasso, "Ricerche", *BSP* xxii 82, no. 148; in 1385: *Antiqua Decreta*, 87. Most of Giangaleazzo's legislation against the "banniti" came in the latter half of his reign.

in 1385. But the introduction of a paid but untrained judicial class presented too many loopholes for inefficiency and abuse in a society where public spirit was little developed, and even judges themselves had to be closely watched;[1] and Giangaleazzo acknowledged as much in the following year, when he reverted to the old procedure.[2] At the same time, he carefully regulated the conduct of appeals; and the tendency to abolish them altogether was confirmed in criminal cases by a decree of 1387.[3]

In 1386, Giangaleazzo organized the "Ufficio delle Bollette", a combination of post office and passport office. All letters brought into the city or sent outside the dominions had to pass through it, and the officers exercised the right of censorship. The office carefully regulated the goings and comings of all citizens and foreigners in and out of each city.[4] We have unfortunately no records of its working, but it was clearly an important feature in the creation of a despotic state.

All officials of the state were subject to strict rules, and an inquest was held into the conduct of every officer after the expiry of his term of office. Edicts were directed against the exploitation of the populace, and others were designed to protect the finances of the state against the frauds of its administrators.[5] A series of regulations was evolved to lessen the opportunities for corruption;[6] but the Visconti had to contend with the common weakness of state systems in the early stages of development— the lack of a trained body of politically-minded men capable of holding office according to the principles which governed the enactments of the central authority.

---

[1] Edict of 2 October 1386, against "sententie inique": *Antiqua Decreta*, 122.

[2] *Ibid.* 69–71, 80–5, 115–23; Rovelli, *Storia di Como*, III, 1, 51–2.

[3] *Antiqua Decreta*, 128.

[4] 26 September 1386: *ibid.* 112–14.

[5] *Ibid.* 27–32, 54–5, 93, 137–8, 152; Osio, *op. cit.* I 256–7, no. 188; Pellegrini, "Documenti relativi al Dominio dei Visconti", *AIV* 3, XIII 1121–2, no. 5; Santoro, "Registri", 36, no. 173; 39, no. 192; 63–4, no. 328; 94–5, no. 136; 475–6, no. 97.

[6] These included, besides the "Sindacato" or inquest, edicts against resuming office in the same district until after an interval of a given number of years—usually three or five; and against holding office in a district where relatives resided.

The Visconti had learnt to depend on the support of the industrial and commercial middle class of the towns, and especially of Milan, which, with its famous industries of cloth and armour, its merchants and international bankers and flourishing trades, had all the aspects of a great capital. But they realized, as the rulers of the Communal age had not, that all this was built upon the foundations of agricultural prosperity. Giangaleazzo continued the work of earlier Visconti in favour of agriculture. He applied to all his dominions an edict to exempt cattle and agricultural implements from liability to sequestration for debt.[1] The building of shacks outside a half-mile radius of Milan received the regular encouragement of tax exemptions.[2] The extent and power of Giangaleazzo's state were in themselves a protection for agriculture. But the economic knowledge of the time was limited; and a severe handicap was imposed by the spirit of intense local protectionism, and by the severe restrictions upon the exportation of corn outside the district in which it was grown —regulations which were suspended only in time of famine.[3]

The feudal landowners of Lombardy, tenacious relics of a past age, were the enemies of peasant and burgher alike. Giangaleazzo was prepared to welcome their co-operation within the framework of a despotic state; for the task of the Visconti lay in the reconciliation of hostile forces. But he continued the unwavering attack on every aspect of feudal privilege which offered scope for abuse. The feudatories had worn themselves out in the self-destructive conflicts and ruthlessly selfish treatment of their subjects which had contributed so large a share to the misfortunes of the Communal age; they had now to accept the lesser position assigned

---

[1] In the revision of the administration of the Milanese "Contado", 1381–4: *Antiqua Decreta*, 49–51, 54, 63. Applied universally to Giangaleazzo's dominions, 13 November 1385: Lattès, *Studii di Diritto Statutario*, 77 and 87. And *v.* Nasalli Rocca di Corneliano, in *Atti del Primo Congresso Storico Lombardo*, 418.

[2] Grants of exemption in 1388: *Inventari e Regesti del R. Archivio di Stato in Milano*, III 9–10, nos. 163 and 184. From 1396 on: Santoro, "Registri", 610–27, passim.

[3] Among many examples, *v.* the regulations of 1386: *Antiqua Decreta*, 103–6. Corn could generally be exported to Milan: *ibid.* 147–8, 152. An example of the relaxation of restrictions, during the plague of 1387: Pezzana, *Storia di Parma*, I 177–8. And *v.* Nasalli Rocca di Corneliano, in *op. cit.* 418.

to them by the logic of political evolution. Giangaleazzo demanded assistance from them for his officers, especially in the pursuit of outlaws and evaders of taxation;[1] for the immunity of certain territories from the judicial competence and police organization of the Communes permitted offenders to escape, with the connivance of the privileged, from the consequences of their crimes. The control of fortified places was another principle which the Visconti always asserted; any stronghold not held by their own troops was a potential centre of disorder and resistance to authority. Giangaleazzo carefully investigated the possibility of destroying all fortresses which did not seem strategically justified by the requirements of defence.[2] The unlicensed construction of castles and unauthorized alienations were forbidden.[3]

The unitary policy of a strong centralized administrative authority aroused resistance from the individual communes. Nevertheless the Visconti gradually acquired by a steady process of attrition a detailed control over the administration and finance of their dominions. The same principle of centralization was enforced in the control of economic policy.[4] Even in the legislative sphere, the steadily accumulating supply of statutes and decrees issued to the whole state brought the cities into closer union; and the general revision of legislative codes initiated by Giangaleazzo,[5] while it preserved local peculiarities, enabled the central government to eradicate any clauses which violated the main principles of its policy.

Administrative independence was lost when nominees of the

---

[1] *Antiqua Decreta*, 125, 190–1, 196, 234–5.
[2] In the *Reggiano*, 1386: Grimaldi, *op. cit.* 112 and note 2.
[3] Edict of 1381: Boselli, *Storie Piacentine*, II 59; of December 1385: Comani, "Usi Cancellereschi Viscontei", *ASL* xxvii, 1, 391; of 1387: *Antiqua Decreta*, 127.
[4] Mira, "Provvedimenti viscontei e sforzeschi", *ASL* NS II 355–6. The economic policy of Giangaleazzo, with which I have not the space to deal here, is discussed in the first two chapters of the recent book of Barbieri, *Economia e politica nel ducato di Milano.* He shows the close relation between Milanese industry and the international trade of which the city was the centre, and illustrates the difficulties with which the directors of economic policy were presented when the protection of one of these interests threatened to conflict with the other.
[5] This revision will be referred to in Chapter xiii.

prince superseded locally elected officials. The Communes made à last effort to preserve their financial independence by retaining the power of the purse. They paid a fixed sum to the ruler, and kept the balance for the expenses of local administration. But as the administration came more and more into the hands of the central government, the share retained by the Communes out of their annual revenue grew smaller; and the Visconti established through their own officials a supervision even over local expenditure. The collection of taxes was farmed out to the highest bidder. The revenues were derived mainly from imposts on the primary necessities of life; the direct levy on property, based on the "Estimo" or assessment of each citizen's means, was reserved as an emergency tax. But Communal finance was haphazard, inaccurate and extravagant; Giangaleazzo's orderly and economical mind resented the waste and confusion caused by local incompetence. In 1384, he took control of all the expenses, and therefore of all the income, of Pavia and probably of his other dominions as well.[1] He no longer received a fixed "salary" out of the revenues of the Commune; the Commune depended, for the unimportant local affairs left in its control, on the sources of income which the prince chose to place at its disposal.

Giangaleazzo did not immediately extend this principle to Bernabò's lands in 1385. The new territories demanded financial concessions, not financial control; and Bernabò's hoarded treasure enabled him to grant the concessions without immediate discomfort. But the unification could not long be delayed; and within a few years the pressure of political events compelled Giangaleazzo to enforce this measure throughout his dominions.[2]

Unity of administration based on a centralized government— so much Giangaleazzo demanded in the interests of his state. He himself looked forward to a more ambitious union—not merely a convenient administrative device, but a bond uniting each subject, independently of his Communal allegiance, in the common allegiance to his prince. Nor was this idea the product of long years of authority and absolute command; it was inherent in Giangaleazzo's political conceptions. In January 1386, he

[1] Tagliabue, *op. cit. BSP* xv 40-7.　　　[2] *V.* Chapter vii.

proposed to break down the prohibitions by which each Commune limited the possession of property within its borders to citizens resident in its territory. "Because the State of our dominions, hitherto divided, is now, by the favour of the Most High, united", he began in his letter to the Communal authorities. Since he has heard that the proposal is contrary to the statutes of some of his cities, he asks for their opinion.[1] Their answers have not survived; but the nature of them may be assumed from a decision, taken a year later by a representative body of Milanese citizens, to retain in force the law excluding a woman who married outside the city's jurisdiction from her paternal inheritance.[2]

Here, too, Giangaleazzo had attempted a settlement. The objections he met with were partly particularist, and partly financial, for difficult questions of the right of taxation were involved; and this exclusive legislation remained in the statute books of all the Communes. The financial aspect of the problem is illustrated by the vexed question whether property, owned by citizens of another Commune, should pay taxes in the locality or in the owner's place of domicile. Giangaleazzo encouraged the Communes to come to a decision by individual agreement, but the result showed no unanimity of opinion.[3]

These tentative approaches to the wider problems of particularism did not reach very far. Municipal jealousies were still unconquered; they remained unconquered when Giangaleazzo died. His own attitude showed, not only an understanding of the drawbacks of particularism, but a remarkable degree of respect for its hold upon the Communes. He would not drive his subjects too far against their will. Perhaps he knew that, in that direction, unity enforced by statute would be of little use to him, a mockery of the goal at which he aimed.

The centralization of government had brought many new duties and problems upon the prince; Giangaleazzo had to create the central organs of government which were thereby made

---

[1] 31 January 1386: Pezzana, *op. cit.* I 162; *Inventari e Regesti*, III 10, no. 179; Santoro, "Registri", 427, no. 16; Lonati, *op. cit.* 68, no. 10.

[2] 14 May 1387: Santoro, "Registri", 451, no. 47.

[3] Comani, "Denari per la dote di Valentina", *ASL* XXVIII, 1, 65–7; Ciapessoni, "Per la Storia della Economia", *BSP* VI 393–8.

necessary. The Councils were the indispensable adjuncts of the
new administrative policy; they marked the inevitable transition
from the purely personal government of the prince and his immediate associates, to the more formal methods demanded of the
ruler of extended territories. Hitherto the Visconti had turned,
when they required counsel, to an undefined body of intimate
advisers.[1] Giangaleazzo instituted a "consilium secretum", or
privy council in personal attendance upon him, and the "consilium justitie", a permanent body established at Milan.[2] He
issued instructions in August 1385 that all envoys, from his own
subjects or from foreign powers, should present themselves first
in Milan "before our Council".[3] Probably the division of functions
between the two Councils was not finally settled until a later
date; certainly their personnel was not yet clearly defined. But
the underlying principle was already apparent. The advisers
surrounding the prince helped him to deal with important matters
of state, and affairs which demanded his direct attention. The
permanent Council in Milan sifted all state business, dealt on its
own initiative with all matters of routine which came within its
competence, and thereby relieved the pressure of work on Giangaleazzo and his immediate advisers; business which needed the
express approval of the prince was forwarded to the secret
Council. A special branch of the Council, known as the "Camera",
dealt with the administration of finance under the direction of the
Masters of the Entries: "Maestri della entrate ordinarie" at
Milan, and the "Maestri delle entrate straordinarie" whose
headquarters were at Pavia. The former directed the financial
policy of the state and supervised the ordinary taxation of the
dominions; the latter received the revenue derived from extraordinary taxation in moments of emergency. Probably a General

[1] Del Giudice, "Consigli Ducali e il Senato di Milano", in *Nuovi Studi di Storia e Diritto*, 227-8.

[2] *Ibid.* 228-32; he accepts, with a reservation, the statement of Giulini, *Memorie*, xii 14, that the first reference to this division into two councils is found in an edict of 1398 (*Antiqua Decreta*, 223). The existence of two councils in 1385-6, not yet perhaps bearing these names, seems clear; cf. Comani, "Usi Cancellereschi Viscontei", *ASL* xxvii, 1, 385-412.

[3] *Ibid.* 394-6. The decree of 29 August was published by Magenta, *Visconti e Sforza*, ii 50, no. 69.

Master of the Entries co-ordinated the control of both departments.

By these means Giangaleazzo was enabled to cope with the ever-increasing stream of business which flowed into the headquarters of his government.[1] He was no longer a petty despot; he ruled over wide territories, of great wealth and strategic importance. He set himself, with wisdom and patience, to convert this agglomeration of cities into something like a state; and the Councils were the most important instruments of his purpose.

They were something more than this. Gathered from all parts of Italy, chosen for their abilities and their experience, Giangaleazzo's counsellors were skilled in diplomacy as well as in administration. The Count of Vertus was not long content with the increased territories which he had gained in May 1385.

[1] A summary in Visconti, *Storia di Milano*, 282–3.

CHAPTER VI

THE POLITICAL DIVISIONS OF ITALY. THE NEW SITUATION IN PIEDMONT; THE BETROTHAL OF VALENTINA, AND THE GREAT SCHISM (1385–1389)

It would indeed have been strange if Giangaleazzo had been lacking in ambition, in an Italy whose political contours changed from day to day. Ill-defined and impermanent boundaries, deeply ingrained traditions of local hostility, lived on side by side with a common language and a fundamental sense of brotherhood which the humanists of the fourteenth century transformed into an active political conception. From the enemy within the city, or the enemy at the gates, an appeal could always be made to a more distant liberator who yet shared the common heritage.

The five states, whose relations with one another formed the history of Italy in the hundred years to come, already dominated the peninsula. Municipalism had broken under the pressure of centralizing forces, and had given way to an epoch of regionalism. But the new regional states were still in process of formation, still struggling to master local resistance and the problems of internal organization; and until this process was complete they could not hope to achieve even the precarious balance among themselves which was the master-work of Cosimo de' Medici in the middle of the following century. During the formative period, each power had ample opportunity to interfere in the sphere of its rivals: the turbulent, feudal state of Naples, ruled by the titular "Kings of Sicily and Jerusalem"; the Papal dominions, temptingly weak in the eyes of their neighbours, plagued by internal dissensions, but destined to survive and know a new glory under the Medici Popes; the democratic Republic of Florence, determined to master the whole of Tuscany; the oligarchy of Venice, newly alive to the importance of a secure footing on Italian soil after the experiences of the war of Chioggia; and the Visconti, rulers of the Lombard plain, eager now to complete the natural borders of their state and to control the roads beyond, which led to and from their dominions. The Counts of Savoy in the north-west hardly entered yet into the direct circle of Italian powers; but they were a dynasty already old in the swift passage of Italian institutions: not brilliant, but steady and persistent, engaged in gaining a strip of land or winning a new allegiance, and always producing sons to carry on the unbroken traditions of their house.

The rivalries of these states formed the main content of Italian politics; the smaller cities and lesser rulers precariously survived by means of a rapid adjustment to the momentary balance of the five powers—turning from one powerful protector to another, using the feuds of their great neighbours to preserve the integrity of their own lands. Giangaleazzo had already shown that he was something more than a novice in this art. The game of politics came to him as a heritage scarcely to be denied. He entered into it, not perhaps with enthusiasm, but with a cool and masterly shrewdness, and a novel skill in handling the customary diplomatic weapons of the period.

His passions seem rather cold in that hot-blooded age. His approach to political problems showed an unrivalled intellectual keenness, but he lacked the active personal zest which a prince more truly typical of his time would have displayed in his enterprises. It was consonant with his rather academic nature, and it characterized his first political action after the events of May 1385—the publication of a "Processus" or trial of Bernabò.

This document summarized the grievances of Giangaleazzo, and of Bernabò's subjects, against the fallen prince, and added a legal argument—although a very weak one—to justify his deposition, on the ground that he had never secured the revocation of the Imperial sentence of deprivation incurred in 1372. The accusations against Bernabò, exaggerated as they were, had a foundation of truth in their picture of his jealousy towards his nephew, and of the ferocity of which he was capable.[1] The same accusations were repeated in the instructions drawn up for the

---

[1] Published in *RIS* xvi 788 A–800 B. And *v.* Romano, "Giangaleazzo Visconti", *ASL* xviii 6–8; Novati, "Cattura di Bernabò", *ASL* xxxiii, 1, 128–9.

envoys whom Giangaleazzo sent to Tuscany at the end of May 1385. Before his messengers had even left Milan, his deed was accepted as irrevocable; but he was none the less anxious to justify himself before the world, and to establish his legal position as firmly as possible.[1]

For thirty years, the Visconti dominions had been shared by two rulers, who recognized the identity of their interests, but who could not always unite their forces in the methodical pursuit of a common purpose. Now, however, the two divisions had recovered their natural unity. The equal distribution of Bernabò's lands among his sons, although it could have no political effect during his lifetime, would have led to grave consequences after his death. Giangaleazzo could depend on the support of all those elements which had favoured the union of the Lombard cities under the Visconti as a guarantee of internal peace and security. The whole resources of Lombardy could now be concentrated on a single policy.

Four main directions of Milanese policy can be discerned amid the tangled diplomacy of Italian statecraft. The four points of the Milanese compass were Genoa, Bologna, the mouth of the Po and the passes of the Alps. These were the commercial and strategic frontiers of Lombardy—access to the Mediterranean in the west and east, the gateway to Tuscany and the south, and the roads to northern Europe. Giangaleazzo, in so far as he had to choose between them, followed the natural destinies of Milan to the east and south. His ambitions were confined to Italian soil. He was heir to Bernabò's political legacy—the claims on Verona, the struggle for Bologna, the Sienese alliance—which took precedence over the interests in Piedmont inherited from his own father.

Giangaleazzo had accepted a reconciliation with the Count of Savoy in February 1385. Immediately after Bernabò's downfall, Amadeus received a present of " certains grans destriers de Lombardie "—probably taken from Bernabò's stable.[2] Amadeus had

---

[1] Novati, *op. cit.* 130–6. The instructions were previously published by Ferrai, " Politica di Giangaleazzo ", *ASI* 5, xxii 62–8.

[2] Camus, " Maison de Savoie ", *BSBS* iv 120 note 3. The exchange of courtesies between Chambéry and Pavia continued through the summer: Id. " Venue en France ", *MSI* xxxvi 9.

other interests to consider at the time: designs on the adjacent Angevin lands of Provence, his promises of service to the French crown, the open hostility of the Marquis of Saluzzo. It was natural, therefore, that the two princes should seek an accord. In November 1385, Amadeus was at Piacenza, where he signed an undertaking with Giangaleazzo to respect their existing boundaries.[1] Four days later, he agreed to accept an arbitration of his disputes with Teodoro of Montferrat; and on his way back to Savoy, he imposed a grand pacification of the feuds which had disturbed the Canavese, the district to the north of Turin, for many years.[2]

Giangaleazzo had clearly set himself to achieve a peaceful settlement of Piedmont. He wished to take Bernabò's place in Italy without fear of a diversion on his western frontier. But the problem was far from easy, for at the same time he had to guard against the steady pressure of Savoy upon his borders. Teodoro of Montferrat and the Marquis of Saluzzo were useful allies, more immediately threatened by the expansion of Savoy, and he did not wish to forfeit their alliance; but they proved embarrassing obstacles to friendship with Amadeus. Giangaleazzo could neither dissuade Teodoro from acting in co-operation with the rebellious subjects of Savoy, nor support him openly against the firm action taken by Amadeus, who for his part naturally resented the use of the Visconti lands of Vercelli as a refuge and place of assembly for his enemies. This dual problem explains Giangaleazzo's perplexing conduct in these years—sincerely discouraging and yet secretly supporting the enemies of Savoy. His real interests were those of a peacemaker; and in August 1387 he tried to solve his difficulties by arranging a truce, and a further arbitration by the Doge of Genoa of the quarrels between Montferrat and Savoy.[3]

Giangaleazzo had also to take into consideration the fact that Piedmont lay directly on the road from France to Lombardy. When Carlo Visconti fled to Verona, his wife Beatrice of Armagnac

---

[1] 25 November 1385: published by Camus, "Maison de Savoie", *BSBS* IV 124–6.

[2] Gabotto, *Ultimi Principi d' Acaia*, 41–2.

Ibid. 67–83. The Doge, Antoniotto Adorno, later resigned this office, which Giangaleazzo took upon himself.

returned to her home in Languedoc, to rouse her brothers against the usurper.[1] At the same time Isabella of Bavaria, a grand-daughter of Bernabò, entered France as the bride of King Charles VI. Although the Angevin marriage of Lucia Visconti had been broken off after Bernabò's fall, the new Queen of France was potentially an even more dangerous enemy for Giangaleazzo in Paris.

The Count of Vertus had only one child whom he could oppose to the ramifications of Bernabò's marriage alliances. Valentina was now the richest heiress in Europe, and her father lost no time in seeking a suitable husband for her. His first proposal, that she should take the place of Lucia Visconti as the bride of Louis II of Anjou, did not find favour in Avignon. Giangaleazzo then turned to Germany, and offered her in marriage to Wenceslaus' brother, John of Görlitz.

While these negotiations were still in progress, a more splendid prospect unexpectedly appeared. Louis of Valois, the brother of Charles VI, had been betrothed to Maria of Hungary. In September 1385, Sigismund of Luxemburg, another brother of Wenceslaus and later to be Emperor, abducted Maria, married her, and in her right ascended the Hungarian throne. Louis of Valois was therefore free again, and Giangaleazzo lost no time in making use of the opportunity. The origins of the proposed marriage between Louis and Valentina are not altogether clear; but it is reasonable to suppose that the first move came from Giangaleazzo, who had most to gain, and that he enlisted the support of Amadeus of Savoy, a friend of the French crown, during their conference at Piacenza in November 1385.[2]

The negotiations proceeded without great difficulty. Wenceslaus was angry at the insult to John of Görlitz, whose prior claims were contemptuously set aside; but he had already demonstrated his incapacity, and a powerful alliance with the French court would more than offset his indignation.[3] Nor was a counter-

---

[1] She had reached Montmélian on 30 June: Camus, "Venue en France", *MSI* xxxvi 50, Doc. 7.

[2] For the proposals relating to Valentina in 1385–6, *v.* Appendix II.

[3] Letter of Wenceslaus, published by Palacky, "Formelbücher", 07–8, no. 26. For its date: Camus, "Venue en France", *MSI* xxxvi 8; and Lindner,

proposal that Valentina should marry Ladislaus of Naples, the reigning prince of the Durazzese house and rival of the Angevins, sufficiently tempting to divert Giangaleazzò from his purpose.[1]

The enormous dowry of 450,000 francs was in itself a great inducement to France. But there were also French interests in Italy to be considered—the claims of the Angevins in Naples, and of the French Pope Clement VII in Rome. An official French document, drawn up nine years later, declared that during the marriage negotiations Giangaleazzo had given some sort of verbal assurance that he would support the French Church policy.[2] To understand his position in this respect, it is necessary to digress for a moment in order to examine his attitude towards the schism of the Church.

Giangaleazzo had steadily refused to intervene in the spiritual questions involved between the two Popes. At first he had accepted the election of Clement,[3] who himself claimed to have Giangaleazzo's support;[4] and the destruction of the Count's ships by the fleet of Aragon in 1379 was held in some quarters to be a triumph for Urban VI.[5] But in fact, when it became obvious that the issue was not to be speedily settled, he imposed on his subjects, by a decree of 24 December 1378, an official and public neutrality which left them free to hold whatever private opinions they chose.[6] He abode by this decision throughout his lifetime, and its effect was that his dominions, predominantly Urbanist in sentiment, continued quietly to pay ecclesiastical allegiance to Rome.

"Geschichte des deutschen Reiches unter König Wenzel", II 459. For the character of Wenceslaus: *ibid.* 170–7. He had already been faced with two plots for his deposition—one in 1384 (*ibid.* I 216–20), the other in 1387 (*ibid.* I 367–71); and the "Diario d' Anonimo Fiorentino", in *Documenti di Storia Italiana*, VI 471 and note 6.

[1] Collino, "Politica Fiorentino-Bolognese", *MAT* 2 LIV 142–4; Mancarella, "Firenze, la Chiesa e Ladislao", *ASN* XLIV 121–6.

[2] Jarry, *Origines de la domination française à Gênes*, 429.

[3] Letter of 28 September 1378: *Repertorio Visconteo*, II 286, no. 2425. His own private assurance to an envoy of the Duke of Anjou has less value: Valois, *France et le Grand Schisme*, I 155, and IV 512.

[4] Sardo, "Cronaca Pisana", *ASI* VI, 2, 205.

[5] Florence to Perugia, 8 May 1379: Romano, "Visconti e la Sicilia", *ASL* XXIII, 1, 44–5.

[6] *Repertorio Visconteo*, II 292, no. 2476; published by Maiocchi, "Scisma d'Occidente e Giangaleazzo", in *Rivista di Scienze Storiche*, II, 1, 469–70.

It is necessary, however, to distinguish clearly between Giangaleazzo's ecclesiastical and political relations with the two Popes. In both his hands were strengthened against them. In the former, he vigorously and successfully asserted his right of provision against the candidates of both Popes when the see of Piacenza fell vacant in 1381;[1] but he always remained aloof from the ecclesiastical disputes which did not immediately touch the interests of his state. On the other hand, his political relations with the Popes were very much more intricate.

Urban VI, after a bitter quarrel with his former ally Carlo of Durazzo, had found a refuge at Genoa in 1385. His suspicions and his megalomania, verging upon insanity, drove him on to excesses against his own immediate supporters. Two of his Cardinals fled from his court to Pavia, whence they despatched to various governments a statement of their grievances and a justification of their flight. They declared that, before these letters were sent, Giangaleazzo's envoys had made a vain effort to recall Urban to a sense of his duties and of the needs of the Church.[2] According to one account, they solemnly burnt their red hats in the great square of Pavia, with Giangaleazzo's approval; and the Count's attitude is attributed to the refusal of Urban to grant him the title of King of Lombardy, to which he aspired after he had united the Visconti dominions.[3]

Professor Romano questioned the truth of this story—whose source is not reliable—on the ground that Giangaleazzo would not have sought from the Pope a dignity which could only be bestowed by the Emperor.[4] But Giangaleazzo did not disdain to use the weakest juridical arguments to support his case; an example has already been noticed in the "Processus" against Bernabò. We shall find further evidence of his desire to secure a nobler and more enduring title.[5] His relations with Wenceslaus grew more strained after the quarrel over Valentina's marriage; and there

[1] Poggiali, *Memorie storiche di Piacenza*, VII 4–6.
[2] 8 August 1386; published by Sauerland, "Aktenstücke zur Geschichte des Papstes Urban VI", in *Historisches Jahrbuch*, XIV 827–31.
[3] Gobelinus, *Cosmodromion*, 267.
[4] Romano, "Valentina Visconti", *ASL* XXV, 2, 12–13.
[5] *V.* pp. 171–2, *infra.*

is nothing fundamentally improbable in the story that he sought from Urban what he could not expect to receive from Wenceslaus.

The existing evidence, however, is very insecure; and the favour shown to the rebel Cardinals was certainly more than an empty gesture of spite. Giangaleazzo had other demands to make to Urban. He wished, for the better organization of his state, to secure control over his higher ecclesiastical officers. In this same year 1386, Urban granted to him the nomination to all benefices within his territory, reserving for himself all the other customary Papal rights.[1]

From the date of this agreement, of whose practical value it would be interesting to know more, their relations were comparatively amicable. But the Count was not bound to any declared recognition of Urban. A loan of 10,000 florins to the Pope in 1387[2] implied nothing more than a similarity of political interests in Tuscany at the time. The most cordial relations existed meanwhile between the courts of Pavia and Avignon.[3] Giangaleazzo recognized the existence of the Schism, and turned it to his own advantage, while he left to the Church the problem of solving its own difficulties. In his negotiations with France, he would have expressed his readiness to accept a settlement imposed by the French; and it was natural that rumours of his Clementist sympathies should have revived at this time.[4] The French marriage was in fact concluded with the full approval of Clement, who granted the necessary dispensation for the marriage of the cousins, and created for the bridegroom a Papal Vicariat in Romagna, to be wrested from the Urbanist lords who ruled over the district.[5]

The marriage contract of Louis and Valentina was drawn up in Paris on 27 January 1387, and ratified by Giangaleazzo in April.[6]

---

[1] "Chronicon Placentinum", *RIS* xvi 547; Giulini, *Memorie*, xi 411–14.
[2] Mancarella, *op. cit. ASN* xliv 142. Carlo Brancacci, Count of Campagna, spent a week in Pavia as Papal nuncio during the summer of 1387: Boselli, *Storie Piacentine*, ii 81 note 108.
[3] Valois, *op. cit.* ii 135–40.
[4] Minerbetti, "Cronica", *RIS* NS xxvii, 2, 20.
[5] Jarry, *Vie Politique de Louis de France*, 30; and 406–7, Doc. 8.
[6] The marriage contract was published by Jarry, *ibid.* 392–406, Doc. 7.

He had chosen as Valentina's dower lands a section of his territories in Piedmont, including Asti, Bra and Cherasco. This choice accorded with his new desire to relieve himself of the burden of defending his western frontier. Louis, with the strength of France behind him, could safeguard the Milanese state, and by the natural development of his own ambitions would keep the Piedmontese princes fully occupied.[1] He would be the instrument of Visconti policy in Piedmont, holding the important Genoese passes open for Giangaleazzo.

Valentina was to receive possession of all her father's dominions if he left no son to succeed him. This famous clause, which brought the French army of Louis XII to Milan a century later, was dictated by the same considerations as the choice of the dower lands. Louis, supported by the forces of France, but not too dependent upon them, could preserve the unity of the Visconti dominions and perpetuate the authority of the house. Giangaleazzo did not foresee the accession of his own descendant to the throne of France. In a later will, he stipulated that, if the issue of Valentina should inherit his dominions through the extinction of the male line, they should take the name of Visconti.[2] They were to be Lombards ruling over a Lombard state, and representatives of a Lombard house; there was no thought in his mind that Milan might become the appanage of a French prince.

The future held something very different from his imagination of it; and even in the present, the creation of a Valois principality in Piedmont failed to achieve its purpose. The authority of Louis, recently created Duke of Touraine, was not welcomed with unanimity in the dower lands.[3] Amadeus, titular Prince of Achaia, a cousin of the Count of Savoy and ruler of the Savoyard territories in Piedmont, claimed the towns of Bene, S. Albano and Trinità, in the jurisdiction of the Bishop of Asti.[4] A little

---

[1] The theory of Camus, "Maison de Savoie", *BSBS* IV 121-3, that the dower lands were chosen with the intention of cheating Savoyard aspirations in Asti, was exploded by Romano, *Matrimonio di Valentina Visconti*, 11-13.

[2] Cusin, "Impero e la successione degli Sforza", *ASL* NS I 51-2 note 66.

[3] Jarry, *Vie Politique de Louis de France*, 39-41. Louis was created Duke of Touraine on 12 November 1386: *ibid.* 26.

[4] Gabotto, *Ultimi Principi d' Acaia*, 88-90.

war raged in Piedmont through the winter of 1387–8. The French made no move, and Giangaleazzo had to assume responsibility for the integrity of the *Astigiano*.[1] Pressure on other fronts forced him to negotiate for a peaceful settlement; he could not afford to fight Louis' battles if the French would do nothing to help. After prolonged discussions, the disputed towns were surrendered to the Prince of Achaia.[2] In the last resort, Piedmont was now a secondary issue, and Savoy must always be placated.

For precisely the same reason, Louis never played the part which Giangaleazzo had designed for him in Piedmont. The stakes were not big enough to draw him away from the French court, where he could take his place as a leader of society and where an immense field of political activity lay open to his talents. The plan failed, because Louis' opportunities in France were so great that his lands in Piedmont were never of as much importance to him as they were to his father-in-law.

From the time of the agreement of 1388, although Giangaleazzo was not free from worry on his western frontier, he never became seriously embroiled with Savoy. He could follow up in comparative freedom the paths which had been set. for him by Bernabò: expansion to the east, the recovery of Bologna, and intervention in the affairs of Tuscany.

[1] Jarry, *Vie Politique de Louis de France*, 39–40.
[2] For the whole incident, *v.* Gabotto, *Ultimi Principi d' Acaia*, 90–106.

MAP IV. Eastern Lombardy and the Veneto in 1385

Land over 3000 feet is shaded

CHAPTER VII

THE CONQUEST OF EASTERN LOMBARDY
(1385–1388)

FOUR states lay between Milan and Venice on the Lombard plain: Verona under Antonio della Scala, Mantua under Francesco Gonzaga, Ferrara with Modena under Niccolò d'Este, and Padua under Francesco Carrara. The Carrarese dominions included in 1385 the cities of Treviso, Bassano, Ceneda, Feltre and Belluno. They were therefore of the first importance to the Venetians, whose trade had to pass through these territories to reach the Alpine passes which led to Germany and Austria. The ambitions and intrigues of Francesco Carrara, and the rapid expansion of his power, had been a continual source of irritation and alarm to the Venetians, who had been compelled on more than one occasion to reduce his pretensions by force of arms. Carrara, however, was reckless of the Republic's hostility; after the War of Chioggia, he began to encroach further on the chosen sphere of Venetian influence in Friuli. Had he succeeded in establishing his authority at the northern end of the Adriatic, the territory of Venice on the mainland would have been hemmed in along a narrow strip of coast-line by an aggressive and formidable neighbour.

The district of Friuli comprised an agglomeration of Communes and feudal lordships under the independent political authority of the Patriarch of Aquileia. The nomination of Cardinal Philip of Alençon as Patriarch in 1381 had aroused the bitter opposition of a large section of his Friulian subjects, who refused to accept his appointment and would not let him enter the lands under his jurisdiction. Carrara seized the opportunities which arose from these dissensions. He championed the Cardinal's cause, and received certain claims over the district in return. Venice, not unnaturally alarmed, gave help freely but discreetly to the Commune of Udine and the other centres of resistance; and in May 1385, while the Paduan army made rapid progress in Friuli, the

Republic enlisted the aid of Antonio della Scala, lord of Verona and Vicenza, Carrara's neighbour in the west. The Venetians were prepared in the last resort to fight for the independence of Friuli; but they preferred to find someone else to fight for them. Antonio della Scala, backed by Venetian gold, was ready to take their quarrels upon himself.[1]

Giangaleazzo's natural policy was to favour Carrara. Bernabò had long coveted the Scaliger dominions; and Giangaleazzo had reason to regard Antonio della Scala as a personal enemy, the one prince in Italy who had offered shelter and what help lay in his power to Bernabò's sons. But the Count's state was too new, his position in Italy still too uncertain, for him to involve himself deeply in the struggle. And behind Verona lay the imponderable might of Venice, which no power in Italy would willingly challenge.

Giangaleazzo therefore chose to appear as the herald of peace, the champion of Italy against the mercenary Companies. It was a device which assured him of a friendly hearing, and of which he made frequent use; the Florentine Chancellor, Coluccio Salutati, acclaimed him in this rôle in an effusive letter, in which the Count is contrasted with Bernabò, protector of the Condottieri.[2] Negotiations between the Lombard powers proceeded at Pavia in strict secrecy and with the exclusion of Antonio della Scala; so that the Venetians, learning of them at the end of July 1385, assumed that they were directed against their ally, the lord of Verona. But Venetian intervention came too late. On 8 August the rulers of Milan, Mantua, Ferrara and Padua signed a League providing for mutual assistance against the Companies and abstention from all favours to other enemies. The Venetian embassy arrived only in time to receive Giangaleazzo's comforting assurances.[3] He had—for the moment—no hostile intentions against anybody; but he had protected himself against his

[1] Cogo, "Patriarcato d'Aquileia", *NAV* xvi 236–56; Paschini, *Storia di Friuli*, iii 8–29.

[2] Salutati, "Epistolario", ii 146–59.

[3] Venetian instructions and letters: Pastorello, *Nuove Ricerche sulla storia di Padova*, 15–16; and 131–9, Docs. 1–5. The pact was published from a copy in Milan by Dumont, *Corps diplomatique*, ii, part 1, 188–90, no. 137. The date, from Muratori, *Antichità Estensi*, ii 152, presumably derived from a copy in the Estensi Archives.

one potential enemy, by an alliance with the three other rulers whose lands separated Lombardy from the *Veneto*.

Giangaleazzo had in fact a difficult problem to solve, before he could embark on an active policy in Lombardy. His immediate enemy was Antonio della Scala; but he did not wish to involve himself in a conflict with Venice, and he could not afford to allow Carrara to found a strong state on his eastern border. He made an alliance with Carrara against della Scala on 26 August 1385;[1] but, knowing his own value, he was content to wait upon events. When the inevitable war broke out in May 1386, he took no part in it. A Veronese force devastated the *Padovano*, and was completely defeated by Carrara's army; but Antonio della Scala, fortified by renewed subsidies from Venice, rejected overtures of peace from Padua, and prepared to continue the struggle. Giangaleazzo made no move. He followed carefully the course of events, and waited, with that patience which contributed in so large a measure to his success, for the situation to develop. Meanwhile, he kept in touch with both combatants, making ingenuous offers of mediation and preparing the way for a more active participation in the dispute.

The Paduan chronicle of the Gatari, whose pro-Carrarese sympathies unfortunately led in some cases to a distortion of the facts, accused Giangaleazzo of offering his alliance to both sides at once.[2] There had been an abortive project of alliance between Giangaleazzo and della Scala in September 1385;[3] and the Count was in communication with della Scala's allies in Udine in the following year.[4] Corio, on the other hand, asserts that Giangaleazzo was already helping Carrara in 1386.[5] Certainly della Scala showed himself throughout as obstinate as he was unwise; there is little doubt that he was in touch with Carlo Visconti, whose envoy had been sent to Lombardy in October 1386, "for my affairs", and who was scheming to return from his refuge in

[1] De Marco, "Crepuscolo degli Scaligeri", *Archivio Veneto* 5, XXII 181, and XXIV 81–2, Doc. 51.
[2] Gatari, "Cronaca Carrarese", *RIS* NS XVII, 1, 278–83.
[3] Pastorello, *Nuove Ricerche*, 15–16 and 134–8, Doc. 3.
[4] Battistella, "Lombardi in Friuli", *ASL* XXXVII, 2, 357, no. 419.
[5] Corio, *Storia di Milano*, II 329.

Bavaria to contest his inheritance at the point of the sword.[1] The abandonment of the exile's cause would have been the first condition of any offers which Giangaleazzo may have made to the lord of Verona. The Count was later to accuse della Scala of plotting against him in favour of Bernabò's heirs;[2] and it is probable that uncertainty over della Scala's relations with Carlo and Mastino Visconti helped to convince Giangaleazzo that the Paduan alliance would better serve his purpose. Having reached this decision, he prepared to overcome the great obstacle of Venetian friendship with della Scala.

This obstacle did not prove insuperable. The war of Chioggia had left the *Serenissima* in a state of exhaustion and indecision. It had given a great impetus to the policy of territorial expansion on the mainland. On the other hand, the government did not wish to be distracted from the protection of Venetian interests in the Adriatic and the Aegean. The Peace of Turin had confirmed Lewis of Hungary in the possession of Dalmatia, the old Venetian province with its valuable naval bases at Zara, Sebenico and Spalato. But Lewis was now dead, and the Hungarian throne was contested between Sigismund of Luxemburg and Ladislaus, the boy King of Naples beset by the Angevin supporters in his own lands. The Venetians, who could not afford to see Hungary and Naples joining hands across the Adriatic, encouraged Sigismund and the Angevins against the house of Durazzo;[3] but the divisions of Hungary awoke fresh hopes in Venice of recovering their former authority in Dalmatia at Sigismund's expense.

The oncoming tide of Turkish invasion, which swept across the Balkans in the second half of the fourteenth century, added to the difficulties of the Republic. The native princes of the Dalmatian and Albanian coast were the more readily persuaded to place their lands under Venetian protection, and in the last decade of the century the Venetians acquired in this way Durazzo,

---

[1] Letter of credence for "Johannes de benedictis dilectus et familiaris meus", addressed by Carlo to Francesco Gonzaga, from Landshut on 26 October 1386: *ASMa*, E. xlix. 2, no. 1606. Cf. Romano, "Giangaleazzo Visconti", *ASL* xviii 17–18.

[2] Giangaleazzo's letter to della Scala, published in *RIS* xvi 779 D–781 B; and his letter to Florence, in Corio, *op. cit.* ii 338–40.

[3] Cutolo, *Re Ladislao d'Angiò-Durazzo*, i 81–3.

Scutari, and other territories; but the resources of the Republic were scarcely able to cope with their new obligations. The finances were in complete disorder; and for forty years after the war of Chioggia, the Venetian battle fleet never put to sea with more than ten " galleys " or ships of war.[1] This was not enough to defend the Adriatic and Aegean possessions against the might of the Ottomans. The Republic was compelled to pursue a cautious and conciliatory policy towards the Turkish power, in spite of the threat which it contained to Venetian security.[2]

In addition, Carrara's armies had to be expelled from Friuli; and Giangaleazzo's plans were forwarded by the other preoccupations of the *Serenissima*. The Venetian admiral Carlo Zeno, who had entered the Count's service in 1385, probably acted as an intermediary between his master and the government of his native city.[3] If the documents of the Visconti chancery had survived, they would tell us how far Giangaleazzo took the *Serenissima* into his confidence, how far he had already planned the campaign against Carrara in 1388 as a deliberate sequel to the campaign against della Scala in 1387. Some private understanding there must have been over Carrara's position in Friuli; for when Antonio della Scala's fall was imminent, the Republic refused to intervene in Lombardy "save with the consent of the Count of Vertus".[4]

Giangaleazzo had made up his mind by the end of 1386. He advanced a loan for the formation of a military company to

---

[1] The details of the financial chaos of Venice are provided in his introductions to "Problemi monetari Veneziani", and to "Regolazione delle entrate e delle spese", by Dr Roberto Cessi. On the other hand, Venetian commercial prosperity was not deeply involved: Luzzatto, "Debito Pubblico nel sistema finanziario Veneziano", *NRS* XIII 623 sqq. The decadence of the fleet was demonstrated by Professor Manfroni, "Crisi della Marina Militare di Venezia", *AIV* 8 XII, 2, 983 sqq. For the revival of Venetian authority on the Adriatic coast-line after the war: Id. *Colonizzatori Italiani*, II 98–105.

[2] Id. "Crisi della Marina Militare di Venezia ", *AIV* 8 XII, 2, 989–1003.

[3] Gatari, *op. cit. RIS* NS XVII, 1, 279 line 42. The "Vita Caroli Zeni", *RIS* XIX 300–7, records that he was serving Giangaleazzo in Piedmont at this time; and *v.* De Marco, *op. cit.*, *Archivio Veneto* 5, XXIV 14–15.

[4] "Nisi foret de beneplacito ipsius magnifici Comitis": Roberto Cessi, "Venezia e la prima caduta dei Carraresi", *NAV* NS XVII 311–13. The possibility of an understanding between Giangaleazzo and Venice was mentioned by Collino, "Guerra Viscontea contro gli Scaligeri", *ASL* XXXIV, 1, 114.

Carrara's general, the exiled Florentine nobleman Giovanni degli Ubaldini, who had fought under Sir John Hawkwood and won the Englishman's highest esteem.[1] In the middle of January 1387, Carrara empowered his envoy to conclude an alliance with the Count.[2] There was still some delay, perhaps because Giangaleazzo had not yet reached an understanding with Venice; and meanwhile the war broke out again, and Carrara was again victorious. Antonio della Scala seemed to lose all power of decision. He refused offers of peace, invoked the intervention of Wenceslaus and then rejected it. Carrara's troops meanwhile penetrated farther into Friuli, and sacked Aquileia at the beginning of April. Hoping perhaps that Venice would now openly join in the conflict, della Scala decided to fight again.[3]

We are unfortunately dependent on the unreliable account of the Gatari for much that concerns Giangaleazzo's policy during this period. Certainly, having decided his course and chosen his moment, he set to work with characteristic thoroughness. In April 1387, he signed the alliances with Carrara and with Francesco Gonzaga, stipulating the terms for the conduct of the campaign and for the partition of the Veronese dominions—Verona for himself, Vicenza for Carrara.[4] Knowing that della Scala and his allies in Friuli expected help from Germany,[5] he came to terms in May with Albert of Austria, who agreed to close the Alpine passes to the enemies of Milan,[6] and in July with the Ghibelline nobility of the Riviera di Trento.[7] An independent observer bears witness to the efficacy of the Austrian action in excluding German money or troops from Italy.[8] Giangaleazzo's allies in Romagna blocked the passage of a strong mercenary force which tried to

---

[1] Pastorello, *Nuove Ricerche*, 140–1, Doc. 6.

[2] 14 January 1387: *ibid.* 141–4, Doc. 7.

[3] *Ibid.* 18–20. For the sack of Aquileia, *v.* Cogo, *op. cit. NAV* xvi 274–5.

[4] With Carrara, 19 April: Gatari, *op. cit.* 274–5. With Gonzaga on the following day: Corio, *op. cit.* ii 330–1.   [5] Cogo, *op. cit. NAV* xvi 278.

[6] 8 May: Lindner, "Geschichte des deutschen Reiches", ii 311, from the copy in Vienna.

[7] Alliance with Carlo d'Arco, 1 July 1387: Verci, *Storia della Marca Trivigiana*, xvi, Doc. 1891, pp. 140–2.

[8] A report from the agent of Lucca in Verona, 6 October: Lucca, *Regesti*, 479, no. 2159 (dated by Fumi, 1398?).

make its way to Verona.[1] Antonio della Scala was practically isolated in his dominions by the thoroughness of Milanese diplomacy.

Giangaleazzo took upon himself the heaviest share of the war. The Milanese army, accompanied by the Veronese exiles Spinetta Malaspina and Guglielmo Bevilacqua, and commanded by Ubaldini, Antonio Porro and his brother Galeazzo Porro, overran the southern end of Lake Garda during the summer.[2] Rocca di Garda fell on 19 June;[3] but Lazise held up further progress until the autumn.[4] Carrara, on the other hand, after a half-hearted attack on Vicenza, transferred his armies to Friuli, where they campaigned with modified success.[5] Giangaleazzo must have encouraged his ally to leave the Visconti troops in full possession of the main theatre of the war; and it was probably more than a coincidence that Carrara's best generals left his service at this time. In Hawkwood's recall to Florence Giangaleazzo could have had no part. But he himself begged for the services of Ubaldini;[6] and Facino Cane entered the service of the Count's friend, Teodoro of Montferrat.[7]

Wenceslaus alone attempted to intervene in favour of Antonio della Scala, whom he officially placed under his Imperial protection.[8] His envoys made two journeys to Italy during the summer.[9] A Sienese, who had taken office in the government of Bologna, wrote on 20 June that "peace negotiations are in full swing, and the general opinion is rather that peace will be con-

[1] Novati, "Trattative di Giangaleazzo con Condottieri", *ASL* xxxix, 2, 572–7.
[2] Cogo, *op. cit.* 277; Galli, "Dominazione Viscontea a Verona", *ASL* liv 479. A letter of 13 June, sent to Francesco Gonzaga from the Visconti camp at Cavaion during the siege of Rocca di Garda, and written by a Mantuan agent named Bernabò da Monte, gives some interesting details of the campaign: *ASMa*, E. xlix. 3.
[3] A note of Novati in *ASL* xxxix, 2, 526.
[4] The report from Verona, 6 October, in Lucca, *Regesti*, 479, no. 2159.
[5] Gatari, *op. cit.* 291–300; Paschini, *op. cit.* iii 40–2.
[6] Gatari, *op. cit.* 284.
[7] Galli, "Facino Cane", *ASL* xxiv, 1, 375. Giangaleazzo's responsibility for these changes was suggested by Pastorello, *Nuove Ricerche*, 21 and note 6.
[8] The letter published in Gatari, *op. cit. RIS* NS xvii, 1, 301 note 1
[9] Lindner, "Geschichte des deutschen Reiches", ii 312.

cluded than not ". He states that " the Emperor has informed the
Count of Vertus and the lord of Padua that the lord of Verona is
under his protection, and that they must abandon their undertaking; and in so far as they do not do so, he will hold himself
offended, as though the damage were to his own possessions or to
his own person. The lord of Verona is reported to be expecting
troops in his support from the Emperor any day now, but
apparently they have not yet arrived."[1]

Giangaleazzo had already tested the strength of Wenceslaus'
authority in Italy during the negotiations for Valentina's marriage. His position was far stronger now; he ignored the menaces
of the Emperor and pursued his course. A very different picture
is drawn three months later, in a letter written by an agent of the
government of Lucca in Verona on 6 October. The Imperial
envoys are still working for a peaceful settlement, but there is
little hope left. The reason is clear; Giangaleazzo no longer has
any need to accept terms other than those which he chooses to
impose. The Austrian blockade has prevented reinforcements
from reaching Verona. Giangaleazzo, on the other hand, enlists
more troops every day, offering twenty florins for every lance
(sixteen was the average pay). The resistance of Verona has
begun to crumble; Lazise has fallen, Torre is expected to
capitulate. "That great bird has established his ascendancy
here, and later he will do so elsewhere." The powers involved
had best look to their defences.[2]

Antonio della Scala's princely days were numbered. His own
crimes and his wife's extravagances had made many enemies for
him. The exiles were in Giangaleazzo's camp; the city of Verona
was full of discontent. Giangaleazzo was master of the situation.
In the middle of October, Veronese ambassadors came humbly
to Pavia, with those of Wenceslaus, to protest that della Scala
was devoted to the Count, and to make offers of peace; Giangaleazzo scorned their proposals. His Council sat with them in prolonged sessions, holding them in play and gradually forcing them
to increase their offers. On the 17th, Giangaleazzo received the

---

[1] "Lo vostro servidore Giovanni de' cacciaconti Capitaneo di popolo in
Bologna", to Siena, 20 June 1387: *ASS*, Concistoro 1821, no. 16.
[2] Lucca, *Regesti*, 478–9, no. 2159.

news for which he was waiting; Bevilacqua and Spinetta Malaspina, who had been proceeding northwards to receive the submission of Riva at the top of Lake Garda, had suddenly turned about, and were marching rapidly on Verona with the whole Visconti army. On that day, Giangaleazzo made known his final terms: the surrender of the district of Lake Garda known as the *Gardesana*, and the banks of the Mincio. He had no serious claims to these territories; but he could afford to make exorbitant demands, because he knew that, before an answer could come, he would have obtained an even greater prize. So well had his secret been kept, that even members of the Council advised him to accept the Veronese offers.[1]

On the 18th, the envoys left Pavia and rode towards Verona, to make known to their master the Count's terms. That night, the friends of Bevilacqua and Malaspina within the city of Verona opened the gate of San Massimo to the Milanese troops. Antonio della Scala fled to Venice on the following day, resigning his authority to the Imperial envoys, who promptly sold it to Giangaleazzo and returned home; it is difficult to see what else they could have done. The citizens of Verona, having no alternative, transferred the dominion of their city to the conqueror. Three days later, Vicenza formally accepted the rule of Caterina Visconti, as the heir òf Regina della Scala, on the condition that Francesco Carrara should not be allowed to take the city as his own.[2]

Once again, Giangaleazzo had triumphed in a manner sudden and unforeseen, by the application of his favourite stratagem;

[1] Report of Galeazzo Busoni, 17 October 1387: *v.* Doc. 1. This letter is worth studying for the picture it gives of Giangaleazzo's methods of diplomacy. Cf. Gatari, *op. cit.* 300–1.

[2] The following table shows Regina's claim to Verona:

Mastino II della Scala

Cansignore (d. 1375) — Cangrande II (d. 1359) — Regina = Bernabò Visconti

Bartolommeo (murdered, 1382) — Antonio (both illegitimate)

Caterina = Giangaleazzo

but his triumph did not spring from mere good fortune, from any brilliant and extemporary employment of a momentary opportunity. He had contacts with the discontented parties of the Scaliger dominions. We may be sure that he waited for months while these contacts were developed, watching his plans gradually come to maturity and carefully guarding the secret of them from all but his most intimate advisers. When the moment came and the word was given, his agents acted swiftly, effectively, and with a minimum of bloodshed. There was no time for protests or for discussion. Giangaleazzo, though he was no man of action, yet preferred deeds to words; he minimized resistance by forestalling it. By carefully preserved secrecy and by rapidity of execution when the moment was ripe, he was able to present the states of Italy with the accomplished fact, which it is always more difficult and more dangerous to dispute. These elements of his policy are essential to an understanding of his achievements.

Having gained his object, he was ruthlessly cynical of his obligations. Carrara, who had been assured of the possession of Vicenza, saw too late the pit he had dug for himself; the accomplished trickster had found his match. Giangaleazzo received his indignant demands and protests with evasion and delay; Vicenza belonged to his wife, not to himself. He deliberately set himself to exasperate his former ally, by laying claim to the Paduan towns of Montegalda and Noale; and, even more significantly, he encouraged Carrara to look for compensation in Friuli, and thereby embroil himself more deeply than ever with Venice.[1]

The wary Republic, however, was not such easy game as the ambitious lord of Padua. Giangaleazzo's triumphant campaign had aroused misgivings among his neighbours. Niccolò d'Este, lord of Ferrara, alarmed for his own safety, took the lead. He enlisted the support of the Florentines, who had already come into conflict with the Count in Tuscany,[2] and summoned a conference at Ferrara in January 1388, to find a settlement in Friuli without Milanese intervention.[3]

[1] Gatari, *op. cit.* 304–11. For the progress of the Carrarese army in Friuli during the winter, *v.* Paschini, *op. cit.* III 43–4.

[2] *V. infra,* Chapter VIII.

[3] Collino, "Preparazione della Guerra Veneto-Viscontea", *ASL* XXXIV, 2, 220–3.

The Venetians were prepared to accept a reconciliation if Carrara withdrew from Friuli and guaranteed to respect its independence under the Patriarch for the future. But Giangaleazzo's problems were promptly made easier by the attitude adopted by Carrara. The Florentines urged him to accept these terms, and thus defeat Giangaleazzo's designs. But he regarded Venice as his chief enemy and Friuli as his real province, and he was prepared to make sacrifices to Giangaleazzo rather than to Venice. It did not, therefore, require the intrigues of Giangaleazzo's agents[1] to produce a deadlock; Carrara would not make the necessary concessions, and the conference broke up.[2]

The negotiations were transferred to Venice in March 1388. Florentine envoys came to plead for Carrara; Giangaleazzo played on the traditional enmity and immediate commercial needs of Venice, fanning the Republic's suspicion of the Paduan's delays and recalcitrance. The Venetians availed themselves of the Florentine intervention to drive as hard a bargain as they could with the Count, but they were resolved now to regain Treviso and restore the liberty of Friuli. On these terms, Venice and Giangaleazzo entered into alliance in May 1388 for the partition of the Carrarese state.[3]

Carrara's obduracy, and the resolution of Venice, had involved Giangaleazzo in a second war before he was fully prepared for it.[4] He had issued instructions in September 1387 for the collection of a "subsidium", a contribution from his subjects towards the payment of Valentina's dowry. The enormous sum of 300,000 florins, which had to go with Valentina to France, in addition to the expenses of a past war and the immediate prospect of another to come, laid a very heavy financial burden upon Lombardy. Giangaleazzo solved one problem by using for the purposes of the

---

[1] This story of Gatari was accepted by Romano, "Niccolò Spinelli", *ASN* xxvi 431–6; but we may reject it in the light of the full and impartial discussion of Dr Cessi, "Venezia e la prima caduta dei Carraresi", *NAV* NS xvii 315, note 4.

[2] For the Conference of Ferrara: *ibid.* 317–22.

[3] *Ibid.* 318–26. The treaty of alliance, 29 May, was published by Pastorello, *Nuove Ricerche*, 156–69, Doc. 13.

Romano, "Tornandoci sopra", *ASL* xxix, 1, 106. The predominant part of Venice in determining the war is emphasized by Cessi, "Venezia e la prima caduta dei Carraresi", *NAV* NS xvii 315, 336.

war the sum raised for the dowry.[1] But the problem of raising a further sum for the dowry remained; and Giangaleazzo was not insensible of the discontent which too heavy pressure would arouse among his subjects.

It is to this period that Tagliabue attributed the completion of the financial reform begun at Pavia in 1384. The central government assumed direct responsibility for the financial administration of the Communes.[2] In evidence of this, we find that Giangaleazzo ordered a general revision of the salaries of his officials in Reggio in May 1388; financial immunities were closely controlled; and in moments of extreme need the income of the cities went straight to the Camera without the usual deduction for the salaries of the Communal officers.[3] War had forced upon Giangaleazzo the need to ensure the most efficient and economical methods of government for this state.

The alliance with Venice protected Giangaleazzo in his new venture. Niccolò d'Este was dead, and his brother Alberto, knowing that no state in northern Italy could hope to resist the combination of Venice and the Visconti, joined with Francesco Gonzaga in the alliance against Padua; Alberto himself accepted an invitation to spend a few days in Pavia, where he had an opportunity of experiencing the lavish hospitality of the court and the persuasive personality of its ruler.[4] The Florentines made no secret of their friendship with Carrara; but, rather from respect for Venice than from fear of Giangaleazzo,[5] the help which they gave to him was confined within the bounds of semi-secret intrigue. Giangaleazzo outbid Carrara—who offered to reconstitute the Habsburg dominion in Feltre and Belluno—and once more secured the promise of Albert of Austria to close the passes to

[1] Comani, "Denari per la dote di Valentina", *ASL* xxviii, 1, 44–5.
[2] Tagliabue, "Politica finanziaria", *BSP* xv 47–55. The actual details of the reform have not survived.
[3] Comani, "Denari per la dote di Valentina", *ASL* xxviii, 1, 45 and note 2.
[4] Cogo, *op. cit.* 291. There is no evidence that either he or Gonzaga made any material contribution to the allied forces.
[5] Speeches in the Council, of Ardinghelli on 17 July; of Cionetti, 19 September; of Sacchetti, 23 November, and of Guasconi and Lorini on the 24: Collino, "Guerra Veneto-Viscontea", *ASL* xxxvi, 1, 15 note 2; 56 note 3; 343 note 1; 347 note 1.

his enemies;[1] and, although one chronicler records that a troop
of German soldiers managed to reach Padua, the report probably
sprang rather from hope than from reliable information.[2] Carrara
was in fact as isolated in Padua as Antonio della Scala had been
in Verona a year before.

Having completed these diplomatic preliminaries with the
thoroughness which characterized all Giangaleazzo's undertakings, the allies declared war at the end of June 1388. At the
same time Carrara, faced by an overwhelming coalition, and
uncertain of the temper of his own oppressed subjects, resigned
his authority in favour of his son, Francesco Novello, and withdrew to Treviso.[3] The young ruler appealed to the Venetians to
forget his father's overweening ambition, and to believe in his
own devotion to their interests; but it was too late to placate the
Republic.[4] Through the summer and autumn, the allied armies
advanced remorselessly upon Padua; all offers of mediation—
from Wenceslaus, from Albert of Austria, from the Florentines
—were politely but firmly refused.[5] The Paduans themselves
awaited the fall of the city, "to be under the rule of the Count of
Vertus, who falsely had won a perfect reputation".[6] Beleaguered
in the city alive with rumours and ill-suppressed excitement, his
water-supply cut off, abandoned by those who considered themselves his friends, and uncertain even of his own counsellors,
Francesco Novello resigned himself to surrender.[7] While he and
his father went to Pavia to treat with Giangaleazzo—preferring
not to trust themselves to the implacable hatred of Venice—a
Visconti garrison entered Padua on 24 November 1388.[8]

Francesco Novello's last hope was gone when he abandoned

[1] Pastorello, *Nuove Ricerche*, 178–82, Docs. 19 and 21; Verci, *op. cit.*
XVII, Doc. 1915, pp. 15–17.
[2] Minerbetti, "Cronica", *RIS* NS XXVII, 2, 62. Germany, in the grip of
the *Städtekrieg*, cannot have had many troops to spare.
[3] Gatari, *op. cit.* 311–17.
[4] 30 June: Pastorello, *Nuove Ricerche*, 172, Doc. 16.
[5] Romano, "Niccolò Spinelli", *ASN* XXVI 443; Cessi, "Venezia e la
caduta dei Carraresi", *NAV* NS XVII 330.
[6] Gatari, *op. cit.* 310.
[7] *Ibid.* 319–29; Cogo, *op. cit. NAV* XVI 293–4.
[8] Gatari, *op. cit.* 330–3. Giangaleazzo to Venice, 27 November: Verci,
op. cit. XVII Doc. 1916, pp. 18–21.

Padua. In Pavia he met with rebuffs and delays, his father with imprisonment; but what small measure of leniency they received came from Giangaleazzo rather than from Venice.[1] Meanwhile, a revolution in Padua restored the institutions of Communal government; the newly revived Commune consigned its standard to Giangaleazzo's victorious general, Jacopo dal Verme, and chose representatives to go to Pavia and offer the dominion of the city to the lord of Milan. The procedure was fundamentally similar to the surrender of Verona. Bassano, Feltre and Belluno submitted to Giangaleazzo's authority without delay. Venice received Treviso and Ceneda in accordance with the terms of the alliance.[2]

The cities of the *Veneto*, accustomed for almost a century to the authority of a prince, had lost the traditions of Communal self-government. They entered the Visconti state as part of a homogeneous organization. The pacts which Padua demanded from Giangaleazzo were intended to secure a measure of independence; but the Count never gave a definite answer, and they were not put into force.[3] Giangaleazzo had his own plans for the government of Padua, as for Verona and his other acquisitions. The city came into the closely centralized system of Visconti administration. But it was far from Pavia, and the central government had no effective means of checking the abuses and corruption of its officials. Padua, deprived of its importance as a capital, rapidly declined in prosperity under the Visconti régime.[4]

---

[1] Cessi, "Venezia e la caduta dei Carraresi", *NAV* NS xvii 336–7.

[2] Venice took over Treviso from the Visconti forces, 12 December: Predelli, "Libri Commemoriali", iii 195, no. 302. The "Chronicon Tarvisinum", *RIS* xix 790, a curious amalgam of fact and legend, relates that Giangaleazzo attempted to keep Treviso for himself, as he had Vicenza. There is no sign, in the relations of the Republic with the Count, of the irritation which such an attempt might be expected to arouse; and if the incident, which I am inclined to discount as fabulous, did actually occur, Giangaleazzo must quickly have transferred the blame to the officers of his army.

[3] Pastorello, *Nuove Ricerche*, 38–48; Ercole, "Comuni e Signori", *NAV* NS xix 308 note 1; or in Id. *Dal Comune al Principato*, 95 note 1. ·

[4] Pastorello, *Nuove Ricerche*, 48–61. The juridical problems raised by the conquest of the Veneto were fully discussed by Ercole, "Comuni e Signori", *NAV* NS xix 302–13, republished in *Dal Comune al Principato*, 91–9.

In two swift campaigns, Giangaleazzo had advanced his eastern frontier from the Chiese to the Venetian coast-line and the borders of Friuli: to the foot of the Brenner pass, the Valsugana and the Pieve di Cadore, "the Keys of Germany" as a Florentine counsellor called them.[1] In spite of his total lack of political scruples, he had acquired—not so falsely as the Gatari claimed— a reputation for justice and clemency as a ruler; so that many citizens of Verona and Padua awaited him as a liberator. Italy knew now the man who had taken Bernabò's place; his ambitions and his quality stood revealed. We have already had occasion to notice his political methods; where deception failed, he could call on his profound political knowledge to convince waverers and bring them to his side.

The birth of a long-awaited son in September 1388 renewed his energy and added fresh ardour to his ambitions. The whole of Lombardy was designed as his prey. Mantua and Ferrara already lay in the shadow of his great state. The day seemed not far distant when every state in northern Italy would obey the commands of the unwarlike prince who dwelt, seldom seen, in the palace of Pavia.

The challenge and the threat of Giangaleazzo's triumphs were read most clearly of all in Florence. The issue was debated in three meetings of the Council, while Francesco Carrara came to terms with Jacopo dal Verme and took the road to Pavia.[2] One counsellor boldly proclaimed that "tyrants, who find cause for fear wherever they turn, are not as powerful as they are believed to be".[3] But the fear of him was in every heart. Amid conflicting counsels and contradictory proposals, one great need was expressed by every speaker. The Republic must prepare to defend itself, must procure by every sacrifice the means to meet the danger which was surely approaching. "Nascitur hora, habeatur de oleo in lampadibus."[4]

---

[1] "Claves Alemanie": Collino, "Guerra Veneto-Viscontea", *ASL* xxxvi, 1, 378.

[2] Consulta of 21, 23 and 24 November: *ibid.* 331–3, 339–47.

[3] Blaxius Bemabuccii, on 23 November: *ibid.* 339 note 6.

[4] Andrea Albizi, on 21 November: *ibid.* 330 note 1.

CHAPTER VIII

GIANGALEAZZO AND FLORENCE: THE DELINEATION OF THE TUSCAN PROBLEM (1385–1388)

To understand the suspicions and fear aroused in Florence by the fall of Padua, it is necessary to trace the history of Tuscany in the past four years, since the failure of Enguerrand de Coucy's Angevin expedition in 1384.[1]

It is an important period in the story of Florentine expansion. The purchase of Arezzo from Coucy was followed by the gradual submission of the communities and Ghibelline lords of the Valdichiana, who had hitherto been subject to Siena. The Sienese protested, but had no remedy.[2] For Florence alone of the Tuscan Republics had not been ruined by the economic decline of the fourteenth century. The "popolo grasso", who regained power after the democratic experiment of 1378–1382, represented the aggressive interests of the commercial oligarchy; and the moderate party among them, led by the Alberti and the Medici, had to cope with the agitations of an extremist section which, under the leadership of Maso degli Albizzi, secured a preponderance in the government during the next few years.[3] Its object was the complete domination of Tuscany by the rulers of Florence; and there seemed to be no grave obstacles to this design.

Pisa, under the rule of Pietro Gambacorta, had abandoned the Ghibelline tradition of centuries, in the hope that a close alliance with Florence would revive the city's economic position. The little Republic of Lucca, restored to independence by the Emperor Charles IV in 1369 after a period of Pisan domination, relied

---

[1] *V. supra*, Chapter III.

[2] Collino, "Politica Fiorentino-Bolognese", *MAT* 2, LIV 123–4. The extent of Florentine acquisitions in the *Aretino* between 1384 and 1387 may be gathered from the documents published in *Capitoli di Firenze*, I 56 sqq., 126 sqq., 161 sqq., 370 sqq., 461–506.

[3] Rado, *Maso degli Albizi*, 96 sqq.

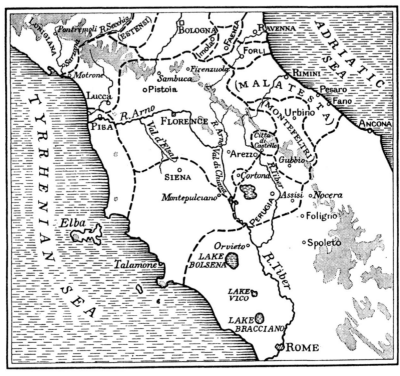

MAP V. Tuscany, Umbria and Romagna in 1386

Land over 3000 feet is shaded

on a policy of neutrality to preserve the integrity of what territories remained to her. The Sienese, with their banks ruined, their woollen industry unable to compete with the scale of Florentine production, and their lands periodically ravaged by the marauding bands of the Condottieri, preserved from the days of prosperity only their fiery pride. Perugia, set among the hills of Umbria, was bitterly divided by the quarrels of its parties, and had lost many of its old possessions. Not one of the Republics of Tuscany could hope to resist for long the aggressive power of Florence.

The Florentines, so favourably placed for the expansion of their authority, naturally resented the interference of other powers in Tuscany, whether it came from the Visconti in the north or from the Popes in the south. Giangaleazzo found favour among many circles in Florence because he had represented himself as having no part in Bernabò's pro-Sienese activities. That had been reasonable enough for the lord of Pavia; but after May 1385 he took Bernabò's place and became the recipient of the appeals of all those who were threatened by Florentine ambitions.

He did not, of course, give any indication of an immediate change of policy; but he secured an entry into Tuscan politics by the one means to which the Florentines could not take exception. He had already made proposals to Florence and Bologna in February 1385 for a League against the mercenary companies. The negotiations were resumed after the fall of Bernabò; and even those wiser citizens, who already suspected the Count's motives, could not object to an alliance against the scourge which afflicted Tuscany far more than the districts which Giangaleazzo ruled. The League was concluded at Legnano on 31 August 1385, between Giangaleazzo and the two Republics. There was no question, as has recently been affirmed, of a grand alliance between all the states of northern and central Italy; only Pisa and Lucca were given the option, of which they quickly availed themselves, of adhering to the League.[1]

---

[1] The documents of the League in Collino, "Politica Fiorentino-Bolognese", *MAT* 2, LIV 164–7, Docs. 56–72. For the legend of a great alliance of Italian states concluded at Pisa on 9 October 1385, v. Appendix III.

The limited composition of the League in fact illuminates two of the salient features of Florentine policy in regard to the Visconti at this period. The first was the emphasis on the close alliance between Florence and Bologna; the Florentines would not accept Giangaleazzo's proposals without the consent of the Bolognese.[1]

Since 1377, Bologna had been governed as a Republic under the nominal suzerainty of the Pope. While the usual quarrels of party divided the Commune, greater rivalries played over it from without. For Bologna was the bulwark of ecclesiastical territory in Romagna and the Mark of Ancona, the gateway into Tuscany through the Apennine passes, the key to the trade routes, and the strategical centre of further Visconti expansion. Bernabò had never reconciled himself to the loss of the city; and the mere exchange of courtesies between the Visconti and the Bolognese aroused the instantaneous jealousy of the Florentines. For the independence and the friendship of Bologna were essential to the safety of Florence; and the Florentine government used every means in its power to link the destinies of the two Communes in the pursuit of a joint policy.

On the other hand, the Florentines firmly rejected the proposal that Siena should be admitted to the confederation.[2] The Sienese disputed step by step the advance of the Florentines in the district of Arezzo. Giangaleazzo had indeed disassociated himself from Bernabò's activities in favour of Siena in 1384; but the Florentines already perceived that he had now taken Bernabò's place in Tuscan politics. The admission of Siena to the League would present Giangaleazzo with an excuse for intervention in a dispute from which they wished to isolate him. The plausibility of his earlier protestations had failed to eradicate the inherent suspicion of Visconti designs in Tuscany. The Florentines were prepared to accept the alliance of Siena against the Companies in November 1385; but this new League comprised only the four

---

[1] Collino, "Politica Fiorentino-Bolognese", *MAT* 2, liv 132–3, and 164, Docs. 56 and 58.

[2] Minutes of the Florentine Council, 3 August: Collino, "Politica Fiorentino-Bolognese", *MAT* 2, liv 133; and 164, Doc. 60.

Tuscan Communes, Perugia, and Bologna—"populos Latini
nominis, et precipue qui libere vivunt".[1] And the Florentines
made their own terms; the possession of Lucignano and the other
disputed towns of the *Aretino* was submitted to the arbitration
of their own allies, the Bolognese.[2] It was a task which Giangaleazzo, had he been able to find a reasonable excuse, would have
been glad to share; but he was not yet strong enough to assert
himself in Tuscany against the will of Florence.

The Visconti had always associated their personal ambitions
with the needs of Milanese commerce. The great merchants of
Florence based their policy more exclusively on their commercial
interests; but they were led nevertheless to seek that expansion
of the Republic's authority, which resembled even in the eyes of
their fellow-citizens a greed for political dominion. They were
already afraid that Giangaleazzo, at the request of those states
whose integrity and very existence they threatened, might take
it upon himself to oppose the development of their hegemony in
Tuscany. Respect for the independence of Bologna, and complete abstention from any form of interference in the affairs of
Tuscany, were the conditions on which the Florentines were
prepared to accept Giangaleazzo's friendship; and if he failed to
observe these conditions, they were prepared to show equal
favour to the Lombard princes menaced by the expansion of the
Milanese state.

Under these circumstances, the ruler of Lombardy and the
Tuscan Republic watched each other with wary politeness during
the year 1386, while Giangaleazzo settled himself more securely
on the throne from which he had deposed his uncle. The Florentines recognized that the wider problems of Italy could not be
solved without his co-operation; they invited him to join with
them in the hopeless, much canvassed plans to suppress the
Companies, and in the settlement of the Neapolitan kingdom
where, after Charles of Durazzo's death, the boy Ladislaus, his
heir, was hard pressed between the supporters of the Angevin

---

[1] 18 November: *Capitoli di Firenze*, II 226–34, no. 45. On 8 November,
Siena had been admitted into an earlier Tuscan alliance: *ibid.* II 223–4, no. 36.
[2] *Ibid.* I 132–3, nos. 37–40; and 146, nos. 77–8.

claimant and the relentless hostility of Urban VI.[1] But when Giangaleazzo offered to co-operate with the Florentines in their own province, he was firmly rebuffed. He intervened on behalf of Antonio Montefeltro, lord of Urbino and Gubbio, at whose expense the more aggressive section of the government, against the will of the moderate party,[2] saw a chance of strengthening the Republic's position on the border of Umbria; and the Florentines finally sent an embassy to Pavia, to persuade Giangaleazzo "to meddle no more in the affairs of the Count of Montefeltro".[3]

In Romagna, Giangaleazzo met with better fortune. The cities between Bologna and the sea on the eastern side of the Apennines were ruled by despotic dynasties owing a nominal allegiance to the Pope: Alidosi in Imola, Ordelaffi in Forlì, Manfredi in Faenza, Polenta in Ravenna, and, most powerful of all, the Malatesta, whose territories included Rimini, Cesena, Pesaro and Fano. The border quarrels of these rival princes and the divergent interests of the neighbouring powers paved the way for Giangaleazzo's intervention. Florence, too, had interests in Romagna, for the territory of the Republic reached across the eastern slope of the Apennines. The Bolognese, on the other hand, were not anxious to see Florentine influence extended in a region so immediately important to themselves; and it was probably for this reason that they accepted Giangaleazzo's mediation in a dispute with the treacherous adventurer Astorre Manfredi of Faenza. The Florentines, whose offer of mediation came too late, did not relish this evidence of Bologna's readiness to accept the Count's friendship.[4]

Giangaleazzo made other contacts with the rulers of Romagna.

---

[1] Collino, "Politica Fiorentino-Bolognese", *MAT* 2, LIV 137–9, and 173–5, Docs. 87–8, 91, 93. Mancarella, "Firenze, la Chiesa e Ladislao", *ASN* XLIV 112–15, and XLVI 208–9, Docs. 5–7.

[2] Rado, *op. cit.* 124 note 2.

[3] Instructions drawn up at the end of March 1386: Collino, "Politica Fiorentino-Bolognese", *MAT* 2, LIV 177, Doc. 99. For the Florentine dispute with Montefeltro: *ibid.* 134–7; Franceschini, "Giangaleazzo arbitro di pace", *ASL* NS III 299–300, where however he seems unaware of the documents published by Collino.

[4] Collino, "Politica Fiorentino-Bolognese", *MAT* 2, LIV 140–1. The "Corpus Chronicorum Bononiensium", *RIS* NS XVIII, 1, vol. 3, 381–2, gives other evidence of this friendship.

He had won, for the moment, the unstable support of Astorre Manfredi, who represented him at a conference on the affairs of Naples at the end of 1386.[1] The Malatesta, too, turned to him rather than to Florence, and accepted his arbitration in a dispute among themselves over the possession of Fossombrone.[2] Carlo Malatesta, the head of the house, was at once a loyal servant of the Pope and the champion of the authority of his own family in southern Romagna. Giangaleazzo appreciated Carlo's worth and made a friend of him; and the value of his good relations with the Malatesta was shown when they prevented a mercenary force from passing through Romagna to the relief of Verona in the war of 1387.[3]

During these years, when the conquest of eastern Lombardy was his immediate object, Giangaleazzo could not develop a positive and continuous policy in other regions; but he lost no opportunity of offering his services in the cause of peace, wherever quarrels arose. He assumed no embarrassing commitments; the Florentine plan for an Italian League, which might have tied his hands in the Scaliger-Carrarese war, petered out after months of weary negotiation;[4] but he steadily increased his influence in Tuscany, Umbria and Romagna: giving no sign of aggressive intentions, uttering no threats against anyone, and adopting the most friendly attitude towards all the powers concerned.

In the early months of 1387, new problems arose to vex the Tuscan cities. Urban VI left Genoa and brought his uneasy presence to Lucca, hoping to settle his differences with Perugia and set up his court there. The perennial Florentine fear of Papal rivalry in Tuscany sprang at once into life. The Republic again made overtures to Giangaleazzo, but the Count was glad enough to know that Florence would be fully occupied while his armies were moving on Verona.[5] Giangaleazzo's relations with Urban

---

[1] *V.* the documents quoted by Mancarella, *op. cit. ASN* xliv 123–4.

[2] Clementini, *Raccolto Istorico della fondatione di Rimino*, ii 174.

[3] Novati, "Trattative di Giangaleazzo", *ASL* xxxix, 2, 572–7.

[4] Collino, "Politica Fiorentino-Bolognese", *MAT* 2, liv 141–2; *id.* "Guerra Viscontea", *ASL* xxxiv, 1, 107–10; Mancarella, *op. cit. ASN* xliv 122–4.

[5] Mancarella, *op. cit.* 127–8; Collino, "Guerra Viscontea", *ASL* xxxiv, 1, 109–12.

were excellent during the summer, although he was in constant touch with the court of Avignon as well. The Florentines, on the other hand, although they never questioned the legitimacy of Urban's claim to the Papacy, formed a thinly disguised alliance against him in August 1387, with Rinaldo Orsini, the Clementist lord of Orvieto and Spoleto.[1]

Graver and more enduring were the disputes between Siena and Florence over the town of Montepulciano. The Florentines had some justification for their interference. Montepulciano resented the overlordship of Siena, whose government seems to have been inefficient and directly contrary to the town's best interests. But Siena, already smarting over the loss of the Aretine lands, was resolved to resist to the uttermost any further encroachment on the part of Florence. In June 1387 the anti-Sienese party in Montepulciano gained predominance, and the Sienese accused Florence of instigating resistance to their authority. Angry words passed; and while the discussions were still proceeding, the lord of Cortona in the Valdichiana dealt a further blow to Siena. Reluctant to renew his obligations to the Sienese, who were no longer masters of the Valdichiana, he persuaded Florence to accept his allegiance.[2]

Florentine ambitions threatened every major state in Tuscany. They encouraged the lesser lords and communities to look to them for protection; and their government, like that of the Visconti in the north, was generally more efficient and more considerate than that of their rivals. But the object of their policy was equally to undermine the authority of their neighbours. Dr Collino, whose articles were based almost exclusively upon Florentine sources and who accepted the full force of Florentine propaganda—a writer who is "visconteggiante" is automatically suspect[3]—maintained that the Florentines were prompted by a

[1] Collino, "Guerra Viscontea", *ASL* xxxiv, 1, 141–2; Labande, "Rôle de Rinaldo Orsini", *MAH* xlix 175–6.

[2] Collino, "Guerra Viscontea", *ASL* xxxiv, 1, 125–32; Favale, "Siena nel quadro della Politica Viscontea", *BSSP* xliii 316–19. The lord of Cortona's pact with Florence: *Capitoli di Firenze*, i 512 (28 August). For the Florentine justification of their attitude, *v.* the instructions of 17 June: Collino, "Guerra Viscontea", *ASL* xxxiv, 1, 127 note 2.

[3] E.g. in "Politica Fiorentino-Bolognese", *MAT* 2, liv 141.

desire for peace and order; but it was an order arbitrarily dictated and imposed by themselves that they wished to promote.[1] He admitted the "audacity of the Florentine government", their determination "to wear away little by little the influence of the Sienese, and to substitute their own".[2] He drew an eloquent picture of a wise and moderate Republic, struggling against the persistent intrigues of an unscrupulous and ambitious tyrant. But the despatches of the ambassadors of Lucca in Siena, during the summer of 1387, present the activities of the Florentine government in a very different light.[3]

These letters leave no room for doubt that the aggressive schemes of Florence lay at the root of the troubles in Tuscany. They reveal the atmosphere of suspicion and fear which enveloped all the Republics save Pisa, faithful still to the Gambacortan policy of subservience to Florence. Even in Lucca misgivings were rife, for the rumour that the city contemplated a closer attachment to Giangaleazzo had attracted the attention of Florence.[4] "It is said by some who have returned from Florence, that they say openly that the first thing they have to do is to settle the question of Lucca. God take from them the power!"[5] The Perugians placed themselves under the protection of Urban VI; but they wished to retain the favour of the Florentines, whom they offered to reconcile with the Pope, explaining that they had invited him to the city only for the impetus to trade which his presence would give.[6] In Siena itself, fury and indignation struggled against the desperate knowledge that a single-handed attack on Florence would spell ruin. "They recognize the trot of the wolf, and put little faith in letters and less in ambassadors;

---

[1] *Ibid.* 145.

[2] *Id.* "Guerra Viscontea", *ASL* xxxiv, 1, 125.

[3] Lucca, *Regesti*, 253–65, nos. 1341–70. Some of the despatches, bearing neither year nor indiction, have been confused by the Editor with those of another embassy to Siena two years later. Nos. 1355–7, 1359, 1361–3, 1371 should be dated 1389. No. 1411, pp. 278–9, belongs to the series of 1387.

[4] Minutes of the Florentine Council, 26 April 1387: Collino, "Guerra Viscontea", *ASL* xxxiv, 1, 121 note 1.

[5] Report from Siena, 5 July: Lucca, *Regesti*, 257, no. 1347.

[6] Minerbetti, "Cronica", *RIS* NS xxvii, 2, 42–3; Collino, "Guerra Viscontea", *ASL* xxxiv, 1, 128.

they are disposed to find their honour in the undertaking, or to lose all that they have." Perugia has given generous assurances. "Every one is dissatisfied with the Florentines; there is talk of a League." Finally comes a passage, in the expressive Italian phrases of the time, which is worthy of the later Florentine tirades against Giangaleazzo. "Per tutto mettono el capo e la coda volpina e sono infiniti loro intendimenti a mal fare. Pregovi che per tutte vostre fortezze facciate avere buona cura, che mai non dorme Giuda maladetto pieno di male e di simonia."[1]

Giangaleazzo is hardly mentioned in relation to Tuscany in these reports. The Florentines made their own difficulties. No statesman of the age, least of all Giangaleazzo, could have resisted the opportunities which the Florentines created for him. While he was concentrating his forces against Verona, however, he could play only a passive part in Tuscan affairs. The Sienese had perforce to accept a joint Florentine-Bolognese arbitration of their differences with Montepulciano. There is no evidence that they even appealed to Giangaleazzo at this stage; he was certainly not in a position to help them if they did. But the moment would come, and meanwhile the Florentines were preparing the way for him; they were driving their enemies into his arms.

The fall of Verona brought home to the Florentines the dangers of their policy. "God help us!" wrote a citizen in his diary when the news came.[2] The shadow of Giangaleazzo fell over them, and wherever they turned, they saw his hand directed against them. But their difficulties were in fact largely of their own making. Giangaleazzo was never precipitate; he built up his position slowly and firmly. He had imperceptibly drawn upon himself the attention of every state which saw itself threatened by Florentine ambitions. He had probably not yet formed a clear policy; he could not make full use of his alliances until he was strong enough to intervene directly in Tuscany. When the time came, all the enemies of Florence would rally to his cause.

The more far-seeing observers in the Florentine Council were already alarmed by the spasmodic symptoms which bore witness

---

[1] Despatch of 6 August: Lucca, *Regesti*, 260, no. 1353.
[2] "Iddio ci aiuti!" "Diario", in *Documenti di Storia Italiana*, VI 474.

to Bolognese jealousy of Florentine influence in Romagna. The Bolognese were as reluctant to permit the expansion of the Florentines in this region, as were the Sienese in the Valdichiana;[1] and the contacts between Bologna and Pavia were watched very closely in Florence.[2] The presence of Ubaldini in Romagna with the troops which had served under him in Giangaleazzo's army during the Veronese war did not ease the tension, for Bologna lay exposed and tempting to an armed attack, and the Florentines believed that Ubaldini's movements were dictated from Pavia.[3]

The Republic of Pisa was uneasy at the failure of Gambacorta's pro-Florentine experiment to restore the city's prosperity, and the old hostility to Florence had begun to raise its head. The activities of marauding companies in Tuscany in the first half of 1388 led to mutual recriminations among the Republics, and provided the anti-Florentine party in Pisa with material for its propaganda.[4] Giangaleazzo had secured an invaluable agent at Pisa in the person of Jacopo d'Appiano, the trusted secretary of Pietro Gambacorta. Appiano was already attached to the Count's service in the summer of 1387, when he forwarded letters to Pavia from the Visconti agents in Tuscany;[5] but his associations with the anti-Florentine party in Pisa, which brought several protests from Florence, may have been due to his own personal ambitions rather than to the deliberate policy of Giangaleazzo.

The Florentines could find little to console them in Umbria. Urban VI was in close touch with Pavia, and Florence dreaded a union of two interests which might so well be exploited at the Republic's expense.[6] Perugia hesitated to take sides, but seemed inclined to prefer the safeguard of Milanese friendship against Florentine ambitions.[7] While Urban left Perugia in September

---

[1] Collino, "Guerra Viscontea", *ASL* xxxiv, 1, 129–30; *id.* "Preparazione della Guerra", *ASL* xxxiv, 2, 241–3, 247–9, 259–61.

[2] *Id.* "Guerra Viscontea", *ASL* xxxiv, 1, 134–5, 137, 140–1.

[3] *Id.* "Preparazione della Guerra", *ASL* xxxiv, 2, 218–19, 225–32.

[4] *Id.* "Guerra Viscontea", *ASL* xxxiv, 1, 154–5; *id.* "Preparazione della Guerra", *ASL* xxxiv, 2, 217, 270–4, 279–81; Silva, "Governo di Pietro Gambacorta in Pisa", 228–32, 236–7, 242–3.

[5] Lucca, *Regesti*, 258, no. 1350; and 250, no. 1332.

[6] Collino, "Guerra Veneto-Viscontea", *ASL* xxxvi, 1, 14–15.

[7] *Ibid.* 55–6 and 333–7.

1388, and moved towards Rome, Visconti envoys came to the city "to do many things".[1]

Finally, the Florentines lived in perpetual fear of a union between Siena and the Count. When the Sienese, like the Florentines themselves, sent an envoy to congratulate Giangaleazzo on his conquest of Verona, great interest was displayed in Florence. "From what we hear from certain friends of ours," wrote the Sienese envoys in Florence, "the rulers of this city find much food for thought in this embassy which you are sending to Milan, and we have been questioned very closely at their request by one of our city. We did not enlarge on the matter, save to say that they go, as we believe, with good purpose, and to honour that lord, and it seems to us that he merits it; and we see that our neighbours do the like."[2]

It is more than probable that the Sienese envoys carried an appeal for help against Florence; but this is not sufficient to justify the assumption[3] that Giangaleazzo was already intervening in the affairs of Tuscany. The Florentines had clearly revealed their attitude towards him, alike by the anxiety which they displayed about his relations with their neighbours, and by their open championship of the cause of Francesco Carrara at the beginning of 1388. Nothing less than a complete renunciation of all alliances and obligations in Tuscany and Romagna would satisfy the Republic. Such an undertaking Giangaleazzo was obviously not prepared to give. But the Paduan situation was developing rapidly; and Giangaleazzo could not be hurried into commitments which he was unable to fulfil. There is every reason to believe that he refused to meddle in Tuscan affairs at the moment.[4] He sent his ambassadors to Florence in March 1388,

[1] Minerbetti, "Cronica", 69–70; Pellini, *Historia di Perugia*, i 1364. The Visconti agents were sent to pacify the quarrel between the Malatesta and Antonio Montefeltro; this they achieved, in spite of Florentine intrigues, on 17 November 1388. For an account of this quarrel, v. Franceschini, *op. cit. ASL* NS iii 300–6.

[2] Despatch of 17 November: *ASS*, Concistoro 1822, no. 3.

[3] Made by Collino, "Guerra Viscontea", *ASL* xxxiv, 1, 152–3; and Favale, *op. cit. BSSP* xliii 320.

[4] This will appear more clearly from his attitude even after the conquest of Padua: v. *infra*, Chapter ix.

to reassure the Republic and to deny the rumours in circulation regarding his intrigues in Siena and Bologna. He offered to join in an effort to secure the pacification of Italy; and the Florentines, preferring to await the issue of the Paduan question, accepted his proposals in principle, and gave a very dilatory attention to the suggested scheme for an alliance.[1]

The fate of Montepulciano arose again to trouble the peace of Tuscany. By the end of May, the city was ripe for rebellion, in spite of official discouragement from Florence.[2] The Sienese, rather than abandon the unequal struggle, offered to accept the dominion of Giangaleazzo on his own terms.[3] But Giangaleazzo was already pledged to the war against Carrara; he could only offer his services to reconcile the two Republics.[4] The Florentines politely declined the offer—on the ground that their relations with Siena were excellent—and prepared promptly and energetically against the possibility of direct interference from Milan.[5] "Hic homo signa multa facit", it was said in the Council.[6] In August, when Montepulciano raised the Florentine banner over the town, the Florentines disclaimed all responsibility, solemnly rebuked their supporters, and sent a small force to defend them from reprisals.[7] The Sienese, unable to obtain active support from Giangaleazzo, agreed to renew negotiations.[8]

Giangaleazzo had nothing to gain by aggravating the differences between Florence and Siena;[9] his offer to try to reconcile them was probably quite genuine. He could only assure the

[1] Minerbetti, "Cronica", 54; Collino, "Preparazione della Guerra", *ASL* xxxiv, 2, 239-41, 249 note 1, 257 note 1.

[2] Collino, *op. cit.* 269-70.

[3] Instructions of 5 June: *v.* Doc. 2. The Florentines showed great interest in the object and the reception of this embassy: Collino, *op. cit. ASL* xxxiv, 2, 281-4.

[4] Minerbetti, "Cronica", 66.

[5] Minutes of the Council, 1 July: Collino, "Preparazione della Guerra", *ASL* xxxiv, 2, 286-9.

[6] The speech recorded by Leonardo Bruni, "Historiarum Florentini Populi", *RIS* NS xix, 3, 242-3; and referred to by Giangaleazzo in a letter of 18 November 1389: Salutati, "Epistolario", ii 380, note 1.

[7] Collino, "Guerra Veneto-Viscontea", *ASL* xxxvi, 1, 34-5.

[8] *Ibid.* 27-30, and 36.

As is suggested by Collino, e.g. in "Preparazione della Guerra", *ASL* xxxiv, 2, 235 6.

Sienese of his friendship and exhort them to be patient. We may be certain that, on the eve of the Paduan campaign, he could afford neither to detach a contingent of his own army to help the Sienese, nor to send an agent into Tuscany to enlist troops on their behalf.[1]

Thus the crisis passed. Opinion in Florence was too divided to permit of any active measures against Milan.[2] Giangaleazzo's offer to give guarantees of his good intentions was accepted;[3] and the Florentines were careful to give no direct cause of offence.[4] They informed Giangaleazzo of the movements of the fugitive Antonio della Scala in Tuscany, and limited the period during which he might remain in their territory.[5] Their representatives were present at the baptism of Giangaleazzo's heir in September 1388.[6]

---

[1] The presence of Visconti troops in Siena in May 1388 is affirmed by Collino, *ibid.* 277–8, on the strength of a reference in the "Annales Sanenses", *RIS* xix 389 E; but an investigation will show that the early chapters of this Chronicle are pre-dated by one year, and that this reference refers to 1389, coinciding with the well-documented arrival of Visconti troops in Siena in June 1389 (*v.* Chapter ix, *infra*). The sending of the Visconti agent Giovanni della Porta to enlist troops in Tuscany is derived by Collino ("Guerra Veneto-Viscontea", *ASL* xxxvi, 1, 12–13) and by Favale (*op. cit. BSSP* xliii 321), from Malavolti, *Historia de' Sanesi*, ii 162 t. Malavolti's exact chronology is often difficult to follow, as he does not give many dates; but in this case he undoubtedly refers to the late summer of 1389. Malavolti states that della Porta accompanied the Condottiere Ugolotto Biancardo, whom the despatches printed in the *Regesti* of Lucca prove to have been in Tuscany in September 1389; and this would correspond very well with Malavolti's further statement that he was sent at the request of Siena conveyed through Battista Piccolomini. Piccolomini was in Pavia in May–June 1389, and two of his despatches survive in *ASS*, Concistoro 1825, nos. 32 and 50, although this would not be conclusive evidence in itself, as Piccolomini had been on at least one previous mission to Pavia, in December 1388.

[2] The division of opinion found in the minutes of the Council, quoted by Collino, confirms the remark of Leonardo Bruni, *op. cit. RIS* NS xix, 3, 244: "Per hanc variationem sententiarum, quamquam frequenter agitarentur consilia, nihil tamen constituebatur."

[3] Collino, "Guerra Veneto-Viscontea", *ASL* xxxvi, 1, 15–18 and 55–6.

[4] Bolognini, "Relazioni tra Firenze e Venezia", *NAV* ix 52; minutes of the Council, 30 May, in Collino, "Preparazione della Guerra", *ASL* xxxiv, 2, 267 note 5.

[5] Collino, *op. cit.* 274–6.

[6] *Id.* "Guerra Veneto-Viscontea", *ASL* xxxvi, 1, 315–8. Rado, *op. cit.* 154–6, without referring to the evidence produced by Collino, sought to discredit the suggestion of Florentine participation in the ceremony.

The Republic, however, was still uneasy. The discovery that a leading citizen was in treacherous communication with Pavia confirmed the resolution to look for new alliances.[1] In August, the Florentines strengthened their position in Romagna by an alliance with Bologna and the lords of Ravenna, Faenza and Imola.[2] Tentative overtures were made in Avignon, in Savoy, in Genoa, in an effort to win new friends in readiness for the outbreak of a struggle which was already foreseen.[3]

Nevertheless Giangaleazzo, who had been playing for time, had played with success. The Florentines understood this when the news of Carrara's surrender reached them. They had encouraged the Paduan resistance without giving adequate support. It is true that a war with Giangaleazzo would have involved them in attacks from every quarter;[4] but this was the result, not of Milanese intrigues, but of their own aggressive policy, whose repercussions threatened at last to overwhelm them. They had not improved their position in Tuscany; in spite of belated attempts at reconciliation, their relations with the neighbouring cities grew steadily worse. They had clearly demonstrated their hostility to Giangaleazzo, without putting any effective obstacle in the way of his plans.

The Count, on the other hand, had made the fullest use of his opportunities. His agents were active in Pisa; Siena and Perugia appealed to him for protection. He had formed an intimate alliance with the French court. Venice was his ally, the Doge of Genoa his friend. The ambitions of Pope Urban promised to further his own plans. After the rapid conclusion of the campaigns against Verona and Padua, he was ready to meet any challenge which the Florentines might offer to the further development of the Visconti state.

---

[1] The carefully suppressed scandal of Buonaccorso di Lapo Giovanni: Romano, "Niccolò Spinelli", *ASN* xxvi 438–9; Collino, "Guerra Veneto-Viscontea", *ASL* xxxvi, 1, 360–2.

[2] Collino, *ibid.* 36; *Capitoli di Firenze*, ii 237.

[3] Instructions of 23 September and 15 October: Collino, "Guerra Veneto-Viscontea", *ASL* xxxvi, 1, 46 note 5, and 323–4.

[4] Collino, *ibid.* 17; and Favale, *op. cit.* 322.

CHAPTER IX

GIANGALEAZZO AND FLORENCE: THE DRIFT TO WAR (DECEMBER 1388–APRIL 1390)

GIANGALEAZZO had hitherto succeeded in isolating his enemies before he destroyed them. Those tactics were no longer open to him. The inevitable coalition, such as had challenged and eventually destroyed the princes who had threatened to overturn the balance of power in the past, began to take shape under the leadership of Florence. The Count's enemies, who saw in the fate of della Scala and of Carrara a menace to their own security, succeeded in confining his ambitions and pinning him to the defensive for ten years after the capture of Padua. Giangaleazzo's unique qualities as a statesman enabled him to survive and finally to overcome their opposition; but the promise of his early triumphs was fatally delayed in its fulfilment. The detailed story of gains and losses, of advance and retreat, of fighting and intrigue and counter-intrigue in the second phase of Giangaleazzo's reign, is one of confusion and bewilderment; but in it may be found the seed of his later achievements.

The decade between 1388 and 1398 falls naturally into three periods, coinciding with the three expedients to which Giangaleazzo resorted in his effort to break the barrier which the Florentines had erected against his further advance: the first war against Florence and Bologna, the negotiations for a French invasion of Italy, and the plan for an active Papal-Imperial-Neapolitan alliance to support Milanese ambitions. Had Giangaleazzo succeeded in any one of these phases of his policy, his power in northern Italy would have become irresistible; but his efforts were not concentrated solely upon these objectives. It was by careful watch and perpetual intrigues among the neighbouring states that he prepared the way for a second period of expansion.

The wide scope of Giangaleazzo's diplomacy leaves an impression of restless ambition expending its energy over too wide a sphere, working without any fixed plan and scattering its resources in too many remote commitments. There was, however, an order behind the confusion of Italian politics. Giangaleazzo's immediate object, after the capture of Padua, was to complete his mastery over the Lombard plain, and particularly to restore the Visconti dominion in Bologna. The traditions of his family, the instincts of the Milanese people, and his own good sense demanded it. But the problem of Bologna, owing to the city's peculiarly important position, was a very delicate one. An open attack would bring not only Florence, but Venice and the Pope as well to the defence of the Republic; the strength of Bologna lay, not in the advantages of strategical protection, but in the number of states whose fortunes were bound up with hers. Giangaleazzo recognized the obstacles in his way; but he had at his disposal more indirect methods by which he could bring his influence to bear on the Republic; and to these he was prepared to resort, rather than embark on an enterprise in which he himself seemed likely to be overwhelmed.

In this case his opportunities lay in Tuscany, where the Sienese were imploring him to help them. A situation had arisen which peculiarly suited the Count's methods. With a minimum of effort on his part, the states most concerned in repressing the ambitions of Florence had been led to regard him as their last refuge; and the Florentines, alarmed at the potential danger of Milanese intervention, had assumed the worst and practically challenged his right to interfere in the affairs of Tuscany and Romagna.

Giangaleazzo always shunned bloodshed as far as possible. He never fought a war if he could avoid it; and when his armies marched against a city, it was generally with the knowledge that the gates would be opened to them from within. At the end of 1388, the leaders of a conspiracy against the existing government of Bologna invited him to co-operate with them and send an army to take possession of the city in his name. Giangaleazzo replied that he could not help them.[1] The Florentines, who had stood aside and watched him devour Verona and Padua, would not

[1] Palmieri, "Congiura per sottomettere Bologna al Conte di Vertù", *AMR* 4, vi 187.

tolerate any movement against Bologna, and he was not yet prepared to fight them; the odds were not heavily enough in his favour. The campaigns of 1387 and 1388 had been rapid but expensive. Giangaleazzo was anxious to send Valentina to her bridegroom in Paris, and that involved the payment of a large instalment of the dowry. The conqueror needed a moment of peace. He did not intend to abandon his friends in Tuscany; but he was not ready to assume the task of defending them.

Nevertheless, his relations with Florence had to be placed on a more regular footing. If he was not prepared to attack the Republic, he was even less anxious for the Florentines, in their present mood of suspicion and defiance, to attack him; they had indeed already begun the feverish search for allies, and were making plans for a powerful League in opposition to Milan. Accordingly, Giangaleazzo sent Bevilacqua from Pavia in December 1388, with an offer to the Florentine government. Speaking in the Council, he gave assurances of his master's peaceful and friendly intentions, demonstrated by the dismissal of the greater part of his troops. Now that the Paduan question, which had prevented an agreement, was resolved, Giangaleazzo offered to join in a pact of non-aggression, or in any other form of alliance to guarantee the peace of Italy. It was not an offer that the Florentines could refuse; they had still to find allies to support them in the event of a war. The councillors were not convinced either that Giangaleazzo had really begun to disband his army after the war, or that he genuinely wanted peace with them; but they decided to test the sincerity of his offer, and appointed envoys to go to Pavia and discuss the question with him in person.[1]

The Florentine representatives, Luigi Guicciardini and Giovanni Ricci, in accordance with their usual practice, showed their instructions to the Bolognese government and urged the importance of common action by the two Republics. The deputations of both cities arrived in Lombardy early in February 1389, and the negotiations began. It was found that the proposals advanced by the parties differed in some important respects. Giangaleazzo wanted a League "ad se non offendendum", a

[1] Collino, "Guerra Veneto-Viscontea", *ASL* xxxvi, 1, 374–85.

restricted formula of non-intervention in quarrels among the allies, who were to promise to submit all disputes to arbitration; the Florentines proposed a League "ad defensionem statum", an alliance of all the lords and Communes of northern and central Italy, pledging them to mutual assistance against attack by any other member of the League. Giangaleazzo offered a vague promise not to accept further jurisdictions in Italy, but he would not undertake, as the Florentines demanded, to abstain from interference in Tuscany, for that would leave his friends at the mercy of Florence; the Florentine ambassadors, on the other hand, were instructed to propose the territory of Modena and the river Secchia as the borders of Giangaleazzo's influence, the limit beyond which he was not to intervene in the affairs of Tuscany and Romagna, in return for a similar guarantee that Florence and Bologna would disinterest themselves in the state of Lombardy. Finally Giangaleazzo, surrounded by the armies of his own generals, could safely advance a plan to drive the unattached mercenary companies out of Italy; but the Florentines, who had no standing army of any size, depended in the event of war on hired troops, and would not commit themselves to a definite line of conduct.[1] Sir John Hawkwood, who had married one of Bernabò's illegitimate daughters, was willing to fight for them at any time against the Count; and they were not sorry to see the Englishman in close friendship with Carlo Visconti, who had returned from Germany and joined Hawkwood's company in the hope of recovering his heritage.[2]

The minutes of the discussions at Pavia would have offered us a fascinating picture: the elected representatives of the Republics, anxious perhaps to return home to their occupations, pitting their wits across the Council table against the wily, experienced statesmen of the Visconti; their interviews with Giangaleazzo himself, flattering, persuasive, convincing. Luigi Guicciardini and Giovanni Ricci proved unable to hold their own. Giangaleazzo himself gave a summary account of the proceedings to his friends the

---

[1] For the Florentine proposals, v. Doc. 3. The nature of Giangaleazzo's proposals is disclosed in the later stages of the negotiations.

[2] Romano, "Giangaleazzo Visconti", *ASL* xviii 26.

Sienese. After long and detailed discussions of each point, it was finally possible to draw up the terms of an agreement, which in fact embodied all the Count's main proposals. The representatives of the Republics sent copies of the document to their governments for approval, "saying that they dared not, and had no power to conclude or sign anything, in a matter of such importance, without the express mandate of their Communes".[1]

This seems reasonable enough; but the Florentines, who learned the news at the end of March, were furious both with their envoys for having yielded where they were instructed to stand firm, and with Giangaleazzo, who had placed them in a false position by having made it known at once that only the consent of the Republics was needed for the conclusion of an accord. They had been prepared, by the middle of March, to accept a simple pact of non-aggression instead of a defensive alliance; but they would not modify the creation of spheres of influence by the line from Modena along the Secchia, since the League could only be made acceptable to them by a complete renunciation of intervention in Tuscany on the part of the Count.[2] They had already had occasion to send a messenger to Pavia, with instructions "severely to reprimand messer Luigi and messer Giovanni, and especially messer Luigi, for having been separated from one another, against the instructions which were given to them".[3] When they learnt that Giangaleazzo, by making known the agreement that had been reached, had publicly placed the onus of refusing a peaceful settlement upon them, they immediately denied his version of the proceedings at Pavia;[4] but privately they were forced to admit that they and their ambassadors had been outwitted. On 10 April 1389, Gherardo Buondelmonti and Lodovico Albergotti were commissioned to join the Florentine representatives in Pavia. They were instructed to reprimand

---

[1] Giangaleazzo to Siena, 13 April, in Professione, *Siena e le Compagne di Ventura*, 135–7.

[2] Instructions to the Florentine envoy to Bologna, 12 March 1388/9: *ASF*, Dieci di Balìa, Legazioni I 174–5.

[3] Instructions to a messenger going to Pavia, 17 March 1388/9: *ibid.* 179.

[4] Instructions of 2 April, published by Silva, "Governo di Pietro Gambacorta", 323–5, Doc. 19.

Ricci and Guicciardini, for having disobeyed their orders. "We are astonished and grieved to think that they pretend to more wisdom and foresight than all the people of this city. And we are forced to conclude, both from this and from the letters we have received from them, that, in defiance of our instructions, they must at least tacitly have agreed to the clauses which the Count demands." No accord could be signed in which the Count did not clearly undertake to refrain from intervention in Tuscany and Romagna.[1]

In Pavia, the envoys of the other Tuscan cities eagerly awaited the Florentine decision. The Sienese envoys wrote on 14 April that the ambassadors of Florence and Bologna had asked their governments to approve the agreement, and were expecting an answer, "which up to to-day they have not had, whereof the lord Count expresses much astonishment; but it is thought that they will have the replies during this week of Easter, and then it will be seen what must follow—God in his pity and mercy grant that it may be for the peace and tranquillity of the whole country."[2] Their hopes were disappointed; Buondelmonti and Albergotti brought the Florentine rejection of the proposed terms of accord, and the negotiations began over again. But the new ambassadors were as incapable as their predecessors of holding their own in the unaccustomed atmosphere of a despot's court, where they were exposed to the concerted pressure exercised by Giangaleazzo's skilful and plausible councillors. The Florentine government wrote on 10 May that "it appears clear to us that you are led by the nose",[3] and commanded them to leave the conference on the 20th, if Giangaleazzo had not accepted the principle of non-intervention in Tuscany and Romagna by that date. They were still in Pavia on the 23rd, however, and were consequently deprived of their ambassadorial office, "because you have chosen to follow your own wishes and not to obey your instructions".[4]

[1] Instructions to Buondelmonti and Albergotti, 10 April 1389: *ASF*, Dieci di Balìa, Legazioni I 185–6.

[2] *ASS*, Concistoro 1825, no. 17.

[3] Florence to Buondelmonti and Albergotti, 10 May: *ASF*, Dieci di Balìa, Legazioni I 191.

[4] The same, 29 May: *ibid.* 196.

Filippo della Molza, who had represented Francesco Gonzaga at the conference, wrote on the 24th: " The Florentine and Bolognese ambassadors leave to-morrow. They say that they wish to go and comfort their governments to accept this League—which would be a holy thing and a good, but, as far as I can see, they seem by no means inclined to accept the agreement, save on conditions that would be too inconvenient and harmful to many parties."[1]

The conference of Pavia had failed, but Giangaleazzo had scored a diplomatic success. Florentine prestige suffered from the Republic's conduct of the negotiations; "and truly, in our opinion they are greatly in the wrong", wrote the ambassadors of Lucca at Pavia.[2] Giangaleazzo pressed home his advantage. The envoys of all the other states represented at the conference—of Siena, Perugia and Lucca, of the Malatesta and the Count of Urbino, of the lords of Ferrara and Mantua—were summoned before the Council on 28 May, to hear proposals for the promotion of peace. The Count offered to make an alliance with all these states, on the terms which he himself had proposed and which the Florentines had rejected, "always with the understanding that he would reserve the right of the Florentines and the Bolognese to join if they wished; and if they were unwilling, it should be done without them." It was decided that the envoys of Perugia and Lucca should seek full authority from their governments to enter the League; "...we for our part said that we have full authority."[3]

Before any progress had been made, however, a herald of peace arrived in Pavia. Pietro Gambacorta, lord of Pisa, had already patched up an agreement between Florence and Siena over the question of Montepulciano;[4] the Florentines were prepared now to make concessions, although the Sienese would probably not have accepted them if they had felt sure of Milanese support. Gambacorta, however, felt that the root cause of the general atmosphere of insecurity lay in Giangaleazzo's relations with

[1] *ASMa*, E. xlix. 3. (The date 1392 has been added by an Archivist at a later period; the despatch clearly refers to the events of 1389.)

[2] Silva, "Governo", 326, Doc. 20.

[3] The Sienese envoys at Pavia to the government of Siena, 30 May 1389: *ASS*, Concistoro 1825, no. 32.

[4] Silva, "Governo", 244 and 246.

the Tuscan Communes. Moved by a sincere désire for peace in the interests of his own state, he determined to go himself and talk to Giangaleazzo. He reached Pavia on 2 June, bringing his own formula for a general appeasement. This included a version of the Modena-Secchia boundary of spheres of influence, modified to allow for possessions already acquired, and concrete proposals to deal with the menace of the Companies. Having acquainted himself with Giangaleazzo's point of view, he returned to Tuscany; the next stage of his mission was a visit to the Florentine government.[1]

Giangaleazzo was genuinely anxious to avoid an open breach with Florence. He preferred to build up his power by peaceful methods, and he was not in any case prepared for war. The French had agreed to reduce the first instalment of Valentina's dowry to 200,000 florins; but Giangaleazzo's subjects had to make a large contribution towards the payment of this sum.[2] Valentina entered Milan on 12 June, and the feasts and ceremonies in honour of her departure lasted for twelve days. "We are to remain here until the 23rd, while the feasts last; then we will return to Pavia, with the lady Valentina. From there she will go on into France."[3] Francesco Gonzaga and the Prince of Achaia were among the noble company who escorted her through Piedmont on the long journey to Paris.[4]

Giangaleazzo, from the country retreat to which he had gone to hide his grief at his daughter's departure, kept his finger on the pulse of Tuscany. The situation grew graver as the summer wore on. Already at the end of May, when the Florentine ambassadors had left Pavia, Giangaleazzo talked in a pessimistic vein to Giovanni and Nicolao, envoys of Lucca at his court. He prophesied that, unless the Florentines accepted his conditions for a League, war would soon break out. He expressed little confidence

[1] *Ibid.* 246–7. Gambacorta's proposals are taken from a copy in the Milanese Archives, dated 7 July: *Inventari e Regesti*, I 122, Reg. 17, no. 2.

[2] Comani, "Denari per la dote di Valentina", *ASL* xxviii, 1, 44–9; Romano, "Tornandoci sopra", *ASL* xxix, 1, 114–15.

[3] Despatch of the Sienese envoys, 16 June 1389: *ASS*, Concistoro 1825, no. 50.

[4] For Valentina's journey, *v.* Camus, "Venue en France", *MSI* xxxvi, 24–31.

in Gambacorta's pacific mission, claiming that his advisers had at least as clear an understanding of the situation as the lord of Pisa. The envoys admitted that this was so, and wrote in admiration of Giangaleazzo's knowledge of local Tuscan politics. "He knows better by name all the rebels of Pisa, than does messer Pietro himself; and similarly of the other lands of Tuscany."[1]

The military precautions taken by Florence after the breakdown of the conference of Pavia were the immediate cause of Giangaleazzo's preoccupations. The Florentine government had recalled Sir John Hawkwood and his troops post-haste from the kingdom of Naples, where they had spent the winter.[2] Giangaleazzo interpreted this action as a threat to his friends in Tuscany, and no longer refused to answer their appeals. He sent 200 lances to Siena under the command of the Roman noble, Paolo Savelli.[3] Another contingent was to go to Umbria and Romagna. "We have heard that the ambassadors of Perugia who are here have asked the lord Count for troops, because of these Companies, and the Count has agreed to place 100 lances at their disposal"; fifty more were to go to Borgo san Sepolcro, to protect the territory of the Malatesta.[4] Hawkwood and the troops in Siena manœuvred on either side of the border, ready to resist the least encroachment, and on one occasion at least came to blows.[5] Giovanni degli Ubaldini moved to Parma, commanding the road to Bologna, enlisting what forces he could, and tempting Lucca to throw off her dependence on Florence.[6] Both sides combed Italy for troops;[7] "if accord with the Count of

[1] Despatch of 31 May 1389: Silva, "Governo", 246–8, and 325–6, Doc. 20.

[2] Mancarella, in "Firenze, la Chiesa e Ladislao", *ASN* XLIV 150, wrongly assumed that Hawkwood was still in the *Regno* in August. The Florentines knew on 1 June that his Company "è giunta presso Tibuli a grande stento": *ASF*, Dieci di Balìa, Legazioni I 196.

[3] Silva, "Governo", 248–9. Lucca, *Regesti*, 279, no. 1412.

[4] Despatch of the Sienese envoys at Pavia, 16 June 1389: *ASS*, Concistoro 1825, no. 50.

[5] Leader, *Giovanni Acuto*, 181–3; Professione, *op. cit.* 138–40; Silva, "Governo", 251–3.

[6] Lucca, *Regesti*, 284, nos. 1420–3.

[7] *Ibid.* 281–4, nos. 1416–7, 1419; and 265, no. 1371 (dated 1387). Silva, "Governo", 244–5.

Vertus be not reached", wrote the Florentine government to Bologna, " we shall have need of soldiers. "[1]

The Florentines had redoubled their efforts to find allies against Milan. Instructions were drawn up in May for an embassy to France, to propose a military alliance for the partition of the Visconti dominions; but the eve of Valentina's departure for Paris was obviously an inopportune moment for such proposals, and the envoy elected for the task probably never left Florence.[2] They appealed to Venice in August for common action in defence of their liberties: "you will expose to the Doge the evil intentions of the Count of Vertus, who proposes to appropriate the dominion of the whole of this country; and that his methods are those of deceit and falsehood, as indeed they must have seen in the past; and that his intention is to take possession of our state, and then of theirs and of the Genoese, because the others are of no account once he has subjugated these. "[3] The *Serenissima* replied with the calm assurance that they saw no cause for alarm.[4] The Doge of Genoa contented himself with an offer of mediation.[5] Only one hope remained. Stephen of Bavaria had already signified his readiness "to come to Italy against the Count of Vertus, on account of the wrongs he has received at the hands of the Count".[6] Florentine envoys were sent to Bavaria at the end of July, to discuss the terms of an alliance; and Francesco Novello da Carrara, who had escaped from his detention in Lombardy and

[1] Florence to Bologna, 11 September 1389: *ASF*, Dieci di Balìa, Legazioni I 216.

[2] Mancarella, *op. cit. ASN* XLIV 31–2, 35, where he makes the suggestion that the envoy probably never went to Paris. The instructions are summarized *ibid.* XLVI, 215–16, Doc. 22; Romano, "Giangaleazzo Visconti", *ASL* XVIII 24, note 1; and Mirot, *Politique française en Italie*, 11–12. They should be dated, from their place in the strictly chronological Florentine codex, 23 May; June was a scribal error, repeated in the copy in the Bibliothèque Nationale in Paris.

[3] Commission of envoys to Ferrara and Venice, 9 August 1389: *ASF*, Dieci di Balìa, Legazioni I 206–7.

[4] Bolognini, "Relazioni tra Firenze e Venezia", *NAV* IX 65; Roberto Cessi, "Politica Veneziana di terra firma", *MSF* v 133–4.

[5] Silva, "Governo", 255.

[6] Commission of envoys to Bavaria, 25 July 1389: *ASF*, Dieci di Balìa, Legazioni I 202.

found his way to Florence after many adventures,[1] offered to go to Bavaria and use his own influence in supporting them.

Meanwhile, Pietro Gambacorta pursued his despairing search for a peaceful settlement. He met with an unfavourable reception in Florence; but he finally managed to persuade both sides to attend a new conference, which met at Pisa in the first days of August.[2] Giangaleazzo made known the terms upon which he was willing to enter into a League with Florence; owing to the modification in the Tuscan situation, he demanded the right to place troops at the disposal of his friends. The Florentines disputed his claims step by step; "and it seems to us", wrote the Sienese delegates on 3 September, "that no conclusion will be reached, although hope has not yet been formally abandoned."[3] A week later, they reported that "up till yesterday evening, no reply had come from Florence, and messer Benedetto [Gambacorta, Pietro's son] said that they expected it to-day, and believed that they would have good news—of which all are doubtful".[4] From Siena, on 21 September, the envoy of Lucca reported in an equally gloomy tone. "As to the conclusion of the League, seeing the many pretexts that are brought up, one can have no faith in it; for they spin out the time with talk at Pisa, while the Companies are being enlisted. For, in conclusion, it is decided by the powers that be, that Mars shall be let loose through our country."[5]

Giangaleazzo's cool judgment held the balance between peace and war. He exercised all his ability to maintain the courage of the Sienese, without accepting extreme measures which would leave no hope of a peaceful solution. The Sienese envoys at Pavia had put forward in June a certain proposition, to which Giangaleazzo answered that "he has well understood us, but that until he knows whether anything will come of this proposed League, he does not wish to take any further steps".[6] It was, in fact, a

---

[1] For which, *v.* Gatari, "Cronaca Carrarese", *RIS* NS xvii, 1, 359–90.
[2] Silva, "Governo", 249–51. Giangaleazzo's delegates were appointed on 20 July: Osio, *Documenti diplomatici*, i 279. The instructions to the Florentine delegates are dated 2 August: Silva, *op. cit.* 327–8, Doc. 22.
[3] *ASS*, Concistoro 1826, no. 22.
[4] From Pisa, 10 September: *ibid.* no. 25.
[5] Lucca, *Regesti*, 282, no. 1416.
[6] Despatch of 16 June 1389: *ASS*, Concistoro 1825, no. 50.

renewal of the Sienese offer, made a year earlier, to accept the
dominion of the Count, whose compliance would certainly have
provoked the Florentines to declare war. Giangaleazzo avoided
the danger and gave no definite reply; but at the beginning of
September, seeing little likelihood of a settlement at Pisa, and
aware of the diplomatic activities of the Florentines, he decided
to take his own precautions. He made known his wishes to a new
Sienese envoy, who brought further appeals and offers of submission. The ambassador reported that "he has most resolutely
determined to seek no lordship or pre-eminence in Tuscany, but
indeed he wishes to defend you and help you with all his power
against those who attack you, and especially against the Florentines. Therefore let no more be heard of your offers. What he
desires of you is, as Battista [Piccolomini], who is fully informed,
will tell you, that you join with him by way of confederation and
alliance against the Florentines for a certain period—although he
intends that it shall be for ever." Let the Sienese declare what
troops they can provide, and the Count will guarantee the rest—
"sufficient to ensure victory over the Florentines, his enemies and
yours".[1] The negotiations were conducted through the delegates
of the two powers at the conference of Pisa, and an agreement was
quickly reached. Giangaleazzo, to protect himself against the
impetuosity of his friends, reserved the right to decide whether
peace or war should be made with the Florentines. The alliance
was signed in Pisa on 22 September 1389.[2]

The conference of Pisa dragged on. The envoy of Lucca wrote
again from Siena in the first days of October, that "a breach is
expected, unless they conclude an agreement very soon; nor is
this thought possible here, unless the Count alters his attitude."[3]
It was not the Count, however, who gave way in the end. The
Florentines had held up the negotiations by every means in their
power, until the end of September. Then at last news came from

[1] Despatch from Pavia, 4 September 1389: *ibid.* 1826, no. 24.
[2] Favale, "Siena nel quadro della Politica Viscontea", *BSSP* XLIII 347–51,
Doc. 1; Malavolti, *Historia de' Sanesi*, II 163t.
[3] Lucca, *Regesti*, 283–4, no. 1419. The letter is undated, but other references which it contains indicate that it was written at the beginning of
October.

Bavaria; Stephen could not come until the end of October, and the conference could not be protracted any further. The Florentine delegates were instructed to secure the best terms they could, and to conclude the League.[1]

The pact of Pisa was signed on 9 October 1389. A modified formula was found for the delimitation of spheres of influence by the Modena-Secchia line; the rights of the allies over dependent lords and Communes were guaranteed; all disputes between the contracting parties were to be submitted to a process of arbitration; and provision was made for abating the menace of the mercenary Companies.[2]

The pact of Pisa was never much more than a figment of Gambacorta's imagination. The temperament and the interests of the ageing lord of Pisa urged him to work for a peaceful settlement; but his whole-hearted efforts produced only a temporary arrangement between two hostile parties, neither of which was ready to fight. The dangerous tension of the summer, when the least incident might have provoked an irrevocable challenge, was eased for a moment; but the intrigues and preparations went on, with scarcely a pause for congratulations over the accord. On the day after the pact was concluded, the delegates of Florence signed a League with those of Bologna, Pisa, Lucca and Perugia—the latter still striving to hold the balance of friendship with both parties—for the preservation of peace, especially in Tuscany, Romagna and the Papal territories. The princes of Lombardy and Romagna were to be invited to join; but the new League was

[1] Florence to the delegates at Pisa, 20 September 1389: Silva, "Governo", 328, Doc. 23. This letter reveals clearly the motives which led the Florentines to accept the League; Silva, however, attributed their decision to the fears aroused by Giangaleazzo's alliance with the Sienese: *ibid.* 254-5. There is no evidence that the Florentines were aware that this alliance had been made; it was probably kept secret, for it contravened the basic principle of Florentine policy, the non-intervention of Giangaleazzo in Tuscany, and would surely have aroused a storm of protest in Florence if its terms had been known.

[2] The pact was published by Osio, *op. cit.* I 278-93, no. 201; and by Favale, *op. cit. BSSP* XLIII 351-70, Doc. 2. The congratulatory letter of 15 October, referred to by Silva, "Governo", 263 and note 1, is sufficient to disprove the theory of de Boüard, advanced in *France et l'Italie au temps du grand Schisme*, 97 note 9, that the pact was merely a project never agreed upon or signed by the parties concerned.

in fact a precautionary measure, a symptom of the doubts which the Florentines entertained of Giangaleazzo's sincerity.[1]

The Count was equally sceptical. Before October was out, he decreed the expulsion of all Florentine and Bolognese citizens from his dominions. An alleged plot devised in Florence to poison the Count provided the pretext;[2] Giangaleazzo himself wrote a little later to Francesco Gonzaga that "we have forbidden their citizens to come and reside in our lands, so that they have not that unimpeded way which they looked for, in conspiring against us".[3] His confidential secretary, Pasquino Capelli, told the Mantuan envoy Galeazzo Busoni in the middle of November that, in spite of the pact, Giangaleazzo "could have no confidence in them".[4] The discovery of the plot which had been brewing in Bologna for the past year, and in which Giangaleazzo had certainly been involved during the critical months of the summer—it is not clear that he had been connected with the conspirators since the pact of Pisa[5]—did not help to improve his relations with the two Republics.

Gambacorta's hopes of peace began to decline. While the Florentines at last sent envoys to France to beg for help,[6] and reopened negotiations with Stephen of Bavaria, Giangaleazzo set out to strengthen his position in Tuscany. The pact of Pisa had disappointed the expectations which the Sienese had formed after their own alliance with the Count;[7] they implored him not to withdraw the troops he had sent for their defence. Giangaleazzo reassured them; and when Benedetto Gambacorta came to Pavia to ask him to revoke the edict against the Florentines and the Bolognese, and to allay the suspicions which the presence of

---

[1] *Capitoli di Firenze*, II 240–3, no. 47; Silva, "Governo", 258.

[2] Frati, "Lega dei Bolognesi e Fiorentini", *ASL* XVI 6–13. Minerbetti, "Cronica", 79, and other chroniclers placed the expulsion in July. A plot to poison Giangaleazzo was discovered in April 1388: Roberto Cessi, "Venezia e la prima caduta dei Carraresi", *NAV* NS XVII 326 note 2.

[3] Letter of 6 January 1390: *ASMa*, E. XLIX. 2.

[4] Despatch from Pavia, 13 November 1389: *ASMa*, E. XLIX. 3.

[5] For the history of this conspiracy, as far as Giangaleazzo was concerned in it, *v.* Appendix IV.

[6] Durrieu, *Gascons en Italie*, 49–50; Mirot, *Politique française en Italie*, 15.

[7] Minerbetti, "Cronica", 81; Bruni, "Historiarum Florentini Populi", *RIS* NS XIX, 3, 245.

his soldiers in Siena aroused at Florence, he replied that "he intended to leave those troops at Siena, and even four times their number if there were need, and the Sienese demanded them".[1]

The time had come when the cities of Tuscany must make their choice. Guglielmo Beyilacqua arrived in Pisa at the end of February 1390 "to learn the intentions of messer Pietro, whether he is disposed to follow the wishes of the lord Count".[2] Gambacorta, perplexed in mind, was heard to mutter after an interview with Bevilacqua: "in truth, in truth, he is wrong;"[3] and, in spite of pressure from the Milanese representatives, he remained firm in his determination to abide by his lifelong policy of friendship with Florence.[4]

Giangaleazzo met with less resistance in Perugia, where the Florentines had taken the unfortunate course of bringing pressure to bear on the government by giving military support to the "fuorusciti", the political exiles who menaced the territories of the Republic. The Florentines officially denied their relations with the "fuorusciti" of Perugia,[5] but no one was deceived; the Sienese ambassador to the Umbrian Commune wrote of "this Company of Florence which is at Cortona with the exiles of Perugia", or again reported that "the troops of the Commune of Florence, with the exiles of this city, made a raid yesterday".[6] It was easy enough for Giangaleazzo to secure the alliance of Perugia, by taking the city under his protection. When Giovanni degli Ubaldini arrived suddenly and unexpectedly in Umbria towards the end of February, "all the citizens were greatly terrified";[7] but they quickly learnt that he had come, not to

[1] Despatch of the Sienese envoy at Pavia, 5 December 1389: *ASS*, Concistoro 1826, no. 44.

[2] Despatch of the Sienese envoys in Pisa, 28 February 1389/90: *ibid.* no. 64.

[3] Despatch of the envoy of Lucca at Pisa, 9 March 1390: Silva, "Governo", 332, Doc. 27.   [4] *Ibid.* 264–8.

[5] Letters of Florence to Perugia during February 1390: Azzi Vitelleschi, "Relazioni tra Firenze e l' Umbria", I 199, nos. 730–1. Minerbetti, on the other hand, admitted the association of the Florentines with the enemies of Perugia: "Cronica", 86–7.

[6] Despatches of 5 and 7 March 1389/90: *ASS*, Concistoro 1826, nos. 68 and 71.

[7] Graziani, "Cronaca", *ASI* XVI, 1, 243; and similarly Pellini, *Historia di Perugia*, II 3–4.

attack but to defend them, and he was followed by a more peaceful emissary from Pavia. The Sienese envoys in Perugia wrote, on 7 March 1390, that "messer Andreasio Cavalcabò has arrived here, and lays the foundations of the League between the magnificent lord the Count of Vertus and this city, and this evening at the 20th hour the terms should be drawn up; the Perugians have made the same agreement that we have with messer the Count, save that messer the Count, seeing the little power of the Perugians, does not require them to employ more troops than they please". On the following day, they reported that "the League with messer the Count was concluded yesterday evening".[1]

The Florentines accused Giangaleazzo of being involved in an intrigue in San Miniato, a town of great strategical importance for the defence of their state, at the end of February. It is probable enough that the Count knew of the conspiracy, although the evidence of his participation in it is contradictory.[2] Certainly the conviction had been forced upon him, not only that war must come, but that it would come very soon; and he prepared for the event with his usual method and deliberation. The Sienese received confirmation of his decision from every quarter. Bevilacqua in Pisa told their envoys that "the lord Count has finally determined to take steps to remedy, at all costs, the hostile disposition of the Florentines; he has sent Ugolotto Biancardo into Romagna and the Mark with more than 20,000 florins, to hire troops up to the number of 2000 lances". His secretary is due in Siena "to learn whether you are able to put troops into the field, and to see that you prepare the Company which, by the alliance you have with him, you are bound to maintain".[3] Cavalcabò in Perugia spoke of the Count's "perfect readiness to defend us and

---

[1] *ASS*, Concistoro 1826, nos. 71 and 72.

[2] The accusation is made in a private letter of 11 March 1390 (Bigazzi, *Firenze e Milano*, 11–12, no. 1), and later in the official correspondence of the Republic. Minerbetti, in the "Cronica", 84, named as Giangaleazzo's agent in the conspiracy Giovanni degli Ubaldini "che allora era a Siena", and then contradicts himself: "egli era ancora in Romagna": *ibid.* 85. Ubaldini only arrived in Perugia on 24 February.

[3] Despatch of the Sienese envoys in Pisa, 28 February 1389/90: *ASS*, Concistoro 1826, no. 64.

do what he can for us ".[1] Sienese envoys, sent to Pavia with fresh complaints of Florentine aggression, reported on 15 March that "his Council has finally decided to make war, and attends with all care to the enlistment of troops, and the arming of ships of war at sea ". A week later, they assured the Republic that "speedy remedy will be found ".[2] Giangaleazzo wrote to the Sienese government on the same day; in answer to their grievances, "within a few days, such remedies will be at hand, as will set your minds at rest ".[3]

The last efforts at mediation foundered inevitably in the midst of these preparations for war. Gambacorta's ambassadors pleaded with the Count "not to wish to instruct them to quarrel with the Florentines, since they have writings and pacts of peace between them ".[4] The Venetian government sent representatives on a mission of peace to both sides.[5] The Pope appointed a special legate to reconcile the adversaries.[6] Their efforts were in vain; the mediators could find no ground for common discussion of the questions at issue.

Giangaleazzo had in fact made his resolve, and pledged his word to the Sienese. The Florentines had accepted with equal vigour the appeal to arms.[7] They had informers at the seat of the Sienese government, and knew all the decisions which were taken by the enemy.[8] It is not surprising, then, that when the citizens of Montepulciano appropriately brought matters to a head by expelling the Sienese officers from the town at the beginning of April 1390, the Florentines did not hesitate to accept responsibility, and welcomed Montepulciano under their own dominion.[9] In doing so, they broke not only the spirit but the letter of the

[1] Despatch of the Sienese envoys in Perugia, 7 March 1389/90: *ASS*, Concistoro 1826, no. 71.

[2] 15 and 22 March 1389/90: *ibid.* nos. 81 and 91.

[3] 22 March 1390: *ibid.* 1828, no. 51.

[4] Despatch of 15 March from Pavia, cit.: *ibid.* 1826, no. 81.

[5] Roberto Cessi, "Politica Veneziana di terra firma", *MSF* v 143–4.

[6] The Papal Legate appointed for the task was Baldassare Cossa, the future Pope John XXIII: Lucca, *Regesti*, 284, no. 1425.

[7] Silva, "Governo", 266.

[8] So Pasquino Capelli told the Sienese envoys at Pavia, according to their despatch of 22 March 1389/90: *ASS*, Concistoro 1826, no. 91.

[9] Minerbetti, "Cronica", 95; *Capitoli di Firenze*, I 114–16, nos. 3–5, from 11 April on.

pact of Pisa. At the end of the month, Giangaleazzo sent a formal declaration of war to the Florentines, and to their allies the Bolognese.[1]

Thus ended the eighteen months of mistrust and hesitation, of parley and postponement, which followed the downfall of the Carraresi. The interval afforded Giangaleazzo a breathing space, in which to refresh and reorganize his forces after the campaigns against Verona and Padua; but all the efforts made by the champions of appeasement only brought out more clearly the irreconcilable differences between the two parties. The conflict between the ruler of Lombardy and the Republic of Florence assumes in retrospect an air of inevitability; and the pessimism of contemporary observers confirms the impression that no peaceful solution was possible. The pen had been enlisted before the sword as a weapon of conflict. Giangaleazzo directed his propaganda against the "Archguelfs" who ruled over Florence with an iron hand; the Florentines raised the banner of liberty against the oppressions and cruelty of the Lombard tyrant.[2] But beneath these *ad hoc* ideological justifications, there lurked the bitter conflict of ambitions and regional interests. The Florentines were eager to secure dominion over their Tuscan neighbours, whose only hope of preserving a precarious independence lay in the strong arm of the Visconti. The fortune of the great mercantile and industrial families of Florence was at stake. Their interests were not entirely selfish; they represented the prosperity and the very life of the city. They were compelled to challenge Giangaleazzo's right to answer the appeals of the weaker Tuscan cities; and Giangaleazzo accepted their challenge. He had long resisted the appeals of the Sienese, and rejected their offers of submission. He had done his best to secure by diplomacy the safety and integrity of the states in Tuscany whom he had befriended; but it became clear at last that no permanent solution could be reached in that way, and Giangaleazzo finally resolved to abandon diplomacy in favour of the active intervention which the Sienese, unable to contemplate a single-handed struggle with

[1] Frati, "Lega dei Bolognesi e Fiorentini", *ASL* xvi 17–20.
[2] E.g. in the declarations of war: *RIS* xvi 815–17.

Florence, had consistently and strenuously advocated for the past two years.

We may be sure that Giangaleazzo took careful stock of the situation, before he let his purpose be known in February 1390. In Lombardy, Alberto d'Este and Francesco Gonzaga had become his faithful satellites, and declared war on his enemies in conjunction with him. The Malatesta in Romagna drew first blood in a skirmish with Giovanni da Barbiano, the captain of the Bolognese army.[1] Their lands, with those of Siena, Perugia and Antonio Montefeltro, Count of Urbino, formed a semicircle to the south and east of the Florentine state from which the campaign against the Republic could be launched. Lucca remained neutral; but the official neutrality of Pisa was a cover, on the one hand for Gambacorta's firm attachment to the Florentine cause, on the other for the activities of Jacopo d'Appiano and Guglielmo Bevilacqua in support of the Visconti army fighting in Tuscany.[2]

Urban VI had carried his tempestuous hatreds to the grave, and his successor, Boniface IX, won the approval of Florence by making his peace with Ladislaus of Naples; but he certainly did not wish to see an increase of Florentine authority in Tuscany and Romagna, and Milanese diplomacy was quickly at work to secure his support. "It really seems that the Count is in agreement with the Church of Rome", wrote an observer from Bologna in June 1390.[3] In fact, however, Boniface had enough to occupy him in the disorders of the Patrimony;[4] he was sincerely anxious to pacify the contestants.

The Genoese, too, had troubles of their own. The Florentines relied on the Ligurian port for the despatch of supplies of corn in case of emergency,[5] and were easily alarmed by rumours of

---

[1] Minerbetti, "Cronica", 91–2; "Corpus Chronicorum Bononiensium", *RIS* NS xviii, 1, vol. 3, 402–3. Florence to the Malatesta, 10 April 1390: Tonini, *Storia civile e sacra Riminese*, iv, 2, 384–5, no. 206.

[2] Silva, "Governo", 267–8. Reports from Pisa, 19 May–2 June: Lucca, *Regesti*, 286–9, nos. 1433–9.

[3] Despatch of 17 June 1390: *ibid.* 299, no. 1482.

[4] Valois, *France et le grand Schisme*, ii 160–6.

[5] De Boüard, *France et l'Italie au temps du grand Schisme*, 119. Letters of March 1390, drawn from the family records of the Acciaiuoli: Bigazzi, *op. cit.* 11–13, nos. 1 and 2.

Giangaleazzo's intrigues with the Doge;[1] but the Genoese took no part during the first year of the war.

The Venetians proclaimed at once a strict neutrality. The elimination of the Carrarese state had created a Veneto-Milanese frontier, and the Venetians mingled a friendly collaboration in the border problems that arose, with a firm insistence on their own rights.[2] They had their hands full with the settlement of Friuli under the new Patriarch, John of Moravia, and with the problems which arose from the overrunning of Bosnia by the Turks after the battle of Kossovo. Political as well as commercial interests therefore fostered a desire for peace, and the Venetians disassociated themselves from the internal affairs of Tuscany; but they had already noted with some concern the growing influence of the Visconti over the lords of Mantua and Ferrara, and their neutrality was occasionally modified, with the utmost caution, in favour of the "Signorotti" of Lombardy. Their attitude in this respect was to cause Giangaleazzo a great deal of perplexity in years to come.

The major quarrels of the Italian states could never be entirely confined to the peninsula. The French were at this moment displaying an increasing interest in Italian affairs. Charles VI had conferred with the Pope of Avignon during the winter on the question of the Clementist and Angevin claims in southern Italy; and the project of sending a French expedition to Rome and Naples had begun to take concrete shape. The friendship of the ruler of Lombardy was of the first importance for such an expedition; and the Florentine ambassadors, who had audience with the King in February 1390, could expect little encouragement. The terms on which Charles offered his alliance to the Republic against Giangaleazzo were in fact such as the Florentines could never accept—the recognition of Clement VII, and acknowledgement of French suzerainty over the Republic.[3] While the Florentine envoys returned home with these evil tidings, French ambassadors left Paris on the road to Avignon and Milan; and

---

[1] Despatch from Florence, 11 June 1390: Lucca, *Regesti*, 293, no. 1463.

[2] Romano, "Niccolò Spinelli", *ASN* xxvi 441–3; Pastorello, *Nuove Ricerche*, 61–5, and 186–8, Docs. 26–7.

[3] Frati, "Lega dei Bolognesi e dei Fiorentini", *ASL* xvi 15; Mirot, *Politique française en Italie*, 16; Mancarella, *op. cit. ASN* xlv 37–8.

Giangaleazzo probably had word of the decisions taken at the French court, before he sent his declaration of war to Florence.[1]

Giangaleazzo, in preparation for the war, renewed his alliance with the Count of Savoy in February 1390;[2] the terms, from which in the circumstances Giangaleazzo alone stood to gain, were confirmed in June of the same year.[3] Amadeus VII fulfilled all his obligations. He sent troops to serve in the Milanese army;[4] he himself spent ten days in Milan in September 1390,[5] and he returned in November to sign a new accord with Giangaleazzo.[6] But his relations with his ally were not entirely wholehearted. He sent a messenger in July "to make enquiries concerning the alliance of the Communes of Florence and Bologna, in order that our lord Count may be informed thereon";[7] and the draft of an accord between Amadeus and the Communes was drawn up, although it probably sprang from the optimism of the allies rather than from the implied consent of Amadeus.[8] It was more in accordance with the Count of Savoy's cautious nature that the negotiations should be merely a precaution taken in case of a Florentine victory,[9] than that they represented a real Savoyard policy which only the attitude of the French court prevented from being put into effect.[10] The Savoyard princes still had difficulties with their subjects in the Valais, but they seemed very willing to accept Giangaleazzo's aid in dealing with them;[11] it was on this business, perhaps, that, as the Sienese envoy at Pavia

[1] Jarry, "Voie de Fait et l'alliance Franco-Milanaise", *BEC* LIII 220–4.

[2] 17 February 1390: Corio, *Storia di Milano*, II 355–6; Gabotto, *Ultimi Principi*, 134–5.

[3] Gabotto, *Ultimi Principi*, 140.

[4] The documents in "Eporediensia", 505–7, no. 212, and 508–9, no. 222.

[5] From 16 to 27 September: Magenta, *Visconti e Sforza*, I 187 note 2, quoting Cibrario, *Istituzioni della Monarchia*, 160. Amadeus passed through Santhià on 13 and 29 September, on his way to and from Milan: "Eporediensia", 454.

[6] Gabotto, *Ultimi Principi*, 143–4; Cognasso, *Conte Rosso*, 143–7.

[7] 10 July 1390: Gabotto, "Documenti Inediti", *MSI* XXXIV 139, no. 48; *Id. Ultimi Principi*, 137–9.

[8] Cibrario, *Operette e Frammenti Storici; il Conte Rosso*, 81–2.

[9] Gabotto, *Ultimi Principi*, 141.

[10] The theory advanced by Romano, "Valentina Visconti", *ASL* XXV, 2, 15–17.

[11] Gabotto, *Ultimi Principi*, 123–4, 128.

wrote in March 1390, "the Prince of Morea [Achaia] and the Marquis of Montferrat have come here, and have been much engrossed with the Count".[1] If Amadeus wavered for a moment, Giangaleazzo was able to persuade him that the best interests of Savoy lay in a close alliance with Milan; and the wise settlement of Piedmontese problems in 1388 brought its reward for the Count of Vertus during the war.

The prospects in Germany were less favourable. Wenceslaus, in spite of his increasingly hostile attitude towards Milan, presented no real threat; but Stephen of Bavaria had concluded a military alliance with the Florentines in April 1390,[2] and Giangaleazzo's relations with the Habsburgs had changed for the worse. After the conquest of Verona, Giangaleazzo gradually mastered the Valsugana, which had formerly belonged to the della Scala, and won the allegiance of the Ghibelline lords of the Bishopric of Trent.[3] In doing so, he encroached on Austrian territory, for the Bishop, who thereby lost his grip on the lands of his Ghibelline subjects, owed allegiance in his turn to Leopold of Austria.

For the moment, however, there is no evidence of conflict between Visconti and Habsburg. The interests of the Dukes of Austria did not at this time lie in the south, and they were not in any case likely to be found in the same camp as their rivals, the Wittelsbachs of Bavaria.[4] Giangaleazzo was more disturbed by the hostility of the Patriarch of Aquileia, a cousin of Wenceslaus. The Count appealed to the *Serenissima* to suggest to Boniface IX that he might see fit to transfer John of Moravia from the Patriarchate to another see;[5] but the Venetians refused to interfere. They had no cause to complain of a ruler in Friuli who distrusted

---

[1] Despatch of 22 March 1389/90: *ASS*, Concistoro 1826, no. 91.

[2] In Munich, in the presence of Francesco Carrara, on 5 April 1390: *Capitoli di Firenze*, II 398–400, no. 58.

[3] Egger, *Geschichte Tirols*, I 442. Giangaleazzo conquered the Riviera di Salò in 1387: Postinger, "Documenti in Volgare Trentino", *AAA* 3, VII 120–7. This important but not easily accessible study treats in detail of the obscure struggles in the Val di Trento at the end of the fourteenth century.

[4] Cusin, *Confine Orientale d'Italia*, I 179.

[5] Romano, "Niccolò Spinelli", *ASN* XXVI 448–9; Roberto Cessi, "Politica Veneziana di terra firma", *MSF* V 143, 104–5, 199.

this powerful and ambitious neighbour. Only when the Patriarch notified them of his intention to receive and make alliance with their old enemy, Francesco Carrara the younger, did they intervene with the recommendation that " it seems to us for the good of the whole Patriarchate, that the said lord Francesco should not conduct his affairs in those dominions ".[1]

Their warning had been delayed until it was too late. Giangaleazzo's fears were justified by the event. Friuli, where the mountain roads from Germany issue into the great Italian plain, was the centre and the base of an alliance which included among its members the Patriarch, with the support of his cousins Sigismund of Hungary and Wenceslaus, Carrara with the friendly or related houses of Ortemburg, Segna and Gorizia on the north-eastern border of Italy, and Stephen of Bavaria, the ally of Florence.[2] Giangaleazzo recognized the danger of invasion through Friuli by a German army; but he did not foresee the form which that danger would take. He had weighed up the chances of war, and found them strongly in his favour. Confident in the strength of his army, in the strategical value of his alliances with the lesser Italian states, and in the assurance of French and Savoyard friendship, he proposed to force Bologna and Florence to accept his terms, before help could reach them from Germany. Stephen of Bavaria's preparations might well be prolonged. In his cold calculations, however, Giangaleazzo failed to take one factor into account: an appeal to old loyalties, a daring less subtle and a courage more open than his own. It was his gravest miscalculation, and led almost to his downfall,

---

[1] 3 June 1390: Roberto Cessi, "Politica Veneziana di terra firma", *MSF* v 193–4.

[2] Cusin, *Confine Orientale d'Italia*, I 176–9.

CHAPTER X

THE FIRST WAR AGAINST FLORENCE
(MAY 1390–JANUARY 1392)

It is not easy to determine the part which Giangaleazzo played in the direction of his army. He took no part in the campaigns, for there was no place for him in the heat of battle. The author of the Minerbetti chronicle, who was usually well informed and did not indulge in fantastic reconstructions of imaginary scenes, records an instance where Giangaleazzo suddenly asserted his own authority in the conduct of the war.[1] It is probable, therefore, that even the broader outlines of military policy were usually left to the decision of the Council. Jacopo dal Verme, the commander-in-chief of his armies, enjoyed his fullest confidence; it was Giangaleazzo's genius to make the best use of other talents than his own. He seems, however, to have been always unwilling to accept the arbitration of battle, unless the numbers were heavily in his favour; a few hours' fighting, in which he took no part, might undo the patient work of years.

In this case, the numbers were fairly even. Minerbetti, the most reliable of the contemporary chroniclers, gives the figure of 3000 lances on each side, at a period of the war when calculations were simplified by the reduction of the fighting to one front.[2]

Bologna, more open to attack than the hill-girt city of Florence, was the main objective of the campaign. Verme and the Visconti army from one side, and a Ferrarese contingent from the other, advanced into Emilia. Giovanni degli Ubaldini, and the Roman Paolo Savelli, created a diversion in Tuscany, keeping the Florentine forces occupied by their raids in the Valdichiana. Ubaldini was brilliantly successful. Lucignano, Palazzuolo, San Brancazio, Vagliano and Marciano fell before his attack. Foiano and Montepulciano were hard pressed; the Montepulcianese, it

---

[1] Minerbetti, "Cronica", *RIS* NS xxvii, 2, 137.
[2] *Ibid.* 137–8; and cf. Leader, *Giovanni Acuto*, 191.

was said, would have surrendered to Giangaleazzo, but Ubaldini
would only accept their submission in the name of the Sienese,
the hated overlords of the past years.[1] Verme, on the other hand,
met with unexpectedly stubborn resistance, and was forced to
withdraw; but he quickly returned with added strength, and
pushed on towards Bologna. The Florentines sent Hawkwood to
conduct the defence of the city, but the Bolognese were hard
pressed, and spoke of desperate remedies.[2] "They speak among
themselves of resisting as long as they can, and when they can
do so no longer, of seeking the protection of the Church."[3]

All hope of relief from Germany had been abandoned. The
envoy of Lucca wrote from Bologna on 17 June that "for the
past month, every day has brought rumours that troops have
entered the *Padovano* against the Count. So far, there has been
nothing to it."[4] Two days later, when it was known in Florence
that Carrara had set out from Friuli with 500 lances and 2000
infantry, "those who are well informed do not believe that he
can make much headway".[5] Giangaleazzo made the same miscalculation. He had left insufficient garrisons to hold the approaches from the north. Francesco Novello marched swiftly and
without opposition through the *Padovano* with his small force,
and entered Padua on the night of 18–19 June amid the acclamations of the inhabitants. The Visconti garrison, taken by surprise,
withdrew into the citadel.[6]

The danger still seems to have been underestimated. Verona
threw off the Visconti yoke, but the Veronese were without unity
or purpose, and the revolt was quickly and ruthlessly suppressed.[7]

[1] Lucca, *Regesti*, 286–8, nos. 1433–8; and 290–5, nos. 1451–66; Minerbetti,
"Cronica", 100–3; Liberati, "Frammento di una Cronica Sanese", *BSSP*
XVII 131–3; the rather confused account in "Annales Sanenses", *RIS* XIX
390–1.
[2] Lucca, *Regesti*, 295–300, nos. 1467–86; "Corpus Chronicorum Bononiensium", *RIS* NS XVIII, 1, vol. 3, 407–16.
[3] Despatch of the envoy of Lucca in Bologna, 17 June: Lucca, *Regesti*,
298, no. 1482.   [4] *Ibid.* 299, no. 1482.
[5] Despatch from Florence, 19 June: *ibid.* 294, no. 1465.
[6] Gatari, "Cronaca Carrarese", *RIS* NS XVII, 1, 394–420.
[7] Verci, *Storia della Marca Trivigiana* XVII, 122–3; Simeoni, "Due Documenti sul sacco di Verona", *ASL* XXXIII, 2, 490–6; Righi, "Amnistia del
1392 concessa ai Veronesi", *ASL* XXXIV, 1, 471–5.

Verme hastily abandoned the siege of Bologna, and marched to the relief of the garrison in the citadel of Padua. Carrara's troops were described as "almost all unwarlike peasants, not accustomed to the exercise of arms ",[1] and the speedy recapture of Padua was foretold; but the partisans of the Visconti were over-confident. Stephen of Bavaria and his promised army, following more slowly in the path of Carrara, arrived in time to intercept Verme and hold his forces in check;[2] and the garrison in the citadel of Padua surrendered at the end of August.

The return of Francesco Carrara to Padua altered the whole complexion of the war. The Florentines jubilantly proclaimed the approaching downfall of the tyrant.[3] Carrara's bold action, against which Giangaleazzo had made no provision in his plans, robbed him of the initiative in the campaign. An active and adventurous enemy was established on his eastern frontier. Carrara wasted no time, but turned against Alberto d'Este, invaded the district of the Polesine, and withdrew only when the Marquis of Ferrara accepted a treaty of neutrality and promised to give no further aid or favour to Milan during the war.[4] Giangaleazzo suffered a serious loss on the Tuscan front, by the death of Ubaldini on 24 June.[5] Henceforth the Tuscan campaign was reduced to a series of raids and skirmishes. Paolo Savelli was summoned to Milan in October, to explain why he had not made the progress "which we hoped for, and might reasonably expect", and to help to find a remedy.[6]

Deprived of the advantages with which he had started the war, Giangaleazzo resorted to methods with which he was more familiar—the weapons of flattery and gold. Stephen of Bavaria succumbed to both, came to an understanding with the Count, and attempted to cover his treachery by an offer to mediate between

---

[1] *V.* Doc. 4, a letter written by the Sienese merchants in Venice.
[2] Rambaldi, "Stefano III, Duca di Baviera", *ASL* xxviii, 1, 287–8.
[3] Florence to Stephen of Bavaria, 10 July: Romano, "Giangaleazzo Visconti", *ASL* xviii 311, Doc. 4. Despatches of the envoy of Lucca in Bologna, 25 and 28 June: Lucca, *Regesti*, 300, nos. 1485–6.
[4] *Capitoli di Firenze*, ii 246–51, no. 49.
[5] Minerbetti, "Cronica", 105; Riva, "Documenti Viscontei", *ASL* xxvii, 1, 262.
[6] *V.* Doc. 5 (Giangaleazzo to Siena, 13 October 1390).

the contestants; but the Florentines were fully aware of his treachery, rejected his pretensions as a peacemaker, and dismissed him from their service.[1] Giangaleazzo also made overtures to Bologna, hard put to find money to pay the army;[2] but the Bolognese, after consultations with their ally, decided to continue the struggle, and rejected the Count's offers.[3]

Giangaleazzo gained some compensation for his reverses by detaching the Bavarian army from the service of his enemies. When winter drew down over the scene, Hawkwood and the allied armies were assembling at Padua for a united attack on Milan; and all eyes were turned, in expectation or in fear, towards France.

The Florentines had made common cause with the pretendants to the Visconti dominions, in the hope that the claims of these exiles might find support within Giangaleazzo's state. The most formidable of them, on account of his family connections rather than of any personal merits, was Carlo Visconti; and it was as the champion of Carlo's rights that his wife's brother, Count John of Armagnac, concluded an alliance with Florence on 16 October 1390, and undertook to bring an army to Italy as soon as possible to combine in the attack on Giangaleazzo.[4]

Giangaleazzo promptly appealed to Charles VI, offering to submit to arbitration any grievances which the Armagnacs might have against him.[5] Thus a curious situation arose. Armagnac's army was composed of the *routiers* of the English war who, left without a livelihood by the peace of Brétigny, had preyed on the

[1] Minerbetti, "Cronica", 111–12. Despatches of Filippo della Molza from Milan, 12 and 14 August, published by Rambaldi, *op. cit. ASL* xxviii, 1, 319–26. Letters of Florence to Stephen, published by Romano, "Giangaleazzo Visconti", *ASL* xviii 311–15, Docs. 4–6.

[2] Despatch from Florence, 19 May 1390: "non sa dove si trarrà il denaro, massime per i bolognesi:" Lucca, *Regesti*, 292, no. 1455. At the end of July, Enghiramo Bracchi, one of the Count's agents in Pisa, told the Sienese envoys that "volendo i bologniesi chella brighata che sono a bolognia chavalcassero, dissero non voleano inperò che none aveano denaio, e che non voleano essare tenuti più in parole". Despatch of 30 July: *ASS*, Concistoro 1827, no. 71.

[3] Leonardo Bruni, "Historiarum Florentini Populi", *RIS* NS xix, 3, 251–2.

[4] Durrieu, *Gascons en Italie*, 50–1; and 232–44, Docs. 4–6.

[5] Jarry, "Voie de Fait", *BEC* liii 234.

French countryside ever since. Both Charles VI and Clement VII
had helped Armagnac to gather these plunderers together and
lead them out of France;[1] but the King was now firmly resolved
to head an expedition to Italy in the cause of Clement and of Louis
of Anjou. Louis of Touraine, Giangaleazzo's son-in-law, and the
Duke of Burgundy had been appointed to go to Milan and secure
the Count's support for the expedition. While the French were
anxious to be rid of the *routiers* at all costs, it was therefore
directly contrary to their policy that they should be used against
Milan.

Giangaleazzo was in a strong position to secure his own terms.
Louis and the Duke of Burgundy arrived at Pavia in March 1391,
and the clauses of a provisional accord were drawn up. Giangaleazzo promised to support the French expedition with his own
troops, and to make public recognition of Clement as soon as the
French had captured Bologna. His absolute authority in Lombardy and the Mark of Treviso was to be recognized in return,
with a hint of the possibility of a more exalted title to confirm his
position.[2] Finally it was agreed that the Dukes, if they could not
persuade Armagnac to abandon his project, would buy off his
troops with Milanese gold, and send them to serve Giangaleazzo
in Italy; thus France would be rid of the *routiers*, and Giangaleazzo's ends would be served at the same time.

The draft agreement drawn up at Pavia formed the basis of
Giangaleazzo's policy for five years to come; but it was destined
never to reach fulfilment. Louis of Touraine returned to Paris to
find that the expedition to Italy had been indefinitely postponed.
The English, prompted by Boniface IX, had intervened with
overtures of peace; and the first interests of France demanded
that their proposals should receive attention.[3] Burgundy, however, fulfilled his part of the agreement; he went to Avignon and,

[1] Circourt, "Duc Louis d'Orléans", *RQH* XLII 43, 45, 47, 51–2; Valois,
France et le grand Schisme, II 184–7.
[2] Valois, *op. cit.* II 187–90: Jarry, "Voie de Fait", *BEC* LIII 230–5,
Romano, "Niccolò Spinelli", *ASN* XXVI 450–2. The draft agreement of
21 March was published by Mirot, *Politique française en Italie*, 49–54.
[3] Valois, *op. cit.* II 180–2; Jarry, "Voie de Fait", *BEC* LIII 237–8, 241–2;
Mirot, *Politique française en Italie*, 28–32; De Boüard, *France et l'Italie*, 126–7.

failing to deter Armagnac from his purpose, bought over a large body of his troops. The deserters never reached Milan, for Armagnac's vengeance overwhelmed them, some before they had left Avignon, others while they were crossing the Alps into Italy;[1] but the attempted mediation of Charles VI and the corruption of the troops delayed Armagnac's arrival in Italy until June 1391, eight months after he had signed the treaty with Florence.

It was just long enough to save Giangaleazzo from the joint attack in the east and the west, by which his enemies planned to overthrow him. Hawkwood, having failed to stir up a new revolt in Verona, or to win Francesco Gonzaga from his understanding with the Count,[2] grew tired of waiting for Armagnac while the campaigning season slipped by. He marched through the *Vicentino* and *Bresciano* in May, driving before him the inadequate garrisons left to hold the river fords, and encamped with the united forces of the allies on the banks of the Adda, within sixteen miles of Milan.[3]

June brought no relief. The Sienese, harassed by Florence and gripped by famine, had once more offered to accept Giangaleazzo's dominion; the Count gave them what encouragement he could, but he could afford little practical help, and this was not the time to accept further responsibilities.[4] The Florentines launched a great offensive in June, hoping that Siena had reached the end of her resistance.[5] They announced confidently at the beginning of July that they had freed Siena from the Visconti yoke;[6] but it was only an expression of their hopes—the Sienese were not yet

---

[1] Jarry, "Voie de Fait", *BEC* LIII 238–40; Romano, "Niccolò Spinelli", *ASN* XXVI 452–6.

[2] Gatari, "Cronaca Carrarese", 434–5; Minerbetti, "Cronica", 115–16; Leader, *op. cit.* 192–5, from letters of the Carteggio Acciaiuoli, of which six were published by Bigazzi, *Firenze e Milano*, 14–19, nos. 5–10.

[3] "Chronicon Bergomense", *RIS* XVI 857 E–858 C; Minerbetti, "Cronica", 124–5; Leader, *op. cit.* 196–8; Vergerio, "Epistolario", 70–4 no. 34.

[4] Riva, *op. cit. ASL* XXVII, 1, 262–3; Favale, "Siena nel quadro della Politica Viscontea", *BSSP* XLIII 328–30, and 370–4 Docs. 3–4. Cf. Minerbetti, "Cronica", 117; Cavalcabò, "Cremonese Consigliere", *BSCr* II 20–5.

[5] Minerbetti, "Cronica", 123–4, 127–30; "Annales Sanenses", *RIS* XIX 393–5.

[6] Florence to Perugia, 4 July: Azzi Vitelleschi, "Relazioni tra Firenze e l' Umbria", I 201, no. 738.

as desperate as that. Meanwhile, the Bolognese created a diversion by ravaging the *Parmense* and the *Piacentino*.[1] Armagnac had already entered Piedmont, and Florentine messengers urged him to march down the Po with all speed and join forces with Hawkwood.[2]

Giangaleazzo moved his court to Milan in this crisis in the history of his state. He strove desperately to control a situation which seemed already to have passed out of his hands. Chaos and dismay threatened to take hold of Lombardy. The wildest rumours circulated along the roads. Uncertainty and suspicion entered even within the circle of the court. Filippo della Molza, arriving at Pavia early in June, was warned by the "amigo" who watched over Gonzaga's interests at the Visconti court, and whose anonymity has been well preserved, that the lord of Mantua would be well advised not to leave his dominions in order to join forces with Giangaleazzo, "for to tell the truth, the situation is not without grave danger to the state of the lord Count". At Cremona, the host of the Wooden Horse had told him that "the greater part of the citizens have gathered arms in their houses, secretly, and their intention is to take such measures that they cannot be robbed; for he said that the citizens are in an ugly temper, on account of the outrageous behaviour of the soldiers billeted in the district and outside it". The Captain of Cremona confirmed the story that the Cremonese were secretly assembling arms, so that "the lord Count has doubts of Cremona". On the road from Cremona to Lodi, Filippo della Molza met an acquaintance from whom he gleaned further stories of doubt and pessimism. "He said to me that the lord Count was certainly in despair, and he told me in secrecy that he had it for certain from a friend of his, that the Count wept every day from fear and from shame."[3]

---

[1] "Chronicon Estense", *RIS* xv 522 E; "Corpus Chronicorum Bononiensium", *RIS* NS xviii, 1, vol. 3, 430–1.

[2] Durrieu, *Gascons en Italie*, 78–81.

[3] These quotations are taken from the first of three despatches which Filippo della Molza wrote to Gonzaga from Milan on 6 June 1391: *ASMa*, E. xlix. 3. The first two letters were written at the eleventh hour of the day, the third "de note".

Such rumours demonstrate the prevalent sense of danger and alarm. Giangaleazzo had too much on his hands, to spend his time in weeping. He prepared with energy and decision to meet the emergency. The incipient discontents of his dominions had to be closely watched, and any murmur of rebellion suppressed; Hawkwood had indeed succeeded in establishing contacts with Venturino Fondulo and other nobles of the *Cremonese*, where his army was encamped.[1] The Florentines had professed to be in touch with "certain Milanese citizens" during the winter,[2] and they still nourished hopes that the city would rise in revolt at Hawkwood's approach.[3] They were doomed to disappointment; the sack of Verona after the rebellion of the previous year had truly been "the re-establishment of the Milanese Empire".[4]

Above all, Giangaleazzo needed troops; and to have troops, he needed money to pay them. A heavy subsidy was imposed upon his subjects, but the government had to admit that its demands were beyond the resources of the dominions.[5] Giangaleazzo had to find other means to make up the difference. Filippo della Molza wrote from Milan on 6 June that, as the "amigo" had told him, "the Doge of Genoa was very anxious to have Serravalle, saying that it would be a great security for his state. So the lord Count, considering how good a friend the Doge is to him, has decided to satisfy him over the said fortress at the price which he paid for it, by way of investiture; and he has invested the Doge and his government in possession of it. I believe that it cost the Count 22,000 ducats and a few hundreds, I know not well how many; but he has not taken more from the Doge than it cost him."[6] Giangaleazzo authorised this tran-

---

[1] Galantino, *Storia di Soncino*, I 144. Filippo della Molza, in his first report (*v.* last note), mentions "the ways which messer Ugolino Cavalcabò has held" in Cremona.

[2] In November 1390: Leader, *op. cit.* 188–9.

[3] In February and March 1391: Bigazzi, *op. cit.* 16–19, nos. 8, 10.

[4] "Il rassodamento dell' Impero Milanese": Corio, *Storia di Milano*, II 359.

[5] 15,600 florins demanded from Milan: Morbio, *Codice Visconteo-Sforzesco*, 14–15, no. 3; and Santoro, "Registri", 21, nos. 80–2. The contribution of Pavia, originally fixed at 10,000 florins, was reduced to 7000 by an order of the Podestà, 30 May: Romano, "Sussidio di guerra", *BSP* II 481–2.

[6] Third report of 6 June, "de note": *ASMa*, E. XLIX. 3.

saction on 22 May, and the sale was completed on the day when this letter was written.[1] Other rumours were afloat, for della Molza added that "as for Sarzana and the Lunigiana, the friend says that it is not true that any word has been said about them". Francesco Gonzaga had promised to add a contingent of his own troops to the Milanese army, but Giangaleazzo, who was still expecting the French troops bought over by the Duke of Burgundy, was more anxious for a loan of cash. Filippo della Molza wrote to Gonzaga on 15 June from Milan "in the matter of the 50,000 ducats". Giangaleazzo had sent a message "to ask me to hasten my return to your lordship, in order that I may beg you to grant the favour that the lord Count asks in this matter of the money, putting aside the despatch of your troops".[2] The deeds were drawn up and the transaction concluded in Milan on 23 June; Gonzaga received in pledge for the loan the town of Ostiglia on the Po, and Asola with other fortresses on the Brescian border.[3]

Meanwhile the army, which these sums were designed to pay, began to assemble. Amadeus of Savoy, in answer to an urgent appeal for another 100 lances,[4] sent a further contingent of troops to Milan.[5] Francesco Gonzaga had not abandoned the idea of joining the army with his soldiers, and the "Armagnacs", as the French troops were called, were expected at Milan, although Filippo della Molza's letters of 6 June show that there was no general confidence in their coming. In Milan, he learnt that, according to the official calculation, "they will all be at Milan within eight days, to the number of 1500 lances"; but owing to the difficulties of communication and the uncertainty of the sources whence this information came, there were those who declared that "they would not believe it until they saw them".[6] Later in the day, della Molza wrote again that Armagnac would not be able to come to Italy for some time owing to the desertion

[1] Stella, "Annales Genuenses", *RIS* XVII 1132 A. Giangaleazzo's procuration: Romano, "Regesto", *ASL* XXI, 2, 21–2, nos. 5–6.
[2] *ASMa*, E. XLIX. 3.
[3] The deeds drawn up "in castro porte iovis Mediolani": *ASMa*, B. XVIII. 4.
[4] Which reached Pinerolo on 17 April: "Eporediensia", 508, no. 220.
[5] They passed through Turin on 19 May: Scarabelli, "Paralipomeni di Storia Piemontese", *ASI* XIII 152.
[6] Second report of 6 June, "ora xi": *ASMa*, E. XLIX. 3.

of his troops, "if the lord Count be not misled by his observers in those parts ".[1]

Giangaleazzo did not place too great a reliance on these reports. He gave orders for the strengthening of the fortifications in the district west of Milan and Pavia,[2] as a precaution against Armagnac's unexpected arrival, while the main army assembled at Lodi to give battle to Hawkwood.[3] Filippo della Molza learnt at Cremona on 6 June that "the Count has finally decided to give battle, and has made the summons throughout all his lands, and has requested his nobles and the governors of his castles to give him reinforcements of troops, as messer Niccolò Pallavicino has done, who has offered 100 well-armed infantry and 10 well-equipped lances, and so with each one ".[4] We find that the Scotti of Piacenza were asked to send "the greatest number they could" of infantry and crossbowmen to the camp.[5] The Commune of Milan, which had already been called on to supply 300 cross-bowmen against Hawkwood, was now summoned to send a further 300 men, "strong and well-armed", to Lodi.[6] From Milan, della Molza wrote that "the order is given that all the infantry and cavalry are to be at Lodi on the 12th of this month [June], to take the field and pursue the enemy ".[7] A report was in circulation that Giangaleazzo himself would be present when the armies joined battle, for della Molza made enquiries on the subject; it was not generally believed, "but it might well be that he would go as far as Lodi, to hold a review, and to make sure that as many come as can, and as quickly as possible ".[8]

The Count did not abate the thoroughness of his methods. He ordered prayers and processions to be held in Milan, betokening the gravity of the moment.[9] Measures were taken to ensure that

---

[1] Third report of 6 June, "de note": *ibid.*

[2] Giangaleazzo to the town of Voghera, 10 June 1391: Sangiuliani, *Agro Vogherese*, I 93, no. 180.

[3] Manfredi, *Storia di Voghera*, 211.

[4] First report of 6 June, "ora xi": *ASMa*, E. XLIX. 3. Cf. Galantino, *op. cit.* I 153.   [5] Boselli, *Storie Piacentine*, II 132 note 3.

[6] Santoro, "Registri", 22 no. 87; Formentini, *Ducato di Milano*, 157–8.

[7] Second report of 6 June, "ora xi": *ASMa*, E. XLIX. 3.

[8] Third report of 6 June, "de note": *ibid.*

[9] Order of 17 June: Osio, *Documenti Diplomatici*, I 300, no. 207.

Hawkwood's army did not intercept the provision of an adequate supply of grain for the capital.[1] Overtures were made to detach Carlo and Mastino Visconti from their alliance with the enemy.[2] But the army at Lodi was not ready to take the field until the end of June; and, by that time, Armagnac's reinforcements were already hastening through Piedmont to Milan.

Giangaleazzo's star did not desert him, nor the skill of his generals. The French troops paused near Alessandria, to await the arrival of Florentine gold deposited at Genoa. They occupied themselves meanwhile in reducing a few of the smaller fortresses of the neighbourhood; but the little town of Castellazzo resisted all their assaults, and postponed any intention they may have had of advancing directly upon Milan.[3]

Hawkwood could wait no longer. His food supplies were exhausted, the country had been carefully evacuated, and the embankments of the rivers had been levelled, so that his line of retreat was threatened by floods. Jacopo dal Verme led the Milanese army against him at the beginning of July. After two or three days of skirmishing, Hawkwood ordered a retreat, and the allied army picked its way with difficulty through the flooded countryside, back towards Padua. Verme watched them go, resisting the temptation to order a general attack; he had to husband his resources for another conflict.[4]

As soon as Hawkwood had passed beyond striking distance of Milan, Verme rushed his army across from Lodi to Alessandria. He arrived in time; Armagnac was still waiting for the convoy which was to bring the pay for his troops from Genoa. When at length it arrived, he prepared to resume his march; but before he set out, he rode with the flower of his men up to the walls of Alessandria, and delivered a scornful challenge to the Visconti army. Verme was prepared for him; he was fighting on his own ground, and Armagnac, who did not understand the conditions

[1] Edict of 21 June: *Inventari e Regesti*, III 11, no. 216.
[2] Romano, "Giangaleazzo Visconti", *ASL* XVIII 43–6.
[3] Durrieu, *Gascons en Italie*, 81–3.
[4] Leader, *op. cit.* 198–203; Bruni, *op. cit. RIS* NS XIX, 3, 255–6, post-dates the retreat, placing it after the battle of Alessandria; and other chroniclers follow him. And *v.* Vergerio, "Epistolario", 74 7, no. 04.

of warfare in Italy, fell an easy victim to the experience and caution of the Milanese commander. On 25 July 1391, beneath the walls of the city which symbolized the spirit of Italy in revolt against the foreign invader, Armagnac and his bravest knights were slain. The rest of the French, scattered in flight among the mountains of Piedmont, were cut down by the peasants, or fought their way back eventually to Provence.[1]

The battle of Alessandria, celebrated as a triumph for Italian arms, was the second turning-point of the war. Giangaleazzo had been allowed to deal with his enemies one by one. The imminent danger was past, the double attack had failed to synchronize and had been beaten off. The initiative which had been gained by the allies when Carrara entered Padua was restored to the Visconti army.

Giangaleazzo was anxious for peace; he did not wish to put too great a strain upon the loyalty of his subjects. On the strength of his victory, he could open negotiations with the enemy from a favourable position; but he did not neglect the military advantages which he had gained. The lands and people of Lombardy had suffered enough from the war. Giangaleazzo ordered Verme to lead his army into Tuscany, and march upon Florence.

The Milanese army won no fresh glory in Tuscany. The city of Florence, well armed and provisioned, was impregnable; and Hawkwood returned, with his army still intact, to defend the Republic. Verme failed to penetrate Hawkwood's defence, and was forced to withdraw, with some loss, to the *Lucchese*. The approach of winter produced a position of stalemate in the military situation;[2] and Giangaleazzo, once more on the offensive, made plans to reduce the Florentines to submission by other methods.

A month before he declared war upon Florence, Giangaleazzo told the Sienese ambassadors at Pavia that, if need be, "such

[1] Durrieu, *Gascons en Italie*, 83–98; Romanelli, *Calata di Giovanni III d'Armagnac.*
[2] Minerbetti, "Cronica", 137–40; Leader, *op. cit.* 204–7. The Florentine letter published by Osio, *op. cit.* I 301–2, no. 209.

provision would be made at sea, that the grain for Florence would not be able to enter Porto Pisano ".[1] He had already envisaged the idea of blockading the enemy to starvation. When war broke out, two ships of war patrolled the mouth of the Arno and entered Porto Pisano "on the business of my illustrious lord the Count", as Guglielmo Bevilacqua wrote to Siena;[2] and Alberto d'Este, in spite of Venetian protests, closed his territories to all trade passing between Venice and Florence.[3] The Florentines understood the danger and, with the full approval of the Venetians,[4] who resented any interference with commerce, signed commercial agreements with the lords of Faenza and Ravenna to assure the passage of supplies to their city.[5] The desertion of Alberto d'Este forced Giangaleazzo to abandon all serious idea of a blockade; but the two galleys remained at the mouth of the Arno to harass Florentine shipping,[6] and when Verme entered Tuscany in the autumn of 1391, the Count returned to the plan of starving the Florentines into surrender.

He found a useful ally in Antoniotto Adorno, who became Doge of Genoa for the second time in 1391. Adorno was a Ghibelline, and the sale of Serravalle to him demonstrated his friendly relations with the lord of Milan. When Giangaleazzo's naval activities were resumed in October 1391—a despatch to Siena mentioned the report that "two ships of the lord Count came to Porto Pisano yesterday, so that the enemy is in evil case"[7]—the Florentines accused Adorno of placing the Genoese fleet at Giangaleazzo's disposal, in order to starve them into accepting an unjust peace.[8]

Giangaleazzo had probably come to an understanding with Adorno, but his most active partisan was Jacopo d'Appiano.

[1] Despatch from Pavia, 22 March 1389/90: *ASS*, Concistoro 1826, no. 91.
[2] A letter from Pisa, 4 June 1390: *ibid.* 1827, no. 34. *V.* also "Chronicon Placentinum", *RIS* xvi 552 d; and Lucca, *Regesti*, 291, no. 1451.
[3] Roberto Cessi, "Politica Veneziana di terra firma", *MSF* v 201.
[4] *Ibid.* 144.
[5] Pagnini, *della Decima*, ii 178–86.
[6] There were complaints from Pisa in March and May 1391: Silva, "Governo di Pietro Gambacorta", 271–2.
[7] From Pisa, 19 October 1391: *ASS*, Concistoro 1829, no. 64.
[8] Minerbetti, "Cronica", 143; Silva, "Governo", 274.

Pietro Gambacorta remained firm, in spite of Milanese pressure,[1] in his attachment to the Florentine cause; but his secretary worked hand in hand with Milanese agents, under cover of the official neutrality of Pisa, in support of Giangaleazzo's army in Tuscany.[2] The army, too, had its part to play in the blockade of Florence. Verme encamped on the *Pisano* in October, and, as a condition of his withdrawal for fifteen days, exacted Gambacorta's promise "that he will not permit supplies or merchandise to be carried from Pisa to Florence, and that within that time he will answer clearly whether he is prepared to support the Count or not".[3] Meanwhile, Gambacorta sent his secretary to lodge a protest at Pavia; Giangaleazzo sent him back with an ultimatum to Gambacorta.[4] The Lord of Pisa refused to agree to Giangaleazzo's demands, and Verme returned to the *Pisano* when the fifteen days had expired;[5] but there was little that he could do. Tuscany was suffering from a severe famine, against which only the Florentines had taken adequate precautions.[6] Conditions in the Visconti camp were far worse than in Florence. Captains of the army came to Pavia to demand remedies, and were answered with "fair words";[7] but as the weather grew more severe, conditions became insupportable. "Many soldiers have fled from the camp in Tuscany, and go away daily, a few at a time, declaring that they can no longer remain in the field."[8]

Verme gained one success in December, when he captured a large convoy of grain bound from Pisa to Florence. Appiano and the "Visconteggianti" in Pisa rejoiced openly,[9] and Gambacorta had once more to seek momentary relief. "Messer Niccolò Pallavicino is here as ambassador of the lord Count, and has

---

[1] Silva, "Governo", 270.

[2] *Ibid.* 267–8.

[3] Despatch of Galeazzo Busoni at Pavia, to Francesco Gonzaga, 26 October 1391: *ASMa*, E. xlix. 3. *V.* also Minerbetti, "Cronica", 142; Silva, "Governo", 273–4.

[4] *V.* Doc. 7. (Despatch of Galeazzo Busoni from Pavia, 28 October.)

[5] Minerbetti, "Cronica", 144; Silva, "Governo", 274.

[6] Minerbetti, "Cronica", 154.

[7] *V.* Doc. 7. (Despatch of Galeazzo Busoni from Pavia.)

[8] Despatch of Galeazzo Busoni from Melegnano, 5 November 1391: *ASMa*, E. xlix. 3.

[9] Minerbetti, "Cronica", 146–7; Leader, *op. cit.* 208. Silva, "Governo", 274–5.

signed a convention with the lord and Commune of Pisa, and presently the troops of the Count ought to leave the lands of Pisa, and the Pisans promise for a certain time not to allow supplies to leave Pisa to go to Florence, and the time I believe to be brief."[1] But the campaign had in fact reached a deadlock with the coming of winter. The problem of feeding a besieging army was no less formidable than that of feeding a beleaguered city; and so other means were used, to bring to an end a war which had already exhausted the resources of the combatants.

Boniface IX and Pietro Gambacorta had constantly renewed their counsels of peace and offers of mediation.[2] The Pope had delegated the task of pacification to the Grand Master of the knights of St John who, with Gambacorta's help, secured the consent of Florence after the battle of Alessandria to the meeting of a peace conference at Pisa; but Giangaleazzo did not favour the idea of holding a conference at Pisa, under the presidency of Gambacorta, who was hostile to him, and of the Grand Master whose attitude was doubtful.[3] He persuaded Adorno to make a counter-proposal that the conference should be held at Genoa. The Florentines showed no eagerness to go to Genoa,[4] and the Bolognese, by their own account, showed less;[5] but eventually the allies had to yield to Adorno's persistence, and the conference opened at Genoa, before the Doge and the Grand Master, in September 1391.[6]

Giangaleazzo was once more in his own element. The choice of Genoa as the seat of the conference was already a first victory. Giangaleazzo claimed Padua, and on that issue the conference nearly broke up; negotiations were repeatedly delayed by the

---

[1] Despatch of the Sienese envoy at Pisa, 22 December 1391: *ASS*, Concistoro 1829, no. 74.

[2] Roberto Cessi, "Politica Veneziana di terra firma", *MSF* v 196–7; Theiner, *Codex diplomaticus Sancti Sedis*, III 34–5, no. 15; Silva, "Governo", 269 and 272.

[3] Delaville le Roulx, "Anti Grand-Maître de l'Ordre de St Jean de Jérusalem", *BEC* XL 529.

[4] Silva, "Governo", 272 note 4.

[5] Bologna to Venice (undated): Zambeccari, "Epistolario", 183 no. 171.

[6] Delaville le Roulx, *op. cit. BEC* XL 528–530. Florence to Adorno, dated 14 August: published by Novati, "Frammento di Zibaldone Cancelleresco", *ASL* XL, 2, 283–5, Doc. 23; Novati, *ibid.* 305, accepts Delaville le Roulx' date, 4 August; Romano, "Regesto", *ASL* XXI, 2, 22, no. 7.

extravagant demands of both parties. But the war had run its
course; neither side knew where to turn for means to keep the
armies in the field; and finally a complete reference was made to
the arbitration of the two presidents of the conference, together
with the Commune of Genoa. Giangaleazzo gave a ready enough
consent to the proposal; he could rely upon Adorno's support, and
hoped that the Doge would secure for him the vote of the Commune as well. The Florentines accepted the arbitration with misgiving, and made overtures to win the favour of the Grand
Master. The difficulties were not yet over, nor the delegates'
threats of withdrawal; but the terms of the peace were at length
made known on 20 January 1392.[1]

Carrara was to retain Padua; but Giangaleazzo kept Bassano,
Feltre and Belluno, and Carrara had to pay an indemnity of
10,000 florins a year for fifty years—a crippling burden for so
small a state. In Tuscany, all the conquests of the war were to
be mutually restored, save that, pending a further award,
Montepulciano was to be retained by Florence, and Lucignano
by Siena. The limits of the political influence of Giangaleazzo
and the Republics were laid down on the model of the pact of
Pisa. The precise status of Alberto d'Este, claimed by both sides
as an ally, was left undecided; but Francesco Gonzaga was
declared to have fulfilled all the obligations incumbent upon him
during the war. The movements of the Companies, especially
dangerous at the end of a war, were to be closely restricted.

Giangaleazzo had to acquiesce in the loss of Padua. These
terms restored, save for that, the conditions which had prevailed
in 1389, giving no greater reason for confidence in the sincerity
of the parties, and no surer means of implementing the terms of
the agreement. They settled none of the fundamental problems
which had caused the war. It was not a peace, but a truce of
exhaustion; and as such it was accepted, both by Florence and
by Giangaleazzo.

---

[1] Published by Rousset, *Supplément au corps universel diplomatique*, I, 2,
247–50. For the Conference of Genoa, the chief sources are the documents
published by Rousset, *ibid.* 229–76; Delaville le Roulx, *op. cit. BEC* XL
525–44 (his chronology requires to be checked by the documents published
by Rousset); Minerbetti, "Cronica", 148–51. *V.* also Doc. 7.

CHAPTER XI

THE VISCONTI DOMINIONS AND THE WAR. THE AFTERMATH OF THE WAR: THE LEAGUE OF BOLOGNA (1392)

Giangaleazzo's calculations had gone astray. When he had declared war in 1390, he had hoped that his army would enter Bologna within a few weeks, and enable him to dictate his own terms to a helpless Florence. Instead, he was faced with the task of financing a war which lasted for twenty months, and in the course of which Lombardy was invaded for the first time since 1373. A contemporary writer estimated the cost of the war to Florence at 2,000,000 florins;[1] and Corio tells us that the burdens placed upon Giangaleazzo's subjects recalled the days of Bernabò.[2] The resources of the Visconti dominions were strained to the utmost limit. A first heavy subsidy, estimated at 300,000 florins, provided Giangaleazzo with the means to fight the opening campaigns.[3] The subsidy, which was raised on the basis of the "estimo", was renewed at the beginning of 1391;[4] and shortly afterwards, we find evidence of an increase of about one-third in the ordinary monthly tribute paid by each of the cities to the

---

[1] Giovanni Morelli, *Cronica*, 293; he gives an account of the privations imposed on his own family in order to meet the needs of the state. 2000 lances permanently in the field—a minimum estimate for both fronts—and 3000 infantry would alone account for half this sum. (The "lance", a cavalry unit of, in Italy, three men, received an average pay of 16 florins a month; the foot-soldier, 3 or 4 florins.) The account books of the Republic give an expenditure of 275,000 florins for the lances during 1391; and an almost equal sum for crossbowmen, from 1390 to March 1392: Salvemini, *Balestrieri di Firenze*, 261 and 265.

[2] Corio, *Storia di Milano*, II 361.

[3] Despatch of a Lucchese envoy from Modena, 20 June 1390: Lucca, *Regesti*, 302–3, no. 1493. No details are known. On 22 March, the price of salt, a state monopoly, had been raised from 40 to 50 soldi a staio: Santoro, "Registri", 14–15, no. 45.

[4] 10 January 1391; 36,000 florins were demanded from Milan: *ibid.* 18, nos. 65–7.

central government.[1] In May, the Commune of Pavia was unable to find its share of the sum demanded to meet the emergencies of that critical moment.[2] Filippo della Molza, gossiping with an acquaintance at the beginning of June, was told "that he had it from a friend of his, that there was undoubtedly no money at all, saying, how are we to pay these Frenchmen who are coming, if we cannot even pay the troops which we have now?"[3] The battle of Alessandria did not bring much improvement, for Galeazzo Busoni, in a more sober report at the end of October, declared that "all here sigh for peace, and pray that it may be made, for the burden of payment is intolerable alike for the clergy as for laymen".[4]

These were the ordinary methods of direct taxation for the financing of the war; but they did not exhaust the ingenuity of the government in finding sources of revenue to meet its needs. It was customary, when the ordinary sources of taxation failed, to raise forced loans from the richer citizens of the state.[5] Giangaleazzo saw possibilities in this beyond the mere extortion of financial help from unwilling subjects. The young and vital forces of capitalist enterprise had always supported the Visconti, and their help was never more needed than now. The enterprises of the state were offered as a profitable field for the investment of the accumulated resources of commerce and industry. The payment of 10 per cent interest to creditors of the state was guaranteed by an edict of 3 November 1391.[6] A regular form of "national debt" had existed in Florence for forty years, and in Venice for over a century;[7] and it was in full accord with Giangaleazzo's political conceptions that he should adapt the idea to the

---

[1] An additional 5000 florins, in the case of Milan: *ibid.* 20–9, nos. 78, 82, 88–9, 111, 119, 130 (cancelled in June 1392).

[2] Romano, "Sussidio di guerra", *BSP* ii 481–2.

[3] First report of 6 June 1391: *ASMa*, E. xlix. 3.

[4] Despatch from Pavia, 30 October 1391: *ibid.*

[5] 10,000 florins were raised thus from Milanese citizens in March 1391: Morbio, *Codice Visconteo-Sforzesco*, 16–17 no. 4.

[6] Osio, *Documenti Diplomatici*, i 298–9, no. 206. Cf. Picotti, "Qualche Osservazione sui caratteri delle Signorie Italiane", *RSI* xliii (NS iv) 24 note 1.

[7] Luzzatto, "Debito Pubblico", *NRS* xiii 632–7.

requirements of his own state. He thereby associated yet more closely the interests of a powerful group of subjects with the preservation of his own strong and secure government.

Another financial expedient was less happily conceived, and met with the failure it deserved. An edict of 25 January 1391 declared the current value of all coins to be 33⅓ per cent above their face value. This may have been intended partly to remedy the scarcity of coinage from which Italian commerce suffered during and after the war;[1] but it was designed to bring immediate benefit to the Treasury, for all taxes had to be paid at the face value of the coins. Private traders, threatened by this double standard with a loss of their profits, immediately raised the prices of their goods. The government, faced with the prospect of commercial disorganization, admitted its mistake and revoked the edict after a trial period of three weeks.[2]

We do not know how far Giangaleazzo himself was responsible for experiments such as these. Niccolò Diversi of Lucca, his "General Master of the Entries",[3] probably formulated the financial policy of the state; and Milano Malabarba, a wealthy "Visconteggiante" from Padua, also became prominent at this period in the Exchequer department.[4] The Milanese bank of the Borromei, growing in importance under Borromeo Borromei and expanding the scope of its enterprises, transacted much of the government's business;[5] and Borromeo himself was in personal contact with the court.[6] Giangaleazzo would certainly have taken the expert advice of men such as these, in the direction of his financial policy.

---

[1] Corio, *op. cit.* II 362.

[2] Argelati, *De Monetis Italie*, III 59; Giulini, *Memorie*, XI 510–12; Motta, "Documenti Visconteo-Sforzeschi", in *Rivista Italiana di Numismatica*, VI 204–6, nos. 40–2.

[3] Romano, "Nuovi Documenti Viscontei", *ASL* XVI 337–9, Doc. 9.

[4] Pastorello, *Nuove Ricerche*, 78 and note 7.

[5] *V.*, for example, *Inventari e Regesti*, II, 2, 135 no. 775; and Lucca, *Regesti*, 320, no. 1561. The branch establishments set up by the Borromei spread across Italy and much of Europe in the first half of the fourteenth century: Biscaro, "Banco Filippo Borromei", *ASL* XL, 1, 39–40.

[6] Giangaleazzo was godfather to Borromeo's children: Romano, "Nuovi Documenti Viscontei", *ASL* XVI 684, no. 30; and *Id.* "Regesto", *ASL* XXI, 2, 33, no. 53.

Giangaleazzo's demands for money were accompanied by
assurances that the interests of his subjects were identical with
his own; he was fighting their battles against the menacing
Archguelfs of Florence, and must call on them, albeit unwillingly,
to bear their share of the burden.[1] These euphemisms were common enough when extraordinary taxation had to be imposed,
even under Bernabò's ruthless régime.[2] Giangaleazzo certainly
did not forget the prosperity which would accrue to his subjects
from the achievement of his grandiose designs; but they were
more inclined for their part to take a shorter view, and to resent
the sacrifices which were demanded of them. Even the more
closely centralized system of financial administration, introduced
by Giangaleazzo in 1388, could scarcely stand the stress of the
war. Busoni's insistence on the need for peace in his despatch of
October 1391 confirms the opinion expressed in Florence a little
later, "that if peace had not been made then, but the war continued even for a few months, we should have achieved his total
ruin".[3] The truth was that the Florentine government was in no
better position, for the people were also beginning to show signs
of a strain that was "unbearable for all the citizens".[4] Wars were
frequent in this age, but they did not last for long; credit was
short, and exhaustion of resources soon enforced a truce.

A brief epilogue to the war showed the temper of Giangaleazzo's
subjects. Six months after the peace of Genoa, the citizens of
Alessandria rose in rebellion and burnt the books of the Commune.
The valiant townsmen, who had helped to defeat Armagnac and
his French army, resented the heavy taxes to which they were
subjected, and felt indignant that peace had not brought the
expected relief from the sacrifices of wartime. The people of
Valenza followed their example; but now, when there was no
enemy at the gates, their cause was hopeless, and the riots were
easily suppressed.[5]

---

[1] *V.* the decrees published by Morbio, *op. cit.* 3–18, nos. 1–6.
[2] Ciapessoni, "per la Storia della Economia", *BSP* vi 185–7; Lonati,
Stato Totalitario, 37.
[3] Giovanni Morelli, *Cronica*, 293.
[4] Minerbetti, "Cronica", 136, 152, 162–3.
[5] *Ibid.* 163–4; Corio, *op. cit.* ii 369; Giulini, *Memorie*, xi 552.

The brutal sack of Verona certainly contributed to the apparent
loyalty of Giangaleazzo's dominions during the war. The Florentines gave the fullest encouragement to all the underlying forces
hostile to the Count—by their intrigues, by the presence of
their army in Lombardy, by the support which they gave to other
claimants of the Visconti heritage. Their faith in Carlo Visconti
was, as they soon learnt, sadly misplaced; Bernabò's heirs repaid
the help they had received from Florence, by accepting Giangaleazzo's propositions as soon as the battle of Alessandria had
turned the scale in his favour. Carlo, by an agreement which
had been concluded by 19 September 1391, promised to live in
Bavaria, and presumably abandoned all rights in his father's
dominions in return for a pension.[1] Nevertheless, Giangaleazzo
had to keep close watch within his state. The feudal nobility were
not entirely loyal; the admission of Bolognese troops into Correggio by the lord of the town, an adherent of the Count, roused
him to bitter anger.[2] Yet considering the opportunities of those
desperate months of May and June 1391, the defections were
remarkably small; and Giangaleazzo knew when he could press
his subjects no further. He reluctantly submitted to the loss of
Padua, and made peace before they were driven to extreme
measures.

The Count must have seen that the unity of his dominions in
a common devotion of every subject to the prince was still an
unrealized dream. Years of thoughtful and efficient government
were needed to arouse a spirit of loyalty, and the passage of time
to give the discipline of habit. But the element of time was
lacking on the overcrowded political stage of Italy; only the
crushing hand of foreign masters eventually succeeded in im-
posing a slower and more steady development, tainted as it was
then by association with the hateful and sterile tradition of
bondage. For Giangaleazzo, the government of his dominions
was not an end in itself; it was subservient to the part which
ambition and circumstance had forced upon him, and in which

---

[1] Brunetti, "Nuovi Documenti", *ASL* xxxvi, 2, 19–27, and 55–6, Doc. 2.
Cf. Leader, *Giovanni Acuto*, 188–9. Minerbetti ("Cronica", 60) described
Carlo as "poco savio uomo, e vile".   [2] *V*. Doc. 0.

the political struggle with other powers absorbed more and more
of his attention.

It is not surprising, therefore, that the early epoch of administrative reform came to an abrupt end. The period of the war
brought no changes of note, save those which were intended to
strengthen the government's financial position; but in the
unsettled years after the Peace of Genoa, Giangaleazzo's system
needed careful supervision. The letter of the law was there, but
the spirit was woefully absent; and it could not be developed, so
long as Giangaleazzo subordinated the internal welfare of his
state to the commitments of his ambitious policy.

It was too late, perhaps, to withdraw from those commitments.
A natural pride demanded that the setbacks of the war should be
avenged; and the Florentines were watching every movement of
their enemy with alert and suspicious eyes. Giangaleazzo's
thoughts were in any case far from withdrawal; but it was by
diplomacy, not by arms, that he proposed to continue the
struggle. He called all his reserves of patience into play. He kept
in mind the idea of starving the enemy into surrender, and the
Florentines themselves did not forget the danger of blockade
which they had experienced "when we had war with that great
lord";[1] but for that purpose the Count had to form new alliances
in Emilia and Romagna, in Umbria and in Tuscany itself. The
hardships of the war had shaken his influence in Perugia and even
in Siena. Galeazzo Busoni wrote from Pavia, in October 1391,
that "in the event of lord Pietro Gambacorta taking the decision
to support the Florentines against the Count, the Sienese and the
Perugians will without doubt do the like;"[2] and Giangaleazzo's
readiness to make peace was in part a recognition of the need to
preserve the friendship of these cities, whose limited resources
could not support the burden of further warfare.

The Peace of Genoa left too much unsettled to afford any
respite on either side; and it was only towards the end of 1392
that the results of the war became at all clear.

---

[1] Referred to by Florentine envoys in August 1395: Bolognini, "Relazioni
tra Firenze e Venezia", *NAV* IX 85.
[2] Despatch of 30 October 1391: *ASMa*, E. XLIX. 3.

The terms of the peace confirmed the most important new factor introduced into the situation by the war, the re-establishment of the Carrarese dominion in Padua. The loss of Padua upset the careful balance of forces on which Giangaleazzo had based his calculations in 1390. It changed the whole aspect of eastern Lombardy, reversed the military position, and shook the loyalty of both Alberto d'Este and Francesco Gonzaga.

Alberto d'Este, who had been compelled to renounce his alliance with Giangaleazzo during the war, ruled over an elongated and vulnerable state. His territories extended from the marshes of the Po delta to Frignano in the Apennines. They lay on the valley of the Po and the estuary of the Adige, across the great highways which ran from Milan to Bologna and Romagna, and from Bologna to Padua and Venice. Bologna, the traditional enemy of the Estensi, had claims on certain border-lands of the *Modenese*. Giangaleazzo had wider ambitions on Modena itself as a step towards the possession of Bologna. The Venetians demanded assurances for their trade along the estuaries of the Po and the Adige. The feudal nobility of the *Modenese*, ensconced in their fortresses in the Apennines, defied their overlord and laughed at his authority.

Between these forces, the Estensi pursued a cautious and conciliatory course. When Alberto accepted the terms dictated by Carrara in 1390, he did not bind himself to any active hostility against Giangaleazzo; and towards the end of the war he spoke to the Milanese agent at Ferrara of his wish to show himself " a friend and a son to the lord Count ". He said that " the Bolognese were outsiders, and had done him great damage, and if they did not give him compensation, he would certainly take measures against them which would leave them little contented ".[1] Giangaleazzo was willing to accept these overtures; but he allowed the opportunity of cementing his friendship with d'Este to slip by, and Alberto quickly changed his mind again.

The attitude of Venice was probably the decisive factor in the

[1] A report of this conversation was given to Galeazzo Busoni by Pasquino Capelli, and related by him in his despatch of 2 November 1391, from Cagnolo: *ibid.*

orientation of Ferrarese policy. Giangaleazzo had forfeited the goodwill of the Venetians, who watched with growing uneasiness the tendency of their neighbours to become satellites of the Milanese power. Their relations with these neighbours were determined by the resolution to obviate the danger at all costs. They accepted the propitiatory overtures made by Francesco Carrara after his return to Padua.[1] Preserving a perfectly correct attitude of diplomatic neutrality in their relations with Giangaleazzo, they encouraged the "Signorotti" of Lombardy to assert their own rights at the peace conference;[2] and Carrara notified them without delay, early in February 1392, that "he has made a complete union with the lord Marquis for the protection of both their states".[3]

The Lombard princes, no longer awed by the irresistible alliance of Venice and the Visconti, drew away from their overpowerful Milanese neighbour. Carrara had deep cause to hate him. Alberto d'Este, who had been left in a most uncertain position by the terms of the peace, needed better securities; assured of Venetian approval, he sought them from the Count's enemies. On 11 April 1392, Carrara and d'Este concluded a League with Florence, Bologna, and the allies of Florence in Romagna, the lords of Imola, Faenza and Ravenna. The League, which was signed at Bologna, made full provision for the protection of the two Lombard princes against aggression.[4]

Francesco Gonzaga had remained faithful to his alliance with Milan during the war. His first marriage, to Bernabò's daughter Agnese, had come to a tragic end; Agnese, discovered in infidelity, paid forfeit with her life.[5] It was suggested, nevertheless, that one of her sisters, now under Caterina Visconti's care at Pavia, should take her place.[6] Whether Giangaleazzo and Gonzaga

---

[1] Roberto Cessi, "Politica Veneziana", *MSF* v 200–2.

[2] *Id.* "Venezia neutrale nella seconda Lega anti-Viscontea", *NAV* NS XXVIII, 233–6.

[3] Pastorello, *Nuove Ricerche*, 200–1 Doc. 38.

[4] *Capitoli di Firenze*, II 352–60, no. 78; Silva, "Governo di Pietro Gambacorta", 278.

[5] Cibrario, *Opusculi Storici e Letterarii*, 16–28.

[6] *V.* Doc. 6. There is further mention of the proposals in later reports of Busoni, and in *Archivio Gonzaga* II 243 note 1.

quarrelled over the proposed match, or over the redemption of the lands which the Count had pledged during the war,[1] and which Gonzaga had hoped to keep permanently in his state, it is impossible to say. Gonzaga's natural affinities lay with the lords of Ferrara and Padua. Giangaleazzo's attitude during the peace conference seems to have aroused his suspicions; he had no intention of allowing Mantua to become a vassal state, and he was a match in ambition and cunning for Giangaleazzo himself. The Count was well aware that Gonzaga was wavering in his allegiance; but he could find no remedy, no offer tempting enough to seduce the lord of Mantua from his purpose. Filippo della Molza wrote from Pavia in February 1392 of the suspicions which were rife in the court; the "amigo" had told him that "he had heard it said that the Marquis of Ferrara had said that you would make accord with the League".[2] Returning in July, after Gonzaga had made a tour of the states of the League on his way to and from Rome, della Molza received a far warmer welcome than usual, "and I believe that you may have every benefit that you wish from the lord Count".[3] But Gonzaga had made up his mind. The ambassador, once more in Pavia, wrote on 4 September that "it has been written to the lord Count, and the letter arrived yesterday, that your lordship has certainly made accord to your advantage with the League, and that the League is giving to you troops and provisions and 18,000 ducats to make the bridge".[4] The report, as della Molza no doubt knew, was true; on 1 September, Florence and a majority of the allies admitted Gonzaga to the League of Bologna; the allies guaranteed the defence of his possessions and the maintenance of his rights.[5]

---

[1] Giangaleazzo's authorization to his delegate to receive back the fortresses, given "in Civitate Papie in castro magno" on the last day of February 1392, the act of restoration of 13 March, and Gonzaga's receipt for "ducatos sexaginta Millia boni auri et justi ponderis" are preserved in *ASMa*, B. xx. 4. The fantastic account given by Platina, "Historia Urbis Mantue", *RIS* xx 755–6, of a personal quarrel between Giangaleazzo and Gonzaga, is clearly legendary.

[2] Despatch of 13 February 1392: *ASMa*, E. xlix. 3.

[3] Despatch of 15 July 1392: *ibid.*

[4] *Ibid.*

[5] *Capitoli di Firenze*, ii 251–5, no. 50.

The bridge of Borgoforte, to which della Molza referred, could close the Po to shipping and facilitate the entry of hostile troops into Milanese territory. The Florentines, who had already established a garrison in Padua on behalf of Carrara,[1] wasted no time; troops were sent at once to Mantua, and under their protection the construction of the bridge was begun.[2] Gonzaga's action was not only a betrayal but a threat; and Giangaleazzo began to build bridges on his side, and strengthened the defences of Verona.[3] "The subjects of Giangaleazzo began to fear that war was imminent."[4] The three lords of Lombardy were now in close alliance; Carrara and Gonzaga were anxious to attack Milan at once.[5] Only the firm authority of Florence and Venice, neither of whom was prepared to countenance an immediate resumption of war, prevented a fresh outbreak of the struggle.

The end of the year saw Giangaleazzo surrounded by a ring of hostile states on his eastern border; insignificant in themselves, they were backed by the powerful protection of Venice. The two allies, whose heralds had so boldly presented themselves together with his own to declare war on Florence and Bologna in 1390, took shelter in the ranks of his more powerful enemies before it was too late.

The League of Bologna, although it was not specifically directed against anybody, was to be the basis of the opposition to Giangaleazzo for the next six years. Its strength lay in the unspoken approval of Venice, and the withdrawal of that approval was to destroy it. It was important to the Venetians that the integrity of the states of Mantua, Ferrara and Padua should be preserved: important, above all, that the independence of Friuli be maintained. The possession of Belluno provided a useful base from which Giangaleazzo could extend his influence in the Patriarchate.[6]

---

[1] Pastorello, *Nuove Ricerche*, 206, Doc. 42.
[2] Lucca, *Regesti*, 304, no. 1500; Azzi Vitelleschi, "Relazioni tra Firenze e l' Umbria", i 204, no. 759.
[3] *V*. Doc. 8. Also Minerbetti, "Cronica", 163; Verci, *Storia della Marca Trivigiana*, xvii 182.
[4] Corio, *op. cit.* ii 369.
[5] Pastorello, *Nuove Ricerche*, 79–83.
[6] Roberto Cessi, "Venezia neutrale", *NAV* NS xxviii 242 and 257.

The Patriarch John of Moravia was not popular in his dominions, and the overtures of his enemies, notably the Commune of Udine and the family of Savorgnano, to the ruler of Milan were observed with suspicion.[1] Giangaleazzo had not established any tangible authority in these parts; but the Venetians had learnt much since 1388, and no rumour or incident which concerned Friuli escaped their attention. They were, however, still deeply involved in the Levant, and they kept their commitments on the mainland down to a minimum. The nature of Venetian neutrality became clear after the war: for Giangaleazzo, a neighbourly courtesy modified by a firm disapproval of any new aggressive movement on his eastern border; for the three "signorotti", the rôle of protector and guardian, assumed not as an ally but as a friend—tempering their impetuosity, encouraging them in moments of weakness, and always emphasizing the importance of their alliance with Florence and Bologna.[2]

The Florentines would have liked to construct a similar barrier against the infiltration of Visconti influence into Tuscany; but the Tuscan cities had less cause to fear Giangaleazzo's power— being more remote from it—and greater need of his protection. The districts of Tuscany and Umbria suffered most severely from the after-effects of the war. The Companies, dismissed from service at the peace, systematically "redeemed" the lands of the Communes, demanding and receiving large subsidies as the price of exemption from invasion. Peace did not bring any immediate relief from the prevalent famine, and the Sienese were forced to appeal to all their friends for assistance, being "in great need of supplies".[3] The Florentines took the opportunity, offered by negotiations for the fulfilment of the terms of the peace relating to the restoration of conquered lands, to seek the favour of their

---

[1] Cusin, *Confine Orientale d'Italia*, I 188, and 191 note 135; Battistella, "Lombardi in Friuli", *ASL* xxxvii, 2, 322 note 1. Florence to Boniface IX, 20 January 1392: Delaville le Roulx, "Anti Grand-Maître de l'Ordre de St Jean de Jérusalem", *BEC* xl 542-3, Doc. 7.

[2] Roberto Cessi, "Venezia neutrale", *NAV* NS xxviii 256-8.

[3] Letters to Siena from the Commune of Perugia, and from the Podestà of Pavia, both dated 28 March 1392: *ASS*, Concistoro 1831, nos. 2 and 4.

former enemies, Siena and Perugia;[1] but the presence of the Companies created fresh suspicions and soon led to mutual recriminations, amid which the chance of arriving at a friendly settlement was lost.

Giangaleazzo did what he could, under these conditions, to preserve the allegiance of his allies and to prevent the formation of a hostile front in Tuscany under the leadership of Florence. He sent his own agent to negotiate with the leaders of the Companies on behalf of his friends. The Sienese envoy in Perugia wrote on 3 June that "Antoniolo Tornielli has arrived here on behalf of the lord Count in the service of this Commune, to see if there is any way by which an agreement can be made with these companies".[2] Perugia had proved a liability during the war, but it was valuable for the control of the southern approaches to Tuscany, and Giangaleazzo made an effort to retain the favour of the Commune. The arrival of Biordo Michelotti, a Perugian exile who had fought for the Count during the war, and who was in touch with all the leading Condottieri, strengthened the position of the rebels who had harassed Perugia with Florentine assistance during the war. The government of the Commune appealed in despair to the Pope to come and pacify their feuds. Boniface IX, surrounded by the hostile princes of the Patrimony, plagued by the Breton troops of Clement VII, and practically powerless against the communal government of Rome, was glad enough to leave his capital. He accepted the submission of Perugia, and arrived in the city in October 1392, amid the rejoicing of the inhabitants.[3]

A little earlier, Giangaleazzo had lost ground in another direction. Antoniotto Adorno had served him well during the peace conference, and received the town of Novi Ligure as his reward;[4] but the feuds of Genoa and the antagonism of the Genoese Guelfs

---

[1] Minerbetti,"Cronica", 152–3. Reports of the Sienese envoys at Florence, in *ASS*, Concistoro 1829, no. 14; 1830, no. 69; and 1831, passim.

[2] *Ibid.* 1831, no. 68. Giangaleazzo to Siena, 22 May, announcing Tornielli's mission: *ibid.* no. 60.

[3] Pellini, *Historia di Perugia*, II 35–6. The pact of August 1392, between the Pope and the city: Theiner, *Codex diplomaticus Sancti Sedis*, III 48–56, no. 20.

[4] Romano, "Regesto", *ASL* XXI, 2, 44 no. 96.

allowed the Doge no peace. Milanese troops helped him to suppress a first uprising against his authority in April 1392; but two months later, he lost his nerve at the approach of a rival, and fled to Pavia.[1] The Florentines lost no time in inviting the new Doge to join the League of Bologna.[2] Giangaleazzo, for his part, set himself to win the favour of the new government. "The former Doge of Genoa has gone to give Serravalle to the forces of the lord Count; and the Doge must not remain in the territories of the Count, as that would not please the Genoese."[3] The same stipulation with regard to Adorno was made when Giangaleazzo succeeded in renewing an old accord with Genoa which was due to expire in February 1393;[4] but it did not involve the withdrawal of Visconti support from the deposed Doge. The Count had made it his business to find friends in all the Genoese parties; but only with Adorno could he rely on a close political collaboration. He continued to favour Adorno's efforts to recover his authority, because they promised to be the most effective means of establishing his own influence in Liguria.

Giangaleazzo resumed apparently courteous relations with Florence and Bologna after the peace. He wrote to Siena on 7 April 1392, to inform his ally of his relations with the two Republics. "We have made known our readiness to bind and ally ourselves with them and others for the restraint and dissolution of the Companies; and not only have we made it known, but we have recommended that this should be done."[5] The atmosphere of mutual suspicion was still too great to permit of the success of this scheme; but Giangaleazzo did not abandon his plans. A fortnight later, the Sienese ambassadors in Florence wrote that "we saw a letter yesterday, from which we understand that the Count of Vertus would be well pleased to make alliance with this

---

[1] Stella, "Annales Genuenses", *RIS* xvii 1132–3; Minerbetti, "Cronica", 156–7. Minerbetti, and the "Chronicon Siculum Incerti Authoris", 106, mention the presence of Milanese troops in Genoa.

[2] Jarry, *Origines de la domination française à Gênes*, 37–8, 50–1.

[3] Despatch of Filippo della Molza from Pavia, 4 September 1392: *ASMa*, E. xlix. 3.

[4] *V.* Doc. 9. The alliance with Genoa was renewed on 8 February 1393: Romano, "Nuovi Documenti Viscontei", *ASL* xvi 320–1, Doc. 2.

[5] *ASS*, Concistoro 1831, no. 15.

Commune and with the other Republics of Tuscany ".[1] He had, in fact, devised a scheme to nullify the effect of the recently concluded League of Bologna, by having himself elected a member. He ingeniously contrived that Boniface IX should put forward his case; but the Florentines were not deceived, and with all reverence rejected the Pope's proposal.[2] The subsequent admission of Francesco Gonzaga to the League naturally produced a stormy protest from Pavia; but the Florentines refused to acknowledge that there was ground for a quarrel, and gave the usual assurances of their friendly and pacific intentions.[3]

The proposal to take measures against the power of the Companies formed part of all the numerous missions which passed between Florence and Pavia during the next five years. There can be little doubt that Giangaleazzo foresaw the ultimate resumption of the armed struggle against the Republic. It is impossible to estimate the number of troops which he kept constantly at his disposal, but it was certainly far greater than that which the Florentines could retain. The Count therefore stood to gain by any agreement for the removal of the independent Companies, from which Florence would have to recruit an army in case of war; and the Florentines, aware of their weakness, were always reluctant to commit themselves to such an agreement without adequate safeguards. Moreover, Giangaleazzo preferred to pursue his intrigues in a friendly atmosphere, until he was ready to strike.

He was very far from ready in 1392. The lords of Ferrara and Mantua had deserted to the enemy, Perugia had accepted a neutral ruler, and Adorno was in exile. Alone among his former allies, Siena still depended absolutely upon his protection. The Sienese treated every overture from Florence as a plot to undermine their independence. The conversations over the mutual restoration of conquests broke down; the attacks of the marauding bands were attributed to Florentine instigation. The Sienese

[1] Despatch of 21 April 1392: *ibid.* no. 42.
[2] Jarry, "Voie de Fait", *BEC* liii 245–6; Romano, "Niccolò Spinelli", *ASN* xxvi 471–2.
[3] Silva, "Governo", 283 and note 4.

Vicar of Poggio S. Cecilia notified the government in August that
"the impious troops of the Florentines yesterday invaded your
territory", and on the following day congratulated them on "the
defeat inflicted to-day on the impious troops of the Commune
of Florence".[1] The relations between the two Republics grew
so bad during the summer, that Pietro Gambacorta, in spite of
his ill-health, once more assumed the task of mediation; but
behind his obviously well-intentioned proposals the Sienese still
saw the shadow of the Florentine menace. They appealed once
more to Giangaleazzo for protection, exposing to him the hostile
attitude of Florence and the incursions of Florentine troops upon
their territory. In the negotiations promoted by Gambacorta at
Pisa, they had been required to make alliance with the Florentines,
"whether we would or no". All this they notified to Giangaleazzo,
"in order that you may be able to provide opportune remedies
in such an emergency".[2]

Giangaleazzo sent a distinguished embassy to Florence in
September 1392, to make proposals for a lessening of the tension
and for a mutual understanding, especially with regard to the
Companies; but he seems to have elicited no more than a promise
that the Florentines, after consulting with their allies, would
send envoys to Pavia to resume the discussions.[3] On 20 October,
while the delegates of the allies were still on their way, Sienese
ambassadors arrived at Pavia to recapitulate the grievances of
their Republic to Giangaleazzo and his Council; they asked for
instant action and pointed out the danger and loss in which any
delay would involve them. Giangaleazzo promised to satisfy
them, but begged them to wait and hear what the Florentine
envoys would have to propose.[4]

The account which was sent to the Sienese government of these
proceedings, as well as the earlier letters of that government, leave
no room to doubt that, if Giangaleazzo decided that he must

---

[1] Letters of 19 and 20 August 1392: *ASS*, Concistoro 1831, nos. 100–1.

[2] Letters of the Sienese government, August and September 1392, in
Silva, "Governo", 281–5; and 337–40, Docs. 35–7.

[3] *Ibid.* 284; Minerbetti, "Cronica", 163. Florence to Carrara, 25 September 1392: Pastorello, *Nuove Ricerche*, 209–10, Doc. 46.

[4] *V*. Doc. 8. (Despatch from Pavia, 26 October 1392.)

increase his influence in Tuscany, it was not out of fear that Gambacorta might succeed in reconciling Florence and Siena, but because the Sienese themselves, resolute in their resistance to the pretensions of Florence in Tuscany, clamoured insistently for his help.[1] Fortunately for Giangaleazzo, he had one card yet to play. Jacopo d'Appiano had managed to strengthen his position in Pisa. The hardships of the war, from which the status of neutrality could not entirely protect the city, had shaken Gambacorta's power. Appiano, who continued to enjoy the implicit confidence of the old ruler in spite of the repeated warnings of the Florentines, skilfully associated the growing economic discontent, and the deep-rooted Ghibelline tradition of hatred for Florence, with his own and Giangaleazzo's cause.[2] Disturbances occurred with alarming frequency during the months after the war, as the "Visconteggianti" grew bolder; and it was clear, even in Florence, that Gambacorta's control in Pisa was slipping.[3]

While the Sienese ambassadors at Pavia pleaded for immediate action against Florence, the measures had already been taken which were to bring relief to their government. Riots broke out in Pisa on 21 October 1392. The ground had been carefully prepared, and the outbreak planned beforehand. Four days later, Gambacorta and two of his sons were dead, and Appiano, granted his titles and honours by the Communal government, ruled in his place.[4]

The aggressive faction in the Florentine government, led by Maso degli Albizzi, immediately proposed to strengthen the forces of the Republic;[5] but Florence formally accepted the friendly assurances of the new governor of Pisa. Certain Visconti circles even displayed symptoms of alarm at these apparently courteous relations; the Sienese envoys in Pisa wrote on 15 November that, to Antonio Porro and Giovanni Rapolano, Giangale-

---

[1] The documents are quite positive. Silva, "Governo", 284–5, leaves rather vague the process by which he supposes Gambacorta's pacific activities to have influenced Giangaleazzo's decision to act without delay.

[2] Silva, "Governo", 278–81.

[3] *Ibid.* 278, 281–2, 285; and 336–7, Docs. 33–4.

[4] *Ibid.* 287–90. The chief source is Minerbetti, "Cronica", 164–6.

[5] Rado, *Maso degli Albizi*, 174–5.

azzo's ambassadors, "it does not look too well, and almost they think that this Commune will make a good accord with the Florentines".[1] Three weeks later, however, the Milanese ambassadors had left Pisa, "and, from what I am given to understand, they have left well satisfied".[2]

The Florentines, indeed, were under no illusions. Giangaleazzo had gained control of the mouth of the Arno, the most vital outlet for their trade, and could now rely on the unquestioning support of two of the Tuscan Republics. It was his sole consolation, among the setbacks which he encountered in the aftermath of the war.

[1] *ASS*, Concistoro 1832, no. 16.
[2] Ghaddo Conte de Ilci to Siena, 6 December 1392: *ibid.* no. 40.

CHAPTER XII

GIANGALEAZZO AND FRANCE: THE "KING-DOM OF ADRIA". GIANGALEAZZO AND THE LEAGUE OF BOLOGNA. GIANGALEAZZO AND GERMANY (1393–MAY 1395)

THE revolution in Pisa, long planned and long foreseen, bore all the signs of Giangaleazzo's guiding hand—the slow and thorough work of winning support and undermining Gambacorta's influence in the city, and the final blow swiftly launched against a weakened enemy. The control of Pisa was obviously a great asset in any struggle against Florence; but it was not enough to restore to the Count the advantages of earlier years. He was weaker than he had been in 1390. The unfriendly states of Padua, Mantua, Ferrara, Bologna and Florence hedged him in in a semicircle to the east and south. After the experiences of the past war, he did not feel strong enough to break through them by force of arms. The active opposition of Florence, the watchful caution of Venice, left no immediate scope for his intrigues. Giangaleazzo was no longer the master of Lombardy as he had been in 1389; and years might elapse before he could recover that position.

These were the circumstances in which Giangaleazzo turned to the great powers of Europe to help him in his plans. The opportunity arose when Charles VI wrote, at the request of Clement VII, to express the hope that Giangaleazzo would not support the anti-Clementist League, which Boniface IX was rumoured to be preparing among the states of Italy. The Count, in reply, renewed the project of a Franco-Milanese alliance, which had been abandoned eighteen months earlier owing to English intervention. Niccolò Spinelli, well known in France as a supporter of the Angevin cause in Naples, led a Milanese mission to Paris at the end of 1392. Giangaleazzo assumed for his own purposes that Boniface IX's reported proposition was practicable, and frankly explained his own position to the French court. He was surrounded by states loyal to the Roman allegiance, and could not expose his subjects to the risk of attack. He could only declare himself in favour of Clement if an adequate French army guaranteed his immunity from the reprisals of his neighbours; and he would repay the protection for which he asked by assisting the French cause in Italy.[1]

Charles VI no longer contemplated a personal visit to the peninsula, and the Count's offer was of no value to him; but it was very important to Clement. To accommodate the Milanese proposals to these conditions, Spinelli revived the rash plan of Clement's earlier days for a "kingdom of Adria"—the infeudation to a French prince of a portion of the States of the Church. The new kingdom would prepare the way for the return of Clement to a subdued Rome and to a Patrimony, very limited in extent, but pacified and obedient to his authority. The identity of the prince whom Spinelli and Giangaleazzo had in mind was beyond doubt; Louis of Valois, now Duke of Orleans, was not only best qualified for the task, but most suitable as a close relation of the ruler of Milan. Independent of France but supported by the might of a French army, independent of Milan but duly submissive to Giangaleazzo's parental guidance, Louis would help the Count to annihilate his enemies.[2]

There were great obstacles to the realization of this plan; and every fresh development proved unfavourable to Giangaleazzo's hopes. It is not necessary to consider in detail the discussions which ensued; they have been fully analysed by the historians of Franco-Milanese relations at this period. Clement VII was horrified at the enormous responsibility involved in the alienation of a large portion of the Papal lands; he would only consent to confer the kingdom of Adria, if Orleans guaranteed a rapid and decisive action in his favour. Meanwhile Charles VI succumbed to his first prolonged attack of insanity, and the court of Paris was thrown into confusion. The office of Regent fell to Louis of

---

[1] Undated instructions, published by Jarry, *Vie Politique de Louis de France*, 419–24, Doc. 14. Cf. Romano, "Niccolò Spinelli", *ASN* xxvi 475–9.

[2] Spinelli propounded this scheme in two able notes, which were discussed in detail by Romano, *ibid*. 479–96; they were published by Durrieu, *Royaume d'Adria*, 41–60, Docs. 1–2.

Orleans, who thereby incurred the jealousy of his powerful uncle, the Duke of Burgundy. The exiled Guelfs of Genoa had added to the difficulties by appealing to Charles VI for his help and protection. The King offered the task of conquering the Ligurian Republic to his brother, as a step towards the acquisition of the kingdom of Adria; and the joint interests of Milan and Avignon were subordinated to the preparations for an attack on Genoa, which appealed to Louis as a simpler and more feasible plan than the conquest of "Adria". Finally, the growing agitation among the French clergy to abandon the "voie de fait" as a means of ending the Schism, in favour of the "voie de cession", the joint renunciation by both Popes of their claims, threatened the whole fabric of the Milanese proposals. The abandonment of the idea of a Clementist expedition would remove the need for an alliance with the Visconti.[1]

Giangaleazzo could find no way out of these difficulties. He had found it convenient to make an open confession of his position in the original proposals to France; he had offered on his side what it was in his power to offer, and could not afford to make any further important concessions. The French mission, which came to Pavia in May 1393, with authority to conclude an alliance if Giangaleazzo would accept in full the modifications suggested by France, returned to Paris without reaching a conclusion. Charles VI wanted an immediate recognition of Clement; but Giangaleazzo could not budge from his original programme: first, the creation of the kingdom of Adria, then the French expedition to Italy, and then his recognition of Clement. His interest in the Schism was subordinate to his own political designs.[2]

The Count sent new instructions to Paris at the end of 1393. He offered to help France in case of a war with England, and

---

[1] For further reference, besides the works of Eugène Jarry and Romano's "Niccolò Spinelli", v. Durrieu, *Royaume d'Adria*; Circourt, "Duc Louis d'Orléans", *RQH* XLV–XLVI; Valois, *France et le grand Schisme*, II 188–200; Mirot, *Politique française en Italie*, 36–47; de Boüard, *France et l'Italie*, 144–95.

[2] Romano, "Niccolò Spinelli", *ASN* XXVI 503–4. Instructions for the French ambassadors, published by Jarry, *Vie Politique de Louis de France*, 426–30, Doc. 15. The envoys were at Pavia towards the end of May: v. Doc. 10.

accepted the exclusion of Bologna, "qui appartient à l'Église de plain droit", from his own sphere of influence in Lombardy and the Mark of Treviso.[1] But these concessions did not convince the Pope of the practicability of the plan. In August 1394, Clement made known his own terms for the creation of the kingdom of Adria; his conditions, which included a demand for immediate action and which ignored the existing rivalries between the Italian states, were acceptable neither to the Duke of Orleans, who was eagerly preparing for his Genoese adventure, nor to Giangaleazzo, who thought primarily in terms of Italian politics.

The Count, however, did not lose all hope of a French alliance, which would gain additional attraction if it were freed from an embarrassing obligation to support the Pope of Avignon. The veteran warrior Enguerrand de Coucy came to Asti in September 1394, to conduct the campaign against Genoa for the Duke of Orleans. Giangaleazzo welcomed him and offered him his full support. Adorno was again Doge; and Giangaleazzo had certainly not forgotten the long tradition of his family, the ambition to secure Genoa as a port for Milan. For Louis, and for him alone, he was prepared to renounce his own claim. Genoa under the rule of Orleans would, he hoped, be at his own disposal and under the protection of France. Giangaleazzo therefore helped to guide Coucy through the intricacies of Piedmontese politics, put him in touch with the Ghibelline exiles of Genoa with whom he maintained relations,[2] and placed his diplomacy, his treasury, and his soldiers at Coucy's disposal.[3] New instructions were sent to the Visconti envoys at Paris; and at the end of December 1394 Giangaleazzo and Coucy prepared the draft of a Franco-Milanese alliance, with a supplementary agreement for military co-operation in Italy.[4]

---

[1] Draft proposals published by Jarry, "Voie de Fait", BEC LIII 549–58.

[2] Romano, "Nuovi Documenti Viscontei", ASL XVI 687–8, nos. 48–9, 54–5; Id. "Regesto", ASL XXI, 2, 62–74, nos. 201, 207, 221–2, 245, 264.

[3] Jarry, Origines, Chapters 3–5.

[4] Three drafts were drawn up at Pavia. The first, published by Romano, "Nuovi Documenti Viscontei", ASL XVI 328–32, was of an alliance between Giangaleazzo and Louis of Orleans for the conquest of Genoa by the latter;

Clement had died in October, and his successor, Benedict XIII, was prepared to reconsider the terms on which he would grant the kingdom of Adria to Orleans. But adverse fortune still dogged Giangaleazzo's plans. The Duke of Burgundy had set himself to counteract the growing influence of Louis of Orleans in French affairs. A convocation of French clergy, summoned by Charles VI in February 1395 to advise him, declared in favour of the "voie de cession"; and the kingdom of Adria thenceforth vanished from the realm of practical politics. In March, Louis was compelled to sell back his claims on Genoa to his brother, and Coucy received instructions to carry on his campaign in the name of Charles VI.

This was a real blow to Giangaleazzo. The identity of French and Milanese interests in Genoa no longer existed; for the Count did not wish the Ligurian Republic to become a direct appanage of the French crown.[1] Giangaleazzo was free henceforth to look after his own interests in Genoa; he had undertaken to help Louis, but not Charles VI.[2]

Thus the opportunity for a positive alliance between France and Milan passed away. It is unnecessary to look for a hidden hand at work in Paris against the Count. The Duke of Burgundy was jealous of Orleans, but there is no evidence of a bitter enmity on his part against Giangaleazzo at this stage, and he intervened in close accord with Milan to pacify the dissensions of the Piedmontese princes in 1396.[3] Queen Isabella, the grand-daughter of Bernabò, certainly represented an element of danger, but she does not seem to have exercised any active power in political

it was dated 27 December 1394, and depended for its validity on the satisfactory conclusion of the other two. These were published by Jarry, "Voie de Fait", *BEC* LIII 558–70, and took the form, the first of a general alliance, the second of a military convention, between Giangaleazzo and Charles VI, similar to those proposed in 1391, 1392 and 1393. This was probably the very secret alliance, confusedly referred to by Corio, *Storia di Milano*, II 372.

[1] Jarry, *Origines*, 124–6, 134–5.
[2] *Id. Vie Politique de Louis de France*, 140–1.
[3] Gabotto, *Ultimi Principi d'Acaia*, 272–6, 281–4. Gabotto himself accepted Jarry's view that Burgundy was already working against Giangaleazzo, without explaining these negotiations in Piedmont.

affairs before 1396.[1] The project for a kingdom of Adria collapsed through its own inherent difficulties, through the obstinacy of Clement, and Giangaleazzo's ulterior motives, and the chaos of France under a mad king.

Giangaleazzo, however, was afraid that his intensive canvassing of the French court might have aroused at Paris an interest in Italian affairs which his enemies could turn to their own advantage; and he was determined to secure some sort of assurance from the French. As an ironical epilogue to the ambitious proposals which had been discussed for the past thirty months, Charles VI and the Milanese representative in Paris exchanged formal declarations of friendship on 31 August 1395. In these mutual assurances—for mutual they were, although some historians have believed that Charles made no promises on his side[2] —simple expressions of goodwill were substituted for the bold clauses of the earlier projects; and Giangaleazzo had to rest content with the hope that, in the event of Florentine overtures to Paris, Charles would abide by his promise of friendship.

The theory of Ferrai, that Giangaleazzo held the French in play for fear of the combination of Isabella and Burgundy, and that he never really intended a French army to set foot in Italy, has been shown by Jarry and Romano to be quite untenable.[3] Professor Romano maintained that Giangaleazzo wanted French help to make himself master of Tuscany; and the value of French

[1] Jarry believed that Isabella, Burgundy and Florence were working in close understanding against Giangaleazzo at this time: "Voie de Fait", *BEC* LIII 508–9, 514–15, 516, 521–2, 526. Valois, *op. cit.* II 199, declared that the evidence was not conclusive.

[2] The Milanese side of the agreement was published by Lünig, *Codex Italie Diplomaticus* I 421–6; the French side by Circourt, "Duc Louis d'Orléans", tirage à part II 71–3. Neither Jarry ("Voie de Fait", *BEC* LIII 546–7), arguing that Giangaleazzo gave a unilateral promise to the French king, nor Romano ("Niccolò Spinelli", *ASN* XXVI 526–7), arguing that it was a bilateral agreement, referred to the document published by de Circourt, who himself seems to have been unaware of its significance.

[3] Ferrai, "Politica di Giangaleazzo", *ASI* 5, XXII 55–7. Durrieu (*Royaume d'Adria*, 15) suggests that Giangaleazzo, having called in the French, would not have hesitated to get rid of them as soon as it suited him; but, as Jarry (*Vie Politique de Louis de France*, 113) pointed out, he would have found this neither easy nor very politic. Cf. Romano, "Niccolò Spinelli", *ASN* XXVI 473.

support in the event of a further war with Florence was certainly in his mind.[1] But his quarrel with Florence was not at this moment primarily concerned with Tuscany. The rivalry between the despot and the Republic, the most striking feature of Giangaleazzo's career, caught the imagination of his contemporaries and of succeeding ages. He himself addressed his attention mainly to Florence, as the head and spokesman of the League of Bologna; but the negotiations between them at this time referred mainly to the Count's relations with the rulers of Mantua and Ferrara. As Dr Cessi has pointed out, the immediate advantage which Giangaleazzo foresaw in an alliance with France was the confirmation of his own authority on the northern side of the Apennines.[2] It was in Lombardy and the Mark of Treviso that he demanded a free hand, in his negotiations with the French. He eventually offered to leave Bologna to the Pope; but Ferrara was specifically mentioned in the discussions as falling within the orbit of Visconti influence.[3] "We shall never have peace together", he remarked to Rinaldo Gianfigliazzi, who came to Pavia as Florentine ambassador in May 1394, "until I am lord of the whole of Lombardy."[4]

A superficial atmosphere of comparative quiet prevailed in Tuscany during these years. The Companies had for the most part found more profitable employment in Papal territories and in Umbria, where the affairs of Perugia were still unsettled. Boniface IX did not remain long in the Umbrian capital, where he had been welcomed so enthusiastically. The exiles, whom he had recalled to the city, rose and expelled their enemies in July 1393;[5] and the Pope fled in terror to Assisi at this new disturbance. The Florentines, having accomplished through Boniface the downfall of Giangaleazzo's friends in Perugia, were not sorry to

---

[1] Romano, "Niccolò Spinelli", *ASN* XXVI 496–7.
[2] Roberto Cessi, "Venezia neutrale", *NAV* NS XXVIII 253–4.
[3] Jarry, "Voie de Fait", *BEC* LIII 555–6, Doc. 1, clause 8. Clement, in the terms which he offered in August 1394, accepted this clause: Durrieu, *Royaume d'Adria*, 35.
[4] From the "consulta" of June 1394: Jarry, *Origines*, 169.
[5] Minerbetti, "Cronica", 170–2, 177–8; Pellini, *Historia di Perugia*, II 35–45.

see him depart.[1] But the real master of Umbria was now Biordo
Michelotti, who governed Perugia under the forms of a Republic.
Biordo was available to the highest bidder; he allowed no bonds
of party allegiance or political gratitude to check the course of
his own aggrandizement. He had been subsidized by Florence
after the peace of Genoa; but he had served in the Milanese army
during the war, and the Count lost no time in cultivating his
friendship. He sent Ambrogio da Viguardo, one of his agents, to
negotiate with the Companies on behalf of his friends in Tuscany
during the summer of 1393;[2] and Biordo described Viguardo as
"my intimate and dear brother".[3] The Count was clearly
preparing the way for an understanding with the ruler of Perugia.

   Giangaleazzo had taken upon himself the responsibility of
defending Siena, and Pisa under Jacopo d'Appiano. Appiano
acted as his chief agent in his relations with both these cities.
The choice was not altogether a wise one. The Count, unable to
exercise a very close control in distant Tuscany, had to leave a
great deal to the discretion of one who, in his relations with his
former master Pietro Gambacorta, had revealed not only his
personal ambitions, but a capacity for base treachery which was
unusual, even in those days, towards the author of his own
advancement. No sooner was Appiano master of Pisa, than he
nearly precipitated a crisis by threatening the security of the
neighbouring Republic of Lucca.[4] He seems to have been reluctant to accept the troops sent from Milan to garrison his city.
The Sienese envoy in Pisa reported, with a "sechondo ò sentito di
verità", that "100 lances of the lord Count have entered the city.
It does not appear that messer Jacopo wanted them here. They

---

   [1] The Florentine government wrote on 4 August 1393 to congratulate
Perugia "inde stetisse factionem nobilium, hinc bonorum civium congrega-
tionem": Azzi Vitelleschi, "Relazioni tra Firenze e l' Umbria", I 209, nos.
779–80.
   [2] *V.* Doc. 10, first paragraph. Viguardo described himself as "familiaris
Illustris domini domini Comitis Virtutum": letter to Siena, dated at Pisa,
7 July 1393: *ASS*, Concistoro 1833, no. 29.
   [3] Biordo to Siena, 8 September 1393: *ibid.* no. 59.
   [4] Silva, "Governo di Pietro Gambacorta", 289–90, and 342–3 Doc. 40.
Forces had marched through the Garfagnana to Appiano's assistance, in
spite of the protests of the government of Lucca: Sercambi, "Cronache",
I 288–9.

entered ten or twelve at a time."¹ If the interests of the lord of Milan and the ruler of Pisa ceased to be identical, there could be no question but that Appiano would follow his own paths; Giangaleazzo, like Gambacorta, seems to have been a little too ready to have confidence in a man of whose treacherous nature he had ample evidence. For the moment, however, Appiano found it necessary to rely on Giangaleazzo's support. Troops paid by the Treasury at Milan garrisoned both Pisa and Siena for the next few years, and the Count's agents sought to protect the two cities from the attacks of the Condottieri.²

Towards Florence Giangaleazzo maintained every aspect of outward courtesy. Pietro da Candia,³ Bishop of Novara and a leading statesman of the Pavian court, visited the Republic in February 1393. He had to explain certain accusations alleged to have been made against Florence by Spinelli in Paris, but the rest of his mission was shrouded in mystery, and apparently met with no success;⁴ perhaps the revelation of its purpose would not have facilitated Spinelli's task.

Maso degli Albizzi gained an unquestionable predominance in the Republic, after internal disturbances which occurred in October 1393;⁵ but the new government continued to use its influence in favour of peace. The Florentines rejected a proposal, whose object remains obscure, for an alliance with Perugia which would have contravened the terms of the peace of Genoa.⁶ The ambassadors sent to Genoa in March 1394 were commanded: "among other things, take good care and diligence that it cannot

¹ Despatch of 13 December 1392: *ASS*, Concistoro 1832, no. 29.
² *V.* Doc. 10. Further references are contained in other letters in *ASS*, Concistoro 1833.
³ The future Pope Alexander V.
⁴ Novati, "Aneddoti Viscontei", *ASL* xxxv, 2, 202–7; Romano, "Niccolò Spinelli", *ASN* xxvi 499–501. Minerbetti has preserved no record of this embassy, and the Sienese envoy at Pavia was not able to glean much information about it: *v.* Doc. 9.
⁵ Minerbetti, "Cronica", 179–83; Rado, *Maso degli Albizi*, 176–94. The version of Pellini (*op. cit.* ii 53–4), that the discovery of a "trattato col Visconti contro lo stato di Parte Guelfa" gave the Albizzi their opportunity, is not supported by other accounts.
⁶ Florence to Perugia, 23 March 1394: Azzi Vitelleschi, *op. cit.* i 214, no. 803.

be said that we send you to defame the Count of Vertus, nor to instil in them suspicion or jealousy of his power. And if you should happen to have occasion to speak of him, always do so honourably, and as of a brother."[1] They sent envoys to Biordo Michelotti and his fellow-Condottieri in July, to ask them not to invade the territories of Pisa or Siena, "for the rumour and slander will run through Tuscany, that we have sent them upon those lands".[2] When they heard a report that the real intention of the Companies was "to pass into Lombardy against the Count of Vertus", their alarm knew no bounds. "For we see that they do this, not for gain nor to offend the Count, for they should do him little harm and would receive not less than they did [a tribute to the security which the government of the Visconti ensured to its subjects] but only to provoke a war between him and us. And they could not do anything which would more greatly displease all the allies, and in particular the Bolognese and ourselves."[3] Giangaleazzo, for his part, seconded the efforts of the Florentines. He forwarded to the government of Siena the complaints which he had received of them from Florence in August 1394, "begging you entirely to refrain from offending the Florentines and their subjects, so that the incidents, which arise on all sides and continually foment bad feeling, may be averted".[4] On receiving the assurances of the Sienese, however, he permitted himself to indicate his real feelings about Florence. "Let your neighbours invent what they please, according to their wonted custom. But since what was told to us about you is entirely imaginary,...then show a calm mind, and take no heed of such studied fabrications."[5]

The mutual show of goodwill was, in fact, only superficial. An undercurrent of suspicion and intrigue flowed beneath the exchange of friendly courtesies. Giangaleazzo and the Florentines were equally anxious to avoid a war; and this fact explains the peculiar relations which existed between them in these years—secret efforts to embarrass the enemy and gain a little ground, but

[1] Commission of 4 March 1393/4: *ASF*, Signoria, Legazioni I 2 & t.
[2] Commission of 19 July 1394: *ibid.* 23.
[3] Commission of 16 August 1394: *ibid.* 29.
[4] Giangaleazzo to Siena, 12 August 1394; *ASS*, Concistoro 1834, no. 48.
[5] The same, 4 September 1394: *ibid.* no. 58.

immediate disavowal when these plans were brought to light. Milanese agents were discovered by Florence to be engaged in intrigues in Pistoia, the key to the western pass over the Apennines to Bologna.[1] On the other hand, the remnants of the Gambacorta family had found refuge in Florentine territory, and gave Appiano no peace.[2] The lord of Pisa had to ask for troops from Siena in September 1393, "on account of the disturbance which recently broke out here".[3]

There was in fact no real feeling of security in Tuscany. The terms of the peace for the restoration of lands had still to be fulfilled, and exiles sheltering in neighbouring territory constantly disturbed the borders with their raids.[4] The occasional invasions of the Companies from the south brought further recriminations. Giangaleazzo had engaged the Condottiere Broglia by means of a "condotta in aspetto", the payment of a retaining fee, usually at half the wartime rate, which left the soldier free to pursue his own affairs until summoned to serve with a full "condotta". Broglia led his Company into Tuscany from the south towards the end of 1394, and both Florence and Perugia believed that he came "a petizione del Conte di Vertù".[5] When Broglia descended upon the Aretine fortress of Gargonza, and

---

[1] Florence to Giangaleazzo, 16 January 1393: Novati, "Aneddoti Viscontei", *ASL* xxxv, 2, 203–4, and 205 note 2. In this respect, it is perhaps significant to find that, on 5 December 1392, Giangaleazzo wrote to Siena that "Egregius miles dominus Rafetus de Marocellis nunc Pistorii potestas devotus amicus et servitor noster" was shortly due to vacate that office, and recommended the Sienese to take him into their service: *ASS*, Concistoro 1832, nos. 37–8 (two copies). Marocelli had been Podestà of Como in 1388, of Piacenza in 1389. He was a citizen of Ferrara: Boselli, *Storie Piacentine*, II 65.
[2] This is admitted even by Florentine writers: Minerbetti, "Cronica", 186; Morelli, "Ricordi", *DET* xix 5.
[3] Appiano to Siena, 20 September 1393: *ASS*, Concistoro 1833, no. 65. Cf. Roncioni, "Istorie Pisane", *ASI* vi, 1, 957–8.
[4] This is clear, for example, from two commissions issued to Florentine envoys, the first going to Siena on 21 March 1393/4, the second to Pisa on 19 July 1394, to answer the grievances and complaints of these two neighbours: *ASF*, Signoria, Legazioni I 6t–8, and 24–25t.
[5] Minerbetti, "Cronica", 189; Pellini, *op. cit.* II 67. Giangaleazzo, writing to Siena on 4 September 1394, referred to the release from captivity of "dilecti nostri domini Brolie et Caporalium suorum": *ASS*, Concistoro 1834, no. 58.

captured it early in the new year, the Florentines prepared to drive him out by force, and wrote in angry protest to Pavia, declaring that Giangaleazzo had guaranteed the immunity of their lands from the Condottiere's attacks. Their resolute attitude procured for once Giangaleazzo's effective intervention, and Broglia withdrew from Gargonza.[1] In this instance, it may be true that Giangaleazzo had prompted Broglia to distract the attention of the Florentines from his own plans in Lombardy;[2] but very little control could be exercised over the Companies, unless they were bound by a full "condotta"; they could be bought, and sometimes persuaded, but they obeyed no man's orders until they were fully paid.

The same rather disconnected efforts to score off the enemy without precipitating an open conflict were applied to the graver problems of Lombardy. The Florentines intervened in the valley of the Po with all the freedom which they so strongly resented in Giangaleazzo's relations with Tuscany; and the effectiveness of their intervention shows how little confidence the Count had in the strength of his own position. His first task was to weaken the influence which the Florentines had gained over his eastern neighbours.

In 1393 occurred the incident which was known as the "fatto del Mencio". The desertion of Gonzaga, in whose devotion Giangaleazzo had had great confidence, was a bitter pill for him. In view of the bellicose attitude adopted by the lord of Mantua, the Count set his engineers to construct a dike at Valleggio, south of Lake Garda, and a new channel to convey the Mincio through Villafranca into the Adige, diverting its course from the city and lakes of Mantua. By closing the dike, he would be able to make Mantua uninhabitable.[3] The members of the League met in Ferrara at the end of April 1393 to discuss the matter;[4] and the

---

[1] Novati, "Frammento di Zibaldone Cancelleresco", *ASL* XL, 2, 307–11, and 287–8, Doc. 26. For the gravity of the situation, *v.* Guasti, *Ser Lapo Mazzei*, II 219–20, no. 444.

[2] As is stated by Bruni, "Historiarum Florentini Populi", *RIS* NS XIX, 3, 266; and Malavolti, *Historia de' Sanesi*, II 180 & t.

[3] Corio, *op. cit.* II 371. "Chronicon Estense", *RIS* XV 529 D–530 A.

[4] "Chronicon Estense", *RIS* XV 530 B–C.

Florentine delegates went on to Pavia, to lodge a protest with Giangaleazzo in the name of Gonzaga and his allies. Giangaleazzo's ambassadors delivered his answer to Florence in June. The works at Valleggio were within his rights according to the peace of Genoa, as the Florentine jurists had to admit. They were an answer to Gonzaga's military preparations, the building of the bridge at Borgoforte and the concentration of troops at Mantua; but the Count was prepared to suspend the work, if Gonzaga reduced his army and gave adequate guarantees for the safety of Milanese territory.[1]

Gonzaga was prepared to settle the matter by force of arms, and he was supported by Francesco Carrara, impatient at the heavy indemnity which he had to pay yearly to Milan; but the Florentines held them both in check.[2] The discussions went on, but neither side was prepared to accept the other's terms. The Florentines suggested that the allies should take an oath, guaranteed by the Pope or the King of France, not to use the bridge of Borgoforte for purposes of aggression against the Count. In May 1394, as Giangaleazzo was not disposed to accept these terms, they made an effort to have the whole dispute referred to the arbitration of Venice.[3]

Giangaleazzo was certainly aware that the decision of the *Serenissima* would not be favourable to him; and it is noteworthy that this was the occasion on which he spoke to Rinaldo Gianfigliazzi, one of the Florentine ambassadors, of becoming master of the whole of Lombardy. But from this moment, the question of the Mincio ceased to disturb the minds of the allies. There is no reason to accept the assertion of a later Mantuan chronicler, that the works at Valleggio were completed, but that the force of the river swept the structure away.[4] A Ferrarese chronicle suggests,

[1] Minerbetti, "Cronica", 174–5.
[2] Pastorello, *Nuove Ricerche*, 84–7.
[3] The commission to Rinaldo Gianfigliazzi and Lodovico Albergotti, "ambasciadori al conte di Virtù", 29 April 1394: *ASF*, Signoria, Legazioni I 14t–16t.
[4] Platina, "Historia Urbis Mantue", *RIS* xx 759–60, under a later year; Verci, *Storia della Marca Trivigiana*, xvii 189. This story probably arose from a confusion with the fate of a later project, the diversion of the Brenta in 1402.

perhaps with good reason, that technical or financial difficulties proved insurmountable.[1] Giangaleazzo himself had assured the Florentines, according to their own words, that "the question of this undertaking on the Mincio must not disturb the peace, or be a cause of discord between him and us";[2] and the persistence of the allies probably helped to avert the danger. That the Florentines themselves believed this, is evident from the curious message which they sent to the Ferrarese government in August 1394, when, as this document tells us, negotiations were still proceeding in Florence. "While the Count abstains from the work, as he still does, this is what we are striving for. And it is a great honour for the League, that so great a lord should abandon his course in the middle of the work, and that from the time of our first embassy he has made no addition to an undertaking launched within his own lands, and begun at such great cost and with such elaborate preparation. It is much better to spend the time in embassies, than to break off negotiations and embark on a war, which would involve more expense every day, than these embassies cost in a year."[3]

Events in Ferrara may also have served to divert Giangaleazzo's attention from the "fatto del Mencio". Alberto d'Este died in July 1393, and left as heir his nine-year-old son, Niccolò. The youth of the new ruler encouraged the nobles of the *Modenese* openly to defy the government, and produced a rival claimant in the person of Azzone d'Este, a distant cousin whose father had found shelter in exile at the Visconti court. Giangaleazzo had no open dealings with the rebels;[4] but he followed the development of the rebellion with close interest and gave what secret encouragement he could. The Regents of the young prince openly accused the Count of supporting their enemies;[5] but both Florence

---

[1] "Quod efficere non potuit": "De Rebus Estensium", in *Monumenta Ferrariensis Historie*: *Scriptores*, fasc. 2, 48.

[2] The commission to Gianfigliazzi and Albergotti, cit.: *ASF*, Signoria, Legazioni I 14 t.

[3] Commission of 16 August 1394: *ibid*. 30 t. Sandri's article (*v*. p. 388, *infra*), which I have not seen, may throw fresh light on this incident.

[4] Delayto, in his long account of these events, only once mentions help received by the rebels from Giangaleazzo: *RIS* XVIII 913 A–B.

[5] Roberto Cessi, "Venezia neutrale", *NAV* NS XXVIII 276-7.

and Venice were more cautious, only commenting upon the remarkable strength of Azzone's forces.[1] Giangaleazzo in fact did not wish to give flagrant offence to the Venetians; and the rebels had to rely mainly on the neighbourly jealousies of Emilia and Romagna for support. The Regents of Ferrara, aided by Florence and Bologna with the full co-operation of Venice, were able to repel the danger; and Azzone d'Este, unable to secure adequate assistance from Milan, was defeated and captured in April 1395.[2]

The prestige of Venice availed to keep the peace. The Venetians kept as much in the background as possible, alike over the Mincio and over Ferrara.[3] They strongly opposed the suggestion that Giangaleazzo should be admitted to the League of Bologna;[4] but they quietly evaded the traps which were set to induce them to join the League.[5] On one occasion, the Florentines secretly proposed that the lords of Mantua, Ferrara and Padua should send messengers to Venice to say that the Florentines and Bolognese had decided to enter into a League with the Count, rather than make war on him, and that therefore the three "Signorotti" were themselves likely to be "constrained to make alliance with the Count, which they do with more ill-will than they can say";[6] but the Venetians were too wily to allow such manœuvres as this to force their hand.

The Florentines, indeed, were envious of the *Serenissima*'s freedom to accept or refuse responsibilities; but the Venetians were determined to fight Giangaleazzo with his own weapons, coming out into the open only when they could not avoid it. They were none the less aware of the Count's private hopes and

[1] The Venetian allegations, 9 and 24 February 1395: *ibid.* 282 note 1; Benvenuto Cessi, *Venezia e Padova e il Polesine di Rovigo*, 60–1 and 64. Florence to Giangaleazzo, 4 February 1395: Novati, "Frammento di Zibaldone Cancelleresco", *ASL* xl, 2, 310.

[2] The fullest account is in Delayto, "Annales Estenses", *RIS* xviii. Also Benvenuto Cessi, *Venezia e Padova*, 50–62; Roberto Cessi, "Venezia neutrale", *NAV* NS xxviii 276–83.

[3] Roberto Cessi, *ibid.* 261 and note 1, 277–8.

[4] Benvenuto Cessi, *Venezia e Padova*, 57 note 2.

[5] Roberto Cessi, "Venezia neutrale", *NAV* NS xxviii 260, note 3, and 270 and note 1.

[6] Commission of 10 April 1394: *ASF*, Signoria, Legazioni i 8 t.

ambitions. He was in close contact with the enemies of John of Moravia, the Patriarch of Aquileia; and when the Moravian's stormy rule ended with his assassination in October 1394, the instigators of the murder appealed for the powerful protection of Milan.[1] Giangaleazzo advanced his own candidate for the see of Aquileia;[2] and the government of Bologna, prompted through Carrara by Venice, wrote in alarm to Rome, exposing to Boniface IX Giangaleazzo's determination to set foot in Friuli in order to gain control of the passes of the Alps, and begging him not to appoint a nominee of Milan to the Patriarchate.[3] The Pope's final choice fell upon a candidate who favoured neither Milan nor Venice, and therefore pleased the citizens of Friuli, who treasured their independence.[4]

Giangaleazzo had too much respect for the power of Venice, to offer excessive provocation either in Mantua, Ferrara, or Friuli. He waited patiently upon the French; and when the negotiations at Paris came to a standstill, he had not yet succeeded in breaking through the ring of his enemies. He had, however, made a beginning. The onslaughts of Azzone d'Este had shaken the government of Ferrara, and the Regents of Niccolò had been forced to pledge the Polesine di Rovigo to Venice in return for a loan. The Venetians thus gained control of the important district lying between the estuaries of the Po and the Adige; but they lost the confidence of the Ferrarese, who resented the alienation of their territory and the constant interference of Venetian agents in the affairs of their state.[5]

It was by such incidents as these that Giangaleazzo hoped eventually to break the unity of his enemies; but the process of disintegration was a very slow one, and meanwhile Giangaleazzo was left without an active and coherent policy. The spasmodic and disconnected character of his relations with the Italian

---

[1] Roberto Cessi, "Venezia neutrale", *NAV* NS xxviii 263–4. The Udinesi to Giangaleazzo (undated): Verci, *op. cit.* xvii, Doc. 1954, pp. 81–2.

[2] Cusin, *Confine Orientale d'Italia*, i 196.

[3] Zambeccari, "Epistolario", 150–6, nos. 134–40; and 159, no. 143.

[4] Roberto Cessi, "Venezia neutrale", *NAV* NS xxviii 266–8.

[5] *Ibid.* 283–4. Benvenuto Cessi, *Venezia e Padova*, 64–78, gives details of the new régime in the Polesine.

states in the years after the peace of Genoa is accounted for by the nature of his task, which was disruptive rather than constructive.

The lack of progress in Lombardy and Tuscany, and the failure of his negotiations with France, impelled Giangaleazzo to look for help in other directions. He had in any case to keep close watch on the relations of the League with the powers north of the Alps. He had friends not only in the *Trentino* but in the upper valley of the Rhine, where the Bishop of Chur and the lord of Sargans both received pensions from him;[1] but the decisive factor in this district was the will of the Habsburgs, for whom it was of the first importance as a link between their lands in the Tyrol and in Suabia,[2] and whose influence steadily expanded alike in the Grisons as in the *Trentino*.[3] George of Liechtenstein, the new Bishop of Trent, received the willing homage of the Guelfs of the district, and encouraged them to resume their struggle with the Ghibellines, who had taken allegiance to Giangaleazzo and defied the episcopal authority;[4] and the troubles spread from the Giudicarie to the *Bergamasco*, where the old party hatred was especially strong.[5] How far these conflicts brought Giangaleazzo into contact with Leopold of Austria, the nominal overlord of the Bishop of Trent, is not known;[6] but the League apparently hoped to make capital out of the disturbances, for Carrara approached the Habsburgs in 1393 with a proposal for a marriage alliance. The burdened treasury of Padua, however, could not endow Carrara's daughter on a scale worthy of the Dukes of Austria,

---

[1] Romano, "Regesto", *ASL* XXI, 2, 48, no. 120; 72, no. 257.

[2] Lichnowsky, *Geschichte des Hauses Habsburg* IV 194–200.

[3] *V.* the register of documents, *ibid.* passim; e.g., nos. 2279, 2380–1, 2493. Also Egger, *Geschichte Tirols*, I 443–4, 446; Huber, *Geschichte Oesterreichs*, II 485.

[4] Postinger, "Documenti in Volgare Trentino", *AAA* 3, VII 146–9.

[5] A particularly violent outbreak of the never entirely quiescent feuds in the Alps of the *Bergamasco* gave a great deal of trouble to the Visconti administrators during the summer of 1393: "Chronicon Bergomense", *RIS* XVI 862–86.

[6] For Leopold and the *Trentino* v. Postinger, *op. cit. AAA* 3, VII 137–9; Huber, *op. cit.* II 494–5.

and fortunately for Giangaleazzo the project was not pursued further.[1]

If the Habsburgs were important for their control of the Alpine passes, the Wittelsbachs were no less so on account of their relationship with Bernabò and with the French court. Giangaleazzo was anxious to settle his differences with them. He made new overtures to Carlo Visconti in 1393,[2] and arranged for the marriage of Carlo's sister Elisabetta, who was under his care at Pavia, to Ernest of Bavaria. The bride remained at Pavia for two or three years, however, while the Wittelsbachs quarrelled among themselves and around the person of the still uncrowned Emperor.[3]

Giangaleazzo's relations with the princes of Austria and Bavaria were natural offshoots of his general policy; but his relations with Wenceslaus assumed at this stage a more fundamental importance. The moment had come for a reconciliation. Ever since Bernabò's fall, Giangaleazzo had sought a nobler title for his great principality. The story of his early rebuff at the hands of Urban VI is supported by a Florentine document of 1389; the Florentine ambassadors in Rome had written that the Count's envoys were constantly with the Pope, offering an alliance and great sums of money in the name of their master, in the hope of obtaining from Urban "a just title for that which he holds, the more easily to make himself king".[4] After the capture of Verona he spoke, according to Minerbetti, of his ambition to assume the royal status of "Re de' Lombardi".[5] His regal ambitions were constantly denounced during the war.[6] Since Rome proved unfruitful, Giangaleazzo turned to Paris. In the four proposals

[1] Carrara to the Dukes of Austria, 19 April 1393: Lichnowsky, *op. cit.* IV 277, and no. 2331 of the documents. Florence to Carrara, 13 March 1393, thanking him for information "de adventu ducis Austrie": Pastorello, *Nuove Ricerche*, 212, Doc. 49. Carrara was also in touch with the Bishop of Chur and with Frederick of Oettingen: *ibid.* 211, Doc. 48.

[2] Romano, "Giangaleazzo Visconti", *ASL* XVIII 299–301.

[3] *Ibid.* 53–7, and 317, Doc. 10; *Id.* "Nuovi Documenti Viscontei", *ASL* XVI 307, and 337–8, Docs. 7–8.

[4] Commission for envoys to Bologna, 12 March 1388/9: *ASF*, Dieci di Balìa, Legazioni I 175.   [5] Minerbetti, "Cronica", 48.

[6] E.g. in the Florentine letter of 2 May 1390: *RIS* XVI 815–17. Florence to Armagnac, 22 January 1391: *ibid.* 818–20.

of alliance drawn up at Pavia between 1391 and 1394, he asked that, if the Clementist party should elect an Emperor of their own choice, the newly elect should be persuaded to confirm the authority of the Visconti in Lombardy and the Mark of Treviso "with that title of honour by which he may wish and require to be entitled".[1]

It was natural that Giangaleazzo, as the hopes of an agreement with France faded, should turn to Wenceslaus, in whose sole power lay the nominal bestowal of such honours as the Count sought. The Bishop of Novara, Pietro da Candia, arrived in Prague in February 1394, but the exact scope of his mission is not known. He found the affairs of the Reich in disorder, for Wenceslaus, in his love of wine and the chase, had allowed the government of Germany to disintegrate; and in August 1394 the King's friends had to take up arms to free him from the clutches of a coalition of discontented princes led by his brother Sigismund of Hungary.[2] But this state of affairs was Giangaleazzo's opportunity;[3] for friends and enemies alike agreed that Wenceslaus ought to go to Rome and be crowned Emperor by the Pope, as the first step towards the restoration of Imperial prestige.

Nevertheless, the Bishop of Novara did not have an easy task ahead of him. His difficulties were not created, however, by Florentine envoys who, as the old story ran, implored Wenceslaus to help the Republic.[4] Wenceslaus himself, still resentful of former wrongs received at the hands of the Count, invited the co-operation of Venice and Florence in his forthcoming journey to Italy. The answers of these governments were polite, but sceptical;[5] they had heard before of the King's projected corona-

---

[1] Mirot, *Politique française en Italie*, 51–2 clause 7 (1391); Jarry, *Vie Politique de Louis de France*, 421–2, clauses 6–7 (1392); *Id.* "Voie de Fait", *BEC* LIII 556–7, clauses 10–11 (1393), and 564–5, clauses 12–13 (1394).

[2] Lindner, "Geschichte des deutschen Reiches", II 193–202.

[3] *Ibid.* 330–2; Novati, "Aneddoti Viscontei", *ASL* XXXV, 2, 208–16.

[4] Corio, *op. cit.* II 394.

[5] Venice, when asked by Sigismund for "auxilium et favorem", replied that "inveniamur parati" when (which implied, if) the Emperor came: decision of the Senate, 6 September 1394, in *ASV*, Senato Secreta, E. 94. A similar answer was proposed in the Florentine Council, 22 September 1394: Jarry, *Origines*, 71 note 2.

tion journey. Wenceslaus persisted, however, and offered to make an alliance against Giangaleazzo, not only with Florence but with the lords of Mantua and Padua as well. It is certainly true that Carrara favoured the acceptance of these offers;[1] and their rejection, therefore, probably followed the advice given by the Florentines to their allies;[2] for the Florentine government decided for its own part, in March 1395, to remain true to the Guelf cause, and to reject the offer of an Imperial alliance.[3]

The way was thus made easy for Giangaleazzo by his enemies. The Bishop of Novara no doubt made it clear that, whatever differences Wenceslaus may have had with the Count, their mutual interests lay now in a close alliance. In January 1395 negotiations had already advanced so far that Giangaleazzo ordered the Imperial eagle to be quartered with the serpent of the Visconti in his armorial bearings upon all public buildings.[4] An intimate counsellor of the King of the Romans arrived in Prague from Lombardy during April;[5] he had probably discussed with Giangaleazzo all the questions which might arise from the plan which the Count had put forward. Wenceslaus was satisfied; on 11 May 1395, for the price of 100,000 florins,[6] he signed the papers which conferred upon Giangaleazzo the title of Duke of Milan.

[1] Pastorello, *Nuove Ricerche*, 89 and note 2.

[2] As related by Bruni, *op. cit. RIS* NS xix, 3, 265–6.

[3] Jarry, *Origines*, 286–8.

[4] Edict of 2 January 1395: Santoro, "Registri", 44, no. 223; "Chronicon Bergomense", *RIS* xvi 887.

[5] Lindner, "Geschichte des deutschen Reiches", ii 334, note 2.

[6] This is the generally accepted price: Romano, "Nuovi Documenti Viscontei", *ASL* xvi 312.

CHAPTER XIII

THE DUKE OF MILAN AND HIS COURT

THE Imperial representative invested Giangaleazzo with the insignia of his Ducal office, in the Square of St Ambrose in Milan on 5 September 1395. The occasion was marked by high pomp and ceremony, and accompanied by festivities which lasted for three or four days. Representatives came from all quarters of Italy and beyond, to offer the congratulations of princes and Republics to the new Duke; and Giangaleazzo, throwing care and economy to the winds, celebrated his elevation to high rank with an outburst of brilliant splendour.[1]

"The tyrant of Lombardy disappears; the legitimate prince and sovereign takes his place."[2] The Visconti had completed the stage of growth in their dynastic history, from elected governor to hereditary prince. The Commune of Milan had already recognized the right of succession in their family; the Imperial diploma consecrated the same right in the Ducal title. A new kind of state appeared in northern Italy—a state which took its place in the framework of the Holy Roman Empire, symbol of medieval traditions, but which was none the less representative of modern needs. The "Ducato" had a dual significance. It crowned the dynastic ambitions of the Visconti, raising them from the status of successful adventurers to the level of the greatest dignitaries of the Empire; and it gave to their state that sense of permanence and stability which was so grievously lacking in the political system of Italy.

Wenceslaus incurred the bitter reproaches of the German princes by alienating one of the largest and richest provinces of

---

[1] The accounts given in Corio, *Storia di Milano*, II 396–401, and in a contemporary letter published in *RIS* XVI 821–6, of the procession to St Ambrose, the coronation ceremony, and the feast and jousts which followed it, are of a rather formal nature, hardly worth repeating here. They are summarized in Visconti, *Storia di Milano*, 288–9.

[2] Romano, "Nuovi Documenti Viscontei", *ASL* XVI 312.

the Empire,[1] although the bond which he created was destined actually to strengthen the hands of the Emperors in their dealings with future Dukes of Milan.[2] The resentment of the Imperial Electors involved the Visconti and the Sforza in difficulties which began, even before Giangaleazzo's death, when the deposition of Wenceslaus raised the question of the validity of the new dignity. In spite of these drawbacks, however, Giangaleazzo could face his political task in Italy with renewed confidence and authority, now that the good pleasure of the Emperor could no longer deprive him of his juridical rights.

The transformation was even more notable within the dominion of the Visconti. The subject communities renewed their allegiance to Giangaleazzo,[3] but his own authority no longer depended on the confirmation of his subjects. When he died, his son's right of succession was recognized; there was no election, and the oath of allegiance was taken to the new Duke, as a sign that his authority was accepted. Only later in the fifteenth century did political circumstances counsel a return to the old custom of election.[4]

Other problems were to arise out of the new investiture; but they did not arise in the time of the first Duke. Giangaleazzo had appealed, from the threats and fear of violence and usurpation which hung over the political organization of Italy, to the old and decadent but traditional sovereignty of the Empire. In that transformation, the rights of the Communes and the freedom of the people disappeared. In the words of Professor Ercole, the cities no longer had rights to assert, but only privileges to beg for; there was no longer authority granted by the subjects, but only concessions granted by the ruler. The political system reverted in appearance to that of an age when the flowering of the Communal spirit had not yet come to revolutionize the earlier medieval conceptions of government.

[1] Lindner, "Geschichte des deutschen Reiches", II 332–3.
[2] Pieri, *Crisi militare italiana*, 137; Cusin, "Impero e la successione degli Sforza", *ASL* NS I 47–9.
[3] Giulini, *Memorie*, XI 583–4; Santoro, "Registri", 52–3 nos. 261–2.
[4] Ercole, *Dal Comune al Principato*, 304 note 2; Cusin, "Impero e la successione degli Sforza", *ASL* NS I 69–70.

Giangaleazzo, however, in seeking and accepting a feudal status in relation to the Emperor, was not a reactionary. It is a far cry from the investiture of 1395 to the unification of Italy, in the attainment of which a vitally important part has been claimed for the newly founded Lombard Duchy. But this much is true; that Giangaleazzo had planned on broad and thorough lines the completion of the work which his predecessors had less con-sciously begun—the effective unification of Lombardy under a strong centralized government; and Wenceslaus, whether he knew it or not, crowned the achievement of the Visconti in the creation of a new form of state in Italy, a phenomenon still imperfect in its institutions, functioning badly, unable to win the full co-operation of its subjects, and uncertain still of its own destiny; but certainly not without its influence in the shaping of the future.[1]

Giangaleazzo did not forget, amid the political advantages which he derived from his new title, that it represented at the same time the personal apotheosis of the Visconti. He secured from the Emperor in the following year the additional title of Count of Angera; and complacent genealogists proved his right to it by tracing the descent of the Visconti from the legendary founder of Angera, Anglus the grandson of Aeneas.[2] Giangaleazzo, not content with the recognition of the achievements of his family, felt the parvenu's need to acquire a fictitious nobility of birth and antiquity of descent; logical and far-sighted as he was, he was bound by the conceptions and prejudices of his contemporaries.

Giangaleazzo was nearly forty-four years old, when the dignity of Duke of Milan was conferred upon him. A miniature, which was drawn within the next ten years, depicts the ceremony. We may imagine that the Duke's physical appearance had now assumed the character which is familiar to us in the surviving representations of him. He seems to have grown rather stout,

---

[1] Visconti, *Storia di Milano*, 287. The juridical aspects of the ducal investiture are discussed by Ercole, *Dal Comune al Principato*, 295–311; Cusin, "Impero e la successione degli Sforza", *ASL* NS i 46–50.

[2] Visconti, *Storia di Milano*, 242.

but the heavy jowl does not detract from the keen intelligence of the face.

Valentina had long since gone to France, and Blanche of Savoy had died in 1388. The Duke's household consisted of his wife and their two sons, together with those of Caterina's sisters who were still unmarried. His sons, Giovanni Maria and Filippo Maria, were born in 1388 and 1392. Nothing is known of their early youth, save that the elder frequently resided in Milan, to please the Milanese; he had a household of his own in the capital under his mother's supervision.[1] On one occasion, we find Caterina sending Giovanni Casate—who later met his death in her service—to Melegnano, for the care of her sons.[2]

Giangaleazzo continued to occupy the palace of Pavia, and his visits to Milan were rare. He made regular seasonal expeditions to his country residences—Melegnano, Abbiategrasso, Sant' Angelo, Belgioioso and Cusago—and, when an outbreak of plague in Pavia forced him to leave the district for a while, would go to Lodi. Although he continued to direct the affairs of state while he was away from Pavia, these expeditions were mainly devoted to hunting; and, as in the time of Bernabò before and of Filippo Maria after him, many decrees were passed to define the territories and the beasts reserved for the Duke's chase, and heavy penalties imposed on those who outraged his privileges.

If Giangaleazzo did not forget to protect his private interests, his administration remained on the whole faithful to the ideas which he had laid down in the early years of his reign. The new statutes of Milan, closely resembling the earlier revisions of the fourteenth century,[3] came into force in 1396. The work of revising the statutes of the other Communes went on steadily;[4] and

[1] Answer of the Venetian Senate in 1392 to a request that Giangaleazzo might be allowed to buy silver in Venice for the young prince's household: Roberto Cessi, "Venezia neutrale", *NAV* NS xxviii 237 note 2. Caterina referred by name, in a letter written in 1396, to the Seneschal of Giovanni Maria's household: Santoro, "Registri", 61, no. 314.

[2] 26 April 1394: *ibid.* 40–1, no. 204.

[3] The resemblance of the Statutes of 1396 to the earlier codes of 1330 and 1351, which have not survived, was proved by Lattès, "Antichi Statuti di Milano", in *Rendiconti del R. Istituto Lombardo*, 2, xxix 1056–83.

[4] Besides the revised Statutes of Milan, those of Cremona, revised in 1388, were published in 1578, of Lodi in 1390 (published in 1537), of Piacenza, an

although the new editions introduced no radical changes, they reveal that there were in many cases striking similarities between the codes of the different cities.

The chief themes of administrative reform—the activities of the outlaws, the building of fortresses, the carrying of arms, the protection of the interests of the "Camera", the abuse of power by officials of the government—all these recur between the years 1392–1396. An edict of 1388 for the proper care of the mentally deficient had to be repeated because it had been largely ignored. Particularly severe punishments were decreed in 1393 against the perpetrators of certain major criminal offences. The feudal nobility were forbidden to give shelter to refugees from justice, and no privilege of exemption was henceforth to absolve them from the task of helping officials in the performance of their duties.[1] But the repetition of old edicts, accompanied in many cases by an increase in the sentence to which offenders were liable, reveals the difficulty which Giangaleazzo experienced in enforcing the law. The wisdom of his policy did not carry conviction to those against whom his edicts were directed; and this constant renewal of decrees bears witness to the difficulty of detecting offenders and bringing them to justice. A detailed examination of Giangaleazzo's policy reveals that, in spite of the firm control which he established over the administrative system of the Communes, he could not put into practice with any completeness the theories of government which undoubtedly underlay his conception of the state. The difficulty was perhaps primarily due to the state's need for money; and particularly in the later years of his reign, when, as we shall see, the financial

apparently unaltered re-issue of an earlier Code, published in 1860, of Pavia (published in 1590), of the Riviera di Garda published by Bettoni, *Storia della Riviera di Salò*, III 204–65, no. 107. The revised Statutes of Brescia came into force in 1385 (Lattès, *Diritto Consuetudinario*, 15); of Verona in 1393 (Galli, "Dominazione Viscontea a Verona", *ASL* LIV 502); of Reggio in 1392 (Grimaldi, *Signoria di Barnabò Visconti*, 81); of Pontremoli in 1391 (Sforza, *Storia di Pontremoli*, 285–6); of Voghera in 1391 (Manfredi, *Storia di Voghera*, 209); of Bobbio in 1398 (Lattès, *Studii di Diritto Statutario*, 96–7). A detailed comparison of these Codes, together with those of other states of the same period, and with the earlier Statutes of the Communal age, should offer scope for some interesting conclusions.

[1] All these edicts may be found in *Antiqua Decreta*, 164–214.

strain increased, Giangaleazzo had to seize whatever opportunities offered, to follow the pressing demands of the moment, to bow before the dictates of economic necessity.[1]

The dangers which accompanied a centralization of government were illustrated by the loss of Padua and the revolt of Verona in 1390. The central government was too remote to exercise much control in these cities, and the corrupt administration of its officials prepared the way for Carrara's return.[2] Giangaleazzo therefore appointed a special Council at Verona in 1392, for his lands east of the Mincio, with full competence to deal with matters which would otherwise have been referred to Milan. A special "master of the entries" supervised financial business;[3] but the "Camera" at Milan, which had acquired from Giangaleazzo's financial reforms a greater integration than the other branches of the Council, continued to exercise supreme control, and it was the Council of Milan which had to unravel the disorders of Communal finance at Belluno in 1401.[4] For the rest, the new Council had the same powers as that of Milan, in disposing of matters which were brought before it, and in transmitting to Pavia the more important business which was outside its control.[5] The new system relieved the congestion at Milan and Pavia, and saved time and trouble for the inhabitants of Giangaleazzo's remoter dominions; and the Council of Verona survived until the Visconti lost possession of the lands east of the Mincio.

Although Giangaleazzo made it as easy as possible for his subjects to gain a hearing, he himself remained remote in his glory, and increasingly difficult to approach. A member of Francesco Sforza's household, who no doubt derived his information from those who remembered the days of the first Duke, has

---

[1] Cf. Ciapessoni, "Per la Storia della Economia", *BSP* vi 396–7.

[2] Pastorello, *Nuove Ricerche*, 54–8.

[3] The first "Maestro delle entrate" at Verona was Lucotto Roncarolo: Verci, *Storia della Marca Trivigiana*, xvii, Doc. 1946, p. 70; Romano, "Regesto", *ASL* xxi, 2, 25 no. 17.

[4] Pellegrini, "Documenti Inediti", *AIV* 3, xiii 1636–8, no. 59.

[5] Giangaleazzo to Belluno, 24 August 1392, announcing the creation of the Council: Verci, *op. cit.* xvii, Doc. 1946, pp. 70–1. Galli, "Dominazione Viscontea a Verona", *ASL* liv 499–500; Comani, "Usi Cancellereschi Viscontei", *ASL* xxvii, 1, 396–7.

recorded that it was only with the greatest difficulty that one could procure an interview with him.[1] He seems to have withdrawn more and more within the intimate circle of his court. Advisers of every kind, indeed, surrounded him. The most distinguished of them were still Pietro da Candia the churchman, Niccolò Spinelli the statesman, Jacopo dal Verme the soldier, and Niccolò Diversi the financier. All these, at one time or another, were also engaged on diplomatic missions for the Duke. But closest of all to him was his confidential secretary, Pasquino Capelli, through whose trusted hands all the routine business of politics and administration passed. Those who desired an audience with the Duke first consulted the secretary.[2] Business which was brought to Giangaleazzo himself would be dismissed with a "speak to Pasquino about that".[3] Pasquino does not appear to have concerned himself with political questions, but was content to be an excellent servant, quiet, discreet and able—a man who performed his own complicated duties efficiently, and did not interfere in matters outside his province. Nevertheless, his friendship was not to be despised, for much was left to his discretion, and his power in the court was far from negligible. He was, as Minerbetti justly wrote, "fattore e ordinatore di tutte le sue cose".[4]

There are symptoms, however, that Pasquino's authority had begun to decline. The Sienese envoys who arrived at Pavia in June 1395 asked Francesco Barbavara to secure an audience for them with the Duke. Giangaleazzo still answered some of their requests by telling them that "we should confer with Pasquino about those matters, and he would give despatch to our business";[5] but it is significant that they should look elsewhere for

---

[1] "Al quale era grande maistro chi gli parlava": quoted by Magenta, *Visconti e Sforza*, i 293 note 5.

[2] *V.* Docs. 8 and 9. Examples could be multiplied, for Pasquino's name constantly appears in despatches from Pavia at this period, as receiving the requests of envoys or expounding Giangaleazzo's intentions to them: v., for example, Doc. 1.

[3] Report presented by Florentine envoys to Pavia, 22 September 1395: "Disse [Giangaleazzo] volerlo fare, et che n'enformassimo Pasquino." *ASF*, Signoria, Rapporti i 2.

[4] Minerbetti, "Cronica", 282.   [5] *V.* Doc. 11.

the most certain means of approaching the Duke. Our first notice
of Francesco Barbavara of Novara is in a document which he
witnessed, as Chamberlain of the Count, in January 1391;[1] but
we already find, later in the same year, that his advice was sought
by those who wished to have audience of the Count,[2] and he
appears at the same time as an adviser on the feminine side of
Giangaleazzo's household.[3] He acted during the following years
in many minor matters to which the Count could not attend
personally;[4] and in January 1395 he received the unusual power
to grant all lands and property of Giangaleazzo in fee in the
Count's name, "as and to whom he please".[5] In the following
year, he laid one of the foundation stones of the Certosa of
Pavia in the name of Filippo Maria Visconti, then only four
years old.[6]

Barbavara's relations with Giangaleazzo were on a different
footing from those of Pasquino. The latter's connection with his
master seems never to have exceeded the bounds of his duties.
Barbavara, in his office of Chamberlain, had a closer, more
personal contact with Giangaleazzo in the domestic life of the
court. The Milanese chronicle declares that he was of low birth;[7]
he was certainly ambitious, and succeeded in gaining the Duke's
confidence, gradually establishing himself as a kind of Ducal
favourite, an indispensable counsellor and friend such as Pasquino
had never been.

These two men were Giangaleazzo's closest political associates.
They were both natives of Lombardy, whom he preferred to
place in his administration; for he stated, in an edict of 1392, that
"we have decided to fill our offices with our own citizens and
subjects, rather than with foreigners".[8] At his council-table, on

---

[1] "Francisco de barbavariis de Novaria eiusdem domini Camerario":
ASS, Capitoli, vol. 103, p. 4 t.   [2] *V. supra*, p. 42.

[3] As a member of the "conscilium muliebrem": *v.* Doc. 6.

[4] Romano, "Regesto", *ASL* xxi, 2, passim (cf. Romano's index on p. 322).

[5] *Ibid.* 28, no. 28.

[6] Beltrami, "Storia documentata della Certosa di Pavia", 60–3.

[7] "Hominem satis parve conditionis": "Annales Mediolanenses", *RIS*
xvi 839; accepted by Maiocchi, "Francesco Barbavara", *MSI* xxxv 259.

[8] 28 November 1392: Pellegrini, "Documenti Inediti", *AIV* 3, xiii
1304–5, no. 12.

the other hand, sat men from every quarter of Italy: Bevilacqua and Malaspina, the Veronese exiles whom he had befriended; Diversi from Lucca and Spinelli from the "Regno"; Paolo Savelli of Rome, the Papal nuncio Carlo Brancacci Count of Campagna, and Baldassare Spinola of Genoa. Many others entered his service; there were the Agnelli and della Rocca from Pisa, the Angevin Louis of Montjoie, the Scrovegni of Padua, the anti-Spanish exiles from Sicily.[1] These men were the instruments of his policy and his ambition—attracted by promises, by persuasion, by the magic of his political vision, to serve his ends.

They were not alone among the distinguished men whom Giangaleazzo attracted to his court. The Duke of Milan was a loadstone, drawing to himself every talent. Although the political situation increasingly occupied his attention, he found the means, in his enhanced glory, to satisfy the respect for learning and the love of the arts which had been bred in him by his parents.

Galeazzo had founded the University of Pavia, and his son proposed to raise its prestige to rival that of Bologna and the other great centres of learning in Italy. He secured special privileges from Boniface IX,[2] and decreed that none of his subjects should study at any other University.[3] The merits of the professors who taught at Pavia have aroused controversy.[4] They cannot for the most part be reckoned among the band of eager scholars who already heralded the revival of classical learning; but there can be no doubt that Giangaleazzo gave every encouragement to the University, and that his careful promotion of its welfare paved the way for the greater glory which it attained in the following century. The University, moreover, served his purpose well. Under the impetus which he gave to it, the faculty of law had

---

[1] The significance of this gathering of Italians at the Lombard court was emphasized by Romano, "Visconti e la Sicilia", *ASL* XXIII, 1, 42–3.

[2] Maiocchi, *Codice Diplomatico dell' Università di Pavia*, I 160–3, nos. 316–17.

[3] In 1392: Osio, *Documenti Diplomatici*, I 305–6, no. 213. A similar decree, less well known, was issued by Galeazzo in 1375: Maiocchi, *Codice*, I 36, no. 46.

[4] The University was judged "riluttante ad accogliere il nuovo avviamento degli studi" by Rossi, "Grammatico Cremonese a Pavia", *BSP* I 39. Cf. the defence of the University by Corbellini, "Appunti sull' Umanesimo", *BSP* XV 342–5.

already taken the lead which it maintained under the Sforza. The civil servants of the time generally held a legal qualification, and Giangaleazzo provided for their training within close reach of his court, by summoning the great jurist Baldo Ubaldi from Perugia to hold the chair of civil law at Pavia.[1] Giangaleazzo stood godfather to Baldo's children,[2] and always showed the greatest consideration for him.[3] The story of Baldo's rivalry with a native professor of civil law, each one striving to secure the bigger attendance at his own lectures,[4] offers an interesting, though not unusual, sidelight on the University life of the time.

Giangaleazzo encouraged other leading scholars to come to his court. Giovanni da Ravenna, a contemporary humanist, praised the generosity, "surpassing that of all others", which he showed to men of learning;[5] and Pier Paolo Vergerio, certainly no friend of the Duke, wrote of him as one who "had no less the will than the means to decorate with honours and load with rewards men who were worthy of them".[6] Poggio, who was not a contemporary of the Duke, added a later tribute. "But this virtue is above all others praiseworthy in him, that he gathered to himself, as though a harbour for the famous, men skilled in all learning and art, and held them in high honour."[7] Giangaleazzo welcomed Manuel Chrysoloras, the Greek teacher, when he came to Pavia in 1400, and addressed him as "egregium familiarem nostrum, dilectum dominum".[8] Marsiglio di Santa Sofia, esteemed as one of the leading physicians of the day, taught medicine at the University, and attended on the Duke himself.[9] Coluccio Salu-

---

[1] Pellini, *Historia di Perugia*, II 121–2; Magenta, *op. cit.* I 253.
[2] Romano, "Regesto", *ASL* XXI, 2, 27–33, nos. 23, 34, 54.
[3] Cf. Giangaleazzo's letter to Baldo, February 1399: Del Giudice, *Nuovi studi*, 284 note 1.
[4] Besta, *Contributi alla Storia dell' Università di Pavia*, 266.
[5] Sabbadini, *Giovanni da Ravenna*, 191.
[6] Letter to Chrysoloras: Vergerio, "Epistolario", 239–40.
[7] Poggio, "Historia Florentina", *RIS* XX 290 D–291 A.
[8] Osio, *op. cit.* I 369–71, no. 245; Chrysoloras came to Pavia to help the Byzantine Emperor in his appeal for aid against the Turks, and stayed there from 1400 to 1403. Corbellini, *op. cit. BSP* XVII 5–51, has shown that there is no foundation for the tradition that he held a Chair at the University of Pavia. For his importance in the revival of Greek learning: Sozomeno, "Specimen Historie", *RIS* XVI 1168 E–1169 A.
[9] Landogna, "Maestro Marsiglio di Santa Sofia", *BSP* XXXIII 175–85.

tati, the secretary of the Florentine Republic and the first
humanist of the period, numbered among his correspondents
Giangaleazzo's secretaries Andreolo Arese, Pasquino Capelli and
Antonio Loschi. Although Loschi and Salutati embarked on a
bitter polemic over the political rivalries of those whom they
served, in times of peace the solidarity of humanistic scholarship
overrode political differences and enmities, and they exchanged
notes on the common ground of newly discovered manuscripts
and other academic topics of vital interest.[1]

The library at Pavia, which ministered to the intellectual
needs of these scholars, continued to expand. Giangaleazzo and
his family were indefatigable in the collection of books. Even
the fruits of conquest found an honoured place in the conqueror's
palace; and it was in this way that a number of volumes which
had belonged to Petrarch were brought from Padua, and remained
in the Visconti library until it was dispersed.[2]

Giangaleazzo wished his possessions to be beautiful, and
miniaturists were constantly at work, embellishing the volumes
in the library.[3] Their work bears many points of resemblance
to that of the contemporary French school which used the style
known as the "ouvraige de Lombardie", but artistic opinion is
not unanimous in attributing the original inspiration either to
Italy or to France.[4] The most notable of these artists working
at Pavia were Michelino da Besozzo and Giovannino da Grassi,
whom tradition has named as masters of a school of art and
sculpture founded by Giangaleazzo in the palace itself. The tradition can be traced back only as far as the seventeenth century, and
sprang perhaps from the knowledge that a school of artists and
sculptors grew up at this moment in Lombardy; but it is certain

[1] Novati, "Aneddoti Viscontei", *ASL* xxxv, 2, 205–6.
[2] Magenta, *op. cit.* I 226–34. For the acquisitions from Verona and Padua:
Schmidt, "Visconti und ihre Bibliothek", in *Zeitschrift für Geschichte und
Politik*, v 452–6; and de Nolhac, *Pétrarque et l'humanisme*, 84–9.
[3] Toesca, *Pittura e Miniatura nella Lombardia*, 279–328.
[4] Articles of Bouchot and Toesca in *l'Arte*, viii 18–32, and 321–39; of
Durrieu on Michelino da Besozzo, in *Mémoires de l'Académie des Inscriptions
et Belles-Lettres*, xxxviii, 2, 365–93; and of Toesca, "Ancora della Pittura",
in *l'Arte*, xvi 136–40.

that this artistic development owed much to Giangaleazzo's steady patronage and encouragement.[1]

Architects, sculptors and engineers had gathered at Milan for the tremendous work involved in the construction of the Duomo. It may be accepted now that the erection of the new cathedral sprang directly from the impulse of the Archbishop and people of Milan; but, in moments of doubt and difficulty, the civic committee appointed to supervise the construction invariably turned to the Prince for help and counsel.[2] The plans of the building were drawn up by a group of local architects—Simone Orsenigo, Marco da Carona, and above all the school of the Campionesi. They were sculptors first and foremost, and their architectural qualifications were frequently called in question, not only by the citizens who had entrusted the work to them, but by the French and German architects who came to share their labours, and who were horrified by what they saw. It has been suggested that Giangaleazzo, conscious of the faults of the original construction, sided with these critics; but that is perhaps to make too much of his desire to be impartial.[3] He appointed his own architect, Bernardo da Venezia, to plan for him the Certosa of Pavia; but at the same time he called three leading architects from Milan to consult with him; and one of them, Jacopo da Campione, remained attached to the construction of the Certosa until he was urgently summoned to resume his duties at the Duomo.[4] Giangaleazzo showed his confidence in the school which represented the achievements of Lombardy in the realms of sculpture and architecture.[5] These late Gothic sculptors, untouched as yet by the reversion to classicism, had been influenced by the earlier Tuscan school, whose pupils had been attracted to Verona in the

---

[1] Borsieri, *Supplimento della Nobiltà di Milano*, 57–8. Cf. Boito, *Duomo di Milano*, 145, for the value of Borsieri's statement.

[2] Visconti, *Storia di Milano*, 289.

[3] Anselmi, *Vero Origine del Duomo*, 16 and 39–43; Ceruti, *Principi del Duomo*, 56–7. Cf. Boito, *op. cit.* 155, 160–2, 164–8.

[4] Beltrami, *op. cit.* 69–72.

[5] For the architects and sculptors of Milan and Pavia, *v.* Calvi, *Notizie dei principali Architetti etc.*; and the works on the Duomo and Certosa, quoted above.

heyday of the Scaligers; their highest achievements are to be found in the work of Giovannino da Grassi.[1]

The decision to build a Carthusian monastery at Pavia received the approval of the Carthusian Order in 1394; but the foundation-stones were not laid until 1396. If the Duomo stood as a monument to the spirit of the Milanese people, the Certosa was a temple of the Visconti, destined to house the mortal remains of Giangaleazzo and his family, and to perpetuate his glory. The work lagged sadly, however, and when the Duke died the chapel had not begun to rise from its foundations.[2]

It was a symbolical failure. Giangaleazzo had planned a system of government, but he could not concentrate his resources on the task of making it secure and permanent. He was prepared to play the part of a Maecenas, in the true tradition of his house; he gathered around himself the talents which he required, but the material resources which he had intended to devote to their activities had finally to be diverted into other channels. The Ducal investiture was a recognition of the position achieved by the Visconti as rulers of an Italian princedom; but it brought no alleviation to Giangaleazzo in his struggle to confirm and strengthen his political position. It did not mark the limits of what he might aspire to, or of what he could achieve.

---

[1] Meyer, *Lombardische Denkmäler*, 133–9. For further details, especially in relation to the Duomo, *v. id., Oberitalienische Frührenaissance.*

[2] Beltrami, *op. cit.* 72–6 and 82–97.

CHAPTER XIV

GIANGALEAZZO AND THE NEGOTIATIONS FOR AN IMPERIAL-PAPAL ALLIANCE. THE DIFFICULTIES OF THE LEAGUE OF BOLOGNA. THE FRANCO-FLORENTINE ALLIANCE (SEPTEMBER 1395–OCTOBER 1396)

THE effect of the reconciliation with Wenceslaus was not confined solely to the acquisition by Giangaleazzo of the "nobler title" which he had so long desired. It inaugurated, too, a new constructive phase of his foreign policy.

The Ducal investiture coincided with the assurances of mutual friendship which Charles VI and Giangaleazzo's representative exchanged in Paris at the end of August 1395.[1] The Archbishop of Magdeburg was in Paris at the same time on behalf of Wenceslaus; and it has therefore been suggested that Giangaleazzo was preparing the way for an alliance which would include both France and Germany, and of which he himself would be in effect the dominant partner.[2]

The prolongation of the Schism, the divisions which arose at the French court on account of the King's insanity, and the weak and ineffective character of Wenceslaus, had combined to produce a complicated and uncertain situation in western Europe; but it does not seem likely that Giangaleazzo could have believed for a moment in the possibility of such an alliance. If he did, the developments of the next few months were to bring disillusionment. Wenceslaus, prompted by the electoral princes of Germany, had conceived the opinion that it was his duty, as lay head of the Christian world, to solve the problem of the Schism; but he was incapable of promoting any concrete measures, and his overtures to France and to Avignon were not relished in Rome.[3]

[1] V. supra, p. 159.
[2] Lindner, "Geschichte des deutschen Reiches", II 340–2; Jarry, Origines, 290–3. [3] Jarry, ibid. 295–6.

The French, having officially adopted the "voie de cession", were turning away from Benedict XIII; but they were not drawing any closer to Boniface IX. Giangaleazzo, on the other hand, was openly seeking the favour of the Roman Pope. He had abandoned all hope of a constructive alliance with France by the end of 1395, and was building up a new policy, based upon the friendship of the powers which opposed the expansion of French influence in Italy.

Boniface IX had recently increased his authority in the states of the Church. His position was not by any means secure, for Breton troops still occupied parts of the Patrimony, and the city of Rome was turbulent and dangerous in its independence; but he had held his own against his enemies, and had reduced a number of rebel princes and communes to submission.

Ladislaus of Durazzo, who in 1388 had been a boy besieged with his mother in the castle of Gaeta by Angevin troops, now led his own army to the attack of the French party. Ladislaus was most intimately associated with Boniface, and received unofficial assistance also from the Florentines; and, although the struggle was not yet over, the fortunes of Durazzo were again in the ascendant.

Maria, Queen of Sicily, who had once been betrothed to Giangaleazzo, had been forcibly abducted and married to a prince of Aragon. The Aragonese invaders succeeded in conquering the island in spite of a stern resistance by the native Catalan party, who enjoyed the full support of Boniface in the struggle against the schismatics from Spain. Giangaleazzo's enemies were anxious to secure the alliance of the King of Aragon, whose fleets controlled the western Mediterranean; and the Count of Vertus, deeming it wisest to give no offence, observed strict neutrality in the Sicilian dispute. In 1395, however, the leaders of the Catalan resistance in the island came to Pavia to appeal for help; and their plea was no doubt seconded by the Count of Campagna, the nuncio who represented Boniface IX at Giangaleazzo's investiture.[1]

Giangaleazzo's new policy was to be based on an active alliance

[1] Romano, "Visconti e la Sicilia", *ASL* XXIII, 1, 27–8.

with Wenceslaus and Boniface, and a close concert with Ladislaus and the Catalan party in Sicily; but any plan which depended for its success on the active co-operation of Wenceslaus suffered from an initial and fundamental weakness. The King of the Romans, who now enjoyed the favour of both Giangaleazzo and the Pope, could at last make his oft-postponed journey to Italy, receive the Imperial crown at Rome, clear the States of the Church of disorderly elements, and set Boniface in full authority over the Papal dominions. He could, in fact, do for Boniface what Louis of Orleans might have done for Clement, and prove scarcely less useful to Giangaleazzo in the process. But Wenceslaus was shut up in his own kingdom of Bohemia, while a storm of discontent was rising in Germany.

His brother Sigismund, King of Hungary, understood the importance of the Imperial coronation, and might have stirred him to action, if he had not himself been distracted by other cares. Giangaleazzo, knowing that Sigismund was the strongest of the Luxemburgers, tried to win his support, and even offered one of Bernabò's daughters to him in marriage. The League of Bologna was equally anxious to secure his help against the Duke. "There is in Lombardy a tyrant well known to him", began the instructions of the Florentine envoys who were charged with an offer to reconcile him with Ladislaus of Durazzo, the rival claimant of the Hungarian throne, and to arrange his marriage with Joanna, the Neapolitan's sister.[1] Sigismund rejected the Florentine proposals. He knew that the friendship of Milan was the first step to Rome and to the Imperial coronation; and if he had already begun to think that his own coronation, rather than that of his incompetent brother, would be the most satisfactory end to such a journey, Giangaleazzo would assuredly have found no difficulty in adapting his own plans to meet this contingency. However this may be, Sigismund was named Vicar of the Empire in March 1396, as the result of an interview arranged between Wenceslaus and the leading princes of Germany.[2] The affairs of Hungary, however, prevented him from turning his attention to

[1] Commission of 26 April 1396, published in *ASI* iv 220–3.
[2] Jarry, *Origines*, 294–5.

the problems of the Empire. He was preoccupied by the growing
Turkish menace, and, on the eve of the campaign which ended so
disastrously at Nicopolis, he had no time even to give the vigorous
impetus which was needed to send Wenceslaus to Rome.[1]

Wenceslaus, left to his own devices, indulged in some diplomatic negotiations, and bestowed favours on the Papal and
Milanese ambassadors at Prague. Giangaleazzo received the
further titles of Count of Pavia and of Angera.[2] He managed to
hold together the threads of Papal and Imperial policy, but his
own designs were dependent on the arrival of Wenceslaus—or
Sigismund—in Italy; and in spite of the close contacts which
were maintained through 1396 between Rome, Pavia, Prague and
Buda, the King's journey remained as problematical as ever.[3]

Meanwhile, Giangaleazzo did not neglect the southern end of
his scheme. In September 1395—a month before Coucy, having
abandoned the enterprise against Genoa, returned to France—
the Duke concluded an alliance with the Genoese, to whom he
promised special trading concessions in Sicily in return for their
aid in the conquest of the island.[4] This did not involve any
Milanese intervention in the domestic affairs of the *Superba*.
Giangaleazzo had not forgotten the importance of Genoa as a
port for Milan; a contemporary pamphlet, probably written in
his chancery,[5] points out the advantages which would accrue to
the city under his rule, and demonstrates that no other prince
was in a position to give the same protection, or to ensure the

[1] An idea of the intrigues which centred around Sigismund, towards the
end of 1395, may be obtained from the reports sent to Francesco Gonzaga by
his ambassador at Buda, and published by Thalloczy, *Mantovai Követjárás
Budán*, 97–112.

[2] The first was published in *RIS* xvi 827–30; the second by Lünig, *Codex
Italie Diplomaticus*, iii 381–6. A third diploma, creating Giangaleazzo Duke
of Lombardy (*ibid.* 386–90), is generally considered to be a forgery: Lindner,
"Geschichte des deutschen Reiches", ii 491; Romano, in *ASL* xxiv, 1, 427
note 1; Cusin, "Impero e la successione degli Sforza", *ASL* NS i 47, note 58.
It may have had some relation to the blank privilege which, according to
reports circulated by Florence, the Emperor sold to Giangaleazzo for 100,000
florins: Lindner, *op. cit.* ii 505–6.

[3] Lindner, *op. cit.* ii 332, 350, 489–90; Jarry, *Origines*, 301–2.

[4] 26 September 1395: Romano, "Visconti e la Sicîlia", *ASL* xxiii, 1,
45–9, Doc. 3.

[5] Novati, "Querele di Genova", in *Giornale Ligustico*, xiii 401–13.

same measure of prosperity. But whatever hopes Giangaleazzo may have cherished of ultimately securing the dominion of Liguria, he had no intention of accepting even the pacific submission of the Genoese, until the French had completely renounced their own claims to the city. The documents published by Jarry prove beyond question that in November 1395, and again in January 1396, the Duke declined the offer, made by the existing government of the city, to place in his hands the lordship of Genoa.[1]

The alliance with Genoa, then, was a political compact between two equal powers, to promote Giangaleazzo's conquest of Sicily. The plan was as fascinating, as full of promise, as it had been in 1379; but the Duke had acquired too many responsibilities since those days, to embark unequipped on a rash adventure in the south; and he therefore began to negotiate for further support.

His plan began to take shape in 1396. Ladislaus of Naples received rich gifts from Pavia at the end of the previous year;[2] and the motive behind the gifts soon became clear. Ladislaus was to place the Neapolitan ports at the disposal of the Duke's fleet; and, to secure his compliance, it was proposed that his sister, Joanna, should marry Giovanni Maria Visconti.[3] The Florentines soon heard of these proposals, and attempted to buy Ladislaus off by offering their official aid in his struggle against the Angevins, on condition that he refrained from helping Giangaleazzo; but Ladislaus, while he did not reject the Florentine offer, continued to allow the ships of the Visconti to take shelter in his ports.[4] The Florentines also learnt that Boniface, who was still in touch with the rebels in Sicily, was to play his part in the scheme. They intercepted a letter from the Cardinal of Bologna to the Duke of Milan, and discovered from it that the

---

[1] Jarry, *Origines*, 160–3, 186–7. This applies even more strongly to further Genoese overtures in September-October 1396: *ibid.* 199–201, 205–7.

[2] "Diurnali detti del Duca di Monteleone", 45; Cutolo, *Re Ladislao d'Angiò-Durazzo*, I 203, and II 86 note 18, gives the correct date as 1395, not 1394.

[3] Romano, "Visconti e la Sicilia", *ASL* XXIII, 1, 29–32.

[4] Mancarella, "Firenze, la Chiesa, e Ladislao", *ASN* XLV 55; Cutolo, *op. cit.* I 214–5.

Pope was prepared to "make him king of the island of Sicily".[1] The Papal suzerainty over the island had never been abrogated, and Boniface was willing to bestow the crown of Sicily upon Giangaleazzo, if the Duke could expel the hated Aragonese and take possession of the kingdom.

Nothing daunted by his failure in Paris, Giangaleazzo had turned elsewhere to seek the advantages which he had hoped to gain by the French alliance. His plans lost none of their boldness. Since France offered no help, he proposed to attain his objects in alliance with Wenceslaus and with the powers of southern Italy. The revival of his interest in Sicily was an incidental development, prompted perhaps by a private ambition to attain the rank of monarchy, by the continued attraction which the strategical idea of ruling both the north and south of Italy exercised over him, and by the fact that the alliances which he sought promised to favour the promotion of the scheme. This ambitious project, however, never passed beyond the stage of preliminary negotiations. Giangaleazzo could not move against Sicily without the help of the Genoese fleet; and his relations with Genoa were still dictated by wider considerations of policy with respect to French objectives in the peninsula. It was, as we shall see, in deference to French opinion that he eventually abandoned his alliance with Genoa, and thereby renounced his plan to secure a crown for himself in the south of Italy.

It is, then, in northern Italy that we must look for the core which gives continuity to Giangaleazzo's policy—to the kaleidoscopic relations between the states of Lombardy and Tuscany and Romagna. There, the League of Bologna had hitherto defeated all Giangaleazzo's efforts to break through the barrier which it opposed to his expansion; but symptoms of disintegration within the League were already beginning to appear.

Giangaleazzo used the ceremonies attending his Ducal investiture, to test the ground and to offer his friendship to those who were prepared to break away from the League.

----

[1] Commission of Florentine ambassadors to the Pope, 9 December 1396: *ASF*, Dieci di Balìa, Legazioni 2, 71.

Francesco Gonzaga remained adamant in his hostility, and he alone sent no representative to the ceremony.[1] He had followed Giangaleazzo's example, and was himself seeking from Wenceslaus an official title to confirm his authority in Mantua.[2] His request was not granted; but he chose this occasion to remove from his coat of arms the serpent of the Visconti, which he had assumed when he was most closely allied to Giangaleazzo in 1389.[3]

Francesco Carrara hesitated for a moment. His ambition and enterprise and very freedom were bound by the annual tribute, the legacy of the peace of Genoa, which crippled his state. The Florentines would not let him fight to be free of it, and an understanding with Giangaleazzo was the only other way of release. The Venetians, however, were aware of Giangaleazzo's plan, and interposed a word of warning, reminding the lord of Padua that his interests were identified with those of the League.[4] Carrara accepted their guidance, and did not go to Milan for the investiture, but sent his sons to represent him.[5]

Giangaleazzo had to recognize that his schemes had once more been circumvented. Direct overtures to the members of the League had failed. But their conflicting interests were his opportunity; and we must leave the Duke for a moment, in order to examine the difficulties in which his enemies were involved.

A grave storm had arisen over the question of Florentine penetration in Romagna. Bologna and the Polentani of Ravenna, threatened on the one side by Florentine expansion, and on the other by the old enmity of the Estensi, came near to renouncing the League, and thereby dividing its territorial extremes from one another. Carlo Malatesta, who was admitted to the counsels of the League on account of his close relations with Francesco

[1] Neither of the lists, in *RIS* xvi 822, and Corio, *Storia di Milano*, ii 396, mentions the presence of a Mantuan representative. The Florentine delegates reported (22 September 1395): "Quello di Mantova non v'era." *ASF*, Signoria, Rapporti i 2.

[2] Luzio, "Corradi di Gonzaga", *ASL* xl, 2, 172–3, Doc. 26.

[3] Platina, "Historia Urbis Mantue", *RIS* xx 759 A–B.

[4] Pastorello, *Nuove Ricerche*, 87–8; Roberto Cessi, "Venezia neutrale", *NAV* NS xxviii 284–5.

[5] The Milanese accounts give to Carrara's sons an honourable place, but not one which would justify the claim that Giangaleazzo showed them especial favour (cf. Gatari, "Cronaca Carrarese", *RIS* NS xvii, 1, 450).

Gonzaga—each had married the other's sister[1]—might also have been expected to resist Florentine ambitions, in his rôle of protector of Papal interests in Romagna; but he seems to have held himself aloof from the dispute, probably at the request of Boniface, who in this case sided with Florence.

The quarrel arose over the fortress of Castrocaro, which Florence received from the Pope in return for a loan. The Florentine alliances in Romagna were a necessary commercial precaution, now that Pisa had fallen into the hands of Appiano; and the purchase of Castrocaro, a few miles from Forlì at the foot of the Apennines, provided additional security for the victualling of the Republic in time of famine or of war. In spite of the re-assurances of this kind which the Florentines gave, the Bolognese regarded the further intrusion of Florence into Romagna as an act of unfriendliness towards themselves. The lords of Romagna were even more alarmed, and refused to believe that the Florentine motives were purely commercial. It was openly said in Bologna that "the Commune of Florence wants Castrocaro in order to have Forlì and Ravenna and the port [of Ravenna] on the sea, and afterwards other things too, and wants to pursue the policy in Romagna, as in Tuscany, of engrossing its neighbours".[2] The government of Ferrara, on the other hand, having much to fear from the proximity of Bologna, and nothing from the remoter power of Florence, supported the Tuscan Republic.

The Venetians eventually imposed a compromise upon the two parties;[3] but the division in the League remained, and the hostility between d'Este and Bologna grew more marked. The Condottiere Giovanni da Barbiano, Count of Cunio, who was nominally subject to the overlordship of Bologna,[4] had given aid to Azzone d'Este, the unsuccessful claimant to the Ferrarese succession.

---

[1] Minerbetti, "Cronica", 163. Carlo attended the conference of the League at Ferrara in April 1393: "Chronicon Estense", *RIS* xv 530 c.

[2] This common opinion was reported to the Florentine government by the envoys at Bologna in August 1395: Bolognini, "Relazioni tra Firenze e Venezia", *NAV* ix 84–6.

[3] *Ibid.* 81–95, for the fullest account of the whole incident.

[4] The lords of Barbiano paid a tribute of one hawk yearly to Bologna, in token of their allegiance: Giorgi, "Alberico e Giovanni da Barbiano", *AMR* 3, xii 106 note 4.

Florence determined to punish the Count, and prompted Astorre Manfredi of Faenza, together with troops from Ferrara, to ravage Barbiano's lands. Giovanni proudly accused Florence of persistent meddling in other people's concerns, and his stand against the Republic was encouraged, according to a Florentine account, by the Bolognese government and by the Polentani of Ravenna.[1]

Giovanni's brother, Alberico da Barbiano, the Grand Constable of the "Kingdom of Sicily", had been ransomed from a Neapolitan prison by Giangaleazzo, who brought him to Lombardy and placed him in command of his own armies.[2] The Duke of Milan saw in the question of Romagna an opportunity to detach Bologna from the League, and his agents lost no chance of working upon the feelings of the Bolognese, and of founding a party favourable to Milan in the city.[3] The Duke appeared, with Florence and Bologna, as arbitrator of Giovanni da Barbiano's disputes with d'Este and Astorre Manfredi in the summer of 1395; but no decision was reached, Giangaleazzo dropped out of the negotiations, and the tension in Emilia remained.[4] Barbiano, in alliance with the Polentani, invaded the lands of d'Este and Manfredi in February 1396. The Florentines held Bologna responsible for countenancing, if not inspiring, the raids. Once more they attempted to pacify the disputes of their allies; but they had to abandon the attempt in August 1396. "No award or sentence was reached in the affairs of Romagna, through the fault of the Bolognese, who would not agree to anything."[5] The Bolognese, in fact, had no intention of accepting the overtures which Giangaleazzo made to them, and which aroused so much alarm in Florence;[6] but they were determined not to renounce their

---

[1] Bruni, "Historiarum Florentini Populi", *RIS* NS xix, 3, 266–7.

[2] Giorgi, *op. cit. AMR* 3, xii 101, and note 1.

[3] This appears from the letters in *ASF*, Dieci di Balìa, Legazioni, vol. 2.

[4] From the reports of the representatives of the Florentine government: Medin, "Rime di Bruscaccio da Rovezzano", in *Giornale Storico della Letteratura Italiana*, xxv 196–9.

[5] Report of the Florentine envoy, 12 August 1396: *ibid.* 199.

[6] Several of the letters and instructions in *ASF*, Dieci della Balìa, Legazioni, vol. 2, bear witness to the anxiety which was felt in Florence at the presence of Visconti agents in Bologna.

relations with Giovanni da Barbiano, who had proved to be a useful instrument in their feud with the Estensi.

The Regents of Niccolò d'Este had no such scruples in dealing with Giangaleazzo. Their immediate ambition was to redeem the Polesine, and break the supremacy which Venice had secured in Ferrara. They were negotiating with Giangaleazzo in October 1395, no doubt with this end in view. The Duke, however, must have demanded an excessive price for his alliance—perhaps the cession of Modena itself; for the Regents chose to keep what they held, and retain the friendship of Venice and the League, rather than sacrifice both in the hope of re-acquiring the Polesine, which Giangaleazzo might never be able to win for them.[1] The financial conditions of the Ferrarese state meanwhile went from bad to worse. The Venetians again intervened, in conjunction with Florence and Bologna, but they could not find an acceptable solution to the difficulties.[2] The Regents turned again to Pavia; but Giangaleazzo apparently refused to modify his demands, for once more the negotiations came to nothing.[3]

The rebels of the Modenese Apennines were still undaunted. Giangaleazzo frowned on the activity of his subjects in their favour, and wrote to the lords of Mirandola, his dependants, asking them to restrain their nephew from helping the rebels;[4] but he did not escape the accusations he had foreseen, that troops formally dismissed from his service fomented the disturbances and found refuge in his lands.[5] The accusation was probably just. The Duke was anxious, if he could not restore his alliance with the ruler of Ferrara, to make sure that he had free passage through the territory of Modena; but he was careful so to restrict his activities that his enemies could bring no proof against him.

Whenever the unity of the League of Bologna was threatened, the Venetians hastened to intervene. They had built the confining wall of the League around Giangaleazzo's ambitions; but its preservation depended upon themselves. The precarious

---

[1] Benvenuto Cessi, *Venezia e Padova*, 82–4; Roberto Cessi, "Venezia neutrale", *NAV* NS XXVIII 282–8.
[2] Roberto Cessi, *ibid.* 293–4.   [3] *Ibid.* 294–5.
[4] In April 1396: "Memorie Storiche della Mirandola", I 78–9.
[5] *V.* Doc. 12.

balance of power created by the unity of the League was the groundwork of Venetian policy; it prompted their advice to Carrara, their intervention in Ferrara, their arbitration of the Castrocaro dispute. Carrara, d'Este and Gonzaga, without the support of the League, would be at the mercy of Milan; and the Venetians would have to abandon their cherished neutrality in order to defend them. "From egoism or prudence, they preferred to have their hands free."[1] When they hinted rather vaguely, in April 1395, that they might reconsider their refusal to join the League,[2] their object was to check the disintegrating tendencies among the allies. Dr Cessi has shown how anxious they were that the "Signorotti" of Lombardy should do nothing to forfeit the protection of Bologna and Florence;[3] it was an insurance against the need to intervene themselves.

The troubles of the League arose within its own borders. Giangaleazzo could not be responsible for them, because, in relation to him, the interests of the allies were identical, and were the basis upon which the League had been formed; but he lost no opportunity of encouraging the discontents which arose. His offers to Carrara and to Bologna, his relations with Giovanni da Barbiano, his designs on Modena, indicated his readiness to help forward the process of disintegration. Until the fabric of the League began to crumble in earnest, there was little else that he could do.

He continued to direct through the agency of Appiano the affairs of Pisa and Siena.[4] He took into his own hands the negotiations of Siena for an understanding with Biordo Michelotti, and with their troublesome neighbour, Count Bertoldo Orsini of Soana.[5] Troops paid by the "Camera" of Milan still garrisoned the two cities; and Pasquino Capelli made the noteworthy, though possibly exaggerated, statement to the Sienese envoys at Pavia in 1395, that "the lord Count has placed many burdens on

---

[1] Romano, "Nuovi Documenti Viscontei", *ASL* xvi 309.
[2] Roberto Cessi, "Venezia neutrale", *NAV* NS xxviii 270–1.
[3] *Ibid.* 258–61, 269–89, 292–5. Dr Cessi does not present the more selfish aspect of Venetian policy.
[4] Professione, *Siena e le Compagne di Ventura*, 147–8.
[5] The letters in *ASS*, Concistoro 1836, give full testimony of his activities.

his own subjects, in order to preserve the state of Pisa and of Siena, which has given rise to much agitation in his lands".[1]

Giangaleazzo remained in almost constant communication with Florence throughout 1395 and 1396—making complaints, answering counter-complaints, and considering or putting forward proposals for improving the relations between them. In February 1395, his envoys were sent to discuss the outstanding differences between Florence and Siena—the unfulfilled territorial settlement of the peace of Genoa, and the raids of bandits who found shelter in neighbouring lands. The Sienese, however, confident of Giangaleazzo's protection, sustained their cause with no less determination than the Florentines; above all, they refused to consider the surrender of Marciano, the fortress of the Sienese family of Pietramala which guarded their outpost of Lucignano on the Florentine border.[2]

The Milanese envoys returned home with nothing accomplished, and the Florentines sent an embassy to Pavia in May, to learn "on what terms they were to live with Giangaleazzo in the future".[3] For a moment, it seemed that some agreement might be reached. The Sienese envoys wrote on 17 June: "Messer Guglielmo [Bevilacqua] told us that they had already begun to draft the clauses to be contained in the League which is to be signed by the lord Count and the Florentines."[4] But the ceremonies at Milan during the summer delayed the negotiations, which were resumed at Florence in the autumn under less favourable auspices. No common ground could now be found. The Florentines finally demanded that the Duke accept their terms or reject them as they stood; and at the end of the year his envoys returned to Pavia.[5] "The ambassadors of the Count have left in confusion, and I hear that they have taken the road to Bologna, for no good purpose."[6]

---

[1] Despatch of 11 June 1395: *ibid.* no. 46.
[2] From letters in the same volume.
[3] Minerbetti, "Cronica", 194.   [4] *ASS*, Concistoro 1836, no. 50.
[5] Minerbetti, "Cronica", 194–5.
[6] "Cioè per seminare il gioglio." This despatch from Florence, although it is dated 23 December 1394, in Lucca, *Regesti*, 308, no. 1519, seems to belong to the year 1395.

The basis on which Giangaleazzo seems to have conducted these negotiations was the old one of union against the Companies. These undisciplined bands of soldiers, who preyed on the countryside under the leadership of unscrupulous Condottieri, exercised a powerful influence on the political life of Italy at the time. The universal hatred and fear in which they were held tended to unite all governments against them, and many Leagues had been formed against the Companies in the past thirty or forty years; but these alliances were never operative, for the states of Italy had no other soldiers to fight for them in their mutual quarrels. Those who could afford to pay the Condottieri found many ways of using them as an instrument of policy, even in times of peace; and the lesser states, which could not pay them, were entirely at their mercy, and therefore dependent on stronger allies who could give them protection. Even Florence lived in the constant shadow of this danger. A curious episode which occurred in March 1396 demonstrates the position. As related a little later by the Florentine government, "Count Giovanni da Barbiano had assembled a great Company...and was treating very closely to unite himself with Biordo Michelotti and with Broglia and Brandolino, and with Bartolomeo Gonzaga and Guido da Correggio and several others. And in Barbiano were the chancellors and ambassadors of the aforesaid, and Guido in person. And also there were the chancellors of Ottobuon Terzo, of Conte da Carrara [an illegitimate half-brother of the lord of Padua] and Mostarda, of the Company of St George, friar Giovanni de' Cani for the Duke of Milan, Count Giovanni da Barbiano, Filippo [da Pisa] and Lodovico [Cantello], who came altogether to more than 2500 lances. And this Count Giovanni did...only to come against us to our damage;...and this he did...secretly, until we had broken up the Company, and afterwards he declared it publicly with proud and poisonous words."[1]

There is no doubt that the Florentines were seriously alarmed. They opened negotiations with Giovanni da Barbiano through

[1] Commission of Florentine envoys to Pisa, 20 June 1396: *ASF*, Dieci di Balìa, Legazioni 2, 28; the envoys were furnished with evidence. The same story had already been told in Perugia: commission of 24 May, in Azzi Vitelleschi, "Relazioni tra Firenze e l' Umbria", I 229, no. 870.

the government of Bologna,[1] and sent an agent to "enlist Lodovico Cantello 'in aspetto'" at all costs and without delay, but in
great secrecy.[2] Another envoy went to Biordo Michelotti at
Perugia,[3] and they wrote to Francesco Carrara, asking him to
dissuade his half-brother from his intention of "joining with
certain enemies of ours during the summer, for the purpose of
invading the lands of our subjects".[4] The adroit but expensive
policy of buying off individual Condottieri succeeded, and any
danger which might have threatened Florence was quickly
removed.

The most interesting detail of this story is the alleged presence
of Giovanni Cane at the conference in Barbiano "for the Duke of
Milan". Giangaleazzo certainly had relations with several of the
Condottieri involved; and in negotiating with Giovanni da
Barbiano, the Florentines had to allow that, "if it cannot be
arranged otherwise", the Count should reserve the right to
attack the Republic, if he were in the active service of the Duke
of Milan.[5] If it is true that the most mysterious and elusive of
Giangaleazzo's agents attended the conference, the alarm of the
Florentines is fully explained; it was no light undertaking to
assemble a force of 2500 lances in time of peace, but the Duke
had unusual resources at his disposal. It is possible, indeed, that
he used this method of bringing pressure to bear upon the Florentines to accept that alliance against the Companies, by means of
which he hoped to confirm the numerical superiority of the forces
which he could command. Simultaneously with the episode of
Barbiano, he appointed new ambassadors to go to Florence; and
on this occasion their mission proved more fruitful.

A treaty between the League, and Giangaleazzo with his
allies, was signed at Florence on 17 May 1396. It did not, indeed,
meet with any greater success than previous agreements of the
same kind. Only a general solution was provided to the issues

[1] They were, as we have seen, in contact with Barbiano, whom they were
trying to reconcile with his neighbours in Emilia.
[2] Commission of 26 March 1396: *ASF*, Dieci di Balìa, Legazioni 2, 9 & t.
[3] Commission of 24 March: Azzi Vitelleschi, *op. cit.* I 228, no. 868.
[4] Letter of 3 April: *ASF*, Dieci di Balìa, Legazioni 2, 11.
[5] Commission of 22 March 1395/6: *ibid.* 7 t.

left untouched at Genoa—restraint of the Companies, and greater security against attack by exiles who had found refuge in neighbouring states;[1] and even these terms were never put into force. The Florentines complained to Giangaleazzo in June of the activities of the Condottiere Broglia, and the Duke also had grievances against troops which were at the disposal of the League. The Republic proposed drastic measures for the total dissolution of the Companies, and for the fulfilment of the territorial settlement of the peace of Genoa. The instructions to the Florentine envoys afford an eloquent illustration of the disturbed condition of the country, and the need for a radical solution.[2]

Giangaleazzo was not inclined to weaken the defences of Siena by enforcing the return of Marciano to Florence; the Sienese had proved adamant on the point in the previous year, and Giangaleazzo wisely refused to insist, during the negotiations for the treaty of Florence, on discussing problems over which neither side was prepared to yield. His envoys demanded, as the Sienese ambassadors wrote from Florence, that "no individual demands should be made by us to this Commune".[3] While this method enabled an agreement to be reached, it gravely limited its scope; and the question of territories arose as soon as the treaty was signed.[4]

On the other hand, the Duke was always ready to negotiate for the dissolution of the Companies. His ambassadors were again in Florence in the middle of August, "to take measures with us for the future against any formation of Companies";[5] and, early in October, they were once more trying to restore mutual confidence and peace, "and among the chief things which would promote this result, would be the dissolution of the Companies".[6]

---

[1] Ammirato, *Istorie Fiorentine*, I, 2, 852; Minerbetti, "Cronica", 195. The treaty is preserved in *ASS*, Capitoli, no. 100.

[2] *V*. Doc. 12.   [3] 26 April 1396: *ASS*, Concistoro 1837, no. 32.

[4] Despatch of the same envoys, 20 May 1396: *ibid*. no. 48.

[5] Commission of Florentine envoys to Bologna, 19 August 1396: *ASF*, Dieci di Balìa, Legazioni 2, 47.

[6] The same, 7 October 1396: *ibid*. 52.

The last embassy was occasioned by an outbreak of the old feud between Pisa and Lucca. Here Giangaleazzo, had he been able to draw the right conclusions, might already have begun to understand the danger of entrusting the care of his interests in Tuscany to a man of great ambition and little faith. At the end of June 1395, while the court of Pavia was occupied with preparations for the ceremony of investiture, Appiano facilitated the entry of Broglia and his Company into the territory of Lucca.[1] The government of Lucca, in self-defence, abandoned its traditional neutrality, and sought the protection of the Duke's enemies, concluding a five-year alliance with Florence.[2]

A year later, a simultaneous movement of the exiles of Pisa, supported by Florence, and those of Lucca, aided by Giovanni da Barbiano with the connivance of Appiano, nearly precipitated a general war. Giangaleazzo took no open part in the dispute, which he regarded as affecting purely local issues, and therefore to be left to Appiano's direction. Nevertheless, he took care that Appiano should not be caught unawares without troops for the protection of Pisa. The Florentines, more closely involved, were equally prepared to assume responsibility for the safety of Lucca; but they were anxious to preserve the peace, and, after six weeks of growing tension, they managed to impose a settlement.[3]

The episode, however, left a legacy of uncertainty and fear; and both sides began to look to their defences. Giangaleazzo had hitherto been content to mark time, while he waited for his European policy to bear fruit in Italy; but the time was coming when he could wait no longer. Each fresh incident heightened the tension; and the next one might set the whole of Italy ablaze.

The spark came from Paris, where the Florentines were now in close touch with the enemies of the Dukes of Orleans and Milan.

---

[1] Zerbi, *Visconti di Milano*, 52–7; Sercambi, "Cronache", I 313–16.

[2] On 19 July 1395: Lucca, *Inventari*, I 63; Ammirato, *op. cit.* I, 2, 848 A–B.

[3] This incident, which is a typical example of the evil influence exercised by the Companies of Venture in Italian politics, cannot be analysed more closely in a work on Giangaleazzo. Besides the accounts of the Chroniclers—

Queen Isabella, aided by her brother Lewis of Bavaria, appears for the first time at the head of the intriguers: not so much, perhaps, from a desire to revenge the death of her grandfather Bernabò, as from more personal motives. She was an ambitious woman who saw in the chaos of the French court an opportunity to establish her own power. Orleans was a rival, and she was jealous, too, of the ascendancy which Valentina Visconti had won over Charles VI in his recurrent periods of insanity.

Isabella achieved her first victory, when a campaign of vicious slander compelled Valentina to withdraw to her country residence at Asnières in April 1396.[1] This retreat, which was a blow to the influence of the Orleanist party in Paris, was the source of more personal grief to Giangaleazzo. The Duke of Milan received other indications that his enemies were drawing closer together, and he belatedly attempted to check them. He made new overtures to Mastino Visconti;[2] but Mastino preferred the alliance of Lewis of Bavaria and of Bernard of Armagnac, who promised to help him in the recovery of his father's dominions.[3] Armagnac, for his part, had already informed the Florentine government of his readiness to lead an army to Italy in their service, to avenge his brother's death at Alessandria.[4]

Enguerrand de Coucy was in Pavia in May 1396, on his way east, and brought an official warning that any interference by the Duke in the affairs of Genoa would be regarded in France as an act of hostility.[5] Giangaleazzo found it necessary to accept this declaration; he was aware of the Florentine intrigues at the French court. To satisfy French opinion, he renounced his

especially Minerbetti, Sercambi, and the confused story of Sardo—and a very brief summary in Guasti, *Ser Lapo Mazzei*, I 151, note 1, many interesting details may be found in the Archives of Florence, Siena, and Lucca (these last published in Lucca, *Regesti*).

[1] Jarry, *Vie politique de Louis de France*, 168.

[2] Romano, "Giangaleazzo Visconti", *ASL* XVIII 299. The Duke's envoy received authority to conduct the negotiations on 9 May 1396: *Id.* "Regesto", *ASL* XXI, 2, 30, no. 39.

[3] On 1 June 1396: Riezler, *Geschichte Baierns*, III 160.

[4] Report of a Florentine ambassador to Avignon, published by Romano, "Giangaleazzo Visconti", *ASL* XVIII 338–9, Doc. 18.

[5] Jarry, *Origines*, 176.

alliance with the Genoese on 1 October 1396.[1] But he had already delayed too long.

Maso degli Albizzi himself had gone to Paris in May, to investigate the possibilities of an accord with France. He was joined in July by Buonaccorso Pitti, with definite proposals for an alliance. He was instructed "in all discussions... to proceed very secretly,...so as not to give any one a chance to spoil or hinder so good a work", and again, he was to ask the King "to commit the negotiation of the business to a few persons, discreet and loyal and in his Majesty's confidence, so that the Tyrant cannot hear of the negotiations and spoil them". The other members of the League of Bologna took no part in the negotiations, and apparently had not been informed of them, "because we did not want it to be revealed, until we knew the intentions of the King".[2]

In spite of this insistence upon secrecy, the Duke of Orleans knew what was afoot. Albizzi, in a letter of 15 July, related how "others seek to spoil our commerce, bringing forward new expedients every day".[3] Nevertheless Isabella, who was the prime mover in the intrigue, managed, with the Duke of Burgundy's approval, to exclude Orleans from the conferences, and in haste and secrecy secured the King's signature to the Florentine terms.[4] Charles probably had little idea of the implications of the document he was called on to sign.[5] France and Florence concluded an alliance for five years, on 29 September 1396. They promised mutual military aid, and arranged for the partition of the Milanese state.[6]

The messenger who bore the news of this alliance to Florence was intercepted in Giangaleazzo's territory in the middle of

[1] Romano, "Visconti e la Sicilia", *ASL* xxiii, 1, 30–3; and 45–6, Doc. 4.
[2] Pitti's commission, 18 July 1396: *ASF*, Dieci di Balìa, Legazioni 2, 35 t–6.
[3] Florence to Albizzi, acknowledging his letter: *ibid.* 49 t (5 September).
[4] Jarry, *Origines*, 170–6 and 189–93. From Pitti's report: de Boüard, *France et l'Italie*, 215–16.
[5] His surprise on learning, in the following year, of the obligations he had undertaken, is recorded by Pitti, "Cronica", 103.
[6] Lünig, *op. cit.* i 1093–1101.

October.[1] Hard on his heels must have come the tidings that the Republic of Genoa had decided to place itself under the dominion of Charles VI.[2]

From that moment, all Giangaleazzo's attention was devoted to the task of anticipating the French menace. He could no longer afford to wait until the League broke up under the stress of conflicting interests. He could no longer satisfy himself meanwhile with indirect activities in Ferrara, in Bologna, in Romagna, with monotonous and inconclusive negotiations for a better understanding with Florence. He forsook his more grandiose schemes in the face of an urgent danger, and took the offensive against his enemies, in the hope that he would be able to cripple their power before the threatened attack from France materialized. The logical consequence of the Franco-Florentine alliance was the Mantuan war.

[1] Florence to her allies, 30 October 1396: Azzi Vitelleschi, *op. cit.* I 230, no. 874.

[2] On 25 October: Jarry, *Origines*, 209 *sqq.*

CHAPTER XV

THE MANTUAN WAR
(NOVEMBER 1396–MAY 1398)

THE months which elapsed between the signing of the Franco-Florentine alliance and the approach of spring, when the war could be begun, were spent by Giangaleazzo in strengthening his own alliances, and in tempting the wavering members of the League to come over to his side. He offered a Visconti bride to Niccolò d'Este, whose advisers had been negotiating without success for a marriage between the Marquis and a daughter of Francesco Carrara.[1] The Florentines, informed by the Bolognese government of Giangaleazzo's proposals, sent an envoy to Ferrara in November 1396. "We have heard that the Duke of Milan was seeking to give a relative of his in marriage to the Marquis, with certain pacts and conditions contrary to his honour and derogatory to his state and that of the League." They urged, instead, the acceptance of the Paduan match.[2] The Venetian government, in answer to an appeal from Francesco Gonzaga, agreed that the proposed marriage "would be harmful to the lord Marquis and to the whole of Italy", and declared that they had used what influence they possessed in opposing it, "and so in this as in other matters affecting him we are disposed to do as much as lies in our power in the future".[3] This intervention defeated Giangaleazzo's purpose, and it seems likely that his proposals were considered by the Regents of Ferrara only as a means of obtaining better terms from Carrara; for the conditions

---

[1] Pastorello, in *Nuove Ricerche*, 92–4, suggests that Florence proposed the Carrarese match to counteract the Milanese offer; but the negotiations between Padua and Ferrara began some time before Florence learnt of the Milanese proposal.

[2] Commission of 11 November 1396: *ASF*, Dieci di Balìa, Legazioni 2, 60 & t.

[3] Minutes of the Senate, 24 November: *ASV*, Senato Secreta, E. 132 t.

of Niccolò's marriage to Carrara's daughter were agreed upon in the following January.[1]

The Milanese agents in Bologna redoubled their efforts, and endeavoured to exploit the doubts aroused in Bologna, which owed a nominal allegiance to the Pope, by the alliance with the schismatical French. The Florentine envoy, on his way to Ferrara, was instructed to thank the Bolognese government for their letter, in which they related " the request which messer Jacopo d'Appiano makes, wishing to join in alliance with them, and the answer which they gave to him". The Florentines added that " messer Jacopo makes these requests only with evil intent, and to bring division and disturbance into the League, because he is (devoted in) spirit and mind to the Duke of Milan, and seeks this under the Duke's instructions".[2] At the beginning of December, an envoy was instructed to speak to Francesco Gonzaga of " the envy and greed which reign among them, and the zeal which the Duke of Milan has shown and shows in flattery and the disbursing of money in Bologna, especially in the case of certain citizens who have power in the state".[3] A fortnight later, " we understand the good intentions of the government of Bologna, and the evil inclination of certain Bolognese maintained by the Duke of Milan, with whom, to fill their purses, they intrigue against the liberty of their city and of the other worthy citizens".[4] This probably represents fairly enough the extent of Giangaleazzo's influence in Bologna; his party in the city did not yet constitute a formidable danger. The Bolognese turned the needs of their ally to good profit, and, in return for their adherence to the French alliance, demanded that Niccolò d'Este should surrender to them the border towns of Nonantola and Bazzano; but they had no wish to forfeit the goodwill of Florence, and were not deceived by Giangaleazzo's offers.

Meanwhile the Duke strengthened the ties which united his friends in Tuscany and Umbria. Biordo Michelotti, earlier in

---

[1] Olivi, "Matrimonio del Marchese Niccolò III", *AMM* 3, v 342–8, and 355–72, Docs. 1–9.

[2] *ASF*, Dieci di Balìa, Legazioni 2, 59 & t.

[3] Commission of 1 December 1396: *ibid.* 66.

[4] Commission of envoys to Bologna, 10 December: *ibid.* 72.

1396, had accepted a "condotta" from him,[1] refused the general-ship of the Florentine forces because "he could not decide on his own account, but depended on the Duke",[2] and directed the Commune of Perugia to adhere to the treaty of Florence as an ally of Milan. His representative, with those of Perugia, of Appiano and of Pisa, of Antonio Montefeltro lord of Urbino, and of Giangaleazzo himself, assembled at Siena in the first days of December,[3] "for the purpose of allying themselves in brotherhood and friendship with the Commune of Siena".[4] The terms of the alliance are not known, but its object was clearly to give greater cohesion to the military forces of the Duke's supporters, in pre-paration for a war which was already foreseen.[5] Montefeltro at the same time united himself with several of the less important lords on the borders of Umbria, and threatened the security of the League's allies in Romagna.[6]

Biordo, however, did not remain faithful for long. His ambitions in Umbria and the Duchy of Spoleto were incompatible with the Pope's determination to re-assert his authority over a renascent Perugia; and as Biordo prepared to renew the conflict with Boniface—a conflict which had been temporarily interrupted through the Duke's mediation—so he drew away from Gian-galeazzo. He entered the service of the League soon after the beginning of the war;[7] but the loss to the Visconti cause was not great, for instead of bringing support to his new allies, he

---

[1] In June 1396, he was stated to be in Giangaleazzo's pay "per tutto Aprile proximo": *v.* Doc. 12.

[2] Commission of Florentine envoys to Perugia, 24 March 1396: Azzi Vitelleschi, "Relazioni tra Firenze e l' Umbria", I 228, no. 868. Pellini, *Historia di Perugia*, II 73–4.

[3] Their credentials are preserved in *ASS*, Concistoro 1838, nos. 90, 94–5, 99.

[4] Minutes of the General Council of Siena, 1 December 1396: *ASS*, Con-siglio Generale, Deliberazioni, CCIII = 198, p. 33.

[5] Pellini, *op. cit.* II 81–2; Malavolti, *Historia de' Sanesi*, II 182.

[6] Franceschini, "Politica di Giangaleazzo e i rapporti Visconti-Monte-feltro", in *Atti del Primo Congresso Storico Lombardo*, 189.

[7] The negotiations, from the first hopes of Florence to Biordo's notification to Giangaleazzo in May 1397 (when his "condotta" had expired), may be traced in Lucca, *Regesti*: e.g. 333, no. 1607; and 323, no. 1567. The commission and report of the Florentine envoys to Biordo are summarized in Azzi Vitelleschi, *op. cit.* I 234, nos. 882–3.

had to appeal to them for help and protection against the Papal armies.[1]

The menace of a French invasion was ever present in Giangaleazzo's mind, and inspired all the military preparations which went on apace during the winter. Even so innocent an event as the arrival of the Count of St Pol in Genoa in March 1397, to assume his duties as governor of the city, awoke profound misgivings in circles devoted to the cause of the Visconti.[2] The Florentine government admitted the fact, and begged Charles VI to send an army to Italy without delay; they declared that the Duke had staked everything on a desperate blow at Florence, before the French caught him in the flank and overwhelmed him.[3] This was not a war of Giangaleazzo's own seeking. He had even appealed to the Venetians to mediate between him and his enemies; but the Florentines would not admit the existence of any quarrel which called for mediation.[4] In the face of this attitude, Giangaleazzo could see no alternative. He put forward his case in an interview which he gave in February 1397, and of which a report was delivered to Francesco Gonzaga. He could not wait tamely to be caught between the forces of France and the League; he must disable the Florentines while there was still time—pin them to the defensive, wipe out their resources by destroying their crops, or bring them to a state of exhaustion before the French could intervene.[5] Therefore he mobilized his forces at Pisa and Siena, and allowed the Condottieri who were in his pay to raid the districts of Florence and Lucca, and to find shelter with their plunder in the territory of his allies.[6]

The lands of Tuscany, however, were not to bear the main brunt

[1] Lucca, *Regesti*, 429, nos. 1958–9; Pellini, *op. cit.* II 94–5.
[2] Letters of Appiano, and of Giangaleazzo's agents in Tuscany: Lucca, *Regesti*, 317–18, nos. 1554 a, c and d.
[3] Jarry, *Origines*, 297–300.
[4] Roberto Cessi, "Venezia neutrale", *NAV* NS XXVIII 302–4.
[5] The gist of this interview was communicated to Francesco Gonzaga, who reported it to his allies in a letter of 24 February 1397: Lucca, *Regesti*, 316, no. 1548. Cf. Jarry, *Origines*, 301.
[6] Many details of these raids are to be found in *ASF*, Dieci di Balìa, Legazioni, vol. 2; also in the despatches in Lucca, *Regesti*, from January to March 1397.

of the war. Giangaleazzo's plan of campaign was dictated by political and strategical considerations. The first war against Florence had been fought, superficially at least, to defend the integrity of the Sienese state; but since 1392, the Count had lost the support of the Lombard princes who had been his allies in the war, and his diplomacy had been directed mainly to re-establishing his supremacy over them. When war seemed inevitable, it was natural that he should concentrate his forces primarily in Lombardy. A direct attack on Florence would leave his dominions exposed to invasion from the east. Mantua, less than 100 miles from Milan, was therefore the first objective of the campaign; and the activities of Alberico da Barbiano and his associates in Tuscany were intended mainly to prevent Florence from sending help to Gonzaga. The Florentine government decided, on 18 March 1397, to answer the raids of the Duke's soldiers by open war[1]—"to stand no longer under water, but to come openly to war", as it was reported to Lucca on the following day.[2] Simultaneously, "the Grand Constable" led the Visconti army into Florentine territory. But the Tuscan campaign proved to be no more than an affair of raids, of cattle stealing and the destruction of crops—a diversion from the main front of the war on the banks of the Po.[3]

Giangaleazzo mobilized his army in Lombardy under the command of Jacopo dal Verme during March 1397; but the concentration of troops in the districts of Parma, Cremona and Verona could not be achieved unnoticed.[4] Gonzaga was able to make his own preparations, and when Giangaleazzo launched his attack, the element of surprise was lacking. The Duke's plans were dominated by the fear of a French invasion, and he relied on the strength of his army to deal a rapid and decisive blow which would break Gonzaga's resistance and secure the eastern frontier. The keys to the defence of the Mantuan district, the "Serraglio"

[1] Minerbetti, "Cronica", 211–12; Jarry, *Origines*, 304–5.
[2] Despatch of 19 March 1397: Lucca, *Regesti*, 344, no. 1679.
[3] Durrieu, *Gascons en Italie*, 202–5; Malavolti, *op. cit.* II 182 t–3; Sercambi, "Cronache", I 370–II 190; and the despatches to Lucca.
[4] Lucca, *Regesti*, 335–6, nos. 1626–9; and 349–50, nos. 1691–2. Pastorello, *Nuove Ricerche*, 232–3, Doc. 64.

as it was called, were the two bridgeheads on the Po, at Borgoforte in the west and Governolo in the east. A joint attack was therefore planned, Verme leading his army from Cremona against Borgoforte, while Ugolotto Biancardo moved with another force from Verona and Ostiglia upon Governolo.

The military events of the war may be briefly described. The campaign opened, apparently without any formal declaration of war, when this joint attack was launched at the end of March; but the defences had been fully manned, and both assaults were repulsed.[1] Giangaleazzo was disconcerted, and is reported to have rated his troops bitterly.[2] The surprise having failed, Verme undertook the systematic reduction of the Mantuan towns outside the "Serraglio", and steadily bombarded the defences of Borgoforte; but it was not until the middle of July that he succeeded in capturing the bridge, and the Milanese army entered the "Serraglio".[3]

Verme marched at once to help Biancardo in the siege of Governolo. This town was Gonzaga's last means of communication with his allies, "and if it is lost, he must needs lose his state".[4] The League made a supreme effort. A relieving army, led by Carlo Malatesta, entered Governolo at the end of August, routed a section of the besieging force during a sally, and, in the panic which followed, drove the whole of Verme's troops in confusion back to Borgoforte and across the Po. Ships, provisions, and a well-equipped siege train were left in the hands of the victors.[5]

The allies made no use of their success. "If they had followed up the victory, the Count of Vertus would have been altogether ruined."[6] But, while Malatesta and Carrara and Gonzaga

---

[1] Minerbetti, "Cronica", 212; Delayto, "Annales Estenses", *RIS* xviii 940 d–941 a.

[2] From the account of a deserter, reported in Florence: Lucca, *Regesti*, 356, no. 1706.

[3] Minerbetti, "Cronica", 212–13; Delayto, *op. cit. RIS* xviii 941 a–942 a; Platina, "Historia Urbis Mantue", *RIS* xx 763–776. The reports to Lucca in Lucca, *Regesti*, e.g. nos. 1703, 1732, 1741, 1744. Frati, "Guerra di Giangaleazzo", *ASL* xiv 241–3.

[4] Giovanni Morelli, *Cronica*, 300.

[5] Frati, "Guerra di Giangaleazzo", *ASL* xiv 243–6.

[6] Salviati, "Cronica", *DET* xviii 185. Similarly Giovanni Morelli, *Cronica*, 300.

quarrelled and debated among themselves, Giangaleazzo gathered a new army and repaired his fleet. Two months after his defeat, Verme recovered Borgoforte and once more entered the "Serraglio". It was too late, however, to make any use of this advantage, for winter was settling down over Lombardy. The Milanese army ravaged the *Mantovano* for a week, and withdrew until the spring.[1]

The results of the campaign were inconclusive, and far from fulfilled Giangaleazzo's expectations; but he had the satisfaction of knowing that the threat of French invasion had not materialized. Preparations had begun in Paris, and Charles had even enlisted the aid of England;[2] but the disaster inflicted on the French crusading army by the Turks at Nicopolis put an end, for the moment at least, to plans for an Italian expedition. The King's reason gave way under the shock. The French even made use of Giangaleazzo's services, to secure the release of the prisoners taken by the Turks.[3]

It was not until July 1397 that the Florentine ambassadors in Paris could make Charles understand the Republic's need and his own obligations. Bernard of Armagnac was then appointed to lead an army into Italy; but the Duke of Orleans placed every obstacle in his way, and there was no chance that the French could arrive in Italy before the opening of the campaign in 1398.[4] Giangaleazzo, however, left nothing to chance. He intervened to settle the disputes of his ally, Teodoro of Montferrat, with the Prince of Achaia,[5] lest the Savoyards might be tempted to make alliance with the League, and facilitate the passage of a French army through Piedmont.

On the other hand, Giangaleazzo's efforts to bring Wenceslaus to Italy were equally unsuccessful. This was his last bid for a

[1] Frati, "Guerra di Giangaleazzo", *ASL* xiv 246–8.
[2] Lucca, *Regesti*, 334, no. 1615.
[3] Delaville le Roulx, *France en Orient*, i 300–4; Froissart, *Chroniques*, xv 354–5, and xvi 31.
[4] Pitti, "Cronica", 104–5; de Boüard, *France et l'Italie*, 221–2. For the hopes and disappointments of the Florentines, *v.* Lucca, *Regesti*, nos. 1634, 1690, 1692, 1695, 1741, 1746, 1760, 1797, 1810, 1813, 1821, 1872, 1877, 1881.
[5] Gabotto, *Ultimi Principi d'Acaia*, 307–8.

triumph engineered from outside Italy—Pope and Emperor in
Milan for the Imperial coronation, a kingdom of Lombardy as the
Duke's reward, and a German army to fight for Boniface and for
himself. The two letters which refer to these proposals, although
they differ in detail, agree in the outline of Giangaleazzo's intentions. Rumours of his plans were already abroad in Florence in
April 1397;[1] and his envoy was still actively engaged in pressing
on the scheme at Rome in December.[2]

Insuperable obstacles arose. Boniface would not move from
Rome until Wenceslaus was well on his way to Italy; he refused
to forfeit the friendship of other claimants of the Imperial crown
until Wenceslaus, fickle and untrustworthy as he was, had gone
too far to withdraw. The King of the Romans, encouraged by
Sigismund,[3] was eager enough to come to Italy; but he could no
longer ignore the discontent aroused by his neglect of German
affairs. The Electoral princes complained of the "alienation" of
Imperial lands by the creation of the Duchy of Milan; prominent
among them was Leopold of Austria, anxious to eradicate Milanese
influence in the *Trentino*. To go directly to Italy as the proclaimed ally of Giangaleazzo, would be to precipitate a revolution
in Germany. Wenceslaus went instead to Germany, and with
unexpected firmness and decision dealt with the problems of the
Reich;[4] but he was fatally ready to be persuaded, and he now
came under the influence of French policy. His barons had
summoned him to deal with the problems of the Church in a
manner befitting his position, and French emissaries suggested
the means. Before the end of 1397, he had agreed to meet
Charles VI in person, and discuss with him the question of putting
an end to the Schism.[5]

---

[1] Information was received "non da homo di Firenze, ma da altro homo
degno di fede et di reverentia et che sa de' facti di corte di Roma assai".
Despatch of 28 April 1397: Lucca, *Regesti*, 360, no. 1716.

[2] Gherardo Aldighieri to Giangaleazzo, from Rome, 8 December 1397:
ibid. 475–8, no. 2156.

[3] Sigismund's approval is shown in his letter to Wenceslaus, undated, but
almost certainly written in 1397: Palacky, "Formelbücher", 71–2, no. 65.

[4] Lindner, "Geschichte des deutschen Reiches", II 361–89.

[5] The Duke of Berri's Chancellor to Jodocus of Moravia, 23 December
1397: *ibid.* 506–7.

The famous conference of Rheims, between Wenceslaus and Charles, destroyed the great combination which Giangaleazzo had worked so hard to construct. The King of the Romans did not abandon either the Milanese alliance or the plans for his coronation—his representatives were in Italy in May 1398, preparing the way for his coming, warning Amadeus of Savoy not to offend the Duke of Milan, "forasmuch as the Duke is his Majesty's baron";[1] but in negotiating with the French, he forfeited the confidence of Boniface IX.

The Franco-Florentine alliance, which was followed within a month by the surrender of Genoa to the dominion of Charles VI, had evoked a violent protest from the Pope. Boniface summoned Wenceslaus to restore Imperial prestige, and drive the French intruders out of Italy.[2] The protests and assurances of Florence —that Boniface and Ladislaus were specifically protected by the terms of the alliance, and that the Visconti were the traditional and most dangerous enemies of the Church—were of no avail; and the Florentines were dismayed to find that the Pope was contributing by indirect means to the strength of the Milanese army.[3] As late as November 1397, Boniface wrote to the Republic that "the King of the French is greedy for the whole of Italy, and threatens our dominion with ruin".[4] The attacks of the Papal Condottieri on Biordo Michelotti[5] in January 1398 were closely related to Milanese policy, and weakened the offensive power of Florence. The activities of the Papal legate, at the peace conferences which sat during the war, were equally partial.[6]

Boniface, however, had no other quarrel with Florence save over the French alliance, and sincerely desired the conclusion of a peace, which would put an end to the danger of French invasion. While he favoured the Milanese cause, he encouraged the work of pacification, and at the same time continued to call on Wenceslaus

[1] Despatch from Pavia, 3 May 1398: *ASS*, Concistoro 1842, no. 20. De Boüard, *France et l'Italie*, 247–8.
[2] Jarry, *Origines*, 302–3. Letter of Boniface to a German prince: Palacky, *op. cit.* 61, no. 53.
[3] Jarry, *Origines*, 303–7.
[4] Fabretti, *Biografie dei Capitanei venturieri dell' Umbria*, I 99.
[5] Lucca, *Regesti*, 429, nos. 1958–9.
[6] Frati, "Guerra di Giangaleazzo", *ASL* XIV 249.

to drive the French out of Genoa. The conference of Rheims, and the fear of an understanding between France and Germany, must have been a grave shock for him. It forced him to rely on the German princes, and especially on the Count Palatine Rupert of Bavaria. The princes had urged Wenceslaus to deal with the problem of the Schism, but they resented any subservience to French policy, and clamoured for the enforcement of Imperial rights both in Genoa and in Milan. Boniface asked them to strengthen the resistance of Wenceslaus against French usurpations. The Florentines, on the other hand, were inciting them against Giangaleazzo and against Wenceslaus himself, whom they represented as a mere instrument of Milanese policy. The princes wished to accept both policies—the anti-French and the anti-Milanese—failing to see that they were at the moment irreconcilable.[1]

One fact emerges plainly from these cross-currents: the collapse of Giangaleazzo's ambitious plan for an alliance with the Pope and the Emperor. A new international situation began to take shape towards the end of 1398: on the one hand Wenceslaus, Giangaleazzo, and the Duke of Orleans, on the other Florence, Boniface IX, the German Electors led by Rupert of Bavaria, and the anti-Orleanist party at the French court, who were connected through Queen Isabella and her brother Lewis of Bavaria with the opposition to Wenceslaus in Germany.

These developments overreach the immediate bounds of this chapter. It remains clear, however, that neither Giangaleazzo nor his enemies could expect any foreign intervention in their favour during the first year of the war; and, since the issue was confined to Italy, the attitude adopted by Venice became all-important.

In war, as in the last five years of peace, the Venetians used all their influence to preserve the uncertain equilibrium between Giangaleazzo and the League. The balance of power created by the formation of the League was far from ideal, but the Venetians were anxious to preserve it from the shocks of war. Peace conferences sat almost uninterruptedly at Imola, Ferrara and Venice, under the presidency of the Doge and the Papal legate; but neither

---

[1] Lindner, "Geschichte des deutschen Reiches", II 366–7, 505–6.

side showed any readiness to accept a compromise, until the
uncertain course of the war had taken a definite turn in favour of
one party or the other.[1]

The Venetians did not intend to allow Mantua to fall to the
Milanese army while the conferences sat. They avoided the commercial dislocation of open war, but stretched the interpretation
of neutrality as widely as circumstances demanded in Gonzaga's
favour. They allowed him to enlist their subjects in his service;
they advanced loans, sent ships up the Po to resist the invading
forces, and constructed new defences on the river in Mantuan
territory.[2] Giangaleazzo's failure to take Gonzaga by surprise
left him face to face with the undefined resistance of the Venetians
who, without recognizing any fixed obligations, enlarged the
extent of their commitments as the danger to Mantua grew.

The need for Venetian intervention increased as the war went
on. The army of the League was paralysed, after the victory of
Governolo, by the quarrels of its leaders. Carlo Malatesta, the
one man who might have led an offensive against Milan, left the
camp "with little love" for Gonzaga, and returned to Rimini.[3]
Bologna did little or nothing to help her allies, and the Florentines, burdened with the defence of Tuscany, spoke in disgust of
leaving Mantua to its fate.[4] Giangaleazzo, thinking to turn these
divisions to his own account, assured the lesser members of the
League that he wished to live at peace with them;[5] but his overtures were premature, and led only to a closer understanding
between Florence and Bologna.[6]

[1] Roberto Cessi, "Venezia neutrale", *NAV* NS xxviii 305. The meetings
of the peace conferences are fully reported in the despatches of this year,
published in Lucca, *Regesti*.

[2] Roberto Cessi, "Venezia neutrale", *NAV* NS xxviii 303–7; Pastorello,
Nuove Ricerche, 96 note 8.

[3] Despatch from Florence, 13 November 1397: Lucca, *Regesti*, 406, no.
1870. Pastorello, *Nuove Ricerche*, 97–8, for the quarrel between Malatesta
and Carrara; but the reasons given are not entirely satisfactory. Cf. Sercambi, "Cronache", II 39, from the despatches published in Lucca, *Regesti*,
397–8, nos. 1831–2, 1834–7.

[4] Reports from Florence, 13–20 November: *ibid.* 406–10, nos. 1870–82.
The quarrels between the allies will be examined further in the next chapter.

[5] Despatches from Ferrara, where the allies were in conference, 16 and 17
November 1397: Lucca, *Regesti*, 407–8, nos. 1874, 1876.

[6] Despatch from Florence, 26 December 1397: *ibid.* 417, no. 1895.

The Duke's predominance over his two allies left small scope for quarrels, but his position in Tuscany was not entirely satisfactory. Biordo's desertion had weakened his strategical strength. "We hear that certain exiles of Perugia would willingly betake themselves to your city [of Siena] with the intention of doing all possible damage to Biordo, with your help and that of your friends. Therefore we recommend you to receive those exiles in your city, and...to afford them all the help which you can conveniently give against Biordo."[1] But the Sienese had no wish to offend Biordo, if we may judge by a letter written a month later by the government of Perugia. "Most dear brothers," they wrote, "We hold for certain that, even as it is shown on both sides, you count the citizens of Perugia as your own, while we declare yours to be citizens of Perugia."[2] The Umbrian Commune, in fact, remained on good terms with Siena, and did not associate itself with the military activities of the League. Biordo himself was held responsible in certain circles for these friendly relations;[3] but the Florentines, who were confident that they would eventually win over the Sienese to the side of the League by a combination of military and diplomatic pressure,[4] may have been glad to use Perugia as an intermediary.

However that may be, the Florentine intrigues failed. Giangaleazzo had to deal with a certain amount of opposition and discontent in Siena; but his agents were active, and the Visconti garrison strong. A plot to admit Florentine troops into the city was discovered, and a brief rising had to be suppressed. Some members of the Piccolomini family went into exile, and offered their swords to Florence. Alberico da Barbiano himself asserted that the troops in Siena were badly paid, and the attitude of the Sienese was not wholly friendly; but all the plots and blandishments and threats of Florence did not succeed in detaching Siena from the Milanese alliance.[5]

---

[1] Giangaleazzo to Siena, 8 September 1397: *ASS*, Concistoro 1840, no. 58.
[2] Perugia to Siena, 13 October 1397: *ibid.* 1841, no. 7.
[3] Despatch from Florence, 26 December 1397: Lucca, *Regesti*, 416, no. 1895.
[4] *Ibid.* nos. 1742, 1763, 1705, 1800, 1811, 1808, 1845, 1848.
[5] *Ibid.* nos. 1555 c, 1561 a, 1564 a, 1568 e, 1706, 1709, 1757.

Giangaleazzo, through an error of judgment on his own part, nearly forfeited the support of his other ally in Tuscany. Jacopo d'Appiano's elder son died in October 1397, and his younger son, Gherardo, showed no ability. Jacopo himself was old, and Giangaleazzo expected to find him acquiescent. The Duke proposed to appropriate the military direction of Pisa and its district. Appiano, in the first moments of grief at the loss of his son, raised no objection; but he soon understood that the control of fortified places was only the first step in Giangaleazzo's plan to assume the direct government of Pisa. Niccolò Pallavicino, Niccolò Diversi, and the haughty Paolo Savelli with 300 lances, came to set these proposals before Appiano.

Giangaleazzo had misjudged his man. The Florentines showed a more acute perception of Appiano's character, and were quick to grasp the opportunity of strengthening their own cause.[1] Appiano, on learning the nature of the Milanese demands, warned his own partisans, drove Savelli's troops out of Pisa, and took captive the Duke's representatives.[2]

For the first six weeks of 1398, the issue of the war was centred on the discussions and intrigues which followed the success of this bold measure in Pisa. Florence and Lucca offered to come to terms with Appiano, if he would undertake to abandon the Milanese cause. Giangaleazzo, on the other hand, was quick to recognize his error; he disowned his agents, and sent Antonio Porro with a free hand to repair the damage they had done.[3] We do not know what terms Porro offered to the affronted lord of Pisa; but old Ghibelline associations, Appiano's long co-operation with Giangaleazzo, and the Duke's ready admission of his mistake, finally won the day. Appiano declared in the middle of February that he could accept no terms with the League, without

---

[1] "Questo si fa molto per noi", it was said in Florence, "per certo si fa per noi: almeno una brigata di traditori non aranno ser Jacopo." Despatch of 2 January: *ibid.* 427, no. 1947.

[2] Minerbetti, "Cronica", 222–6; Sercambi, "Cronache", II 67–75. A Florentine letter of 11 January 1398: Scaramella, "Dominazione Viscontea in Pisa", *SS* III 465–7, Doc. 3. Despatches in Lucca, *Regesti*, nos. 2152, 1931, 1948–51.

[3] *Ibid.* nos. 1902, 1905, 1911, 1913, 1918, 1920; Scaramella, "Dominazione Viscontea in Pisa", *SS* III 431–2.

the consent of his ally the Duke of Milan.[1] "The agreement with Pisa is entirely broken off, and messer Jacopo is indeed that traitor for which we know him."[2]

The Florentines had contributed to their own failure, by their refusal to accept anything less than the privileges which they had enjoyed in Porto Pisano under Gambacorta's rule. Giangaleazzo benefited in two ways from their obstinacy; for they lost, not only the chance of a reconciliation with Appiano and the reopening to their trade of the vitally important Porto Pisano, but also the friendship of Lucca, whose rulers would have welcomed the opportunity of making peace with a dangerous neighbour, and who felt that the interests of their community were being sacrificed to the greed and ambition of Florence. From this moment, Lucca began to move steadily back into the orbit of Visconti influence.

Giangaleazzo, having retrieved his position in Tuscany, prepared to renew the campaign against Mantua. The peace conference had meanwhile resumed its meetings in Venice, and the Venetian government now advanced its own proposals for a settlement, including the renunciation of the old claims which Giangaleazzo had revived to Gonzaga's homage, and the surrender of the conquests which he had made during the war. Giangaleazzo, confident in his strength, rejected these terms; but once again he reckoned without the *Serenissima*. Mantua was in danger, Gonzaga wavered, and his allies were divided. The Venetians agreed, as a last resort, to become an active member of the League. The peace conference was transformed into a council of war, and Venice took the lead with energy and resolution.[3] The clauses of the new alliance were drawn up and signed on 21 March 1398.[4]

One clause in the new alliance awoke some misgiving in Florence. The government wrote to their envoys that "where it

[1] Minerbetti, "Cronica", 226; Sercambi, "Cronache", II 75–9; Lucca, *Regesti*, nos. 1899–1929, 1950–62, 1937, 2151. Letters and instructions of the Florentine government: *ASF*, Signoria, Legazioni I 173–7.

[2] Florence to her envoys in Venice, 19 February 1397/8: *ibid.* 177.

[3] Despatches from Venice, January and February 1398: Lucca, *Regesti*, 430–4, nos. 1962–71. Frati, "Guerra di Giangaleazzo", *ASL* XIV 248–53.

[4] Published by Veroi, *Storia della Marca Trivigiana*, XVII, Doc. 1965, pp. 97–112.

is shown that the Venetians wish to take pre-eminence, in being able to make war and peace at their own disposition, it seems to us that their claim is not just, nor one which good and reasonable allies ought to make. Do you then abide firmly by the decision of the allies, or the greater part of them, showing that we are disposed to peace, and do not need any one to be our guide in this resolution."[1] They accepted this condition in the end, but only with reluctance; and their hesitation was soon shown to be only too well justified.

The Venetians decided to send an ultimatum to Giangaleazzo, demanding that he should accept the terms which he had formerly rejected. Meanwhile, they took upon themselves the direction of the war, united the allies under their determined leadership, and prepared to enlist 6000 lances for a double attack on Milan. The forces of the League, which Giangaleazzo had confidently been preparing to assail and defeat, suddenly threatened to overwhelm him. Under the spur of the Venetian example, his neighbours on every side offered their services to his enemies.[2] Leopold of Austria volunteered to bring 3000 lances to fight for the League, in return no doubt for concessions in the Val di Trento. The Count of Savoy, prompted perhaps by Philip of Burgundy, his wife's father, offered to attack Giangaleazzo from the west, and acquire for himself the Visconti territories between the Po and the Ticino. The lands of the Malaspina, whose many branches were scattered through the Apennines of the Lunigiana, and along the rocky coastline between the Genoese Riviera and Tuscany, had been included by Wenceslaus in the dominions of the Duke of Milan;[3] and some of them turned now to Venice, in the hope of securing their independence from the Visconti. Serious revolts, fostered by the League, the Bishop of Trent,[4] and Leopold of Austria, had already broken out among the Guelfs in the mountains of Ber-

---

[1] Letter of 10 March 1397/8: *ASF*, Signoria, Legazioni I 177 t–8.

[2] From accounts of the deliberations of the League in Venice, given in despatches from Venice, February to April 1398: Lucca, *Regesti*, 434–8, nos. 1972–9; Frati, "Guerra di Giangaleazzo", *ASL* xiv 270–7, Docs. 5–6.

[3] *V. RIS* xvi 827 c; Lucca, *Regesti*, 318, no. 1556.

[4] "Giorgio di Liechtenstein voleva eziandio concorrere con la lega alla distruzione del Visconti": Postinger, "Documenti in Volgare Trentino", *AAA* 3, vii 160–1.

gamo and Brescia.[1] Buonaccorso Pitti arrived post-haste from
Paris to complete the arrangements for Bernard of Armagnac's
expedition, which was nearly ready to set out against Milan.[2]

Thus the action of Venice turned the tide. Wenceslaus, from
whom alone Giangaleazzo could expect help, was in conference
with Charles VI in the distant city of Rheims. The Duke could not
hope to stand alone against the gathering forces of Florence,
Venice, Austria, Savoy and France. The only course open to him
was to sue for peace.

Here the superiority of his diplomacy over that of his enemies
became apparent; and, by a curious accident of good fortune, it
was precisely the open adherence of Venice to the cause of his
enemies that enabled him to extricate himself from the dangers
which threatened him, and opened a new era of success and
triumph. The League in desperation had made a false step, of
which the Florentines were uneasily aware. The slip did not
escape Giangaleazzo's watchful eyes, and he seized his opportunity
with both hands. It was his only chance of emerging from the
war without material loss.

The Duke received the Venetian envoys, who came to deliver
the Serenissima's ultimatum, in a spirit of friendly co-operation.
He knew that the Venetians did not want to fight if they could
avoid it. He knew, too, that Gonzaga's faith in his allies was
badly shaken;[3] for Carlo Malatesta arrived in Pavia at the heels
of the Venetian ambassadors,[4] apparently bringing overtures of
peace from the lord of Mantua.[5] Giangaleazzo, with the Venetian
ambassadors and Carlo Malatesta, who knew and respected him,

[1] "Chronicon Bergomense", RIS xvi 893 E sqq.; "Annales Mediolanenses", ibid. 831 D.

[2] Pitti, "Cronica", 105–7; Lucca, Regesti, nos. 1872, 1877, 1881, 1889,
1895, 1952, 1976, 1978.

[3] Gonzaga's grievances are recorded in a despatch from Florence, 21 December 1397: ibid. 413–15, no. 1889.

[4] "Domani s' attendono qui l' imbasciadori Venegiani senza fallo; el
signore Carlo malatesti s' attende qui lunedì o martedì." Despatch from
Pavia, 29 March 1398: ASS, Concistoro 1842, no. 1.

[5] Platina, op. cit. RIS xx 789 D–790. This seems the most likely explanation
of Carlo's presence in Pavia, in view of his intimate relations with Gonzaga.
Cf. the story told from the Paduan angle, by Gatari, "Cronaca Carrarese",
RIS NS xvii, 1, 464.

quietly arranged between them the terms of a truce based on purely Veneto-Lombard interests.

The Florentines had foreseen, but could not guard against this eventuality. "You know how hard are Venetian heads," they had written as early as 15 January; "they are often incapable of subtle argument!"[1] Later, their reproaches grew more bitter. "We thought by the alliance with Venice to have exalted the League to the skies; and these first negotiations bury us, and the League, and all honour and advantage which we ought deservedly to have.... If the Commune of Venice alone were at war with him, they would not suffer that a settlement should be negotiated with him in his own house, as it seems that they do when they are negotiating for us. This is not that which they said to us, that although they desired authority to make peace and truce, it was not their intention to do anything without our consent; and that, in evidence and guarantee of this, they wished that our ambassadors and those of the other allies should always be at hand to confer with their government and decide whatever should be necessary....And now their ambassadors, without any consent of ours, and to our shame, have gone to the enemy's house....We see well that the Duke our enemy has but a poor opinion of the League; and he is right."[2] Early in May, they renew their complaints. "We do not object to their sending to Pavia, but the whole foundation of our grievance is in the discussions. For we thought, and so you gave us to understand, that their ambassadors would inform the enemy of the alliance they had made, and of the authority reserved to their government of making peace; and that they would offer him peace on good and reasonable terms. But that their ambassadors should negotiate in his house,...this is what displeases us, alike for the honour of the League and for the good of the business. For, although the Venetian ambassadors are good and most prudent gentlemen, and competent for the greatest affairs, yet it is impossible for them to know and understand all the particulars which affect each ally....We are sure

---

[1] "Della suttilità della ragione." Florence to her ambassadors in Venice: *ASF*, Signoria, Legazioni I 173 & t.

[2] The same, 24 April 1398: *ibid.* 180t–181.

that their government is well-disposed, and would regret an
undesirable settlement; but the other side does not deal straight-
forwardly, as they do, but in sophistry and malice, against which
those who have not experienced their methods would never be
on guard."[1]

Their reproaches and warnings went unheeded. The Venetians
took command of the situation, as the terms of the League allowed,
and concluded a truce for ten years at Pavia on 11 May 1398.[2]
Giangaleazzo, flattering and deferring to their wishes, emerged
from the war without loss. He agreed to surrender the captured
castles of the *Mantovano* to Carlo Malatesta, pending the conclusion of a definitive peace. Gonzaga was to surrender others of
equal value, and might repair the fortifications of his lands and
rebuild the bridge of Borgoforte. Giangaleazzo promised not to
tamper with the course of the Mincio. The indemnity, which the
peace of Genoa had imposed on Carrara, was suspended until a
final settlement was made. For Tuscany, no provision at all
appears in the truce.

---

[1] The same, 5 May 1398: *ibid.* 181 t–2.
[2] Giangaleazzo to Siena, 11 May, notifying the government of the truce:
ASS, Concistoro 1842, no. 30. The terms of the truce were published by
Dumont, *Corps diplomatique*, ii, 1, 266–9, no. 194, erroneously dated 17 May.

CHAPTER XVI

LOMBARDY DURING THE MANTUAN WAR.
THE COLLAPSE OF THE LEAGUE OF BOLOGNA,
AND GIANGALEAZZO'S POLICY AT THE TRUCE
OF PAVIA (1397–*MAY* 1398)

THE prosperity of Lombardy was on the decline. The dominions of Milan had been asked to contribute to too many extraordinary expenses since 1392—the works on the Mincio, Coucy's campaign against Genoa, the celebration of Giangaleazzo's investiture in 1395, and the defence of Pisa and Siena. As late as August 1394, a levy had to be ordered, to settle up the accounts of the previous war.[1] The mantle which Giangaleazzo assumed among the other insignia of his Dukedom, was alone estimated to be worth 200,000 florins.[2] In March 1396, the Duke had to dismiss part of the troops which garrisoned Siena, "for the abatement of the great and manifold expenses which fall upon us".[3] Even the financial privileges enjoyed by the Duomo of Milan were suspended in the same year.[4]

Apart, then, from any other considerations, the financial condition of his state was sufficient to explain Giangaleazzo's reluctance to go to war, and his anxiety to reach a quick conclusion. His hesitation was fully justified, for ordinary methods were not sufficient to meet the heavy demands of the Mantuan campaign. According to Corio, 800,000 florins were raised by extraordinary taxation.[5] It is more likely that this was the sum which the taxes were estimated to yield; but money was very scarce, the value of the florin was rising, and the government

---

[1] Morbio, *Codice Visconteo-Sforzesco*, 17–19, nos. 6–7.
[2] Corio, *Storia di Milano*, II 398.
[3] Giangaleazzo to Siena, 26 March 1396: *ASS*, Concistoro 1837, no. 2.
[4] Nava, *Memorie del Duomo*, 64.
[5] Corio, *op. cit.* II 408–9. And *v.* Santoro, "Registri", 79–82, for taxation.

found it impossible to meet their requirements in this way.[1] Giangaleazzo offered the town of Serravalle in the Ligurian Alps for sale, but he does not seem to have found a purchaser.[2] He had to increase the commitments of the state by renewed borrowing, which was accompanied by a reduction of the interest on state loans from the rate of 10 to 8 per cent.[3] A percentage tax was taken on legacies to the foundation of the Cathedral of Milan;[4] and the plans of the Certosa of Pavia, which had already been rigorously curtailed in 1396,[5] were now almost completely held up by lack of funds. The army had to be paid before it would fight; but grave difficulty was experienced in securing money in cash for the purpose, especially for the troops in Tuscany.[6] On the other hand, the sailors of the river ports were compelled to serve in the Milanese fleet; and many of them were still clamouring for their pay, a year after the end of the war.[7]

An appeal, written in March 1398, called the attention of Francesco Barbavara to the penury of Pavia;[8] and official letters in the following year declared in terser but equally effective terms that the Commune was unable to meet its expenditure or pay its debts.[9] Pavia was certainly not the only city to find itself in this predicament; nearly all the historians of the Communes record the financial oppressions of these years. The Mantuan war marks a definite stage of the decline in the prosperity of the Visconti

[1] Pezzana, *Storia di Parma*, I 254, and note 1, from a manuscript chronicle. According to a report drawn up by Galeazzo Maria Sforza's treasurers, seventy-five years later, the value of the florin rose from 34 soldi in 1397 to 36 in 1398: Argelati, *de Monetis Italie*, III 35. Its exchange value was fixed at 32 soldi.

[2] Niccolò Diversi to Francesco Barbavara, undated: Lucca, *Regesti*, 323, no. 1568 b. Jarry, *Origines*, 250.

[3] Ordinance of 19 April 1398: *Antiqua Decreta*, 218–22.

[4] Nava, *op. cit.* 74.

[5] Romano, "Bolla dell' Antipapa Clemente VII", *BSP* II 418–19.

[6] Letters of Niccolò Diversi and of Giovanni Borromei: Lucca, *Regesti*, 318 and 320, nos. 1555 c, 1561 a.

[7] In the *Archivio Notarile* at Piacenza, "ci sono molte procure di Piacentini dell' armata navale, per esigere il loro stipendio" in 1398–9: Rossi, "Eustachi di Pavia", *BSP* XIV 48, note 2.

[8] *V.* Doc. 13.

[9] Published by Magenta, *Visconti e Sforza*, II 78–9, no. 104; and 83–4, no. 110.

state. Giangaleazzo's ambitions had involved him in a struggle from which he could no longer withdraw, and in which he was steadily using up the capital resources of his dominions.

These conditions were not likely to promote the happiness and contentment of the people. Lombardy owed much to the powerful protection of the Visconti: the suppression of crime, the limitation of abuses in the exercise of privilege and authority, the freedom of the ordinary citizen to pursue his affairs in security; but the affection and gratitude, which these benefits might have earned, were alienated by the constant financial pressure which was exerted in the concomitant struggle for further dominion. The Florentines, indeed, no longer spoke of the possibility of revolts in the central nucleus of Visconti territory. The rebellion of the Guelfs in the mountains behind Bergamo and Brescia arose from special circumstances, the survival in the remote and inaccessible valleys of more primitive social and political conditions, in which the feuds of Guelf and Ghibelline were enshrined. In the cities of the Lombard plain, the war passed without incident. The Communes and districts renewed their homage to the Duke of Milan and Count of Pavia between February and June 1397.[1] Although Communal independence hardly survived, the people enjoyed the reflected glory of their ruler. But they grew passively discontented, under the burdens to which the Duke's foreign policy subjected them. The economic pressure of war forced Giangaleazzo to abandon the standards of good government which he himself had set in his earlier years; and the forces of disorder bided their time, awaiting the moment when they could resume the freedom they had lost.

The struggles between city and "contado", between feudal proprietors and Communal governments, between wealthy merchants and industrial labourers, had begun long before the Visconti had come to power; they had to direct the energies of the contestants as best they could, without being able to impose a final solution in accordance with their own principles. They had to rely on the co-operation of some sections of the population

---

[1] The list of Communes is published by Romano, "Regesto", *ASL* xxi, 2, 80–5.

within their dominions, in order to be free to pursue unhampered the fulfilment of their ambitions. Giangaleazzo had not been able to achieve as complete a unification and co-ordination of the life and government of his territories as he desired; beyond a certain point, he was faced by an opposition which he did not dare to defy. He relied on the profits of commerce and industry, to finance his enterprises. As we have seen, he adapted the fiscal policy of the state, to provide for the profitable investment of capital resources in the undertakings of the government; and the owners of capital, the youngest and most vital element of society, demanded protection for their own interests, and concessions in the ordinary routine of taxation, in return for their help.[1] Hence perhaps arose the complaint from Pavia at the end of the war, that the poorer citizens had many of them been driven from their homes by the pressure of taxation, while the rich paid nothing.[2] In spite of Giangaleazzo's wish to distribute the burden fairly according to each man's capacity, necessity forced him to respect certain interests, at the expense of those whose resistance he least feared. In 1392, he had commanded that, in the payment of a special levy, those whose assessment fell below a fixed level in the "estimo" should be exempt;[3] but he rebuked the Milanese government for issuing a similar order on their own initiative, three years later.[4] An exemption of the same kind, made in September 1397, had to be revoked within a fortnight.[5] Thus inclination and expediency struggled within him.

The "Contado", too, suffered from the distribution of taxation. In 1416, the city of Pavia contributed only a third of the total sum which the whole district of the Commune was called upon to

---

[1] Picotti, "Qualche Osservazione sui caratteri delle Signorie Italiane", *RSI* xliii (NS iv) 24, note 1. Ciapessoni, "Per la Storia della Economia", *BSP* vi, 613; Barbieri, *Economia e Politica*, 41–4.

[2] *V.* Doc. 13. Barbieri traces the depressive effect on the working classes of the international economic policy pursued by Giangaleazzo in alliance with the great merchant-bankers of Milan, and refers to wage limitations which were imposed in order to keep down prices: *op. cit.* 45–6, 55–6.

[3] Santoro, "Registri", 34–5, no. 162. Cases in which the interests of the consumer and of the workers received special protection from the government are quoted by Barbieri, *op. cit.* 54–8.

[4] Santoro, "Registri", 52, no. 250.   [5] *Ibid.* 79, nos. 46, 48.

pay;[1] and the rural districts were probably little better off under Giangaleazzo's rule. The "Comuni rurali" had, indeed, found a measure of protection under the Visconti from the oppressive authority imposed by the victorious cities during the Communal epoch. In the case of many localities, allegiance was transferred directly to the ruler, and centres of resistance were thus created against the great Communes, with their traditions of independence and self-government;[2] but the issue was by no means settled, and the Communes were constantly striving to retain or renew their supremacy in administration, jurisdiction, and finance, over the districts which they had formerly ruled.[3] In spite of Giangaleazzo's efforts to promote the prosperity of agriculture, the burden of taxation still fell unduly on the countryside.

The same character of opportunism distinguishes the fight against privilege. The Visconti had taken drastic measures, by revoking grants and by the less arbitrary method of investigation "quo Warranto", to check this abuse; and the campaign against privileges reached its height at the time of Giangaleazzo's reform of financial administration in 1387–8; but the problem was not solved. Giangaleazzo himself granted many privileges and rights of exemption, on the new basis of "famigliarità", the reward of personal service to the prince; but they were not fundamentally different from the old feudal model, and complaints were heard that the Count undid the good work of revoking the old immunities, by the creation of new ones.[4]

It may perhaps be true that the Visconti never hoped entirely to eradicate feudal privilege; their object was to use it, as they wished to use local particularism, in the service of their despotic state. The efficiency of his government, combined with an understanding of the need to compromise with the elements whose support was indispensable to him, enabled Giangaleazzo to hold together the great Lombard state; but, while he succeeded in uniting conflicting interests, he did not reconcile them in a mutual

[1] Ciapessoni, *op. cit. BSP* vi 229–31.
[2] Tagliabue, "Politica Finanziaria", *BSP* xv 56–60.
[3] This is clearly shown, for example, by Lonati, *Stato Totalitario alla fine del secolo XIV*, 29–30, 35–6, 41.
[4] Boselli, *Storie Piacentine*, ii 66–7; Tagliabue, *op. cit. BSP* xv 69–75.

acceptance of his own political ideas. The political education of his subjects, as well as the sound economic prosperity of his dominions, had still to be achieved.

Giangaleazzo had ruled alone over the territories of the Visconti for thirteen years. This is a factor which cannot be ignored, in discussing the sudden change which came over the political situation of northern Italy in 1398. The Duke had twice faced the united onslaughts of his enemies, and emerged unscathed. There seemed no hope of overthrowing his firmly established power. The allies had borne the sacrifices of war, and had gained nothing in return. Only the prospect of defeating the common enemy had held them together, in spite of their own differences and quarrels, for six years; and that hope was frustrated by the truce of Pavia.

The war had thrown a glaring light on their egotism, on their inability to frame and execute a joint policy to promote the general objects of the League. The quarrels of Carlo Malatesta, Gonzaga and Carrara have already been mentioned. Far more serious was the lack of confidence shown between Florence and Bologna. The Bolognese, who at first seemed disposed to take their full share in the war,[1] soon revealed the combination of selfishness and fear which lay at the root of their policy. They demanded "that all the troops of the League should be sent to Mantua",[2] expecting that Florence would bear the brunt of the Lombard as well as of the Tuscan campaign. They fully appreciated the importance of protecting Mantua, but they refused to become involved in the plan to save Mantua by launching an offensive against Milan.[3]

The Florentines, whose faith in an offensive sprang partly from a desire to keep the stress of war away from Tuscany, grew bitter in their reproaches. They instructed their ambassadors at the end of July: "Especially, you are to see and hear whether the Bolognese are prepared to help the lord of Mantua, and to make war

[1] In April 1397: Lucca, *Regesti*, 351 and 353, nos. 1695, 1700.
[2] Commission of Florentine ambassadors to Bologna, 30 June 1397: *ASF*, Signoria, Legazioni I 86.
[3] Lucca, *Regesti*, nos. 1705, 1785–6, 1789, 1808, 1811, where the opinions current in Florence from mid-April to mid-August 1397 are recorded.

openly on the enemy, and not to stand under water and advance now one pretence and now another, as they have done hitherto."[1] They dreaded above all the insidious influence of Visconti propaganda in the allied city; they insisted that the peace conference should not meet in Bologna, "so that the Duke cannot sow more poison in Bologna".[2] And each incident nourished the old distrust and suspicion in which their policy was held by the Bolognese.[3]

The victory of the allies at Governolo seems to have brought a momentary truce to these bickerings; but once more, in November 1397, the Florentines were saying that "all are agreed that, if they had done their duty, things would be in better shape, as far as the war is concerned, than they are";[4] and it was questioned in Florence whether it would not be wiser to leave the fate of Mantua in the hands of those whom it more nearly concerned.[5]

Even within the walls of Florence, there was some murmuring against the government. The allies had as much difficulty as the Duke in financing the war. Money was lacking, and taxation oppressive;[6] and the people began to ask for whom or for what they were making sacrifices. Many of them regarded the war as a political intrigue of a governing clique, of Maso degli Albizzi and his supporters who were bent on securing their own commercial interests, their personal ambitions, or their political dogmas, against the rivalry of the Duke of Milan. The reports which came from Paris, relating the progress made in the preparation of the French expedition, were dismissed as a device of the rulers to delay the conclusion of peace. The people could find little consolation in the plausible argument that, after a few years of peace, Giangaleazzo would be able to renew the struggle with replenished resources, or in the more specious pretext that peace

[1] Commission of 30 July 1397: *ASF*, Signoria, Legazioni I 94.
[2] Despatch of 5 May 1397: Lucca, *Regesti*, 362, no. 1722.
[3] Two letters of Bologna to Florence during June 1397 are also relevant to these disputes: Frati, "Raccolta di lettere politiche", *ASI* 5, XI 138.
[4] Commission of ambassadors "per lo fatto della pace", 21 November 1397: *ASF*, Signoria, Legazioni I 101.
[5] Despatches from Florence during November: Lucca, *Regesti*, 407–10, nos. 1877–81.
[6] Despatches of 14 and 16 November 1397: *ibid.* 407, nos. 1871, 1874. Minerbetti, "Cronica", 223.

would involve Tuscany in invasion by the large armies engaged in the Mantuan campaign.[1]

It is not surprising that, while Florence and Bologna quarrelled and the Florentine people murmured against their rulers, the lesser allies lost faith in the virtue of the League as a bulwark against Milan. Giangaleazzo had waited for six years, watching for a sign of weakness in the unity of his enemies; his patience had its reward. Niccolò d'Este officially co-operated with his allies, although he remained in the background during the war. Francesco Carrara was still the most inveterate of the Duke's enemies. But the Bolognese envoy at Venice noticed, during March 1398, that two links in the chain of the League threatened to break under the strain.[2] These were Gonzaga, beset in Mantua, and the Commune of Lucca, disillusioned by the failure of Florence to profit by the opportunity of coming to terms with Jacopo d'Appiano.

Thus, by the dissolvent force of the war combined with a constructive revision of his diplomatic aims, Giangaleazzo was able to reverse the consequences of the peace of Genoa in Lombardy, and to secure the restoration of his own position, for which he had been struggling during the past six years. He emerged with an altered policy from the conference at Pavia with Carlo Malatesta and the Venetian envoys. Gonzaga was once more his good friend, to help and share in his triumphs. Niccolò d'Este might well be won over in the near future. For Giangaleazzo had convinced the Venetians of his readiness to fulfil the terms of the truce, and to respect the integrity of the states of Mantua, Ferrara and Padua. In Friuli, too, where he had not abandoned his intrigues during 1396 and 1397,[3] nothing is heard of his ambitions for two or three years after the truce of Pavia. By his reconciliation with Gonzaga and his recognition of Venetian interests in these districts, the Duke destroyed the menace of the League on his eastern frontier.

---

[1] Lucca, *Regesti*, nos. 1874, 1886, 1895, 1942.

[2] Frati, "Guerra di Giangaleazzo", *ASL* xiv 253.

[3] An offer of alliance and protection to the Patriarch in December 1396: Roberto Cessi, "Venezia neutrale", *NAV* NS xxviii 301–2. A threat, real or imagined, to the integrity of the Patriarchate, in May 1397: Cusin, *Confine Orientale d'Italia*, i 197 note 158.

In return, he secured a free hand in Tuscany; the Venetians were not prepared to fight in defence of the hegemony of Florence.

The Florentines sent an embassy to Venice in July 1398 to protest against the terms of the truce, as being fatal to the objects of the alliance which they had formed.[1] The tone of the instructions is mild, in comparison with the indignation expressed by contemporary Florentine chroniclers;[2] for the government knew that the truce had only brought a pause in the long conflict with Milan. Whether they believed that the *Serenissima* had been outwitted at Pavia, or had deliberately betrayed the allies, they gave no sign of distrust; for their hopes in the future must depend on the friendship of Venice. But Giangaleazzo had measured the extent to which the Venetians were prepared to help his enemies; by yielding the necessary minimum, he effectually put an end to the active alliance of March 1398. The Venetians resumed the policy of "no commitments"—not unwilling to accept Giangaleazzo's friendship, but watching his activities in their own territorial sphere with great care. They were determined to prevent him from dominating eastern Lombardy; but, as long as they found his assurances acceptable, they were not prepared to oppose his progress elsewhere. A short-term policy was typical of Venetian methods. They rejected the Florentine thesis that the interests of the two Republics were closely bound by the menace of Milanese power, and that it was short-sighted for one of them to allow the Duke to devote his whole resources to the annihilation of the other. In spite of the respect which the strength and reputation of Venice commanded on the mainland, the Venetians themselves were only too well aware of the insecurity of their colonial empire, especially after the battle of Nicopolis had revealed the weakness of Christendom in the face of the Turkish advance to the west.[3] They could not afford to accept the earnest and self-interested protests of Florence, that the policy of preserving a balance of power only allowed Giangaleazzo

---

[1] *V*. Doc. 14.

[2] E.g., Dati, *Istoria di Firenze*, 55–6; Pitti, "Cronica", 108; Salviati, "Cronica", *DET* xviii 186.

[3] Manfroni, "Crisi della Marina di Venezia", *AIV* 8, xii, 2, 987–9.

to recover from the strain of war, and to establish himself yet more firmly in northern Italy.[1]

Not only in Lombardy but in Romagna Giangaleazzo had undermined the ascendancy of Florence. Carlo Malatesta, having made peace between Gonzaga and the Duke, was able to resume his friendly relations with Milan. The Ordelaffi of Forlì ratified the truce as adherents of the Duke.[2] So, too, did Astorre Manfredi,[3] although he seems to have been engaged at the same time in a typical piece of trickery, and gave another ratification as "allied with Bologna".[4] Lodovico Alidosi of Imola was represented at Pavia during the negotiations for the truce;[5] his ratification was given on the side of the League of which he was a member,[6] but he had perhaps begun to look to the Duke for the powerful protection which the ruler of a small principality needed, in order to defend himself against the petty jealousies of his neighbours in Romagna.

The truce, moreover, marked the successful anticipation of the threat which had immediately brought about the war. The Florentines had been irritated by the delays and postponements in the arrival of the French army which had been promised to them. Charles VI and Bernard of Armagnac, on the other hand, were indignant that their allies should have made a truce without consulting them, at the moment when the French troops were almost ready to march.[7] They would not accept the excuse that the fault lay with the Venetians. The truce, which had revealed the conflicting purposes of Florence and Venice, also brought to an abrupt end the Franco-Florentine alliance, which had caused so much anxiety and alarm in Pavia.

[1] Roberto Cessi, "Venezia neutrale", *NAV* NS xxviii 304–7.
[2] Predelli, *Libri Commemoriali*, iii 265, no. 139.
[3] At Pavia, 31 July 1398: Romano, "Regesto", *ASL* xxi, 2, 295, no. 391. Manfredi passed through Parma on his way to Pavia on 14 July: Pezzana, *op. cit.* i 264.
[4] Dated 10 September, and recorded in the manuscript catalogue of *ASV*, "Miscellanea atti diplomatici e privati", no. 859.
[5] "Et qui...è uno ambasciadore del signor d' imola." Despatch from Pavia, 29 March 1398: *ASS*, Concistoro 1842, no. 1.
[6] Predelli, *op. cit.* iii 260, no. 119.
[7] Pitti, "Cronica", 109; Jarry, *Origines*, 308–9 and note 1; de Boüard, *France et l'Italie*, 228–30.

Thus, within three months of the day on which Venice had made alliance with his enemies, Giangaleazzo succeeded in the task which had perplexed him for six years. The unity of the League was broken, and the threat of French intervention ended. The alliance of the three Lombard princes against him was dissolved with the approval of Venice, and the danger to his eastern frontier was removed. Giangaleazzo could proceed to create new nuclei of supporters in Tuscany, Umbria and Romagna. His power and authority were no longer confined by the hostility of the League of Bologna.

The Florentines were generally shrewd interpreters of the motives which lay behind their enemies' actions. It is likely enough that Giangaleazzo had not abandoned, but only postponed, the establishment of his complete authority in eastern Lombardy. However weak and indecisive the rulers of Venice may have shown themselves to be in their oriental policy, there was no lack of determination to protect their interests in the *Veneto* and its immediate neighbourhood. The Duke set out to acquire fresh strength elsewhere, before he challenged them. Gonzaga was once more an ally. Niccolò d'Este hesitated, but he seemed inclined to adopt an attitude of neutrality, rejecting all obligations but recognizing the need to accept the dictates of a stronger power. The non-committal policy of Venice might be expected to exercise a restraining influence on the impetuous nature of Francesco Carrara. On the basis of these fresh circumstances, Giangaleazzo completely reversed his policy of the last six years. Instead of seeking to strengthen his authority in the east, in order to be free to help the threatened victims of Florentine aggression in Tuscany, he was now able to concentrate his forces on Tuscany and secure his southern flank from attack, in preparation for the rounding off of his dominions to the north of the Apennines.

It is interesting to find an alteration in the inner circle of the Duke's court, accompanying this change of policy; but it is impossible to make any definite connection between the two. A despatch from Fornuovo to the government of Lucca on 12 June gave the news that "Pasquino è preso di volontà del signore con

gran chaso ".[1] The powerful secretary was charged with the
betrayal of secrets to the League, and put to death. The true facts
of his downfall will probably never be known. Corio believed
him guilty of the treasonable acts of which he was accused. Of
the two contemporary accounts, that of the Milanese chronicle,
which relates that he fell through a stratagem, designed by
Francesco Gonzaga and revealed by him to Giangaleazzo at the
time of the truce, is clearly incompatible with the chronology of
events. The Veronese writer Marzagaia, although he is not a
reliable historian, makes the interesting suggestion that the
accusations against Pasquino were made by jealous rivals at the
Duke's court.[2]

At the same time, Niccolò Diversi disappears from among the
number of the Duke's advisers. He had been made the scapegoat
of the incident in Pisa at the beginning of the year, and only
secured his liberation from a Pisan prison early in June, on payment of a large ransom.[3] It does not seem likely, therefore, that
Giangaleazzo would have wished to punish him further for his
failure. But if he did not share in Pasquino's downfall, he must
have fallen from favour very soon afterwards; for it is recorded,
a year later, that he escaped from the prison in Pavia in which he
had been confined.[4]

Pasquino and Diversi were among the most important officials
of the court. Their simultaneous disgrace may have been a
coincidence, and it would certainly be rash to put forward
anything more than a conjectural explanation. But it is worth
noting, particularly in view of Marzagaia's comment, that the
removal of Pasquino left Francesco Barbavara without a rival as
the Duke's most favoured servant. The First Chamberlain had
won his master's confidence to a unique degree. Barbavara had

---

[1] Lucca, *Regesti*, 426, no. 1944.

[2] The scanty evidence was carefully analysed by Romano, "Regesto",
ASL xxi, 2, 295 note 2. Minerbetti, "Cronica", 282, gives the typically
biassed Florentine legend: "per torli il suo, ch'era molto ricco." But the city
of Cremona received Pasquino's property as a gift from the Duke.

[3] Sercambi, "Cronache", ii 195–6. He left Pisa on 7 June 1398.

[4] Known in Bergamo on 23 June 1399: "Chronicon Bergomense", *RIS*
xvi 916 E. He made his peace with the Visconti three years after the Duke's
death: Santoro, "Registro di Giovannolo Besozzi", 60 and note 4.

his own rooms in the palace, and even his own chancery above that of the Duke.[1] Much of the business of the state seems to have passed through his hands; thus in one instance, his chancellor was sent in person to convey instructions which emanated from the Duke.[2] The appeal which the Commune of Pavia addressed to him is a recognition of his influence and power at court.[3]

Although he is sometimes described as "Chamberlain and Secretary", he performed no such regular secretarial duties as Pasquino had done. He had far greater freedom, however; and he wrote letters and gave instructions in his own name, as Giangaleazzo's deputy and director of his affairs.[4] He received power "ad permutandum, et ad investiendum" the states, lands and goods of the Duchy in Giangaleazzo's name;[5] and almost the last act of the Duke was to confer upon him the title of Count of Pietre Gemelle in the Valsesia.[6] The memory of the Chamberlain's power survived to the days of Francesco Sforza, when a counsellor recalled how "he disposed of the state of the Duke as seemed good to him, and his friendship was sought rather than the Duke's, especially because it was easier to have speech with him than with the lord Duke".[7] The letters of the government of Lucca to Pavia during the years 1401-2 fully substantiate this later record of his influence.[8]

[1] "Ma certifichiamo la Signoria vostra che neuna cifra del mondo è in cancellaria di vostro, nè Francesco nè suoi cancellieri di sopra n'ànno niente." Despatch of the Sienese ambassadors at Pavia, 6 March 1397/8: *ASS*, Concistoro 1840, no. 16. Another document of the same year was drawn up in the palace, "super salla ante aulam Francischi Barbavarii"; it is the one indexed in *Inventari e Regesti*, I 3, no. 27.

[2] For the payment of the salaries of the professors at the University of Pavia: Maiocchi, *Codice Diplomatico dell' Università di Pavia*, I 339-40, no. 546.   [3] Doc. 13.

[4] Letters of Barbavara to Belluno, in 1398 and 1402: Pellegrini, "Documenti Inediti", *AIV* 3, XIII 1617-19, nos. 25-6; and XIV 16, no. 97. Two written to Gonzaga, 26 June and 27 July 1402, are preserved in *ASMa*, E. XLIX. 3.

[5] In August 1398, two months after Pasquino's fall: *Inventari e Regesti*, I 2, nos. 3-4.

[6] 23 August 1402: Bianchetti, *Ossola Inferiore*, I 322 note 1.

[7] Magenta, *op. cit.* I 293 note 5.

[8] *Carteggio di Paolo Guinigi*, 3-4, nos. 2, 6; and 177-85, nos. 92, 112, 140, 149.

There is no evidence that Barbavara used his influence to shape the course of Giangaleazzo's political affairs. The statesmen and advisers who sat in the Duke's Council were well qualified for that task. The Florentines had not forgotten their experience during the conference of Pavia in 1389; and they warned the Venetians, during the negotiations for the truce in 1398, that Giangaleazzo's counsellors were as dangerous as his armies. "There are on the enemy's side men skilled in argument and in action, and who know well how to direct things to the Duke's favour, covertly and one by one, so that in good faith, even if all who are concerned were represented, it would be difficult to avoid committing mistakes."[1] Eighteen months later, on the occasion of some new negotiations, they were writing again in the same strain. "The Duke has taken to himself many wise men, who direct all his affairs with great skill and cunning, and never agree to anything that does not lead to his advantage."[2] It was indeed a rather jealous tribute to Giangaleazzo's wisdom in selecting his advisers, and to the skill with which they served their master; and it is interesting to observe that the Florentines attributed the Duke's triumphs in diplomacy not, as might have been expected, to his own superior cunning and deceitfulness, but to that of his counsellors.

Giangaleazzo, indeed, needed men whom he could trust. There was a limit to the control which he could exercise in person over every aspect of politics and administration. He placed full confidence in his servants, and gave them scope to display their own particular talents. The responsibilities borne by the chief private secretary and by the director of finance must have made them all the more easily vulnerable; once suspicion had been implanted in the Duke's mind, their position might quickly become untenable. Giangaleazzo, who was not really suspicious by nature, must have suffered a severe shock when he became convinced that Pasquino had betrayed him.

It would be all the more interesting to know what part Bar-

---

[1] Florence to her ambassadors in Venice, 5 May 1398: *ASF*, Signoria, Legazioni I 182.

[2] The same, 16 November 1399: *ibid.* Legazioni 3, 12.

bavara played in the events of June 1398, for henceforth he enjoyed unchallenged the Duke's fullest trust. His position was unique in the story of the reign. Giangaleazzo may have begun to feel the need for some one who could lighten his duties; and his sons were still too young to share in the tasks of government. He therefore delegated to Barbavara much of the ordinary supervision of administration, while he himself, remote within the inner circle of his court, devoted an ever increasing amount of his attention to the new situation in northern Italy, and to the new opportunities which were open to him. Free from the danger of French invasion, and secure in his reconciliation with the Venetians, he concentrated his efforts on a struggle to overthrow the hegemony of Florence in Tuscany.

CHAPTER XVII

FROM THE TRUCE OF PAVIA TO THE PEACE OF VENICE: THE ACQUISITION OF PISA, SIENA AND PERUGIA (MAY 1398–MARCH 1400)

As a prelude to the more serious tasks which awaited him after the truce of Pavia, Giangaleazzo quietly took possession of the district of the Lunigiana, where the branches of the Malaspina family had their home. The negotiatjons of these princes with the League in the early months of 1398 had not escaped his attention, and provided him with an occasion to assert that authority over the district, which Wenceslaus had confirmed to him in 1395. Very few details of the struggle have survived;[1] the Milanese campaign was brief and efficient; it has left no trace in the diplomatic records of the time. Some of the Malaspina did homage to the Duke, in the hope of profiting from the destruction of their neighbours;[2] but, according to Corio, friends and foes alike had forfeited their lands before the end of 1399. Some afterwards gave assurances of their fidelity, and were restored to their possessions;[3] but Giangaleazzo had gained complete control of the road across the Apennines from Pontremoli to Sarzana, the western gateway into Tuscany from the Lombard plain.

In accordance with the new policy adopted at the conference of Pavia, Giangaleazzo raised no difficulties in eastern Lombardy during the two years after the truce. He strengthened Francesco Gonzaga in his friendship, tempted d'Este to draw closer to Pavia, and gave no offence to Carrara; and if his activities in Bologna were more invidious, they were too obscure and indefinite

---

[1] Sercambi, "Cronache", ii 163, 176–80, 403; Corio, *Storia di Milano*, ii 416; Porcacchi, *Historia dell' Illustrissima famiglia Malaspina*, 202–3; Manfredi, *Storia di Voghera*, 218.

[2] The Marquis of Fosdinovo, of Castel dell' Aquila, and of Olivola and Varano: Romano, "Regesto", *ASL* xxi, 2, 316–17, nos. 453–6 (25–26 February 1399).

[3] Corio, *op. cit.* ii 416; Porcacchi, *op. cit.* 203–4, 214–15.

to justify any positive action against them on the part of the *Serenissima.*

Gonzaga had decided that the protection and friendship of the Duke offered the surest guarantee for the safety and development of his state. He was wily enough to appreciate and take advantage of Giangaleazzo's anxiety to remain on good terms with Venice. Platina records that Gonzaga visited Pavia after the truce was made, and that he was received with all honour and affection.[1] Henceforth he followed the Duke's lead and fought in his army, renewing the close alliance which had united them in earlier days. Carlo Malatesta was in Pavia at the beginning of 1399, to negotiate in his behalf a settlement of the territorial questions arising from the war.[2] An agreement was reached in the summer of that year; the complete documents have not survived, but Gonzaga apparently received back the towns captured by the Milanese army, and did homage to Giangaleazzo for them, at any rate until the truce was superseded by a more lasting peace.[3] Giangaleazzo on his side assured the lord of Mantua that, if this homage involved him in any trouble from any quarter—"which we do not believe"—he would take action on his behalf, "even as we would act for the preservation and defence of our own rights".[4]

Niccolò d'Este pursued a more cautious policy; the pressure of hostile ambitions steadily drove him towards complete neutrality. Giangaleazzo's plans, however, received a fillip from an unexpected quarter, when Niccolò's father-in-law, Francesco Carrara, made an attempt to usurp control of Ferrarese affairs at the end of the Mantuan war, by dismissing the counsellors of the young Marquis and setting his own agents in their place. Giangaleazzo could not contemplate with equanimity the dominance of his confirmed enemy in Ferrara; but the prospect was equally

---

[1] Platina, "Historia Urbis Mantue", *RIS* xx 791 c–d.

[2] Gonzaga's ratification of the promises made by Carlo Malatesta in his name, 1 February 1399: Osio, *Documenti diplomatici*, i 344–5, no. 228.

[3] Gonzaga received the investiture of Luzzara from Giangaleazzo, 11 August 1399: *ibid.* i 344 note 1. The document is in *ASMa*, B. xi, together with Gonzaga's oath of homage to the Duke for the town, 10 July; and the annulment of the homage, 15 August 1400, after the peace of Venice.

[4] Giangaleazzo to Francesco Gonzaga, 13 August 1399: *ASMa*, E. xlix. 2.

intolerable to the Venetians, who encouraged d'Este to resume his independence; and the deposed counsellors were recalled in May 1399. D'Este, however, was not satisfied by the prospect of continued subservience to Venice, and still hoped to redeem the Polesine di Rovigo.[1] He proposed to keep the friendship of both Venice and the Duke, to play one off against the other in order to improve his own precarious position, and yet be able to rely on both of them when danger threatened him. Giangaleazzo could not depend on his support as he could on that of Gonzaga; but he had no cause to fear his hostility, and when Venetian susceptibilities need no longer be considered, further pressure could be brought to bear on him.

Meanwhile, the Florentine government had several opportunities, during the winter of 1399–1400, to notice the gradual severance of d'Este's relations with the League, and the encouragement given by Giangaleazzo to the process. In October 1399, they instructed their envoys in Venice to beg the *Serenissima* to exercise their influence "in the affairs of the Marquis and of the Bolognese, for there seems to us great need of it".[2] Three weeks later, a fresh request was to be made "to restrain the Marquis from allowing himself to be deceived by the Viper".[3] Within a fortnight, they were asking the Bolognese "to send an embassy to the Marquis, to rescue him from the flatteries of the Duke".[4] Florentine envoys presented a request three months later "at Ferrara, to the council of the Marquis", for his cooperation against the Duke, "e non si optenne".[5]

The affairs of Bologna were almost ripe for Giangaleazzo's intervention. Carlo Zambeccari had obtained in the government of the Commune a predominance which stirred resentment among other prominent citizens, opposed to the faction of the *Maltraversi* which Zambeccari represented. Two of these citizens, Nanne Gozzadini and Giovanni Bentivoglio, plotted to over-

---

[1] Benvenuto Cessi, *Venezia e Padova*, 86–9.
[2] Letter of 23 October 1399: *ASF*, Signoria, Legazioni 3, p. 11.
[3] The same, 16 November 1399: *ibid.* 12 t.
[4] Florence to the envoys at Bologna, 27 November 1399: *ibid.* 14 t.
[5] Report of 15 May 1400: *ASF*, Signoria, Rapporti I 37.

throw the government with the aid of Giovanni da Barbiano; but the troops of the Condottiere arrived too late, and the leaders of the conspiracy were sent into exile.

The Florentines insinuated that Giangaleazzo was responsible for the plot.[1] Their ambassador to Bologna spoke of many things "relating to their and our neighbour, who seeks with all industry and by every means things which are and would be against the peace of their state and of our own".[2] The legend of the Duke's ubiquitous hostility was already growing, and Florence attributed every movement in Bologna to the impetus of his intrigues. In this case, the family of Correggio and the Pii of Carpi, dependents of Giangaleazzo, seem to have been involved with Giovanni da Barbiano in the plot;[3] and it is not difficult to imagine that the Duke quickly established contacts with Bentivoglio and Gozzadini in exile.

They were not in exile for long. At the end of September 1399, Giovanni da Barbiano paid the penalty for his many treacheries. He was captured, laden with booty after a raid on Bolognese territory, and put to death by order of the Bolognese government; and the common report ran that Astorre Manfredi of Faenza had instigated the execution of his old enemy.[4] The Condottiere's death caused as much disturbance as his exploits while he was still alive. Alberico da Barbiano, Giangaleazzo's general, proclaimed a vendetta against his brother's murderers, obtained leave from his master the Duke, and marched on Bologna. Meanwhile, the strength of the governing party in Bologna had been undermined by the plague, which ravaged the district in the autumn, and numbered among its victims Carlo Zambeccari and his leading supporters. The people rose against the *Maltraversi* at Alberico's approach, established a more

[1] Bosdari, "Comune di Bologna alla fine del secolo XIV", *AMR* 4 IV 161-2.

[2] Report of 21 April 1399: *ASF*, Signoria, Rapporti I 28 t.

[3] A private letter of 24 March 1399, which shows knowledge of Giovanni's movements: "Memorie Storiche della Mirandola", I 82.

[4] Corio, *op. cit.* II 420; Delayto, "Annales Estenses", *RIS* XVIII 956 A; Griffoni, "Memoriale historicum", *RIS* NS XVIII, 2, 89.

democratic government, and recalled the exiles, among them Gozzadini and Bentivoglio.[1]

Alberico, his grudge against Bologna satisfied by the downfall of the former rulers of the Commune, joined with the new government in an alliance against the remaining object of his vendetta, Astorre Manfredi. In December 1399, Bentivoglio and Gozzadini organized another revolution in the city, and, probably with Alberico's support, took over the government from the men who had recalled them from exile.[2] Meanwhile Manfredi, by one of those acts of petty treachery which helped to keep alive the flames of local hatred and particularism, had annexed the Bolognese border fortress of Solarolo. Alberico had no difficulty, therefore, in coming to an agreement with the new rulers of the Republic for a joint attack on Faenza; and preparations for the campaign were set on foot in Bologna during the winter, under the supervision of the Grand Constable.

The Florentines followed these events with not unnatural bewilderment and alarm. The successive governments of Bologna renewed their predecessors' assurances of fidelity to the principles of the League; but no amount of assurances could lull the fears which prevailed in Florence. The rulers of Bologna were in communication with Pavia, and the Duke's general had entered the city—the pretext scarcely mattered—and was preparing to fight, as an ally of the Republic, against Manfredi. Giangaleazzo was feeling his way towards the dominion of Bologna; and he moved so plausibly and so imperceptibly that the Florentines, well aware of his intentions, could do nothing to stop him. Alberico was pursuing his own vendetta, in which his master was graciously helping him; and remonstrances to Pavia would no doubt have met with assurances that the Duke had no interest in the Grand Constable's relations with Bologna.

Although the presence of Milanese troops in Bologna was particularly alarming to the Florentines, they were not themselves able to strengthen the defences of their ally. "If they complain that we did not send troops to help them against the Count

---

[1] Corio, *op. cit.* II 420–1; Sercambi, "Cronache", II 390–2; Bosdari, "Comune di Bologna", *AMR* 4 IV 167–9.

[2] Bosdari, *op. cit.* 169–70; Sercambi, "Cronache", II 090.

Giovanni, make our excuses, on the grounds of the smallness of the forces at our disposal."[1] It is not then surprising that the Bolognese, in the unsettled condition of the country, made over-tures to their more powerful neighbour. "We hear from a trust-worthy source", wrote the Florentine government two months later, "that this Commune [Bologna] has sent ambassadors to the Duke, a thing which is highly displeasing to us."[2] But this displeasure, which was aggravated by the success of Bentivoglio, was not translated into any positive action. The Florentines could only accept the assurances of the new Bolognese governors with as good a grace as possible, and warn them to put no trust in the common enemy at Pavia.[3]

If Giangaleazzo profited in Lombardy' from his new under-standing with Venice, the disinterestedness of the *Serenissima* in the affairs of Tuscany was even more valuable to him; it left him free to strike at the very heart of Florence.

Many of the old Ghibelline families, who had submitted perforce to the Florentine Republic, still dwelt in the Casentino and in the Apennine ranges to the east of the city. Their Ghibelline sym-pathies, and their resentment of Florentine dominion, had never been entirely extinguished; and Antonio Montefeltro, lord of Urbino, worked upon these sentiments on behalf of the Duke of Milan during the Mantuan war.[4] The Florentines learnt of these activities when the Ubertini, the Counts of Bagno and Palaz-zuolo and Modigliano, and above all Count Roberto da Battifolle, lord of Poppi, quietly renounced their allegiance to the Republic in May and June 1398, and ratified the truce of Pavia as adherents of Giangaleazzo.[5]

The Florentines protested to Venice; their suspicions and mistrust revived in full vigour. It was intolerable, they said, that the Duke should win by a stroke of the pen, without a blow given or taken, the allegiance of lands which had been ruled for centuries

---

[1] Commission of envoys to meet those of Bologna, 7 October 1399: *ASF*, Signoria, Legazioni 2, p. 7 t.

[2] Florence to the envoys at Bologna, 4 December 1399: *ibid.* 3, p. 15.

[3] Bosdari, "Comune di Bologna", *AMR* 4 iv 172–3.

[4] Franceschini, "Politica di Giangaleazzo Visconti", in *Atti del Primo Congresso Storico Lombardo*, 189–90.

[5] Ratifications in Predelli, *Libri Commemoriali*, iii 265, no. 139.

by the Republic.[1] But the Venetians would not interfere; they accepted the formal protest of Florence, and Giangaleazzo's equally formal protest against the reservations made on the subject by Florence in ratifying the truce;[2] they refused to see cause for breaking off the good relations they had established with the Duke, in a question which in no way involved their own interests.

If the Venetians hoped to hear no more of the matter, they were disappointed. Giangaleazzo encouraged his new friends to harass the Florentines by raids on the territories of the Republic; a long series of complaints and a full account of the rebels' activities reached Venice during the year 1399. Roberto of Poppi even appealed to the *Serenissima* against the persecutions of Florence.[3] The Venetians tried to find an accommodation; but the danger was too great for Florence to consider any terms short of complete submission. If the rebels would return to their allegiance and sever all connection with the Duke, they would be forgiven. The Republic introduced an economic boycott of the rebel lands, to hasten their acceptance of these terms.[4] The plague, which reached its height in Tuscany during the summer of 1400, made the boycott more severe; and Roberto of Poppi, realizing on his deathbed that his young son could only rule securely after him under the aegis of Florentine protection, made his peace with the Republic. Some of the rebels followed his example; but others remained faithful to the Duke until the day of his death.[5]

Giangaleazzo could not make full use of these valuable outposts in Florentine territory, until he had mastered all the roads leading

[1] *V.* Doc. 14.

[2] Predelli, *op. cit.* III 265–6, no. 139; Bolognini, "Relazioni tra Firenze e Venezia", *NAV* IX 102–3.

[3] "Commendiamo la risposta faceste alla signoria del ramarichio di quel bugiardo conte Roberto." Florence to the envoys at Venice, 23 October 1399: *ASF*, Signoria, Legazioni 3, p. 11.

[4] The instructions to the Florentine commissioners in the Casentino, *ibid.* I 142 t, 137 t, 145, and the letters to the envoys at Venice, *ibid.* 3 1–10 t passim, reveal the relations of Florence with the Casentino in 1399. Also Minerbetti, "Cronica", 236–7; Bruni, "Historiarum Florentini Populi", *RIS* NS XIX, 3, 275; "Commissioni di Rinaldo degli Albizzi", in *Documenti di Storia Italiana*, I 3–4.

[5] *ASF*, Signoria, Legazioni 3, especially pp. 29–32; Minerbetti, "Cronica", 283–4; Giovanni Morelli, *Cronica*, 304–5; Bruni, *op. cit. RIS* NS XIX, 3, 280.

to Tuscany; and this was the task which he now undertook. The ground had been carefully prepared during the past ten years, and the Duke had no difficulty in manufacturing the opportunities which he required.

Jacopo d'Appiano, knowing that he had not long to live, turned to Milan for the protection which, he believed, would be necessary to secure the succession of his son. Even before the truce of Pavia had been proclaimed, he concluded an agreement for ten years with the Duke, who gained fuller control over the military arrangements of Pisa, and who assumed certain financial obligations for the defence of the city;[1] and when Jacopo died, in September 1398, Gherardo d'Appiano succeeded to the lordship of Pisa with the support of Milanese troops.[2]

Gherardo had ample time, during the five months of his rule, to reveal his weakness and incompetence. He opened conversations with Florence for the renewal of the commercial relations which had made Porto Pisano the port of Florence; but he would not accept the essential condition of breaking off his political relations with Pavia.[3] The Pisans themselves had little faith in him, and openly demonstrated their hostility.[4] "From a trustworthy source", wrote the Florentine government in the middle of November 1399, "we have it that affairs in Pisa have taken a turn for the worse, and that messer Gherardo, who follows the advice of Stranbo de' Calci and of others in whom he has great faith, is not satisfied with the Pisans, nor they with him; and it is thought certain that matters cannot remain as they are, and doubt is felt that the situation may not turn to the advantage of those who desire that the Duke shall attain his object in that city. And in witness and evidence of this, it seems that Lombard troops

---

[1] In Pavia, 24 May 1398: Romano, "Regesto", *ASL* xxi, 2, 290–1, no. 385. De Boüard, *France et l'Italie*, 250.

[2] Minerbetti, "Cronica", 231; Sercambi, "Cronache", ii 226; Scaramella, "Dominazione Viscontea in Pisa", *SS* iii 433.

[3] *ASF*, Signoria, Legazioni i 124–6 t, 156 t–9 t. These letters disprove the view of Bruni, accepted by Scaramella, "Dominazione Viscontea in Pisa", *SS* iii 433, and support that of Sercambi, "Cronache", ii 242, on the origin and nature of these negotiations.

[4] Sercambi, "Cronache", ii 243.

have come from Urbino, and that messer Antoniolo Porro, messer Antonio Balestraccio and further troops are expected."[1]

Antonio Porro, in fact, was sent by Giangaleazzo to turn the situation to account. The Duke was determined that the fiasco of a year earlier should not be repeated; but Gherardo was easier game than his father, and Porro made no mistake. Gherardo rode through Pisa with his Milanese troops on 21 January 1399, and received the resignation of the *Anziani*; the dualism of government, to which Pietro Gambacorta had always adhered, was abolished, and Gherardo notified his neighbours that he had assumed the absolute dominion of the city. From that moment the affair passed beyond Gherardo's control; the city was sold to Giangaleazzo for 200,000 florins, and the expostulations and promises of the Florentines, who clearly foresaw this sequel, could not arrest the fulfilment of the Duke's plans. On 19 February, Gherardo formally surrendered the staff of dominion to Antonio Porro, who accepted it in Giangaleazzo's name.[2]

The Duke was not content to base his claims on purchase alone. Porro immediately recalled the *Anziani* to their office, and on 31 March the representatives of the Commune did homage in Pavia, recognized Giangaleazzo's lordship, and signed pacts for the government of the city. The Duke permitted his new subjects to retain as much of their independent communal administration as was compatible with complete political subservience.[3]

The Sienese had clung faithfully to their alliance with Milan, in spite of the wars, famine and pestilence which it had brought in its train. But the spirit which had sustained them against Florence was almost exhausted after the Mantuan war, and they welcomed Florentine offers of a commercial alliance. They soon perceived, however, that political dependence was still one of the essential terms of the offer; the Florentines would not grant

---

[1] Florence to the envoys in conference with those of Pisa at Empoli, 15 November 1398: *ASF*, Signoria, Legazioni I 158.

[2] Sercambi, "Cronache", II 241–3; Minerbetti, "Cronica", 234; Sardo, "Cronaca Pisana", *ASI* VI 2, 244–5.

[3] Published by Rousset, *Supplément au corps universal diplomatique*, I, 2, 299, no. 157, and discussed at length by Silva, "Ordinamento interno in Pisa", *SS* XXI 5–22.

privileges to a state which flaunted the banner of the Viper from
its towers.[1] Rather than renounce the Milanese alliance and leave
themselves at the mercy of their hated neighbour, the Sienese
appealed again to the Duke; and Giangaleazzo's new policy
allowed him to accept the responsibility which he had formerly
refused. His enemies declared that he forced the Republic's hand
by letting loose the Companies on Sienese territory; but nothing
in his relations either with Siena or with the Condottieri suggests
that this was likely or necessary.[2] Visconti commissioners
already held the key positions in the government of Siena, and
nothing could be done without their consent; the city had long
been his for the taking.[3] His decision was known at the end of
July 1399. The General Council of Siena voted the "translatio
dominii" on 6 September; and the proceedings followed closely
the precedent of Pisa. There was no previous signorial régime on
which to base the new constitution, but the final agreement
adhered to the same principles which had governed the settlement
with the neighbouring Republic.[4]

The administration of Pisa and Siena under the Visconti
differed in some respects from that imposed on the cities of the
Duchy of Milan. The fact that they were outside the Duchy, and
that they were neither inherited, nor conquered by force of arms,
gave them an advantage in negotiating with the Duke. They were
not prepared, neither was he in a position to compel them, to
abrogate the apparent integrity of their communal institutions.
The *Anziani* of Pisa and the Priors of Siena maintained their
position as instruments of domestic government. Giangaleazzo's
nominees held the highest executive offices, but they were
expected to secure the execution of the Duke's wishes by persuasion, not by force. The *Anziani* in Pisa retained some control

[1] *ASF*, Signoria, Legazioni I 120–1 t, 125, 126, 128 t, 156 t, 157, 158–9.
[2] The accusation was made by Florence in a letter to the envoys at Venice:
ibid. 3, p. 5. Cf. Minerbetti, "Cronica", 238; Sercambi, "Cronache", II
279–83; Malavolti, *Historia de' Sanesi*, II 184 t–5.
[3] *V.* a letter quoted in Salutati, "Epistolario", III 485 note 2.
[4] Malavolti, *op. cit.* II 185 & t; Sercambi, "Cronache", II 286–8. The oath
of homage (18 November 1399) and the *Pacta* (11 December) published by
Rousset, *op. cit.* I, 2, 294–9, no. 166.

over finance, and in Siena a surplus income could be devoted by the city to its own needs.[1]

Giangaleazzo was tactful, and left much unchanged, because he knew that his wishes would be carried out. The Sienese had long been accustomed to look to him for guidance; and "he regarded the Sienese more in the light of comrades and friends, than of subjects or vassals".[2] Even the contemporary Florentine Giovanni Morelli confirms this: "he did not need to build a fortress at Siena, because they were so devoted to him, and had given themselves to him so freely, that he had no cause to suspect them".[3] His first task was to attempt to restore the shaky balance of the Commune's finance; and with this end in view, he introduced thorough reforms and new economies during the year which followed the surrender of the city.[4]

The Pisans were more restless under their new lord, and Giangaleazzo had to deal very carefully with the conflicts between different groups of citizens. That he encouraged their divergencies of opinion, in order to strengthen his own position in Pisa, has been suggested and denied;[5] it fits ill with his wish for unity, which led him even to the length of recalling the Gambacorta to the city.[6] Disputes between merchants and artisans there certainly were; and rumours of revolt more than once reached Pavia during 1401.[7] The Florentines did all they could to add to the difficulties of the Visconti government;[8] but the ducal officials gradually strengthened their control over the affairs of Pisa, as of Siena, at the expense of local autonomy. They directed all the business between the cities and the neighbouring states; and Giangaleazzo hoped that, with the steady development of his

---

[1] Silva, "Ordinamento interno in Pisa", *SS* xxi 9–22; Salzer, "Anfänge der Signorie", 263–6.

[2] Malavolti, *op. cit.* ii 198.   [3] Giovanni Morelli, *Cronica*, 303.

[4] Malavolti, *op. cit.* ii 190 & t; Favale, "Siena nel quadro della Politica Viscontea", *BSSP* xliii 342–3.

[5] Silva, "Ordinamento interno in Pisa", *SS* xxi 24–38; Scaramella, "Nuove Ricerche sulla Dominazione Viscontea in Pisa", *BSP* xiv 13–24.

[6] The disturbances which arose from their recall are referred to by Roncioni, "Istorie Pisane", *ASI* vi, 1, 969.

[7] Letters from Lucca, April and May 1401: *Carteggio di Paolo Guinigi*, 3–4, nos. 2 and 6.

[8] E.g. the plan described by Sercambi, "Cronache", iii 49–51.

authority, Pisa and Siena would become as integral and uniform parts of his dominions as any city of the Duchy.[1]

The assurances of Giangaleazzo's agents, that the two cities would continue their peaceful and friendly relations with Florence under the new régime, kindled no enthusiasm in the Republic; they were indeed belied by disturbances and incidents which arose on Florentine territory, and whose origins were traced back to the government of Siena.[2] Giangaleazzo, without exposing himself to attack, was in a position to create innumerable irritations and difficulties for the Florentines.

The rulers of Florence were determined to save Perugia from the fate of Pisa and Siena. Biordo Michelotti had been assassinated in March 1398, and the brief moment of glory, which the Umbrian Commune had enjoyed under his rule, quickly faded. Assisi elected the Condottiere Broglia as lord and protector. Todi, Orvieto and Nocera returned under the dominion of the Pope. Braccio da Montone and other enemies of the Michelotti ravaged the countryside and reduced the city to starvation. The government appealed desperately on all sides, for money and troops to resist the exiles and the Pope.

The Florentines did not dare to provoke Boniface again by helping Perugia against him, as they had by the French alliance; but they could not stand aside and allow the Umbrian Republic, through whose territory ran their lines of communication with Rome and the south, to fall quietly under the standard of the Viper.[3] They begged their allies to bring Perugia under the protection of the League; but the Venetians, who had no immediate interests at stake in the district, refused to interfere, alleging that such an action would constitute a breach of the truce of Pavia.[4] The Florentines twice managed to patch up an understanding

---

[1] Scaramella, "Dominazione Viscontea in Pisa", *SS* III 439. Letters from Pisa and Siena in 1400–2, e.g. in *Carteggio di Paolo Guinigi*, bear the signatures of the Visconti officials.

[2] Minerbetti, "Cronica", 243; Salutati, "Epistolario", III 485 note 2. And *V*. Doc. 15, p. 368.

[3] Pellini, *Historia di Perugia*, II 99–100; Graziani, "Cronaca", *ASI* XVI, 1, 269–73.

[4] Azzi Vitelleschi, "Relazioni tra Firenze e l' Umbria", I 240–4, nos. 899–900, 904, 907. Further letters in *ASF*, Signoria, Legazioni I 183 t–4, 164–6 t.

between Boniface and Perugia; but they worked unaided, and the accords were not lasting. Boniface was reluctant to abandon any part of his claims, and the Perugians soon found themselves no better off than before.[1]

The Florentine letters of 1398–9 were full of warnings against Giangaleazzo's ambitions, and his wish to enslave Umbria; the Duke had received an embassy from Perugia with his usual show of favour in the autumn of 1398.[2] He was forestalled by the swift action of Florence in making peace between Boniface and the Republic; but as they drew apart again, a fresh opportunity arose for him to profit by the Commune's difficulties. The arrival in Perugia of the mysterious Giovanni Cane, whose presence was dreaded as the herald of Giangaleazzo's bold and sinister designs, elicited a protest from Florence in the summer of 1399; but the warning went unheeded.[3] Cane secured the support of Ceccolino Michelotti, Biordo's brother, and of the *Raspanti*, who feared the consequences to themselves of the traditional alliance of the rival party, the *Beccherini*, with Florence and the Pope. At the end of November, while Boniface and the Florentines still had no immediate suspicions, Giangaleazzo appointed Pietro Scrovegni to accept the dominion of Perugia in his name.[4]

Troops began to gather to the north of the Apennines; but the Florentines imagined that their own lands were threatened. "Now you know", the government wrote, "that these Counts [of the Casentino] and the troops of the Duke are certainly putting themselves in readiness to raid us....We hear indeed that at Parma and Reggio and in Romagna troops are assembling, and we believe that it is only for this purpose....And we have it that messer Ottobuon Terzo is coming into Tuscany with a very great force, of more than 2000 lances."[5] They did not grasp the truth

¹ Pellini, *op. cit.* II 100–12. The documents summarized by Azzi Vitelleschi show the diplomatic activity of the Florentines in Perugia and Rome during 1398–9.

² Pellini, *op. cit.* II 104–5.

³ Instructions and report, 7 August and 24 September 1399: Azzi Vitelleschi, *op. cit.* I 245–6, nos. 911 and 913.

⁴ On 23 November 1399: *ASI* XVI, 2, 565.

⁵ Florence to the envoys at Venice, 6 December 1399: *ASF*, Signoria, Legazioni 3, pp. 15 t–16.

until the end of the year, when it was already too late to save Perugia. Then their entreaties to the Republic, and the renewed offers of accommodation which Boniface was persuaded to make, met with no response. Ottobuon Terzo led the Milanese army into Umbria. Under its protection, Ceccolino Michelotti and his friends declared their allegiance to Milan, and won a majority for the Duke in the General Council of the city. Scrovegni received the submission of Perugia to Giangaleazzo on 21 January 1400.[1]

The surrender of three great cities to the Duke, within a year and without a blow struck, tremendously increased his prestige at the expense of Florence. Giangaleazzo was now firmly established in Tuscany and Umbria, to the south and east of Florentine territory. Ottobuon Terzo remained with his army in Umbria, to consolidate the position that had been gained. Assisi, Spoleto and Nocera quickly surrendered to him, and accepted the lordship of the Duke.[2]

The lord of Cortona also made a bid to free himself, with Sienese support, from the dependence on Florence which he had eagerly accepted twelve years before. In this case, however, the Florentines were close at hand, and acted promptly and firmly; they soon convinced him that his action was premature, and induced him to repent and submit to their authority.[3]

Such methods could not be invoked against an allied Republic of equal status, and Giangaleazzo openly sought the friendship of the government of Lucca. He wooed the favour of the Guinigi, who practically controlled the affairs of the Commune; and Lazzaro Guinigi, the head of the family, went to Pavia in May 1399, in spite of grave warnings from Florence.[4] The outcome of his visit was not fully comprehended, however, until eighteen months later, when the Duke was able to turn the situation to account.

¹ Graziani, "Cronaca", *ASI* xvi, 1, 274 note 2; Minerbetti, "Cronica", 244–5; Pellini, *op. cit.* ii 117–21.

² Pellini, *op. cit.* 120; Corio, *op. cit.* ii 423; Minerbetti, "Cronica", 249. The acquisition of Nocera and Spoleto is proved by a Papal letter of 28 January 1403, in Raynaldo, *Annales Ecclesiastici*, viii 100.

³ Giovanni Morelli, *Cronica*, 304; Bruni, *op. cit.*, *RIS* NS xix, 3, 280–1; Pellini, *op. cit.* ii 122–3.

⁴ Sercambi, "Cronache", ii 264–72.

Lazzaro Guinigi was assassinated in February 1400.[1] The exiles of Lucca gathered throughout the summer on the borders of the Republic, and the predominance of the Guinigi seemed to be on the point of crumbling.[2] The supporters of the family decided to anticipate the action of their enemies. They obtained the support of Milanese troops from Pisa, and secured the election of Paolo Guinigi, a young cousin of the dead ruler, as governor of the city. A few weeks later, Paolo deprived the *Anziani* of power, and proclaimed himself the absolute sovereign of Lucca.[3]

His action must have recalled to the Florentines unfortunate memories of Gherardo d'Appiano. They exhorted Paolo never to surrender the glorious position he had acquired, and offered their alliance to strengthen his resolve. The new lord of Lucca assured them of his determination to rule until his death, and affirmed his friendship towards Florence; but the silence with which he received their offer of alliance indicated only too well the trend of his policy.[4] Lucca, as an ally of Florence, was cut off from expansion, and confined to the narrow territory restored to the city by the Emperor in 1369; but Lucca, as the ally of Milan against Florence, might still hope to expand.[5]

Four independent chroniclers, in commenting on the sale of Pisa by Gherardo d'Appiano, assert that the Pisans only accepted Giangaleazzo's rule as an alternative to Florentine dominion.[6] The Tuscan Communes chose the distant master rather than the near one; and the Florentine propaganda, directed against the tyrant who was bent on exterminating liberty, awoke little

[1] *Ibid.* II 406–10. His account reveals no evidence to support the statement of Minerbetti, "Cronica", 246, that the deed was prompted by Giangaleazzo; and Sercambi played an important part in the affairs of Lucca at this time.

[2] Letter of 9 July 1400: Lucca, *Regesti*, 439, no. 1986.

[3] Sercambi, "Cronache", III 6–22.

[4] De Boüard, *France et l'Italie*, 251 note 2.

[5] This argument was expounded by Sercambi, "Cronache", II 259–63. He gave further evidence of his hostility towards Florence: *ibid.* II 247–8, 283–4, 287; and he was probably expressing the sentiments of the majority of the citizens of Lucca.

[6] Sercambi, "Cronache", II 253; Gatari, "Cronaca Carrarese", *RIS* NS XVII, 1, 465–6; Bruni, *op. cit. RIS* NS XIX, 3, 276; and Platina, *op. cit. RIS* XX 791 E.

response in governments which lived in perpetual fear of Florentine hostility and aggression. The expressions of friendship and offers of alliance, which the Florentines extended to their neighbours on condition that all ties with Milan be broken, came too late. Giangaleazzo had matured his plans, and put them into execution with all his old decision as the opportunities arose, while his enemies talked.

The Florentine government was handicapped by the dilatory procedure imposed by the constitution. The speech which is recorded to have been made in the Council by Rinaldo Gianfigliazzi during 1399, but which bears traces of Leonardo Bruni's clear and orderly thought, is filled with that spirit of impatience which moves an undespotic state to abrogate the popular safeguards of the constitution in the face of a crucial emergency. Gianfigliazzi spoke of the dangers which threatened the city. "Although I confess them to be great, yet I fear them, not so much on their own account, as on account of our own methods. For I see, as far as my memory goes, that always and in everything, we have sluggishly lost the moment to make provision and to act, on account of our own delays and heedlessness....For so much licence is there in our city for cavillers, that as soon as any one points out the dangers and proposes to avoid them, many declare that he wants war and cannot rest at peace, and they hedge everything in with petty laws, and envelop them in a thousand difficulties and restraints, so that, even if any one wishes to provide for the safety of the Republic, no way is open for him to do so....When indeed the dangers are on our very threshold, and can now by no means be evaded, then at last we consult in agitation, then we summon the Council of the 200 and of the 131, we enter on interminable discussion. And I would not think this serious, if our struggle were with another people; for then conditions would be the same, or almost the same, on both sides. But now our struggle is, not with another people, but with a tyrant, who watches continually over his own affairs, who has no fear of cavillers, who is not hampered by petty laws, who does not wait for the decree of the masses nor the deliberation of the people. And so it is not surprising if he anticipates us in action, while we ponder over remedies after our cause is lost."[1]

Gianfigliazzi's warning produced no concrete results. The diplomatic methods of Florence were no longer able to put a check to the Duke's triumphant course. By the end of 1400, there was no route on which the Florentines would be able to rely with absolute confidence for the needs of their commerce, in the event of a war with Milan.

Giangaleazzo had triumphantly vindicated his new policy, within two years of the truce of Pavia. His achievements were crowned on 21 March 1400, when the Venetians proclaimed the definitive peace between the Duke and the League, in the teeth of Florentine opposition. Every stage of the preliminary negotiations marked a new victory for Milanese diplomacy, and provided fresh evidence of Venetian indifference to the affairs of Tuscany. Giangaleazzo had manœuvred the *Serenissima* into acquiescence in his dominant position, because the fate of peace or war in northern Italy was in his hands. Therefore, although the Venetians professed their desire to see the unity of the League maintained—"that their government is wakeful for the unity of the allies, gives us great pleasure", wrote the Florentines in September 1399[2]—yet each step they took in 1399 weakened the strength and prestige of Florence, on whom the power of the League depended. In their determination to secure a settlement of the issues which divided them from Giangaleazzo, they ignored the claims of their allies, treating them without even the natural consideration that courtesy demanded. Giangaleazzo was the first to learn the intentions of the Venetian arbitrators, and inexplicable delays occurred before the proposed terms were revealed to the allies. "And if the Duke says 'yes'", wrote the Florentines, "and gives his consent—which he will never do save with his own profit and honour, and therefore with loss and shame for the League—their lordships will say to us: 'you can have peace if

[1] Bruni, *op. cit. RIS* NS xix, 3, 276–7.
[2] Florence to the envoys in Venice, 13 September 1399: *ASF*, Signoria, Legazioni 3, p. 7.

you want it'—a peace not negotiated by us, as is usual, but dictated to us by our adversary.... And if there is any disadvantage in it, great or small, we do not see how a single comma can be changed, but that it will at once be said: 'it is better to have peace with this disadvantage, than not to have peace at all.' "[1]

When the proposed terms were at last made public, the Florentines wrote to Venice to demonstrate in detail the injustices contained in them. "We have always feared that there might be in them things which detract from our rights."[2] Their protest received scant attention; and they learnt with dismay, a few weeks later, that Venice had decided to send ambassadors to continue the negotiations in Pavia. "Say how, hearing that they have decided to send ambassadors to Pavia, we feel great discouragement and regret, in view of the example of the truce."[3] And their misgivings were justified, for Giangaleazzo was once more able to use all the arts of persuasion on the Venetian representatives in his own palace.

By the terms of the peace, which was concluded at Venice in March 1400, Carrara, the closest ally of Florence, was required to continue the payment of his crippling indemnity to Giangaleazzo, although at a reduced annual rate. The Duke and Gonzaga were reciprocally to restore the conquests of the Mantuan war, and all discussion of legal claims to the disputed territories was postponed. The allegiance of the Counts of the Casentino was left to the arbitration of the heads of the two alliances—Venice and Giangaleazzo himself, whose joint decision would almost certainly be unfavourable to Florence.[4] All conquests made during the war in Tuscany were to be restored; but no mention was made of certain fortresses which had been snatched from the possession of Florence and Lucca by surprise attacks after the truce of Pavia had been signed. Acquisitions of the previous war, including Lucignano and Montepulciano, were to be retained for ten years

[1] The same, 13 July 1399: *ibid.* p. 1.
[2] The same, 22 October 1399: *ibid.* 9 t.
[3] The same, 16 November 1399: *ibid.* 11 t–12.
[4] There is no evidence that any steps were taken to proceed with this arbitration.

by their present owners, notwithstanding the provisions laid down in the peace of Genoa.[1]

The peace was, as Florence had feared, practically dictated by Milan. Giangaleazzo's relations with Venice and the intervening states were for the moment satisfactory. There could no longer be any mention of spheres of influence, for the recognized lord of Pisa, Siena and Perugia could not be excluded from participation in the affairs of Tuscany. His triumph may be measured by the outcry of Florence at this peace "which may rather mean war", at this foolish and dangerous condonation of Visconti greed and trickery.[2] The Florentine government sent new ambassadors to Venice with a long list of grievances—over the independent action of the *Serenissima* in announcing the peace without the advice or consent of the allies, over the inequable clauses regarding the lords of the Casentino and the restoration of conquests, over the undue deference shown to the Duke of Milan. Finally they referred to plots hatched against them in their own territories, to the harrying of their dependents, the lords of Cortona and Foligno, and to the persistent and threatening activities of Ottobuon Terzo in Tuscany and Umbria. It was not enough "to live in the hope of God and wait for God to provide", nor to rely on the fact that "the enemy of liberty cannot live for ever". It was the duty of Venice, as head of the League, to assemble the allies in conference and to propose practical measures for the defence of Tuscany against the tyrant.[3]

The answer of the Venetians was tantamount to a declaration that the *Serenissima* would not incur any liabilities in Tuscany. For a moment, indeed, the Florentines had hoped that God had provided. In October 1399, while the plague ravaged every quarter of Italy, a rumour arose of Giangaleazzo's death. "In many places and from many signs, it is thought that the Duke no longer lives."[4] The Guelfs of the *Cremonese* took up arms—a

---

[1] 21 March: published by Helmolt, *König Ruprechts Zug nach Italien*, 165–81; summarized by Predelli, *op. cit.* III 273–4, no. 174.
[2] Florence to the envoys in Venice, 1 April 1400: *ASF*, Signoria, Legazioni 3, p. 24.   [3] *V.* Doc. 15 (Commission of ambassadors to Venice.)
[4] Florence to the envoys in Venice, 22 October 1399: *ASF*, Signoria, Legazioni 3, p. 10t.

grim presage of the task which would face the Duke's successor; but the revolt, if it deserves that title, was quickly suppressed.[1] The Florentines regretfully surrendered their illusion. "We believe that the Duke is alive, as you write; but there were many signs to the contrary."[2]

Giangaleazzo prepared a new will at this time, so that he may have been seriously ill.[3] But he did not deviate from the course which Venetian eagerness to postpone the day of reckoning had made easy for him. The understanding with Venice, which allowed him to concentrate his efforts in Tuscany, had succeeded so well that Florence was almost isolated. The process of mastering Tuscany in order to acquire complete control of Lombardy was a lengthy one; but Giangaleazzo had not yet attained his fiftieth year, he had always possessed infinite patience, and the new policy had proved brilliantly successful. He only needed now the surrender of Bologna to his authority; then the Republic of the Archguelfs, the last centre of resistance in Tuscany, the great rival of his state and the bitter enemy of his house, would be at his mercy.

[1] "Annales Mediolanenses", *RIS* XVI 831 E–2 A, 832 A–3 A, under both 1398 and 1399.

[2] Florence to the envoys in Venice, 9 November 1399: *ASF*, Signoria, Legazioni 3, p. 11 t.

[3] The undated will published by Osio, *op. cit.* I 318–38, no. 223. It was drawn up between the acquisition of Siena and of Perugia: Romano, "Nuova Ipotesi sulla morte di Giangaleazzo", *ASI* 5, XX 251; Manaresi, in *Inventari e Regesti*, I XIV–XIX; Romano, "Testamento di Giangaleazzo", *BSP* XVII 121–3.

CHAPTER XVIII

GIANGALEAZZO AND THE STATES OF WESTERN EUROPE: THE DEPOSITION OF WENCESLAUS AND THE ITALIAN EXPEDITION OF RUPERT OF BAVARIA (1400–APRIL 1402)

Giangaleazzo's progress was carefully observed in Rome and Naples, in Germany and in France; and a survey of his position at the time of the peace of Venice would be incomplete, without some consideration of the attitude adopted by these powers towards his new bid for dominion.

Boniface IX was no longer a virtual prisoner of the Roman mob and of the disorderly vassals of the Patrimony. He deposed the Communal government of Rome in 1398, and made himself unquestioned master of the city. He recovered the Umbrian cities that had been taken by Biordo Michelotti. He reduced to obedience Onorato Caetani lord of Fondi, the Prefect Francesco Vico, and other old adherents of the Popes of Avignon. He drove the rebel Colonna back to their lairs, and forced them to submit to his authority.[1]

The renewed strength of the Papacy impelled Boniface to reconsider his relations with the states of northern Italy. There were, indeed, limitations to the revival of Papal power; the poverty of the Curia, the Pope's hesitant character, and the ambitions and intrigues of his brothers made it almost impossible to adopt and carry through a consistent Papal policy. Yet it was clear that Giangaleazzo no longer enjoyed the Pope's full confidence. Boniface was alarmed by the Duke's rapid expansion southwards after the Mantuan war; and his fears were fanned by the unremitting accusations and insinuations of Florence. Finally the Pope agreed to investigate the possibilities of a League of Italian powers, directed against the Duke.[2] "The Pope hints

[1] Gregorovius, *History of the City of Rome*, vi, 2, 549–61.
[2] Jarry, *Origines*, 306–7.

once again", wrote the Florentine government in March 1399, "that he would like to make a League, and join himself in close union with the allies, because he has taken alarm, and with good reason, on account of the occupation of Pisa, and these intrigues in Perugia."[1] In the following month, the envoys in Rome were instructed to suggest that Boniface "may see fit to send his messenger, for the good of Italy, to make proposals for this union, especially to the Venetians and the other allies".[2]

The Pope's ally, Ladislaus of Durazzo, entered Naples in triumph in July 1399, and quickly destroyed the last centres of Angevin resistance in his kingdom. In announcing his victory to Florence, he made offers of alliance to the Republic.[3] They were received with friendly reserve, for the Florentines were not certain what policy he would pursue, now that he was undisputed master of the "Regno". Ladislaus, having conquered the Neapolitan kingdom, was in fact bent on asserting his claims to the throne of Hungary; and his proposals to the Florentines were probably intended rather to secure their help against Sigismund, than to encourage them in their struggle against Milan. Nevertheless, when Boniface invited Florence to send ambassadors to Rome to discuss the situation with him and the Neapolitan envoys, visions were entertained of a great alliance which would unite Naples, Rome, Florence, Bologna and Venice against the tyrant.[4]

Giangaleazzo's agents in Rome did what they could to obstruct the designs of Florence. Their task was not easy, for the Duke wished to retain the friendship of Boniface, while he steadily encroached upon the sphere of Papal authority. The acquisition of Perugia naturally increased the suspicion with which he was regarded in Rome. The Florentines, making the most of their opportunity, assured the Pope that he could win back Perugia

---

[1] Florence to the envoys in Venice, 22 March 1398/9: *ASF*, Signoria, Legazioni i 164 & t.

[2] Florence to the envoys in Rome, 26 April 1399: *ibid.* 169.

[3] "Commissioni di Rinaldo degli Albizzi", in *Documenti di Storia Italiana*, i 5–7; Pitti, "Cronica", 111.

[4] Instructions of 19 October 1399, summarized in Ammirato, *Istorie Fiorentine*, i, 2, 874 B–D; and Mancarella, "Firenze, la Chiesa, e Ladislao", *ASN* xlv 60. De Boüard, *France et l'Italie*, 235–8.

without difficulty; "if his Holiness were willing, it would be a light matter to recover his own."[1] But Giangaleazzo had a great asset in the character of Boniface himself. The Pope, after long discussions with the envoys of Ladislaus and of Florence, decided that he could not approve of all the proposals made by the Republic. Finally, alleging the pressure of other business, he promised to send representatives in due course to renew the discussions in Florence. "On account of his many affairs, he was not able to bring the matter of the League to its conclusion", reported the Florentine envoys.[2]

Boniface was in truth uncertain of his own position. He would have been glad to drive Giangaleazzo out of Umbria; but he feared the Duke's strength, and did not dare to join forces with the Duke's enemies, who were manifestly weaker than the Duke. He could not afford to lose the allegiance of Lombardy, nor to incur the hostility of its ruler. So the Pope and Ladislaus were still associated with Milan in 1400. Giangaleazzo was accepted as arbitrator of the disputes between his friends, the Colonna, and Boniface.[3] The Pope would scarcely have been willing to accept his mediation if, as it has been alleged, the Duke himself instigated the revolt of the Colonna; but this friendship at least enabled him to exercise some influence over the affairs of the *Patrimonio* whenever he wished. The relations between Milan, Rome and Naples were outwardly so close, that Martin of Sicily spoke of negotiations for the marriage of one of the Duke's sons with Joanna of Naples, and a renewal of the danger, which had accompanied the same proposal in 1396, of a united attack by the three powers upon his island kingdom.[4] His fears may have been exaggerated; but Giangaleazzo could at least feel reasonably sure that neither Boniface nor Ladislaus would throw in his lot with the enemies of Milan, until the League could find its unity of

---

[1] Florence to the envoys in Rome, 1 February 1399/1400: *ASF*, Signoria, Legazioni 3, p. 21 t.

[2] Reports presented on 1 and 14 February 1399/1400: *ibid.* Rapporti I 36 & t.

[3] The accord published by Theiner, *Codex diplomaticus Sancti Sedis*, III 111–16, no. 59.

[4] Romano, "Visconti e la Sicilia", *ASL* XXIII, 1, 35–7.

purpose again, and greatly strengthen its forces on its own account.

This was the position in Italy, when the Electoral princes informed Boniface of their decision to depose Wenceslaus, and to choose a new King of the Romans, better qualified to govern Germany and to maintain the prestige of the Empire. The Electors threatened to withdraw their allegiance from the Pope, and to support the French plan of the "voie de cession", if Boniface refused to countenance their plot against Wenceslaus.[1] Boniface had abandoned all hope of securing through Wenceslaus a solution of the Schism favourable to himself; but with his usual caution, he refused to commit himself too precipitately to the support of the King's enemies. The Florentines, on the other hand, were closely bound to the Electors by their common hostility to the Duke of Milan.[2]

Giangaleazzo, who could not renounce his allegiance to Wenceslaus without forfeiting his Ducal title—which constituted one of the main grievances of the German princes—made an effort to break up the hostile coalition, and to secure allies for himself in Germany. He proposed marriage alliances for princes of Meissen and Thuringia with two of Bernabò's daughters; but only one of them reached the stage of a formal betrothal, and the growing agitation against Wenceslaus prevented its further consummation.[3]

In May 1400, Giangaleazzo exchanged undertakings of friendship with Leopold of Austria and other Habsburg princes, in the hope that they would close the Alpine passes against his enemies if the need arose.[4] Any promises that Leopold may have given, however, were soon broken. According to Corio, Leopold, "poco amico del duca", accepted the agreement "in return for a certain

[1] *RTA* III 162–3, nos. 114–15.
[2] Lindner, "Geschichte des deutschen Reiches", II 505–6.
[3] Romano, "Matrimonio alla corte de' Visconti", *ASL* XVIII 601–28; Wenck, "Mailändisch-thüringische Heiratsgeschichte", in *Neues Archiv für sächsische Geschichte und Alterthumskunde*, XVI 1–42.
[4] Giangaleazzo's promises to the Habsburgs, given at Pavia, 4 May 1400: Kurz, *Oesterreich unter Herzog Albrecht IV*, I 212–14, Doc. 15.

sum of money", and then, "not keeping faith", increased his demands.[1] He was among the Electors who, by a majority vote, decided on the deposition of Wenceslaus, at Oberlahnstein on 20 August 1400, and who on the following day elected Rupert of Bavaria, Count Palatine of the Rhine, as King of the Romans in his stead.[2]

Florence rejoiced at the election of Rupert, who was bound by oath[3] to recover from Giangaleazzo the Imperial rights which the Duke had "usurped". The new King could not come to Italy, however, until he had settled some of the outstanding problems which faced him in Germany. Wenceslaus and the House of Luxemburg did not accept the verdict of Oberlahnstein, and they still had many supporters, especially in the German towns. The Florentines could not expect immediate relief from Germany, but they waited eagerly for a sign from the new King; and when his envoys arrived in the city in January 1401, on their way to Rome to seek the Pope's confirmation of Rupert's election, the government of the Republic took heart and began to formulate new plans for a great alliance against the tyrant. They sent Buonaccorso Pitti to Germany, to hasten the King's coming. Pitti did not hesitate to contrive a convincing story of a plot against the King's life, implicating Giangaleazzo as its prime mover.[4] Rupert, against his own inclination, finally yielded to the urgent appeals of Florence. He agreed to leave Augsburg for Italy at the end of September 1401; and the Florentine contribution to his expenses was fixed at 200,000 florins.[5]

Giangaleazzo had steadily increased his pressure upon Bologna during the year 1400; but Rupert's decision interrupted his plans.[6] Measures had to be taken to meet the threat of invasion from Germany. The Duke strengthened the garrisons of Verona and

[1] Corio, *Storia di Milano*, II 423–4.
[2] Lindner, "Geschichte des deutschen Reiches", II 430–3.
[3] In the "Wahlkapitulation" of 11 August 1400: *RTA* III 248, no. 200.
[4] Discussed in detail by Romano, "Giangaleazzo Avvelenatore", *ASL* XXI, 1, 309–60.
[5] Pitti, "Cronica", 117–19. Rupert to Florence, 22 and 23 May 1401, and the first draft of a treaty between them: *RTA* IV 365–8, nos. 305–7.
[6] Giangaleazzo's relations with Bologna during 1400–1 will be discussed in the next chapter.

Vicenza, and set his engineers to work on a scheme to divert the
course of the Brenta and the Bacchiglione, whose waters fer-
tilized the territory of Padua; during the summer of 1401, he
assembled his army around Brescia and Verona, to meet the
coming attack.[1] The leading Condottieri of Italy—the Grand
Constable and the veteran Jacopo dal Verme, Pandolfo Malatesta, Facino Cane and Ottobuon Terzo—were in his service, and
prepared to resist the challenge of the German forces. So strong
was the army which gathered on the Veronese frontier in September, that Francesco Carrara, and even the Venetians, felt
obliged to take counter-precautions.[2]

Giangaleazzo did not neglect other measures which might lessen
the danger. The attitude of the states of Italy to the rival Emperors
was determined by their position in the struggle between Florence
and Milan. Bologna and Carrara supported Rupert. Gonzaga
remained loyal to Wenceslaus. Niccolò d'Este and Paolo Guinigi
reserved their judgment.[3] These decisions were not unforeseen,
and were of small importance, compared to those of Venice and
of Boniface IX.

The Duke sent Carlo Malatesta to Rome, to beg Boniface not
to give his support to Rupert. The choice of an envoy was a wise
one, for the lord of Rimini had always served the Pope loyally,
and had defended his interests in Romagna. But Boniface would
not listen to Carlo's proposals; in April 1401, the Florentine
government expressed gratitude to the "Cardinal of Florence"
for his effective intervention with the Pope "in the matter in
which Carlo Malatesta was occupied".[4] Boniface privately urged
Rupert to hasten to Italy, and sent him a Bull of Approbation.[5]
He signed no alliances and gave no undertakings—only his
goodwill, and the assurance that success would win recognition
in due course. Florentine envoys were sent to Rome, in a fresh

---

[1] Pastorello, *Nuove Ricerche*, 103, and 253–4, Doc. 72; Corio, *op. cit.* II
427; Benvenuto Cessi, *Venezia e Padova*, 90 note 1.

[2] Benvenuto Cessi, *op. cit.* 149–52, Doc. 16; *RTA* v 87–8, no. 40.

[3] *RTA* IV 227–32, nos. 193–6, 199. For Bologna and d'Este, *v.* further in
the next chapter.

[4] *RTA* IV 359, no. 301. Minerbetti, "Cronica", 260–1, says that Carlo's
object was to make a Papal-Milanese alliance.

[5] *RTA* IV 22–35, nos. 4–7, 10, 16.

effort to form an alliance with Boniface in Rupert's favour;[1] but the Pope could not be brought to give an open pledge of his support. "Finally we revealed the clauses which were given to us by the 'dieci della balìa';...some of them were accepted, and others not."[2] When the envoys were recalled in September, "leaving the business suspended",[3] Boniface still had not made up his mind. The Duke's designs upon Bologna, and the strong position which he had already won in Umbria, were matters which called for a remedy; but the Pope did not dare to defy him, until the strength of Rupert's expedition to Italy was known.

The decision of Boniface was all the more important, because Ladislaus of Naples followed the Pope's lead. Ladislaus was already preparing, in spite of Florentine counsel, to assert the rights of the Durazzesi to the Hungarian crown. He may not have been anxious to interfere in northern Italy; but Giangaleazzo was closely associated with Sigismund of Hungary, and Ladislaus was therefore prepared to support any action which the Pope might take in favour of Florence. "He answered again that he was well disposed, and that it seemed to him that these three named [himself, Boniface and Florence] should make alliance together", wrote the Florentine envoys.[4]

The Venetians decided to preserve complete neutrality. While Florence and the Duke plagued them with requests and entreaties and demands to support or oppose Rupert, they displayed consummate ability in avoiding any obligations, or even the expression of an opinion; the Senate debated for five days before a suitably non-committal answer could be drawn up to a letter from Rupert. They assured Giangaleazzo that they could find no reason to suspect an aggressive purpose behind the relations of Florence with the Bavarian; they recalled to the Florentines the terms of the Peace' of Venice, and hoped that they would be observed.[5]

---

[1] Commission of 4 April 1401: *ibid.* iv 357–60, no. 301.
[2] Report of 16 July 1401: *ASF*, Signoria, Rapporti i 38 t–9.
[3] Report of 26 September 1401: *ibid.* 39 t.
[4] Report of 16 July 1401: *ibid.* 38 t–9.
[5] Minutes of the Venetian Senate, especially in *RTA* iv 306–12, nos. 260, 262–3; 371, no. 310; 436–7, nos. 362–3; *ibid.* v 81–8, nos. 37, 39–40; and 106–25, nos. 58–66.

Giangaleazzo had perhaps imagined that the Venetians, who resented any foreign interference in Italy, would join in his resistance to Rupert; but their neutrality was a sufficient advantage in itself. The renewal of the Veneto-Florentine alliance, in support of Rupert, would have involved him in grave difficulties. The wisdom of deferring to the wishes of the *Serenissima* during the past three years now became apparent.

Giangaleazzo had to meet the intrigues of his enemies, not only in Italy but in the whole of western Europe. Rupert at one moment contemplated the possibility of a flank attack on Milan through Savoy;[1] but Amadeus VIII would not give him the necessary support. The Count of Savoy was working in apparent harmony with Pavia, to preserve the peace of Piedmont. His decision to remain loyal to Wenceslaus was perhaps prompted rather by his native caution than by any attachment to the Duke of Milan; but it served none the less to simplify the problems with which Giangaleazzo had to deal.[2]

Rupert also sought to enlist the sea-power of Aragon in his cause. Giangaleazzo made counter-proposals of alliance to King Martin of Aragon, who was a cousin of the Bavarian. Martin refused to consider the Duke's proposals, so long as the court of Pavia continued to offer a refuge for the Catalan rebels from his son's kingdom of Sicily. Moreover, he recognized the legitimacy of Rupert's election; but he was not prepared to squander his naval resources in support of a rash German adventure in Italy.[3]

Giangaleazzo had renewed his relations with the French court soon after the Mantuan war. The French had found that, without the support of Milan, their dominion in Genoa was bound to be precarious; and Giangaleazzo helped the French officials to keep the turbulent city quiet.[4] He had never been indifferent to the value of a friendly France; and relations had so far improved, by

---

[1] Rupert's proposals of May 1401: *ibid.* IV 374–6, no. 314.

[2] Gabotto, *Ultimi Principi d'Acaia*, 423–43.

[3] *RTA* IV 313–8, nos. 254–8; *ibid.* V 209–12, nos. 167–8. Romano, "Visconti e la Sicilia", *ASL* XXIII, 1, 38–9.

[4] Jarry, *Origines*, 345–9, 366. The document to which he refers (*ibid.* 354 note 2), as evidence of a mission of Pierre de Craon to Pavia in this year, is dated 1390.

August 1400, as to permit of negotiations for the marriage of Giovanni Maria Visconti to a daughter of Charles VI. "There is no other news here," wrote a Sienese ambassador from Pavia, "save that the hand of the King of France's daughter is sought for the Count of Angera, and they have good hopes. There is also discussion of the daughter of the 'conte d'universo' [Jean de Nevers, the Duke of Burgundy's eldest son] for the other son of the lord Duke, messer Filippo Maria."[1]

Charles VI, who still adhered, in his moments of sanity, to the ambition of ending the Schism of the Church, required that any such agreement should include a promise of support for his ecclesiastical policy. Giangaleazzo accepted the principle of the resignation of both Popes, but he stipulated that his consent should remain a secret until he had had an opportunity to consult with his allies, Wenceslaus and Sigismund.[2] He was playing for time. The publication of these proposals would inevitably drive Boniface into the arms of his enemies; on the other hand, he had to circumvent the designs of Rupert's friends at the French court —Queen Isabella and her brother Lewis of Bavaria, the Duke of Burgundy, and all the enemies of Louis of Orleans—who were eager to place the forces of France at Rupert's disposal.[3]

Giangaleazzo therefore gave no definite answer to the French requests, but kept the negotiations open. Charles VI was unwilling to help Rupert, who depended on the favour of Boniface IX;[4] and the Duke of Milan could also rely on the hopeless division of the French court between the factions of Orleans and Burgundy, to defeat the objects of Rupert's friends in Paris. Marshal Boucicault, on his way to take up the office of governor

[1] Despatch of 6 August 1400: *ASS*, Concistoro 1848, no. 18. The envoy adds the curious remark: "che all' altra sua sorella ch' è moglie del figliuolo[!] del re di Francia succede essare reyna di Francia, che tutto sarebbe a grande exaltamento del Signore nostro."

[2] From the "Responsum domini Mediolanensis", of which a copy, made in October 1400, is preserved in the *Archives Nationales* in Paris: Jarry, *Vie Politique de Louis de France*, 247.

[3] Romano, "Giangaleazzo Visconti", *ASL* xviii 302–6; Jarry, *Vie Politique de Louis de France*, 246–7, 253–6; de Boüard, "Empereur Robert et le grand Schisme", *MAH* xlviii 219–22.

[4] Leroux, *Nouvelles recherches critiques*, 42–3. Charles wished to mediate between Rupert and Wenceslaus: *RTA* iv 210, no. 100.

of Genoa, stopped at Pavia in October 1401, to renew the discussions on the Schism and on the proposed betrothal of Giovanni Maria.[1] His mission does not seem to have advanced the negotiations any further; but it must at least have brought to Giangaleazzo the relief of knowing that Rupert had failed to win any official help from France in support of his expedition.

The deposition of Wenceslaus had momentarily united the house of Luxemburg in his defence. Sigismund, as Giangaleazzo recognized, was the strongest member of the family, and it was to him that the Duke appealed to stiffen the resistance to Rupert in Germany. Sigismund, however, had difficulties enough of his own. The Hungarian nobility had grown restless under his rule, and were negotiating with William of Austria, with the King of Poland, and with Ladislaus of Naples, all of them prospective candidates for the Hungarian throne. Sigismund was actually held a prisoner by his subjects for a few months, and did not secure his release until August 1401.[2] Meanwhile Wenceslaus, deprived of his brother's encouragement and support, allowed offers to be made to Rupert in his name, for a division of the powers and titles of the Imperial office. Rupert had been unable to bring the war against Wenceslaus in Bohemia to a satisfactory conclusion; but he hoped that the troubles and divisions of his enemies would render them powerless while he was away from Germany, and that success in Italy would obviate the need to bargain with his rival.[3] He therefore refused the offer, and set out from Augsburg for Italy on 25 September 1401, leaving his enemies in Germany to do their worst while he was away.

His arrival had been anticipated by a fresh uprising of the Guelfs in the Brescian Alps. Encouraged by their old friends of the Mantuan war, who were now Rupert's allies—Francesco Carrara, the Bishop of Trent and Leopold of Austria—the rebels took the initiative even before Rupert's coming was

---

[1] Commission of 14 August 1401: Doüet d'Arcq, *Choix de pièces inédites*, i 204–7. Jarry, *Origines*, 353.

[2] *RTA* v 178 note 4; Lichnowsky, *Geschichte des Hauses Habsburg*, v 36–7; Huber, *Geschichte Oesterreichs*, ii 360–4.

[3] *RTA* iv 395–8, nos. 337–40; 470–3, nos. 392–5. Jarry, *Vie politique de Louis de France*, 268.

announced.[1] Giovanni Ronzoni, their leader, raided the *Bergamasco* in May 1401, captured a force sent against him in August, and defeated another expedition in September.[2] But his forces were limited; although the government could not capture him, the area on which he inflicted damage was very small. This was only the vanguard of the German attack.

The whole of western Europe had been canvassed by both sides before the struggle began; but the part which Rupert played, on the stage so carefully prepared for the vindication of Imperial rights in Lombardy, was quite unworthy of the preliminary dispositions. He was fully justified in the forebodings which he had felt, when he allowed Pitti to persuade him to go to Italy. The expedition, hastily prepared and crippled by lack of money, arrived in Italy at the beginning of the winter, when the campaigning season had already ended.

Rupert's army, joined by a small Italian force under Francesco Carrara, encamped a few miles north of Brescia on 21 October 1401; but it was not the army which Florence had expected. A third of the troops had been left behind at Augsburg for want of money to pay them. The season was late, and provisions were scarce.

Giangaleazzo had every reason to be confident. Brescia, strongly fortified and garrisoned by the armies of Facino Cane and Ottobuon Terzo, could easily defy the assaults of the Germans. A conspiracy to admit the invaders into the city was discovered, and quickly suppressed; Rupert's Italian friends had assured him that the discontent of the Duke's subjects would lighten his task, but this hope proved false. The superiority of the Italian cavalry, with the heavy bridle which brought a quicker response from the horse,[3] was demonstrated during a sortie from Brescia in which a

---

[1] Rupert's letters to the Guelfs of the *Bergamasco*, addressed particularly to Pietro Lodrone (whom Corio, *op. cit.* II 428, describes as their leader) were dated 9 July 1401: *RTA* IV 439–40, nos. 366–7.

[2] "Chronicon Bergomense", *RIS* XVI 923 E–924 E; "Annales Mediolanenses", *ibid.* 834 B; Minerbetti, "Cronica", 266.

[3] The explanation of Bruni, "Historiarum Florentini Populi", *RIS* NS XIX, 3, 282–3.

large German foraging party, whom necessity made overbold, was put to rout. This was the battle of Brescia, which the Paduan chronicler magnified into an heroic struggle between the two armies.[1]

Its results were in fact as conclusive as if the whole forces of both sides had been engaged. Divisions arose in the German camp; Leopold of Austria and the Archbishop of Cologne turned back and led their large contingents homewards. Rupert, faced by the limitations which had contributed to the failure of so many earlier German adventures in Italy, followed the deserters northwards as far as Trent. Only the desperate entreaties of his Italian advisers induced him to turn back to Italy; making a wide detour through Friuli, he rejoined Carrara in Padua with the sad remnants of his army.[2]

The Bavarian's efforts to find backing and support need not be related in detail. Florence refused to spend another penny, until Rupert had crossed the border of the Milanese state at the head of a powerful army. Boniface and Ladislaus refused their support until Rupert could guarantee to put into the field an army five or six times as numerous as the depleted forces left to him. The Venetians, who had it in their power to unite all these forces, gave only the minimum of encouragement needed, to delay Rupert in Italy as a check upon Giangaleazzo, without involving themselves in a quarrel with Milan. After five months of fruitless discussion, Rupert sailed to Friuli in the middle of April 1402, and crossed the mountains again to Bavaria.[3]

The battle of Brescia had been little more than a skirmish, but for Giangaleazzo it represented nevertheless "a new legitimation".[4] He had done remarkably little to account for the total

---

[1] Winckelmann, *Romzug Ruprechts von der Pfalz*, 48–62; Gatari, "Cronaca Carrarese", *RIS* NS xvii, 1, 472–3. A full review of the evidence against Gatari's account is given by Lindner, "Schlacht bei Brescia", in *Mittheilungen des Instituts für Oesterreichische Geschichtsforschung*, xiii 377–94.

[2] Winckelmann, *op. cit.* 63–70. His theory that Leopold's departure was due to a quarrel with Francesco Carrara over his claims to Verona was developed by Pastorello, *Nuove Ricerche*, 105 note 3.

[3] Winckelmann, *op. cit.* 71–117. The attitude of Florence is made clear by the minutes of the Council, which he quotes, *ibid.* 130–44.

[4] Romano, "Giangaleazzo Visconti", *ASL* xviii 306–7.

failure of Rupert's expedition. Adequate precautions had been taken; but his strength was never seriously tested, his state never in the least danger, his reserves of power never called into use. He had triumphed with scarcely an effort, not only over his immediate enemies, but over the might of Germany. The great effort to overthrow him proved to be little more than an interlude in the development of his own policy. His declared enemies had shown to the world that their resources were pitifully inadequate, and that they did not know how to make the most even of those they had. Others, who would have been glad to see his power curtailed, were quite simply afraid to declare their hostility and join forces with his enemies. Instead, they looked to Venice to give them a lead; and the only danger which Giangaleazzo had to fear was that the Venetians would abandon their neutrality and turn against him.

This danger could no longer be ignored. The Venetians had followed Giangaleazzo's activities in Emilia, before and after the German expedition, with the closest interest. For the Duke was gradually maturing his plans against Bologna. With the added prestige which he had gained from Rupert's defeat, he decided that he could afford, for once, to force the issue with impunity.

CHAPTER XIX

THE RULE OF GIOVANNI BENTIVOGLIO IN BOLOGNA. THE POLICY OF VENICE DURING THE GERMAN EXPEDITION, AND GIAN-GALEAZZO'S CONQUEST OF BOLOGNA
(1401–*JUNE* 1402)

THE government of the *Scacchesi*, established in Bologna in December 1399, with the connivance of Alberico da Barbiano, was disturbed by the rival ambitions of its leaders. Nanne Gozzadini represented the more democratic elements of the party. Giovanni Bentivoglio professed aristocratic principles; he also made overtures, in his own interests, to the Duke of Milan.

Giangaleazzo was willing to rule Bologna through Bentivoglio, as earlier he had ruled Pisa through Appiano. And when Bentivoglio recalled the exiled *Maltraversi*, and with their support proclaimed himself lord of Bologna in March 1401, he acted with Giangaleazzo's encouragement and approval.[1]

The Duke sent his agent, Pietro Corte, to Bologna, to make offers of friendship, alliance and military support to Bentivoglio; and Corte returned to Pavia, without a signed agreement, but well satisfied with the result of his talks.[2] Bentivoglio, however, did not trust the Duke; and the Florentines, although they regarded the new ruler of Bologna with suspicion as a friend of Milan, exhorted him none the less warmly to return to the true Guelf alliance.[3] Bentivoglio accepted the Florentine troops sent to strengthen his defences, and was tempted to increase his reliance on the Republic. The Florentine ambassadors, who had

---

[1] Bosdari, "Giovanni I Bentivoglio, Signore di Bologna", in *AMR* 4, v 205–13. The help received from Pavia is referred to in Sercambi, "Cronache", III 31–2; Dati, *Istoria di Firenze*, 66; Corio, *Storia di Milano*, II 427; Ghirardacci, *Historia di Bologna*, 517–18.

[2] Bosdari, "Giovanni I Bentivoglio", *AMR* 4, v 231.

[3] Minutes of the Florentine Council, 9 April onwards, published by Winckelmann, *Romzug Ruprechts von der Pfalz*, 125–6.

been in Bologna at the time of Bentivoglio's seizure of power, reported that "we pursued our object of giving unity to the city; but, notwithstanding that we did what we could, Giovanni Bentivoglio took the dominion". They then congratulated Giovanni, and broached the subject of an alliance, to which the ruler replied through his Council that "considering the newness of his dominion and the nearness of the Duke of Milan, and of Astorre and of Carlo Malatesta, to strengthen himself with troops, as he was doing, seemed to them at present to come before the making of alliances. They said, however, that if the Venetians should be willing to join, he would be able the more securely and the more readily to make alliance."[1] Bentivoglio would indeed have preferred to steer a middle course between Florence and Milan, basing his policy on close co-operation with Venice;[2] but the Venetians refused to be drawn too deeply into his affairs. They contented themselves with diplomatic mediation. On learning from the Bolognese ambassadors in Venice that "their lord was ready to make peace, and accepted our intervention in good spirit", they elected two envoys to join those of Florence and of Milan in the task of finding a solution of the quarrel between Bologna and Astorre Manfredi of Faenza, which still dragged on under the impetus of Alberico's thirst for revenge.[3]

Bentivoglio had to choose between Florence and Milan; when Pietro Corte returned to Bologna, in June 1401, he found that the choice had already been made. The Florentine ambassadors were evidently enjoying the complete confidence of the ruler. Two days after his arrival, Corte left the city, having delivered a dramatic warning to Bentivoglio.[4] It was without the participation of a Milanese representative that a peace between Bologna and Manfredi was proclaimed, in the following month.[5]

Bentivoglio was quickly reminded of the implications of his

---

[1] Report of 29 March 1401: *ASF*, Signoria, Rapporti I 38 t.
[2] "Corpus Chronicorum Bononiensium", *RIS* NS XVIII, 1, vol. 3, 474; Minerbetti, "Cronica", 260; Sercambi, "Cronache", III 41–2; Bruni, "Historiarum Florentini Populi", *RIS* NS XIX, 3, 281; Corio, *op. cit.* II 427.
[3] Minutes of the Senate, 17 May 1401: *ASV*, Senato Secreta, F. 3 & t.
[4] Bosdari, "Giovanni I Bentivoglio", *AMR* 4, v 235.
[5] On 7 July; published *ibid.* 279–89, Doc. 7.

choice. He had tricked the Duke, accepting his help and then betraying him to the Florentines. Alberico da Barbiano raided Bolognese territory a few days after Pietro Corte's second return to Pavia, and again on his own account a month later, when Bentivoglio made peace with their joint enemy.[1] The Grand Constable now had his own feud with Bentivoglio, and Giangaleazzo could rely on him to harass Bologna, while his own attention was turned to meet the danger from Germany. Their interests seemed identical. Bentivoglio, appealing to Venice for help against the Condottiere, referred to Alberico as "the man and creature of the lord Duke of Milan";[2] and the Milanese chronicle records certain losses inflicted on Alberico by the Bolognese, as a defeat for the Duke.[3]

Since he had failed to obtain control of Bologna through Bentivoglio, Giangaleazzo resorted to other means. He did not rely entirely on Barbiano's inadequate military power. Bentivoglio's despotic methods of government quickly antagonized his former associates. Nanne Gozzadini left Bologna, and soon found his way to Pavia. Others followed him, while some remained at Bentivoglio's side, apparently supporting him, but secretly in close touch with their friends at the Duke's court.[4]

The approach of Rupert's army momentarily relieved the pressure on Bologna. The German invasion drew Giangaleazzo's attention to the north-eastern corner of Italy. There, the attitude of Carrara on the one side, as of Gonzaga on the other, was beyond doubt. Niccolò d'Este, however, still hesitated between his fears of Venice and of Milan; he was anxious not to offend either power, until the outcome of Rupert's expedition could be foreseen.[5]

---

[1] For the raid in July, *v.* Bosdari, "Giovanni I Bentivoglio", *AMR* 4, v 236–7. Bosdari does not refer to Alberico's first raid, in June, which is mentioned in "Corpus Chronicorum Bononiensium", *RIS* NS xviii, 1, vol. 3, 474–5; Sercambi, "Cronache", iii 41; and in a minute of the Venetian Senate, 23 June, "ad primam partem damnorum datorum et incursionum factarum per gentes domini Octoboni tercii et Magni Comestabilis": *ASV*, Senato Secreta, F. 6.

[2] Minute of 12 July: *ibid.* 9 t.

[3] "Annales Mediolanenses", *RIS* xvi 834 E–5 A.

[4] Bosdari, "Giovanni I Bentivoglio", *AMR* 4, v 235–6.

[5] D'Este was very frank in explaining his neutrality: *v.* his letters to Venice, 21 October 1401 and 23 February 1402, in *RTA* v 151–2, no. 96; 165, no. 119.

Giangaleazzo invited him to a hunting party at St Angelo in September 1401, and the young Marquis did not dare to refuse. He assured Venice, on his return to Ferrara, that he had given no pledges and undertaken no obligations; but the Duke had at least confirmed him in his resolution to preserve absolute neutrality during the coming struggle.[1]

The roads to Germany sprang into prominence again. The Patriarch of Aquileia was absent from his lands, and Giangaleazzo had little difficulty in winning the favour of a powerful league of the lords and communities of Friuli;[2] the distant power of Milan held the same attraction for them as for the Tuscan Republics, as a bulwark against a nearer tyranny. The records of the Venetian Senate reveal with what close attention the Duke's activities were followed in Venice. The first note of alarm was sounded at the beginning of May 1401: "We were recently told that friar Giovanni Cane, 'famigliare' of the lord Duke of Milan, was in the country of Friuli some days back."[3] The Venetians were anxious that Friuli should adopt their own policy of complete neutrality towards Rupert;[4] and they were so far successful, that the German was able to pass through the district without hindrance, on the way to Padua after his failure before Brescia. But the answers which they received from the pro-Milanese party, formed in Friuli under the leadership of Tristan Savorgnano, were by no means sufficient to allay their suspicions. The final reply, that "they would more willingly oblige us and our government, in their affairs, than any other government or person", was too vague and indefinite to convince the Venetians that they had nothing to fear from a renewal of Giangaleazzo's intrigues in their own sphere of influence.[5]

There was nothing tangible enough, in these intrigues, to bring

[1] Benvenuto Cessi, *Venezia e Padova*, 90–3.
[2] Paschini, *Storia di Friuli*, III 100–1.
[3] Minute of the Senate, 2 May 1401: *ASV*, Senato Secreta, F. 2.
[4] Cusin, *Confine Orientale d' Italia*, I 217–18. In November, a Parliament was summoned to make provision for defence in case of an invasion "de Alemania": *Parlamento Friuliano*, 395–6, no. 418.
[5] Minute of the Venetian Senate, 15 October 1401: *ASV*, Senato Secreta, F. 25. Among other references to the affairs of Friuli between May and October, from the same volume, v. *RTA* v 141–2, nos. 85–6.

about an open change of front on the part of Venice; but the significance of the Duke's new approach to Friuli was not allowed to pass unnoticed. When Rupert arrived at Padua in November 1401, Giangaleazzo allowed Alberico da Barbiano to resume his attack on Bologna; but Alberico had to rely on his own forces, for the greater part of the Milanese army had necessarily to be concentrated in the *Veronese*, on the border of Paduan territory. Venice chose to regard this essential measure of precaution as a threat to Carrara, and took the unusual step of hiring 300 lances for the defence of Padua.[1]

After the Duke's triumph at Brescia, his ambassadors in Venice claimed from Florence and from Carrara the penalty for violating the peace of 1400, and declared before the Venetian Senate their master's proud intention to preserve Italy from foreign invasion.[2] The Duke also made offers of alliance to the Venetians. He hoped that the victory over Rupert might have impressed upon them the value of his friendship. But the moment was ill-chosen; the Venetians showed themselves suspicious of the Duke's relations with the rulers of Mantua, Ferrara and Ravenna; they demanded explanations of his policy in relation to these states, all within the sphere of Venetian influence, and they pointed out his responsibility for the war against Bologna.[3] If Rupert's expedition accomplished nothing else for the allies, it crystallized the suspicions of the Duke which had recently revived in Venice.

While this lack of sympathy existed between Venice and Giangaleazzo, there could be no sense of security on the Paduan border. While Francesco Gonzaga and the Malatesta joined in the attack on Bologna, Giangaleazzo began in April 1402 to build a dam at Noale, near Bassano, to check the waters of the Brenta and divert them along a new channel into the Bacchiglione near Vicenza.[4] Carrara, who was loyally supporting Bentivoglio

---

[1] Pastorello, *Nuove Ricerche*, 255–6, Doc. 73; "Copialettere", 42–3, no. 70 and note 1; *RTA* v 136, no. 79.

[2] Bruni, *op. cit. RIS* NS xix, 3, 284–7.

[3] Minute of the Senate, 14 February 1402: *RTA* v 136, no. 78.

[4] "Annales Mediolanenses", *RIS* xvi 835 c; Corio, *op. cit.* ii 433–4; Cena, "Ponte Visconteo presso Bassano", in *Bollettino del Museo Civico di Bassano*,

in the defence of Bologna, would have answered this threat to
interfere with the waters of the *Padovano*, by launching an attack
upon Milan. He did, indeed, lend his encouragement to plots
against the Visconti government in Verona and the *Veronese*; but
the plots were abortive, and the Venetians restrained him from
taking active measures against the Duke.[1] Instead, they decided,
no doubt with some reluctance, that the time had come for them
to intervene once more in the affairs of northern Italy.

The Venetian ambassadors, who arrived in Pavia at the end of
May 1402, delivered a warning which the Duke could not afford
to ignore. They invited him to send his representatives to Venice,
for a conference to discuss means of pacifying Italy. They made
it quite clear that both the campaign against Bologna and the
works on the Brenta were regarded in Venice as contrary to the
terms of the peace of 1400; and they asked the Duke to suspend
them both, as a sign of his goodwill, and as a first step towards
the happy issue of the proposed conference.[2]

Giangaleazzo gauged on the one side the length of the resistance
that Bentivoglio could oppose to his armies, and on the other the
patience of the Venetians, whose neutrality was essential to his
plans. The campaign against Bologna was proceeding satisfac-
torily; and the Duke decided to play for time. The Venetian
government did not receive his answer until the middle of June,
when the ambassadors at Pavia reported the reply of the Duke's
Council, that "their lord, who was disposed and ready for the peace
of Italy, and especially to preserve himself in love and favour with
our dominion, had decided to send his ambassadors at once...
with full freedom and mandate alike on the matter of the Brenta
as of Bologna". The Venetians at once issued similar invitations
to the allies,[3] who had perforce to accept, although they had no

---

v 1–2; "Copialettere", 82, note 1 to no. 135; 103, no. 165 and note 2; 124,
no. 194 and note 3; 129–30, no. 199.

[1] Pastorello, *Nuove Ricerche*, 110–19.

[2] Instructions of 20 May 1402, summarized in *RTA* v 140–1, no. 84; and
published by Cena, *op. cit.* 4–6.

[3] Minutes of the Senate, 14 June 1402: *ASV*, Senato Secreta, F. 66 & t;
the invitation to the allies was published in "Copialettere", 240, note 1 to
no. 404; and cf. nos. 409, 424, 431.

illusions as to the Duke's sincerity. The Florentine ambassadors in Venice declared, with some insight into the Duke's character and methods, that "he does not wish to have peace, but instead he wishes to draw out the discussions, while he obtains his purpose in the affairs of Bologna, and also for the purpose of reducing others to submission". But the Venetians rejected their protest, and refused to abandon their plan of pacification "for the present".[1]

Meanwhile, the pressure on Bentivoglio had steadily increased. Within Bologna, there was no enthusiasm for his arbitrary rule; without, the allies of Milan were gathering their forces. The Malatesta had declared war on Bologna in March; Francesco Gonzaga sent his "sfida" to Bentivoglio in April. Giangaleazzo's army assembled against Bologna in May, when Rupert had returned to Germany and the Paduan frontier no longer needed to be so carefully guarded. The war was nominally fought by Gonzaga, the Malatesta and the Grand Constable, in pursuance of their several grievances against Bentivoglio, and in support of the Bolognese exiles who had been driven out of the city by his despotic acts; but behind the leaders were the dominant will and the guiding hand of the Duke; and against them were the Duke's enemies, Florence and Carrara, who denuded their own defences in order to strengthen the resistance of Bologna to the banner of the Viper.[2]

In spite of the superiority of his forces, Giangaleazzo's task was far from simple. The dominions of Niccolò d'Este separated Bologna from the Milanese state; and the allies tried, although without much success, to cut off the supplies which Giangaleazzo's forces were receiving from Ferrarese territory.[3] The Duke had to sustain a large army on foreign ground for the prolonged period needed to starve out a great city, and at the same time to satisfy the demands of Venice for tangible evidence of his goodwill and desire for peace. The patience of Venice was not inexhaustible; on 25 June, the Senate rejected by only a small majority a motion

---

[1] Minute of the Senate, 16 June 1402: *ASV*, Senato Secreta, F. 66 t.
[2] Bosdari, "Giovanni I Bentivoglio", *AMR* 4, v 254–8.
[3] Letter of Carrara, 3 May 1402: "Copialettere", 160–1, no. 249.

to send help to Bentivoglio, proposed on the ground that the *Serenissima* would eventually have to intervene, with greater expense and in less favourable circumstances, if Bologna fell.[1]

The Duke could not hope to hold the Venetians in play much longer; and it must have been with great relief that he learnt that Bentivoglio had finally solved his problems for him. The ruler of Bologna could not trust even his own subjects; rather than remain shut up with them in the city, with his water-supply already threatened, to resist a siege, he decided to give battle to the numerically superior Milanese army.[2] The Florentine captain, Bernardone, protested that this course would be fatal; and so it proved. The battle was fought at Casalecchio, a little way outside the city on the banks of the Reno. The Visconti army triumphed, and at the end of the day Bentivoglio fled back to Bologna with the remnant of his forces.[3]

In the night that followed, the Bolognese rose against their ruler; and on the following day, they opened the gates of the city to the exiles who had gathered at the court and in the camp of the Duke. Bologna was proclaimed to be a free Commune once more.

It is not quite clear whether Giangaleazzo had envisaged the restoration of a Communal government in Bologna; he may have encouraged it, as he had restored the *Anziani* in Pisa three years before, for the purpose of strengthening his own juridical authority. In that case, the events which followed in Bologna must have been carefully planned beforehand in Pavia.

There were still divisions and party quarrels among the Bolognese. The aristocratic party, Bentivoglio's former associates, feared the ambitions and the democratic tendencies of Nanne Gozzadini. In conjunction with Francesco Gonzaga and the other Condottieri, they admitted the Milanese army into the city, pro-

---

[1] Cusin, *Confine Orientale d' Italia*, I 228 note 256.

[2] Bosdari, "Giovanni I Bentivoglio", *AMR* 4, v 260–1. His calculation that the forces were about equal, seems to have been made without distinguishing between the knight ("eques", "cavallo") and the lance, the unit of three horsemen.

[3] Durrieu, *Gascons en Italie*, 210–13; Bosdari, "Giovanni I Bentivoglio", *AMR* 4, v 263–5.

claimed Giangaleazzo as "Signore", and appointed Pandolfo Malatesta his governor.[1] One account of these events records that the Milanese troops met with some resistance from the citizens;[2] but an important section of Bolognese opinion was not displeased to accept Giangaleazzo's rule.[3] In the second week of July 1402, the representatives of the recently elected Communal government formally transferred the "dominium" of Bologna into the hands of the Duke of Milan.[4]

[1] Bosdari, "Giovanni I Bentivoglio", *AMR* 4, v 265–9. An account in "Copialettere", 279–80, note 1 to no. 484; and *ibid.* 295, note 1 to no. 520, in a letter to Rome.

[2] *Ibid.* nos. 496, 502.

[3] *Ibid.* 287, note 2 to no. 502.

[4] Mattiolo, *Cronaca Bolognese*, 114–17; "Corpus Chronicorum Bononiensium", *RIS* NS xviii, 1, vol. 3, 482–3.

CHAPTER XX

GIANGALEAZZO AND FLORENCE (1402)

THE fiasco of Rupert's expedition to Italy had given new confidence to the Duke of Milan. He conquered Bologna by force of arms, in spite of the defence sustained by the Florentine army, of the veiled hostility of the Pope, and of the open expression of Venetian disapproval. His natural caution had not forsaken him; but he was conscious of his own strength, and his neighbours might find in his easy triumph over the Germans a warning of the fate which awaited those who opposed his designs. The possession of Bologna brought him a step nearer to the realization of his ambition to rule unchallenged over the Lombard plain from the Alps to the Apennines. He had won an important strategical advantage over Florence by cutting the direct road of communication between Tuscany and Venice; and by taking the crossroads of northern Italy into his own hands, he had prepared the way for a fresh expansion of Milanese trade.

There were no evident symptoms, at the end of June 1402, to suggest that Giangaleazzo's hopes would never find realization. The forces of Florence were dispersed on the field of Casalecchio, and the passes into Tuscany lay open to the Milanese army. The lands of Pisa, Siena, Perugia and Urbino formed an impenetrable semicircle, blocking the outlets of Florence to the Tuscan ports and to Rome. Transit through Bologna was forbidden to the Florentines when Giangaleazzo captured the city.[1] With Rupert of Bavaria fully occupied in Germany, Venice bent on keeping the peace, Boniface apparently afraid to forfeit the allegiance of the Milanese Church, and Ladislaus engaged in winning Venetian support for his claims on Hungary,[2] Florence seemed to be at the mercy of her enemy.

---

[1] Delayto, "Annales Estenses", *RIS* XVIII 971 E. This decision was known in Rome on 12 July: "Copialettere", 295, note 1 to no. 520.

[2] "Copialettere", 345, no. 632; 374, no. 693. Carrara wrote on 2 September: "per quello che me pare, el re Ladislao e la Segnoria da Venesia sono facti una anima e uno corpo": *ibid.* 385, no. 713.

Giangaleazzo's first task, however, was to consolidate his position in Bologna. Many citizens regretted their lost liberty; and the Duke decided to secure his authority by the erection of a strong fortress in the city. The building of the citadel, which was begun in August and completed with all speed, aroused fierce resentment among those who had prized their former freedom;[1] but many others welcomed with joy the favours bestowed by the Duke on his new subjects.[2] The attraction of Visconti rule, to those citizens who suffered most from the internal disorder and frequent revolutions of Communal government, had not lost its force, even in a city of great and independent traditions.

Having secured possession of Bologna, Giangaleazzo was anxious to come to an understanding with Boniface IX, the nominal overlord of the city. He approached the Pope through the Bishop of Cervia, Carlo Malatesta's envoy in Rome, and offered to restore the freedom of Perugia, if Boniface would grant an appropriate title to confirm his authority in Bologna. We cannot tell how sincere this offer may have been; it suggests that Giangaleazzo recognized the limits of his expansion southwards; and wished to consolidate his authority to the north of the Apennines, but it seems unlikely that he would have abandoned control of the road between Tuscany and the south until the issues between him and Florence had been finally settled. Boniface, at least, was unwilling to trust him, or to relinquish the Papal claims of suzerainty over Bologna; there were skirmishes between Papal troops and the Visconti garrisons in Umbria,[3] and the Pope gave ear to Florentine proposals of alliance against the Duke.[4] The discussions in Rome continued throughout August; but the Florentines considered that the Pope's demands placed too heavy a burden upon the Republic, and they had little confidence in the

---

[1] "Corpus Chronicorum Bononiensium", *RIS* NS XVIII, 1, vol. 3, 483–4, 486–7.

[2] A contemporary letter published by Gozzadini, *Nanne Gozzadini e Baldassare Cossa*, 168–70.

[3] Pellini, *Historia di Perugia*, II 128–9. Carrara reported news of a victory over Giangaleazzo's troops in Umbria, in letters of 10 and 11 July: "Copialettere", 365–7, nos. 548, 552–3.

[4] *V*. Doc. 16. (Despatch from Rome, 9 August.)

wavering and mutable Boniface, whose policy was governed by the intrigues of his brothers.[1] The Pope refused to modify his terms; and at the beginning of September, in reply to a new overture from Milan, he decided to give further consideration to the Duke's proposals. "We told you in our other letters", wrote the Florentine ambassadors in Rome on 5 September, "how the negotiations entrusted by the Duke to the Bishop of Cervia and to Carlo [Malatesta] for an agreement over Perugia and Bologna had been broken off, and so they certainly were; but yesterday evening the proposal was discussed afresh, that ser Niccolò da Imola should go to Carlo Malatesta on that business, and he leaves tomorrow morning, although not with authority to sign any binding agreement. This has happened because of letters which the Pope received yesterday from the Duke, and we believe that he will draw out our talks until an answer comes."[2]

While Giangaleazzo and the Florentines sought the favours of the Pope, a similar rivalry was in progress at Venice. The Duke had at last sent the representatives whom he had promised, to enter into conversations with the *Serenissima*. They arrived in Venice on 4 July,[3] when no amount of discussion could any longer deprive him of Bologna; and they were instructed to propose an alliance between Milan and Venice, as the best means of securing the peace of Italy.

The Venetians, however, were on their guard. The new Patriarch of Aquileia, elected in April 1402, was wholly devoted to the interests of the pro-Milanese party.[4] Between May and August, envoys from the communities of Friuli, from the Savorgnano

---

[1] *Ibid.*; and further despatches of the Florentine envoys in Rome, 19 August-5 September: *ASF*, Legazioni 7 bis, 3 t–6 t. "El respondere vostro fa tale che possiamo conchiudere o romperci senza più rescrivere", they wrote with some exasperation on 19 August: *ibid.* 4. "Attento quod papa non est talis quod de ipso sperari possit", declared Filippo Corsini in the Council on 18 July; and Filippo Magalotti, on 24 August: "liga Pape propter mutabilitatem Pape et condicionem fratrum eius, et quia cardinales non concurrant ad ista colloquia, non est speranda nec utilis": *ASF*, Consulte e Pratiche, xxxv 139 t, 148 t.

[2] *ASF*, Legazioni 7 bis, 6 t.

[3] "Copialettere", 337, note 1 to no. 620; "Commissioni di Rinaldo degli Albizzi", in *Documenti di Storia Italiana*, I 17.

[4] Cusin, *Confine orientale d' Italia*, I 219.

clan, and finally from the Patriarch himself, went to Pavia to seek an accord with Giangaleazzo.[1] Visconti troops were reported to have entered Friuli, and, according to a rumour circulated by Francesco Carrara, a good half of the district had been offered to the Duke in the course of the negotiations at Pavia.[2]

Giangaleazzo had not abandoned the works on the Brenta, in spite of Venetian protests; but when the dam was finished, and the gates were closed at the beginning of August 1402, the waters broke through and the whole construction was ruined.[3] The *Serenissima* found a further cause for alarm in the growing influence which the Duke exercised over the Marquis of Ferrara; the momentary fear, which d'Este showed when he found his Modenese territory sandwiched between the dominions of the Visconti after the fall of Bologna, was quickly allayed, and he was drawn closer than ever to the orbit of Milanese policy.[4] Almost it would seem that Giangaleazzo, sure of his unchallengeable power, no longer thought it necessary to conceal his designs from the Venetians.

The *Serenissima* saw the danger, but still hoped to avoid it without undue exertion—the Florentine ambassadors were to report that the Venetians "are all cordial enemies of the Visconti, but they shun trouble as much as they can".[5] When the Milanese envoys arrived in Venice at the beginning of July 1402, the proposal set before them was for an alliance between Venice, Florence, the Duke, the Marquis and the lord of Padua, to guarantee the peace of northern Italy. Giangaleazzo, who did not wish to bind himself in any way to Florence or to Carrara, replied that this League would be "neither useful nor honourable", and declared that he wanted only an alliance with the *Serenissima*, "for such an alliance seems to him to be that which can give peace and repose to Italy"; and the Venetians, while

¹ "Copialettere", 322, note 3 to no. 591; 367–8 no. 677. Verci, *Storia della Marca Trivigiana*, XVIII 59, from a manuscript chronicle of Belluno.
² Cusin, *Confine Orientale d' Italia*, I 229–30.
³ Verci, *op. cit.* XVIII 57–8; "Copialettere", nos. 656, 667 (letters of 7 and 11 August).
⁴ Benvenuto Cessi, *Venezia e Padova*, 94–100.
    ·Report of 16 October 1402: Bolognini, "Relazioni tra Firenze e Venezia", *NAV* IX 109.

repeating that their object was a general League, expressed their readiness to discuss the terms he wished to propose for a particular alliance.[1] Three days later, however, they decided to enter into negotiations for an alliance with Florence.[2]

The Venetian proposals, both for a general accord and for an alliance with Florence, were ready by 11 August;[3] but the latter met with a mixed reception from the Florentine government. The Venetians, resolute in the defence of Padua and Ferrara, were not concerned in the affairs of Tuscany; and their proposals were thought to place too heavy a burden on Florence in the event of war. After the bitter experience of 1398, the Florentines were chary of giving too much power to Venice. An alliance with the *Serenissima* would be an extra guarantee of peace, if the conference at Venice were successful; but the Venetians would not commit themselves to a large enough share in a military alliance, in case the conference failed. The Florentines decided to postpone their answer, while they explored the possibilities of reaching an agreement with Boniface IX on more equal terms.[4]

The determination of the Florentines to secure their own terms from Boniface and from Venice is the more surprising, because none realized better than they the acute danger in which they stood. The support given by the Republic to Rupert of Bavaria was a challenge too open to be ignored. Giangaleazzo did not declare war on Florence; but he was in a position to put into effect the plan that had failed in 1391. Reprisals were imposed on Florentine merchants in Perugia during Rupert's expedition;[5] Giangaleazzo placed a ban on Florentine trade in Pisa in April 1402.[6] After the conquest of Bologna, there were

---

[1] Minutes of the Senate, 28 July: *ASV*, Senato Secreta, F. 70; and "Copialettere", 337, note 1 to no. 620. Further mention of the negotiations, *ibid.* nos. 507, 579, 639, 670, 684, 693.

[2] On 31 July: *ibid.* 337, note 1 to no. 620.

[3] Pastorello, *Nuove Ricerche*, 263–4, Doc. 78.

[4] "Pacta certe non satis equa": Bruni, "Historiarum Florentini Populi", *RIS* NS xix, 3, 288. That this was the general verdict in Florence is shown by the debates of the Council, especially on 24 August: *ASF*, Consulte e Pratiche, xxxv 148 t–149.   [5] Pellini, *op. cit.* ii 128.

[6] Piattoli, "Problema Portuale di Firenze", *RSAT* ii 162–4.

only two roads by which the commerce of the Republic could avoid the Duke's territories, and the embargo which he had placed upon Florentine trade.

Paolo Guinigi, lord of Lucca, refused to join in the blockade of Florence, whose trade was indispensable to the prosperity of his state. In April 1402, he gave a verbal promise of security to the Florentines who used the port of Motrone;[1] but he would not commit himself to a written contract. Giangaleazzo was a dangerous neighbour, and the state of Lucca was uncomfortably wedged between his lands in the Lunigiana and Pisa. Guinigi probably assured the Duke that he had refused the Florentine request;[2] but Giangaleazzo did not allow the matter to rest there. He staged a military demonstration on the Pisan border;[3] and when the Milanese envoy returned to Lucca in June, he found Guinigi far readier to comply with the Duke's demands.

The lord of Lucca, like the Marquis of Ferrara in Lombardy, was playing a waiting game—unable to resist the demands of either of his powerful neighbours, anxious both to preserve his independence and to ensure that the stronger party should have no grievance against him. A Milanese ship, stationed in the mouth of the Magra, enforced the blockade of Motrone;[4] and Guinigi had no alternative but to submit to the Duke's terms. It is not clear whether any definite agreement was drawn up, and Guinigi may once again have avoided giving a written promise;[5] but, albeit as

---

[1] "Commissioni di Rinaldo degli Albizzi", in *Documenti di Storia Italiana*, I 10–11; "Copialettere", 147, note 2 to no. 227; Piattoli, "Problema Portuale di Firenze", *RSAT* II 167–8. Guinigi's letter to Giangaleazzo, 6 April 1402: *Carteggio di Paolo Guinigi*, 5–6 no. 10; Zerbi, *Visconti di Milano*, 62–3. Cf. *Carteggio di Paolo Guinigi*, 177–80 nos. 94, 96, 109, 113, for the use which the Florentines made of their right of transit to Motrone from April to June 1402.

[2] Corio, *Storia di Milano*, II 434; he asserts that Guinigi refused the Florentine request.

[3] Sercambi, "Cronache", III 59.

[4] "Il tiranno à ghalea armata nella Magra": a letter of 28 July, in Piattoli, "Problema Portuale di Firenze", *RSAT* II 165.

[5] Seregni, "Documenti Viscontei", *ASL* XXVI, 1, 256, refers to a definite pact, which does not appear from the summary of the document of 27 November in *Carteggio di Paolo Guinigi*, 196, no. 233. Barbavara's letter of 17 June (*ibid.* 185, no. 149), on the other hand, implies a clear understanding. And cf. *ibid.* 181, no. 120; 6, no. 11; and Zerbi, *op. cit.* 64.

unobtrusively as he could, he obeyed the Duke's instructions, and joined in the blockade. He detained the Florentine merchandise in Lucca, alleging as his reason the dangers and insecurity of the road; and the Florentines, after repeated and unavailing requests for its release, understood that their goods had been sequestered, and that they could no longer rely on Motrone as a port for their commerce.[1]

Only the long and arduous road across the Apennines to Romagna remained open. Carlo Malatesta was a friend of Giangaleazzo, but he was not so easily coerced as Guinigi; and, in answer to a request of the Florentines, he placed the port of Rimini at their disposal.[2] He was not at war with the Republic; and Florentine trade was profitable. But the road to Rimini, valuable as an additional outlet, was too difficult to cope with the bulk of the Republic's commerce. Giangaleazzo's blockade of Florence achieved a large measure of success. "Our trade is asleep, the losses of our merchants and of the city are inestimable", wrote the Florentine envoys from Rome in August 1402;[3] and letters from other sources speak of the famine and hunger in the city, and of the impossibility of guaranteeing the safe passage of merchandise to and from Florence. "These are in great dearth, one could almost say famine, and it seems that it is going to last."[4]

While Giangaleazzo's attention was concentrated on the capture of Bologna, he confined the expression of his resentment against Florence to these commercial reprisals; but he allowed his friends in Tuscany to harass the Republic as much as they could. Riccardo Cancellieri of Pistoia, after a quarrel with the rival family of the town in the summer of 1401, took to the hills and seized the fortress of Sambuca, on the pass leading to Bologna;

[1] Piattoli, "Problema Portuale di Firenze", *RSAT* II 167–70; Instructions of 27 September, in Salviati, "Cronica", *DET* XVIII 207–8; *Carteggio di Paolo Guinigi*, 184–90, nos. 144, 147, 183.
[2] "Commissioni di Rinaldo degli Albizzi", in *Documenti di Storia Italiana*, I 12–19.
[3] Despatch of 21 August 1402: *ASF*, Legazioni 7 bis, 4 t.
[4] A private letter from Florence, 3 June 1402: "Copialettere", 389, note 1 to no. 723. Cf. a letter from Genoa, 28 July: Piattoli, "Problema Portuale di Firenze", *RSAT* II 165–7.

abetted by the Duke, he carried out raids on Pistoia and the neighbouring Florentine lands, and resisted all efforts to dislodge him.[1] In May 1402, Florence foiled a conspiracy to place San Miniato in Giangaleazzo's hands;[2] in the following month, it was discovered that Giangaleazzo's agents were in touch with the Guazzalotti, who had governed the little town of Prato, in the hills above Florence, when it was a free Commune, and who were still the first family of the town.[3] The Florentines, for their part, were not idle. They encouraged the exiles from Pisa to raid Pisan territory; and when the fortress of Bientina was captured in one of these raids, it was at once placed under the dominion of the Republic.[4]

When Bologna fell at the end of June 1402, it seemed clear that Giangaleazzo would turn at once, with all his strength, to settle his account with Florence. The first reports received by the Duke's enemies from the Milanese camp indicated that one half of the army was to march on Florence, the other half on Padua;[5] the two enemies, divided and unprotected, were not expected to offer much resistance. On the following day, however, a fresh rumour was circulating. A spy, who claimed to have been present at a conference of the generals, declared that Jacopo dal Verme and Facino Cane, with 1600 lances and the garrisons of Verona and Vicenza, were to attack Padua; Alberico da Barbiano, on the other hand, had declared that "he had a mote in his eye, which was Faenza"; and he was determined to deal with his old enemy, Astorre Manfredi, before he moved against Florence.[6]

In fact, the Milanese forces remained inactive around Bologna. Facino Cane went off to Milan; Verme, after a brief absence, was

[1] Sozomeno, "Specimen Historie", *RIS* XVI 1172c–3c; Minerbetti, "Cronica", 262–3, 278–9; Sercambi, "Cronache", III 42–3, 58–9.
[2] Minerbetti, "Cronica", 277.
[3] Piattoli, "Ignoto Tentativo di Giangaleazzo", in *Archivio Storico Pratese* x 37–41. The incident is not recorded by any chronicler; a letter of 9 June told of the failure of the Duke's plot: *Carteggio di Paolo Guinigi*, 180, no. 118.
[4] Minerbetti, "Cronica", 277.
[5] Carrara, at second hand from "quodam viro fide digno, veridico et conducte", 1 July 1402: "Copialettere", 284, no. 498.
[6] *Ibid.* 285, no. 500 (letter of 2 July).

soon back at Bologna; and the main body of the army did not move.

The Florentines, granted an unexpected respite, hastily repaired their defences, gathered in the harvest, and assembled what troops they could.[1] Fresh reports came, at the end of July, that the Milanese army was about to move against Florence. Giangaleazzo warned the government of Siena to expect a visit from Francesco Gonzaga; and Carrara, in conveying this news to Florence, warned his ally that it was connected with a plan to attack the Republic.[2] From Genoa, it was reported that "many believe they will pay us a visit, but it is not known for certain";[3] and the Florentine ambassadors, on their way to Rome, "have received a letter from the 'dieci della balìa' of our Commune,... in which they write that truly they suspect that the enemy forces of the Duke of Milan, which are fighting in the lands of Bologna, may at any moment cross our borders with hostile purpose".[4] Yet still the Duke's army did not move. Accounts of a brief expedition of the Grand Constable in Tuscany find no confirmation in Florentine sources.[5] The only attack which the Florentines had to meet was that of the Ubaldini, who, from their fortresses in the Alpi di Podere and the Mugello, had renewed their old feud with the Republic.[6] Verme, according to Francesco Carrara, had placed a force of 400 men at the disposal of the Ubaldini;[7] and the reported defeat of the Milanese army by the Florentines, on 23 August 1402, can only refer to this small detachment.[8] Once

---

[1] Giovanni Morelli, *Cronica*, 313–14.

[2] Letter of 23 July: "Copialettere", 325, no. 595 and note 3; cf. 351, no. 641.

[3] Letter of a Florentine citizen, 28 July: Piattoli, "Problema Portuale di Firenze", *RSAT* II 166.

[4] Letter to Boniface IX, from Todi, 31 July: *ASF*, Legazioni 7 bis, 1 t.

[5] Malavolti, *Historia de' Sanesi*, II 191 t, and Pellini, *op. cit.* II 130, record this expedition.

[6] Minerbetti, "Cronica", 279; Delayto, *op. cit. RIS* XVIII 971 E–2 A; Malavolti, *op. cit.* II 191 t.

[7] Letter of 22 July: "Copialettere", 322, no. 591.

[8] For a summing-up of the evidence relating to the battle of 23 August: *ibid.* 322–3 note 4. Delayto, *op. cit. RIS* XVIII 971 E–2 A, refers to a defeat of the Ubaldini and Facino Cane near Firenzuola; cf. also Minerbetti, "Cronica", 279.

again, at the beginning of September, the rumour spread that the main force of the Milanese army was about to enter Tuscany, this time through the Lunigiana;[1] and once again the danger never materialized.

Various arguments have been advanced to explain the inactivity of Giangaleazzo's forces during the months of July and August 1402. One is that he had to assimilate Bologna into his state, before he could attack Florence;[2] but this would hardly account for the delay. Bologna needed a garrison, not an army. The Grand Constable is said to have protested against the proposal to attack Florence, on the ground that it was impossible to ensure the supply of provisions necessary to feed a large army in Tuscany;[3] and this argument may well have helped to deter Giangaleazzo from immediate action. The Duke was also awaiting the outcome of the negotiations in progress at Venice and Rome; but if he hoped to secure the neutrality of the Pope and the *Serenissima* before he attacked Florence, that expectation was not in itself enough to account for his delay. The issue of the negotiations was uncertain, and the interval would allow reinforcements to reach his enemies. If all had been ready for an attack on Florence, it is not likely that Giangaleazzo would have hesitated to give the command to go forward.

All this is a matter of conjecture; but it seems a reasonable conjecture, not unsupported by evidence, that conditions existing within the Milanese army were immediately responsible for the delay. Alberico da Barbiano had once, perhaps, hoped to make himself lord of Bologna;[4] foiled in this ambition by the Duke, he had now set his heart on winning Faenza for himself. Astorre Manfredi, despairing of being able to resist after the downfall of his ally Bentivoglio, appealed to Florence for protection. The Florentines were not anxious to have dealings with

---

[1] Bruni, *op. cit. RIS* NS xix, 3, 288.

[2] Pastorello, in "Copialettere", 389, note 1 to no. 723.

[3] Possevinus, *Gonzaga*, 472-3.

[4] Cf. his ambition "dictam civitatem Bononie sub suo tirapnico periculosiximo et tremendo regimine reducere et subjugare": from the indictment of a Bolognese conspirator, in January 1402. Giorgi, "Alberico e Giovanni da Barbiano", *AMR* 3, xii 287, Doc. 12.

a man whose trickery was well known to them; but in the discussions which ensued on Manfredi's request, it was most clearly stressed that any course which they adopted should have the approval of Carlo Malatesta.[1] Not only was Carlo interested in anything which concerned Romagna, but his sister had married Manfredi's son, and he felt himself obliged to intervene in favour of the lord of Faenza. Lodovico Alidosi, lord of Imola, had placed himself under Giangaleazzo's protection immediately after the conquest of Bologna;[2] and Carlo's intention was probably that Manfredi should follow his example, rather than enter into relations with Florence.[3] This would have made it all the more difficult for Alberico to carry out his own designs on Faenza, and it was natural that he should resent the opposition of the Malatesta to his plans. Reports of a quarrel between him and the Malatesta reached Florence at the end of July.[4] Alberico entered into relations with Boniface IX, and the Florentines rejoiced in the hope of seeing the Duke's army reduced in power by his withdrawal. The Pope also hoped to win over to his own service Paolo Savelli and Giovanni Colonna, two Roman Condottieri who had fought in the Duke's army. "We hear that the Pope will take into his service Count Bertoldo [Orsini, lord of Soana], Paolo Savelli and Giovanni Colonna", wrote the Florentine ambassadors in Rome on 9 August;[5] and, later on the same day, "he is making overtures, and feels confident of having Count Bertoldo, Paolo Savelli and Giovanni Colonna, and, weakening the enemy by these methods, if the Grand Constable also withdraws, to have the victory over the enemy".[6] Twelve days later,

[1] This appears clearly in the debates of the Council, 6–18 July: *ASF*, Consulte e Pratiche, xxxv 133–139 t passim.

[2] Corio, *op. cit.* II 439; "Copialettere", 42, note 1 to no. 69; 296, note 1 to no. 520.

[3] Giovanni Morelli, *Cronica*, 315, records that Manfredi, having accepted Florentine protection, deserted Florence on receiving more tempting offers from Milan (*v.* also Minerbetti, "Cronica", 279–80). Corio, *op. cit.* II 439; he places Manfredi's desertion of Florence after the Duke's death.

[4] The "discordia inter Malatestas et Comitem Albericum" was discussed, in its effect on Florentine policy, in the debate of 28 July: *ASF*, Consulte e Pratiche xxxv 143.

[5] *ASF*, Legazioni 7 bis, 2 t.

[6] *Ibid.* 3.

Boniface is still negotiating with the three noblemen, "and he has good hopes, from news that he has already received, of the Grand Constable".[1]

The personal ambitions and jealousies of the Condottieri were a common source of difficulty to the states of Italy; a quarrel between Carlo Malatesta and the Grand Constable would have been sufficient to immobilize the whole Milanese army. On this occasion, Giangaleazzo had to contend at the same time with another and no less common difficulty. Giovanni Morelli, a contemporary Florentine, records that Alberico, the Malatesta, and other commanders left the camp "per isdegno", not only on account of differences between themselves, but also because they had no money to pay their troops.[2] Giangaleazzo did not attack Florence, he suggests, because his financial condition would not permit him to do so; and here, perhaps, we may find the fundamental cause of the inaction of the Duke's armies, in the two months after Bologna fell.

---

[1] Despatch of 21 August 1402: *ibid.* 4 t.
[2] Giovanni Morelli, *Cronica*, 315.

CHAPTER XXI

THE STATE OF LOMBARDY AT THE TIME OF GIANGALEAZZO'S DEATH (1402)

The struggle between Giangaleazzo and Florence had reached its climax; the end was to come, swiftly and unexpectedly, little more than two months after the fall of Bologna. The dramatic effect of the sudden solution makes a strong appeal to the imagination, and even a recent historian of the events of this year speaks of the Duke's soldiers "drunk with victory, marching upon Florence";[1] but this is romance. Miss Pastorello more cautiously estimated that Giangaleazzo was not in a position to fulfil his task in the summer of 1402;[2] and an analysis of the evidence supports her conclusion. The Milanese army did not march upon Florence, because the Duke could not find the means to pay it.

Giangaleazzo's dominions were not spared during the last years of his reign. The resources of the land were nearly exhausted; the severe epidemic of plague, which ravaged Italy in 1399–1400, had taken a heavy toll of the population of the countryside, and reduced the yield of taxation.[3] The cities of Tuscany did not know how to meet their expenditure; Perugia sent a special ambassador to beg for the Duke's assistance,[4] and the Sienese government adopted drastic measures of financial economy, "in view of the serious debt which our Commune has, and since the entries do not cover our expenses".[5] Milanese trade suffered too, from the reprisals imposed by Rupert of Bavaria and by Leopold of Austria;[6] the Germans interfered with commerce along the

---

[1] Valeri, "Stato Visconteo", NRS xix 470.
[2] "Copialettere", 389, note 1 to no. 723.
[3] Riboldi e Seregni, "Documenti Viscontei", ASL xxxiii, 1, 202 note 3.
[4] Pellini, Historia di Perugia, ii 126.
[5] Resolution of 27 January 1401/2: ASS, Consiglio Generale, Deliberazioni, ccv = 200, 60 t–1.
[6] Schulte, Geschichte des mittelalterlichen Handels und Verkehrs, i 512; Mone, "Handelsgeschichte der Städte am Bodensee", in Zeitschrift für die Geschichte des Oberrheins, iv 33–7, Docs. 10 20.

valley of the Rhine, and Milanese merchants could no longer rely on the safety of the roads through the Tyrol.[1]

An unsound currency aggravated the economic disorders of Lombardy. Giangaleazzo had resorted to the expedient of debasing the coinage, to an even greater extent than his predecessors.[2] He issued new coins of a baser alloy, and called in all the old; but the distrust which the innovation aroused among his subjects compelled him to give to the new coinage a current price below its nominal value.[3] Prices began to rise, and money became scarce. "After a little, there was so great a scarcity of coins, that few could be found, indeed almost none; and this scarcity lasted for several years to come."[4]

Rupert's expedition to Italy had demanded a special effort from the Milanese dominions,[5] and a levy, at the high rate of 4 lire for each florin of the "Estimo", was imposed in September 1401;[6] but the victory of Brescia did not save the Duke's subjects from further exactions during the months that followed.[7] The eastern frontier had to be protected, and the campaign against Bologna imposed further demands; the works on the Brenta cost up to 200,000 florins, the citadel of Bologna over 100,000.[8]

Giangaleazzo tried out a system by which the expenses of his army devolved directly upon his subjects, each citizen being held responsible for the upkeep of so many lances; but the experiment was not a success, for it was quickly abandoned in favour of a general levy. The dominions were unable to cope with the Duke's needs, and the sum demanded had to be reduced;[9] even so, if the

[1] Giangaleazzo to Belluno, 10 February 1402: Pellegrini, "Documenti Viscontei", *AIV* 3, XIII 1641–2, no. 62.

[2] Mulazzani, "Studii economici sulle Monete di Milano", in *Rivista Italiana di Numismatica*, I 47–8 and 51, gives some details of the debasement of coinage under the Visconti.

[3] Documents published by Verci, *Storia della Marca Trivigiana*, XVIII, Docs. 1970–3, 1975, 1978–9, pp. 8–16.

[4] "Annales Mediolanenses", *RIS* XVI 833 D–E. [5] *Ibid.* 834 C.

[6] On 16 September: Santoro, "Registri", 134 no. 28.

[7] In November and December 1401: Corio, *Storia di Milano*, II 431.

[8] *Ibid.* 435. According to Gatari, "Cronaca Carrarese", *RIS* NS XVII, 1, 491, the works on the Brenta cost 150,000–200,000 florins.

[9] To 70,700 florins, from Milan. The levy was imposed in February 1402: Santoro, "Registri", 136–7, nos. 92–3, 96–7, 99; "Chronicon Bergomense", *RIS* XVI 928 B–C, D–E.

other Communes paid in proportion to Milan, the new tax should have raised well over 300,000 florins. Some financial relief of a minor nature was granted at the beginning of July 1402, to celebrate the capture of Bologna;[1] but, a week later, Giangaleazzo decreed the appointment of a financial committee in Milan, to investigate the resources of the citizens, and to ensure that each one contributed the most that he could afford to the general burden.[2] We can understand that the Milanese chronicler complains in this year of taxation "truly insupportable".[3]

Once more the Duke turned to those capitalist elements, whose commercial and industrial enterprise he had always encouraged, to supplement the insufficient revenues yielded by normal methods of taxation. Forced loans and other impositions were levied on the wealthier citizens of the state;[4] but the rich merchants resisted the effort to deprive them, in view of the general need, of those privileges and exemptions to which they had grown accustomed. The Duke had, in some cases, to resort to unusual methods of violence and persecution, which reveal the grave straits to which he had been reduced, before he could overcome the opposition of the subjects on whose support he should have been able most confidently to rely.[5]

Giangaleazzo had, indeed, overtaxed the resources of his dominions, to finance a policy of conquest and dynastic glorification. There were no general symptoms of revolt, however; his authority was accepted now, for good or ill, as firm and irrevocable. The rebels in the Valcamonica, deserted by Rupert of Bavaria and their other allies, and too weak to resume the attack, were on the point of submission.[6] An interesting but obscure and unique reference reveals that, in 1401, Giangaleazzo had revoked certain discriminatory legislation, which had hitherto

---

[1] Letter of Giangaleazzo: "Annales Mediolanenses", *RIS* XVI 836 C–E.
[2] On 7 July: Santoro, "Registri", 142, no. 130.
[3] "Annales Mediolanenses", *RIS* XVI 835 B.
[4] "Chronicon Bergomense", *RIS* XVI 926 D–7 A; Santoro, "Registri", 134, no. 78; Giulini, *Memorie*, XII 56; Pezzana, *Storia di Parma*, II 2.
[5] Pezzana, *op. cit.* II 6–7.
[6] "Copialettere", 18. The appeals of the rebels to Rupert, through Carrara and the Florentines: *ibid.* passim.

remained in force against the Guelfs in Piacenza.[1] He needed their help, and was too strong to fear their hostility; it was almost a challenge to the old party feuds and distinctions. They were no longer powerful enough to harm the state.

Nevertheless, there are symptoms, not of revolt, but of exhaustion in Lombardy. The problems of population faced the rulers of that age. When financial oppression grew heavy, emigration meant, for the subject, a way of escape from the burdens of taxation; but to the state, it meant so many less heads to tax, and so many less hands to till the fields. Flight from the land had always been forbidden by Visconti law;[2] in 1401, Giangaleazzo issued a decree forbidding any of his subjects to go out of his dominions without express permission from the government.[3] He had to appeal once more to the municipalities, for lists of those suitable for service in civil offices and in the army.[4] He offered a full remission of sentence to outlaws who were willing to pay a fine and return to his dominions;[5] this was the recognized method of replenishing a diminished population, and the remission did not apply to those who had been condemned for the most serious offences. In 1402, the Duke offered a free pardon in return for three months' service in his army[6]—the last resort of a bankrupt government.

The finances of his enemies were equally strained. The debates of the Florentine Council, after the battle of Casalecchio, revealed the nature of the problem which confronted the Republic; where could they find the money, to supply the needs of defence?[7] Soldiers did not fight without pay; and neither side knew where to look for the cash, without which a war could not be fought. The position

---

[1] Poggiali, *Memorie storiche di Piacenza*, VII 72.

[2] Nasalli Rocca, "Decreti Signorili Visconteil", in *Atti del Primo Congresso Storico Lombardo*, 420–1.

[3] 20 May 1401: *Antiqua Decreta*, 235–6.

[4] To Pavia, 7 May 1402: Magenta, *Visconti e Sforza*, I 289.

[5] "Annales Mediolanenses", *RIS* XVI 834 D–E; some subsidiary documents were published by Pellegrini, "Documenti Viscontei", *AIV* 3, XIII 1648–52, nos. 68–71.

[6] 20 April 1402: *ibid.* 1658–61, nos. 75–7.

[7] Minutes of the Council, 27 June: "Commissioni di Rinaldo degli Albizzi", in *Documenti di Storia Italiana*, I 11; Ammirato, *Istorie Fiorentine*, I, 2, 890 A.

of stalemate, which had been reached in 1392 and again in 1398, was repeated. The Florentines regarded with bewilderment and suspicion Giangaleazzo's apparent readiness to discuss a peaceful settlement at the conference of Venice; but Venetian circles expressed confidence in the outcome of the conference.[1] The Duke, maintaining a show of force to convince his enemies of his power, sent his ambassadors to Venice in the hope of being able to secure a temporary arrangement on good terms; a settlement would at least have to incorporate and recognize his conquest of Bologna. His treasury was empty;[2] but very soon, when his lands had recovered their prosperity, he would be able to complete his work.

These were the thoughts which seem to have dictated Giangaleazzo's policy after the battle of Casalecchio. There had been a revival of the plague in Pavia, and he was anxious to escape from the city; but the settlement of Bologna under his sovereignty delayed his departure until the end of July. On the 26th of that month, he was at last able to leave the city for the purer air of Melegnano, a favourite hunting resort on the Lambro.[3] In the brief intervals which he snatched between the transaction of affairs of state, he found relaxation in riding through the woods which surrounded his castle. He had fled from the plague; but he reckoned without the treacherous climate of the Lombard plain in the height of summer. A fever came upon him in the middle of August. At first, he took slight notice of it. After some days, as he grew worse, the doctors recommended a change of air; but it was too late. He was already too ill to be moved.[4]

The Duke felt that his end was near; but his instinct as a

---

[1] The rise in the price of "danari del monte" in Venice was regarded as a hopeful sign of peace: "Copialettere", 339, note 2 to no. 639 (July 1402).

[2] "Unde mortuo nullus repertus thesaurus est": Valeri, "Stato Visconteo", *NRS* xix 462, from the manuscript "Cronica bossiana". Caterina, after Giangaleazzo's death, had to pledge lands to raise money—an expedient which the Duke had avoided as far as possible: *Id., Guelfi e Ghibellini in Val Padana*, 6–7.

[3] From the contemporary poem of Cinuzzi: Romano, "Nuova Ipotesi sulla morte di Giangaleazzo", *ASI* 5, xx 260.

[4] From Cinuzzi's poem: *ibid.* 260–1. For the evidence that he died of fever, not of plague: *ibid.* 257 and note 3.

statesman did not desert him. No rumour of his illness could be allowed to get abroad; and it is not even certain that his family was with him at the end.[1] He made a new offer to Boniface IX, and probably hastened on the negotiations at Venice, in the hope of easing the task of his successor after his death; but the time left to him was too short. On 3 September, before anything could be accomplished, he knew that his end was at hand. He had made some final alterations in his will, and now reconciled his soul with God.[2] Towards the evening of the same day, the first Duke of Milan died.

The widow Caterina and her advisers recognized at once the gravity of their task. Only Wenceslaus was notified of the Duke's death;[3] in Italy, the secret was closely guarded, while the Milanese army was recalled in haste from Bologna, to secure the succession for his sons. But a fact, which reversed the whole political situation of the peninsula, could not be kept secret for long. Official notification was given to the Duke's subjects a week after his death; but the news had already reached his enemies. Paolo Guinigi was the first to send the tidings to Florence, in two allusive and gleeful lines of verse;[4] by 8 September, Francesco Carrara was writing to assure his allies that the news was true.[5] The Florentines, who had lived for fifteen years in terror of his name, were at first incredulous; not until the evidence was overwhelming, did they fully accept their good fortune.

On 20 October 1402, with unprecedented pomp, the funeral ceremony of Giangaleazzo Visconti was performed in the Cathedral of Milan,[6] to whose erection he had contributed his encouragement and protection and support. It was attended by members of the many branches of the Visconti, by representatives

---

[1] Cf. Romano, "Nuova Ipotesi", *ASI* 5, xx 258 and note 1. The notification sent to Wenceslaus on the day of the Duke's death was written from Milan; and a hasty departure of the Duke's family, without him, from Melegnano to Milan, would not have helped to keep the secret of his death.

[2] *Ibid.* 261–3. The codicil was signed on 25 August; its terms are described in Corio, *op. cit.* II 438.

[3] Letter of 3 September, summarized in *RTA* v 416, no. 309.

[4] Giovanni Morelli, *Cronica*, 315.

[5] "Copialettere", 388–90, no. 723.

[6] *RIS* xvi 1025–36; Corio, *op. cit.* II 439–47; Minerbetti, "Cronica", 280.

of all the cities of his dominions, and by the princes of Italy who were his allies; but they were assembled to celebrate a greatness which had passed away with the man who had achieved it. The Duke's death had restored hope and confidence to his enemies. Niccolò d'Este planned to recover Parma and Règgio.[1] Francesco Carrara's ambitions in the Mark of Treviso soared again, cloaked as a championship of the rights of Antonio della Scala's heirs in Verona; but Venice, no longer threatened by the waning might of Milan, compelled Carrara to lay down arms.[2] The Florentines recalled their ambassadors from the conference of Venice, as soon as the news of the Duke's death was confirmed, concluded an alliance with Boniface IX,[3] and assailed the dominions of the Visconti in Tuscany, in conjunction with the Papal army.

The Regents might have cut their losses and saved Lombardy for the two young princes, if they had been opposed only by external enemies; but Giangaleazzo's death acted as a signal, to set free all the forces of disorder which he had kept firmly under his control. A year before, he had confidently challenged the spectre of the old party feuds. On his death, the Guelfs rose against the tyranny of the Visconti, who, however impartial their government might appear, were bound to the Ghibellines by tradition and by common interests; and the Ghibellines in many places anticipated the attacks of their enemies, in the hope of destroying the Guelfs to whom Giangaleazzo had, in their opinion, allowed too much licence.[4]

The Council of Regency helped, instead of restraining, this reaction. The widowed Caterina relied entirely on her husband's most confidential servant, Francesco Barbavara. The Ghibelline nobles resented the upstart's ascendancy; they ranged themselves, in Milan, under the leadership of Antonio Porro, and of Francesco and Antonio Visconti, two distant cousins of the Duke

---

[1] Letter of Carrara, 8 September: "Copialettere", 392, no. 726.
[2] Pastorello, "Preliminari della pace", *NAV* NS XXII 289–305. More briefly in *Id., Nuove Ricerche*, 124–5.
[3] On 19 October 1402: *RTA* v 412, no. 303.
[4] Valeri, *Guelfi e Ghibellini*, 12–16; Maiocchi, "Francesco Barbavara", *MSI* XXXV 262–4. "Così stando le cose, si comprende che la lotta era tutta fra Ghibellini e Guelfi, ed era lotta per il potere". *ibid.* 265.

whose influence lay chiefly in the name they bore.[1] While the Council was divided between these parties, the cities chose their own course. Carrara threatened them from the east; the Marquis of Montferrat, and Boucicault, the ambitious French governor of Genoa, prepared to make the most of their opportunities in the west. The trade routes to Germany were lost. The Swiss from Uri and Unterwalden invaded the Valtellina; the Count of Mesocco took Bellinzona; and Milanese influence in the Val di Trento evaporated.[2] The leading families of the Lombard cities strove among themselves for mastery—Soardi and Colleoni in Bergamo, Scotti and Anguissola in Piacenza, Cavalcabò and Fondulo in Cremona, Rossi and Correggio in Parma. Giovanni Vignati acquired Lodi, the Tornielli mastered Novara, and the Beccaria made themselves powerful in Pavia. Of the great Condottieri who had served Giangaleazzo, only Jacopo dal Verme remained disinterestedly loyal to his heirs. Carlo Malatesta and Alberico da Barbiano took service with the Pope; and in August 1403 Caterina had to make peace with Boniface, giving back to him Bologna, Perugia, and the other conquests of her husband in Umbria.[3] Siena elected to regain her independence, and seceded from the Visconti state. Carrara prepared a new attack on Verona and Brescia, in conjunction with Carlo and Mastino Visconti and Guglielmo della Scala, who claimed to be Antonio della Scala's heir. Pandolfo Malatesta anticipated the attack on Brescia, and took the city for himself. Ottobuon Terzo, after defending the Milanese possessions in Umbria for as long as he could, returned to Lombardy and gained the mastery of his native district of Parma. Facino Cane, most ruthless and unpredictable of them all, returned to Piedmont to carve out for himself, from the Visconti dominions· which had hitherto sheltered him from his enemies, an appanage worthy of his sword.

In this desolation of wars and bloodshed and cruelty, the whole of Lombardy was given over to the ravages of armed bands,

---

[1] Maiocchi, "Francesco Barbavara", *MSI* xxxv 261 sqq.; Valeri, *Guelfi e Ghibellini*, 10–12.

[2] Schulte, *op. cit.* I 441–2; Huber, *Geschichte Oesterreichs*, II 495–7.·

[3] Visconti, *Storia di Milano*, 297.

which wandered across the countryside unrestrained by the helpless forces of authority—"all reins of government broken, all security destroyed".[1] It is small wonder that men began to look back with affection and regret to "the days of the good Duke",[2] who had ruled them with firmness and sometimes made harsh demands upon them, but under whom they had reaped their harvests and pursued their business in security. Giangaleazzo Visconti was remembered above all for the peace which he gave to his dominions, and which an impartial contemporary, who held high office in the administration of a neighbouring state, contrasted with the disorders which followed upon his death. "From the death of this Prince came the source of the desolation and destruction of the whole of Lombardy, through the discord and slaughter which arose among the peoples. But he, while he lived, held all things subject to him in tranquillity and peace."[3] "Tranquillity and peace"—it is a strange and significant comment on the man whose ambitions had kept Italy in suspense for fifteen years.

[1] Romano, "Nuova Ipotesi", *ASI* 5, xx 275–6.
[2] "Il tenpo del bon ducha": Valeri, *Guelfi e Ghibellini*, 10. They are the words of Gatari ("Cronaca Carrarese", *RIS* NS xvii, 1, 496–7), certainly no friend of "the good Duke".
[3] Delayto, "Annales Estenses", *RIS* xviii 973 A–B. The French "Chronique du religieux de St Denys", iii 130, also emphasized the peaceful nature of his rule: "Maxime partis Lombardie possessor pacificus".

CHAPTER XXII

CONCLUSION

THE polemics of his own and of succeeding generations have helped to obscure Giangaleazzo's character and achievements. He was in some respects a precursor of the many-sided princes of the Renaissance; but he lacked their physical vigour and restlessness, the perpetual thirst to add to their glory by their own deeds. It was this personal inactivity which accounts for much of the difficulty in relating his life to the events of his reign. He directed and decided the course of his policy from the shelter of his palace at Pavia; he never appeared at the head of his armies or at the courts of his friends. The seclusion of his life encouraged the development of the enigma and the legend, which have distorted the true nature of the first Duke of Milan.

Giangaleazzo emerges, therefore, as a curiously impersonal figure, from the records of his own age. Even the virtues and vices with which he has been credited have assumed an abstract quality, as a result of his tendency to withdraw from personal contacts. He has been portrayed as a monster of treachery and greed, and as a model of Italian patriotism, but seldom as an individual, because only rare traces have survived to guide us in the interpretation of his character. He was ambitious, and treacherous in his political dealings to a degree of cold thoroughness which startled even his contemporaries. But he had finer qualities—the tact and sympathy which won allegiance in many quarters, a warm affection for those who were nearest to him, and some sense of his responsibility as the ruler of a state. His judgment of men and forces was seldom at fault; when he erred, it may be that the remoteness of his life at Pavia from the reality of the events which he sought to control was responsible for the mistakes which he made.

The story of Giangaleazzo may be read as a failure. He devoted all his ambition and greed and energy to the task of securing the political supremacy of his dynasty in Italy; but the work of his life was never completed, for the power of the Visconti crumbled suddenly after his premature death, and was never wholly restored. The bitter destiny which decreed that the three sons of Isabella of Valois should die, while the children of Caterina lived to reap the evil harvest of inbreeding, was fatal to the fortunes of the house. After the death of his two sons, no descendant of Giangaleazzo was left to carry on the name and the traditions of the Visconti.

It is no longer possible, however, to dismiss Giangaleazzo as a greedy and ruthless tyrant, bent only on personal aggrandizement. The political significance of his reign did not end with the collapse of his state after 1402; enough was preserved to form the nucleus of a Lombard state which, held together by the system of government first given a logical coherence by Giangaleazzo, continued as a free, and later as a dependent province to share in the historical development of Italy for more than four centuries.

What then were Giangaleazzo's ambitions? How far across Italy had the net of his intrigues been spread? Did he propose to win a kingdom for himself, and how would he have governed it when it was won?

It is necessary, first of all, to recall the circumstances which shaped his policy. The Communal age was past. Six states, if we include Savoy, had secured a preponderance of power in their respective parts of the peninsula. The Republics of Venice and Florence already favoured the perpetuation of this "regionalism" by the preservation of a balance of power between the six governments. But the boundaries between them were still undefined. Venice had only recently embarked on the conquest of a state on the mainland; the hegemony of Florence was still opposed by the other Republics of Tuscany, which had preserved their independence and were determined to resist the encroachments of their powerful neighbour; the Pope of Rome and the King of Naples were both challenged by rival claimants, backed by the authority of France. There was ample opportunity for intervention and intrigue; the balance of power could not be preserved until each state had secured complete control of its own sphere of influence, and had overcome its own internal dissensions. The transition was still being made at the end of the Trecento. By the middle of the following century, the authority of the Papacy had been restored in central Italy; Venice had consolidated her position in eastern Lombardy; and Florence under the Medici was approaching her "golden age". Cosimo de' Medici's policy effectively guaranteed the preservation of the balance of power, and not even the genius of Francesco Sforza could restore the greatness of Milan as Giangaleazzo had conceived it.[1]

Giangaleazzo was more fortunate in his time. Within his own dominions, which included the greater part of Lombardy, he had little to fear from the intrigues of his enemies; and he was quick to grasp the opportunities of extending his power by intervention in other regions, where union under one authority had not been so easily or so rapidly accomplished. His first task was to complete his dominion over eastern Lombardy, and in this he was successful up to the point where his ambitions were openly challenged by Florence. After the check which he received in the first war against the Republic, he sought the alliance of foreign powers to help him towards his ends in eastern Lombardy; he could not deal single-handed with the opposition both of Florence and of Venice, whose Empire on the mainland would have been confined, if he had achieved his ambition, to a narrow and isolated strip of the Adriatic seaboard. Finally, he postponed a settlement of the issues at stake in Lombardy, and took the offensive in Tuscany; this was the period of his greatest triumphs—the submission of Pisa, of Siena, of Perugia, the defeat of Rupert and the capture of Bologna.

M. Eugène Jarry has made the interesting suggestion that Giangaleazzo would have been content to rule over the whole of Lombardy, from Como to Bologna and from Verona or Padua to Parma; and that his intervention in Tuscany was prompted only by the relentless opposition of Florence to his designs.[2] Certainly

---

[1] Cf. Visconti, *Storia di Milano*, 366; and *Id.* "Politica Unitaria Italiana dei Visconti", in the *Atti del Primo Congresso Storico Lombardo*, 168.

[2] Jarry, *Origines*, 169–70. Cf. Romano's criticism in *ASL* XXIV, 1, 427–8.

the emphasis lay, during the early and central periods of the Duke's reign, on his plans in Lombardy; and for a long time he showed his reluctance to accept the desperate offers of Siena. It was not until 1401, when a large part of Tuscany had already accepted his dominion, that he publicly expressed his determination "that Lombardy and Tuscany be made one".[1]

On the other hand, there were forces at work which neither the Duke nor the Florentines could ignore. The ambitions of the Visconti and the interests of Milan crossed the path of the Republic both in Bologna and in Genoa, and the hostility between the two states had begun before Giangaleazzo was born. Luchino Visconti made a premature attack on Pisa in 1348; Bernabò devised a scheme for the economic blockade of Florence in 1369.[2] The independence of Bologna was an issue over which the Florentines could admit no compromise; and the wiser of them understood, as early as 1385, that the friendship of Giangaleazzo was therefore dangerous and impermanent. Giangaleazzo inherited a policy; he brought to its pursuit his own peculiar gifts of organization and of intrigue.

The struggle with Florence was a form of flank attack, undertaken to sap the resistance of Bologna and of Ferrara to the designs of the Visconti; but it did not exclude the possibility of bolder adventures. Wherever a government found itself in difficulties, Milanese agents could be discovered at work: in Genoa, in Umbria, in Romagna, in Sicily. The exiles, who gathered at the Duke's court, brought him into touch with elements of discontent in every quarter of Italy. The projects of alliances outside Italy, with France and with the Empire, were designed to make Milan the decisive factor, not only in the north, but in the south of the peninsula as well. Giangaleazzo missed no opportunity of strengthening his power and increasing his dominion, even in the most distant parts of Italy.

The Duke's achievements, remarkable in themselves, were nevertheless limited, in comparison with the extent and variety of the schemes on which he embarked. He lacked the gambler's

---

[1] "Quod Tuscia cum Lombardia fiet unum et idem": Professione, *Siena e le Compagne di Ventura*, 160 note 4.   [2] Leader, *Giovanni Acuto*, 52.

spirit: "timid in adversity, most bold when fortune favoured him". He never attempted the improbable—save once, perhaps, on that morning in May 1385, when he staked his fortune and his life on his own political judgment. He always counted the numbers, and waited patiently until the greater strength was on his side; the respective values of sacrifice and gain were always carefully weighed. Giangaleazzo never embarked blindly on an enterprise without counting the cost. His caution is most clearly illustrated by his relations with Genoa. He refused to accept the dominion of the Ligurian port, in spite of its great importance, because he could not foresee the effect of such an action on his relations with the French court; he preferred to base his policy on calculable forces. The hesitant character of his relations with Genoa arose from his failure to reconcile in a firm and bold policy the claims of Milanese commercial interests and the political fear of French hostility.

He was an opportunist, moreover, and probably did not allow his plans to run too far ahead. At the time of his death, his thoughts were concentrated on the conquest of Florence, and he had already organized an economic blockade of the Republic; but he was faced once again with the possibility of Venetian intervention in favour of his enemy. The streak of caution in his nature, which had contributed so largely to his success, must have warned him of the dangers in which a direct attack on Florence might involve him. Many a prince had met his downfall in Italy by overweening ambition, which had found its nemesis in the formation of a powerful coalition against him. It was a fault which Giangaleazzo had always been careful to avoid. There were powerful factors in his favour during the summer of 1402—the uncertainty which prevailed in Florence, the lack of union among his enemies, and the added prestige which he himself had gained in the past year. But there was also, among the greater states of Italy, a growing feeling that his progress must at all costs be checked; and it is unlikely that the Duke, whose whole policy had been designed to prevent the formation of coalitions against himself, should have completely forsaken caution for self-confidence, and have been ready to defy this feeling.

It must be remembered that Giangaleazzo himself lost ground,
in directions vital to the economy of his state. The pressure of the
Habsburgs on the Alpine passes weakened Milanese control of
the trade routes to the north. The growing power of Savoy
encroached on the western border, annexing parts of the *Vercellese* by peaceful penetration; in spite of the government's
special care, frequent desertions drove the western boundary of
the Dukedom back towards the Sesia, and many subjects found
a refuge in Savoy from the heavy taxation of Giangaleazzo's last
years.[1] Expansion in these directions had to be sacrificed, when
Giangaleazzo united Bernabò's dominions with his own. In other
directions, too, his difficulties grew after every success; for more
than purely political boundaries divided the north of Italy from
the south. The States of the Church formed a central strip which
divided the highly developed lands of Tuscany, Lombardy and
the Veneto from the backward kingdom of Naples.[2] The diversity
of their traditions and of their economic needs could only enhance
the political difficulties of uniting them under one rule.

The union of the whole peninsula under the rule of one man was
not, in fact, a political idea capable of realization; and Giangaleazzo cannot have failed to recognize the fact. The motives of
the expansion of the Visconti dominions were dynastic ambition
and commercial rivalry; the opportunities arose from the peculiar
circumstances of Italian politics—the legacy of Guelf and
Ghibelline traditions, of Communal pride and particularism, of the
highly developed though not always efficient system of government which the great Communes had evolved each for itself—a
legacy which brought resentment, jealousy and war in its train,
as the surviving states expanded and met in conflict with one
another. But the recent tendency to identify these forces with a
conception of national unity as an active political influence[3] must
be examined with reserve, if we are to avoid the danger of attri-

[1] *V.* Appendix I, p. 328.
[2] Pieri, *Crisi militare italiana,* 52–3.
[3] This tendency is exemplified in the article of Ginevra Zanetti on "La
'Mediolanum' medioevale", in the *Atti del Primo Congresso Storico Lombardo,* 145.

buting to Giangaleazzo motives which were foreign to his character, and ideas which were beyond his understanding.

The political unity of Italy, on which the career of Cola di Rienzo had provided an ironical commentary, was cherished as an ideal in the writings of Italian poets and humanists; and it was natural that they should summon Giangaleazzo to assume the mission of ending the bloodshed and ruin which each Italian state inflicted on its neighbour—the mission in which Frederick II and Charles of Anjou, Henry VII and Rienzo had all failed. Giangaleazzo, for his part, used the writers who gathered at his princely court to answer the bitter attacks which issued from the chancellery of Florence; both the despot and the Republic appreciated the value of political pamphleteering. The polemic between Coluccio Salutati and Giangaleazzo's secretary, Antonio Loschi, the anonymous "Dream" in which Genoa appealed to him as the one ruler worthy to receive and capable of retaining the sovereignty of the city—these were accompanied by a stream of sonnets and poems, acclaiming Giangaleazzo as the destined unifier of Italy, the saviour of desolate Rome, the restorer of the Italian name:

> Et un signor avrà Italia bella
> che tanto tempo è stata vedovella.
> De conte, duca e poi sarà reale
> un ch'è tiranno nella gran pianura.

One poet proclaims that "Roma vi chiama: Cieser mio novello". A new Caesar—this was

> il bel destino che dal ciel t'è dato,
> re nostro sacrosanto.

As Dante appealed to Henry VII, and as Petrarch pinned his faith for a moment on Rienzo, so Vannozzo and Saviozzo and Loschi and the rest, less talented and more subservient than their great predecessors, but animated in part by the same spirit, hailed Giangaleazzo as the saviour of Italy.[1]

This feeling of a great national destiny, still to be fulfilled,

---

[1] Medin, "Visconti nella poesia contemporanea", *ASL* XVIII 758–95; Levi, "Francesco di Vannozzo", 254–74. For the importance of political pamphlets, cf. Novati, "Querele di Genova", in *Giornale Ligustico*, XIII 403.

played an important part in the literature of the time. A sense of national consciousness certainly existed, indissolubly bound up with the idea of a heritage of civilized life, and contrasted especially with the "barbarism" of the Germans. All who came from the north were barbarians—the spirit was exemplified in a letter written by Pier Paolo Vergerio at the time of John of Armagnac's expedition to Italy.[1] But this was not yet synonymous with a sense of Italian patriotism. Coluccio Salutati expressed the sentiments of a cultured Italian when he wrote, in one of his early letters: "sum denique gente italicus, patria florentinus".[2] His political loyalty belonged to Florence. The sense of brotherhood among Italians could not overcome the spirit of particularism which divided the peninsula against itself.

The poets urged Giangaleazzo towards a goal, which was beyond the scope of his more practical aspirations. His secret ambitions are not known to us. He may have cherished, as an ultimate hope, the idea of mastering the whole of Italy; but to assert that he did so from a sense of his political duty as an Italian, is to ascribe to him a motive for which there is no real evidence in his career.

Much has been said of Giangaleazzo's employment of Italian soldiers. But the epoch of the great foreign Condottieri and Companies had come to an end; after Hawkwood's death in 1394, the only foreign commander of importance in Italy was Bernardone da Serres, who led the Florentine army in the Mantuan war and the Bolognese campaign of 1402. The Italian school of warfare, which owed so much to Alberico da Barbiano and which had won its spurs at the battle of San Marino in 1379, had taken the place of the foreigners, and it was only natural that Giangaleazzo should make use of Italian soldiers.

Much has been said, too, of the part played by the Visconti as the bulwark of Italy against foreign invasion. Giangaleazzo did not hesitate to claim this honour for himself, when he rated the Florentines for bringing Armagnac to Italy in 1391, and Rupert of Bavaria in 1401. In a memorial oration to the Duke, Andrea

---

[1] Vergerio, "Epistolario", 77 no. 34.
[2] Quoted by Ercole, *Dal Comune al Principato*, 211 note 1.

Biglia echoed his words;[1] but they seem to have had no more practical significance than the acclamations of the poets. The sense of racial unity was used as political propaganda on both sides; and the Florentines made the same accusations, with equal justification, against the Duke. He would have brought the French to Italy if he could, not only to fight his battles for him, but to conquer Italian soil for themselves; he invited and encouraged Wenceslaus to come to Italy. When his ambitions were held in check by the League of Bologna, he turned as freely as Florence to foreign powers, for help against the enemies who encircled him.

The nature of Giangaleazzo's designs may be gauged more surely by a reference to past traditions, than by an anticipation of future developments. The crown of Italy had been an appanage of the Emperors for four centuries, but the Visconti had at last succeeded in restoring unity to the greater part of the old Lombard state. It may have been Giangaleazzo's intention, if Wenceslaus had come to Italy during the Mantuan war, to confront him with a demand for the iron crown of the Lombards, in return for his services in persuading Boniface IX to perform the Imperial coronation elsewhere than in Rome. In 1402, the Duke is said to have ordered a crown and royal robes to be ready for his own coronation, as soon as Florence had fallen. There is no evidence that this story is true; but it is significant that Sigismund, in full accord with the Duke, was at this moment making a last effort to send his brother to Italy for the Imperial coronation. The Commune of Pavia wrote in the same year that Giangaleazzo was held to be "not unworthy of the crown of all Italy".[2] If that was clearly beyond his reach for the moment, the iron crown, which conveyed authority over Lombardy and Tuscany, represented closely enough the immediate scope of his ambitions; and Wenceslaus, to whom it rightly belonged, was not strong enough to resist the wishes of the Duke of Milan, the powerful defender of his authority in Italy.

[1] It seems to me that undue importance was attributed to them by Professor Romano, "Giudizio di A. Biglia", *BSP* xv 141 and 143–5.

[2] "Totius Italie Diadematis non immerito digno": Magenta, *Visconti e Sforza*, I 210 (18 May 1402).

Whatever hopes the Duke may have entertained, his death left his successors in no position to realize them. Giangaleazzo had spoken from the first of his desire to win a nobler title; and after ten years of intrigue, he had succeeded in transforming himself from an appointed official to an hereditary vassal of the German Emperor. This was not national pride, but dynastic ambition using every means to secure its own ends. Yet it was the "Ducato" that, of all Giangaleazzo's work, survived to influence the future course of Italian history. It gave a sense of unity to the group of Communes, which had hitherto been associated only in their allegiance to a common lord. That sense of unity was still very weak, as the events of 1447 were to show; but it was destined to grow. The will of the Visconti had never met with any combined resistance from the cities over which they ruled. This may have been a source of security to the ruler, but it was an element of weakness in the composition of a state; and it was also a source of irritation, for it involved the partial survival of Communal independence, with all its inefficiency and waste. The Visconti had been compelled step by step to reduce the disorders which arose from the lack of a unified government in their dominions; and Giangaleazzo completed their work by a radical process of centralization. The erection of his lands into an Imperial Duchy set the seal upon his work, and recognized the stability and permanence of the Visconti state in Lombardy.

As their political dominion expanded, the Visconti built up a system of government and internal organization for the administration of their state. Their power grew largely from the realization of economic needs, and the development of their domestic policy sprang from the peculiar circumstances and requirements of the lands which recognized their sovereignty. They had no direct precedent on which to found an administrative system. While the kingdom of Naples retained the characteristics of its feudal organization, and the Communes and princes of the Papal dominions owed little more than a nominal allegiance to their overlord, the northern cities surrendered a large part of their independence when they accepted the rule of a despot. The exceptional extent of the Visconti dominions created special needs, which could not be met by the intimate personal system of government sufficient to deal with the problems of the smaller Lombard states, of Mantua under the Gonzaga or of the Scaliger possessions. The growing complexity of their administrative obligations forced the Visconti to review the task of government from a new angle, and to build up, slowly and experimentally, a system adequate for the requirements of their state. But their administrative system was designed, above all, to promote the greater glory of the dynasty, and to extend yet further its authority. The Visconti harnessed the fertility, the industrial and commercial prosperity of the Lombard plain, to the exigencies of their political ambitions. Even Giangaleazzo introduced his reforms primarily as a means to the achievement of his more grandiose aspirations of political supremacy.[1]

Centralization was the keynote of the new system, and nowhere more than on the financial side. The waste and extravagance of communal government, the obstructions of class privilege, were incompatible with the demands of an efficient and powerful state. Order and authority, honours and exemptions must all emanate from the prince. The new state was to transcend the old party strife, which tradition had perpetuated and family vendetta kept alive: to transcend, too, the clash of class interests, which lay at the root of so many of the troubles which had vexed the Communes in the past two centuries.

The Visconti, however, combined a theory of absolutism with a respect for tradition and a sense of responsibility towards their subjects. They yoked their ideas to a practical opportunism, which enabled them to recognize the limits of their own power. They secured their authority with as little innovation as possible upon the political structure of the communal age. They had often to bow before the compulsion of a force greater than their own; they could influence, but not control the struggle between the reactionary feudal nobility on whose services they were dependent, and the young, active, ambitious power of mercantile capitalism

[1] Cf. Tagliabue, "Politica finanziaria di Giangaleazzo", *BSP* xv 24.

to which their house was closely allied. The suppression of criminal disorder, the reduction of class distinctions to secure equality of rights and responsibilities, centralization especially in the financial sphere—these were the leading principles of their rule; but the application of them was incomplete, and they had sometimes to make concessions to forces which were antagonistic to the ultimate fulfilment of their purpose.

Giangaleazzo, too, had to accept inevitable modifications, which hampered the realization of his plans; but he approached the problems of government with a wider understanding than his predecessors. The systematic revision of the communal statutes throughout his dominions, the reform of the financial system and the setting up of the "Camera" under the "Masters of the entries", the formation of the Councils—these reveal that instinct for organization, which led him to revise and co-ordinate the work already accomplished by the Visconti. The work of con-solidation, by which he endeavoured to impose a uniform order on the foundation of his predecessors' reforms,[1] had its lacunae; the more pressing demands of war and policy compelled him to seek a compromise in domestic affairs, and prevented him from making the sacrifice and effort needed to eradicate the surviving forces of resistance—local particularism, feudal privilege, and the irresponsibility of officials with no bureaucratic tradition of service behind them.[2] The task of creating a trustworthy band of subordinates, to help in the work of government, was perhaps the most difficult problem with which Giangaleazzo was faced. He had to keep a constant watch over local administration, to circumvent slackness, inefficiency and corruption.[3] One dis-gruntled citizen openly declared that the Ducal court itself was ruled by influence and bribery, and requested a personal interview

---

[1] "Egli raccoglieva l'eredità di un lavoro politico quasi secolare": *ibid.* 22.

[2] "Varietà di legislazioni e di norme, magistrature communali indipen-denti dal potere centrale, autonomie amministrative, arbitrii di singoli e di ufficiali dello Stato, una quantità di esenzioni, privilegi, abusi, prepotenze in cui rivivevano i mal domi odi di campanile, e di fazione": Valeri, "Stato Visconteo", *NRS* XIX 464.

[3] E.g. close supervision of the government of Milan during the plague of 1400: Santoro, "Registri", 99–120 passim.

with the Duke, in order to open his eyes to the abuses which went on around him.[1]

The process of unification had territorial limits as well as limits of degree. The Lombard Communes, and the lands acquired from other despots north of the Apennines, had grown accustomed to some form of signorial government; they could be moulded with comparative ease into the form of a state. The Communes of Tuscany presented a more difficult problem. Giangaleazzo recognized a limit, beyond which he was prepared to respect the wishes even of the Lombard Communes; and he showed himself unwilling to force allies, of whose support he stood in need, to accept a form of government which they might deem to substitute liberty by servitude. He hoped, in time, to bring the Tuscan cities within the general framework of his administrative system; but it was a slow and delicate task, which was cut short, when it had scarcely begun, by the Duke's death and the subsequent loss of Pisa, Siena, Perugia and Bologna.

These cities were not included in the Duchy of Milan. As Giangaleazzo had sought the ducal rank which had transformed him from the lord of many cities to the ruler of a Lombard state, so we may imagine that he sought a new title, which would give cohesion to his later acquisitions, and which would recognize the enhanced authority which he derived from them. If he had won the iron crown of Italy, he would have been able to claim the same absolute authority in his new lands that he exercised in the Duchy of Milan.

All his hopes and plans and achievements collapsed when death intervened. But the Lombard dominions remained. Andrea Biglia, who extolled Giangaleazzo as the defender of Italy against foreign invaders, recognized at the same time the practical achievement of the Visconti. A century earlier, the agents of Pope John XXII had first heard the opinion expressed that Lombardy would never find peace save under its own king, a "dominus naturalis", a natural lord of native blood, the founder of a dynasty.[2] Biglia proclaimed the accomplishment of this

---

[1] The "frottola" of Giuliano da Galliano: Levi, "Francesco di Vannozzo", 276–8.   [2] V. supra, Chapter I.

task by Giangaleazzo. The Visconti had built an order of peace and justice out of a chaos of party quarrels and local jealousies, out of the general confusion and strife of the communal age. Giangaleazzo, filling the rôle of natural prince, whose own virtues formed an inherent part of his office as head of the state, gave peace to Lombardy, "so that law and equity prevailed at once among all men".[1]

The "natural prince", whose state is founded on justice, was a common conception among the humanists of Pavia. Niccolò Spinelli spoke of it in his pamphlet on the kingdom of Adria;[2] Uberto Decembrio, the Bishop of Novara's secretary, in his treatise *de Republica*, placed "justitia" first among the qualities needed in government.[3] The idea naturally focused itself upon the person of the Duke. This would be strange, if he were the ruthless and oppressive tyrant of popular imagination. Utterly unscrupulous in his foreign policy, he gave to his own subjects the benefits of his far-sightedness, his love of order, his powers of organization, his sense of the state's responsibility to the subject as well as of the subject's duty to the state. He failed them only when he had to choose between their immediate interests, and the political greatness of the Visconti.

The efforts, which Giangaleazzo made to promote the unification of Lombardy, received recognition in the Ducal investiture. The Visconti state meant to Giangaleazzo, not only the proud heritage of family possessions, but a Lombardy closely united under a centralized government—a state, in fact, as well as a dynastic heritage. The terms of Giangaleazzo's wills are important in this respect, because they have been adduced as proof of the purely dynastic motives of his policy.[4] The conditions of the Imperial grant of the Duchy permitted the alienation of territories to other members of the Duke's family; but it proposed, at the same time, that an annuity of 12,000 florins would be a

---

[1] "Ut simul inter omnes ius et equitas valerent": Romano, "Giudizio di A. Biglia", *BSP* xv 141–3.
[2] *Id.* "Niccolò Spinelli", *ASN* xxvi 482, 493, 495.
[3] Borsa, "Umanista Vigevanesco", in *Giornale Ligustico*, xx 102.
[4] E.g. by Medin, "Visconti nella poesia contemporanea", *ASL* xviii 770.

suitable provision for the brothers of the Duke's heir.[1] Giangaleazzo was a shrewd judge of men; and as he watched his children grow up, he may well have regretted the need to transmit the succession to the elder.[2] Even so, he never contemplated the separation of his dominions into two parts, save as an extreme resort. Filippo Maria inherited the County of Pavia, with the Veronese and the Piedmontese lands, as a feudal grant from the Duke of Milan, to whom in all things he owed homage and obedience. The terms of the will of 1399 are explicit in this respect. It names Giovanni Maria "heredem universalem et in solidum". Precautions were taken, so that Filippo Maria "may have reason to remain in obedience, love and devotion" to Giovanni; and all the younger brother's lands and cities "he is bound and ought to recognize and receive in fee from the aforesaid lord Giovanni Maria".[3]

No possibility, however, against which Giangaleazzo may have thought to provide by the bestowal of so large a portion upon his younger son, could have been worse than the reality. In the midst of reaction and crime and the resurgence of every element of disorder and resistance which Giangaleazzo had believed crushed, the real hope of the Visconti lay in Pavia. Whether Giangaleazzo foresaw the course which events would take or no, the division of his state into two separate parts was not a provision of his will, but a practical necessity, imposed by the complete breakdown of all efficient government after his death.

Giangaleazzo's system of government was designed to work smoothly with a minimum of personal intervention—to be a state rather than a despotism. That was demanded by the extent of his dominions, but it was precisely that system which he failed to secure. Although he left so much to the discretion of his soldiers, his counsellors, his officials, it was his own character, his faculty

---

[1] *RIS* XVI 828 B; Giulini, *Memorie*, XII 40–1.

[2] So at least Filippo Maria's biographer, Pier Candido Decembrio, asserted: Valeri, "Insegnamento di Giangaleazzo", *BSBS* XXXVI 459.

[3] Osio, *Documenti diplomatici*, I 320–3; and v. Valeri, "Stato Visconteo", *NRS* XIX 473. The lands of the Visconti in the *Astigiano* and in Piedmont were added to Filippo Maria's share in the final codicil of 1402: Corio, *Storia di Milano*, II 438.

for commanding and ensuring service, that gave life and strength to the organization of the state. When he died, his son, just completing his fourteenth year, was not old enough, even if he had possessed the virtues or the ability, to take his place. Giangaleazzo, by continuing in the constitution of the Council of Regency the combination of diverse interests and talents which had worked together under his own directive genius, hoped to perpetuate the order he had created;[1] but the Council of Regency was a breeding ground of jealousies and rival ambitions. Giangaleazzo had not entirely reconciled the divergent interests of classes, of old party divisions.[2] He left behind an organization, but he failed to infuse into it the spirit which alone could keep it alive. He assembled many talents, but he had not taught his collaborators to serve an abstract idea. It was the force of his will, and not the nature of his system, that suppressed disorder, reconciled diversities, and imposed a superficial unity of order and purpose. When he died, unity vanished and disorder reigned.

The territorial expansion of the Visconti state had reached its natural limits in 1385. Giangaleazzo's hopes and ambitions, his intrusion in the political affairs of other regions, his schemes of expansion, his wars and intrigues spread the glory and terror of his name; but his hard-won rewards were lost within a few years of his death. The core of his work remained, however; and his children still bore, in their deepest tribulations, the name of Visconti which had become a portent in Italy. The cultured eloquence of his court, turned to the exaltation of its patron, fostered the legend to which his political achievements had given rise. His character, versatile yet solitary, the ubiquity of his agents and his influence, the extent of his success, had puzzled and terrified and fascinated his contemporaries; and his sons, in their personal dealings with their subjects and in their diplomatic relations with other powers, inherited the respect commanded by his name.[3]

Giangaleazzo combined a political imagination beyond that of

[1] Valeri, "Stato Visconteo", *NRS* xix 473.
[2] Cf. Anzilotti, "Per la Storia delle Signorie", *SS* xxii 83.
[3] Valeri, "Insegnamento di Giangaleazzo", *BSBS* xxxvi 457–03.

his time with a mastery of the political instruments which the age placed at his disposal; and the principles of his government were not entirely lost in the decade of chaos and reaction which followed his death. The practical expression of what Professor Romano has called the "social justice" inherent in the person of the prince was summarized after his death as a counsel and a warning to his son. Peace rather than war, equality and impartial justice rather than personal inclination and private favour, respect for the law rather than violence, deference to the advice of his counsellors, close supervision of officials, taxation as low as the needs of the state allowed, and imposed according to the means of his subjects so that the burden fell on those most capable of sustaining it, swift and efficient collection of taxes so that the accounts should balance, and no grants of exemption—these, according to a memorandum drawn up by Carlo Malatesta for the benefit of Giovanni Maria, were the lessons which the young Duke could learn from his father's example for the government of his state.

The lord of Rimini, who maintained his own independence of outlook in the turmoil of Italian politics, had observed with a calm judgment and unprejudiced respect the methods by which Giangaleazzo governed his extensive realm. His advice, never heeded by Giovanni, was accepted by Filippo Maria, who followed it to the best of his ability when he succeeded his brother.[1] On these principles, Filippo Maria restored the basis of the Visconti state: the fertile, industrious, populated and naturally prosperous area of Lombardy, hemmed in between the expanding dominions of Venice and Savoy. This was the state whose political organization had been fashioned and moulded by his ancestors, and of whose economic needs they had been the chosen representatives. Their work survived the dynasty which bore the name of Visconti, survived even the betrayal by their successors of the wider vision of national independence and resistance to foreign invasion. The basic instruments of law and government,

---

[1] The memorandum of 1408 was republished by Valeri, "Insegnamento di Giangaleazzo", *BSBS* xxxvi 483–7. For Carlo Malatesta's relations with Giovanni Maria, and the importance of this document: *ibid.* 472–83; it was first published by Giulini, *Memorie*, xii 612–7.

deriving from the order established by Giangaleazzo, were preserved even under the Spanish and Austrian dominion.[1] With unusual historical vision, Andrea Biglia had seen the destiny of the Visconti come to realization, under Giangaleazzo's guiding hand, in the unity of Lombardy. That work lived on, through momentary disintegration, through intrigue and invasion and conquest, until the armies of Napoleon marched over the Alps, and the spirit was born which saw, beyond Lombardy, the outline of an Italian kingdom.

[1] Cf. Valsecchi, *Assolutismo illuminato in Austria e in Lombardia*, II, 1, 28.

APPENDICES

APPENDIX I

GIANGALEAZZO AND PIEDMONT
(1391–1402)

I have shown, in Chapter VI, how Giangaleazzo adapted his policy in Piedmont to the greater responsibilities which he assumed in 1385; and, in Chapter IX, how the Count of Savoy fulfilled the obligations of his alliance with Milan during the war against Florence in 1390. From that moment, the affairs of Piedmont played so minor a part in Giangaleazzo's policy, that they may conveniently be discussed as an isolated incident, influenced by but scarcely affecting the course of his career.

The roads from France were full of soldiers marching into Italy in the spring of 1391. First came the contingent which Bernard de la Salle was leading to the service of the Count of Vertus. Amadeus, Prince of Achaia, as befitted an ally of the Count, prepared to welcome them in Turin; but when he found himself confronted instead with the army of John of Armagnac, who had overtaken and destroyed the troops of la Salle as they crossed the Alps, neither he nor the Count of Savoy offered any resistance. They satisfied the demands of their alliance by sending frequent reports of the invader's progress to Milan.[1]

The suggestion that Giangaleazzo deeply resented the failure of his allies to put any obstacle in the way of Armagnac's passage has been discredited; if his relations with Savoy were less than cordial in the following years, other explanations must be sought. Of the three aspects of Milanese policy in Piedmont—the importance of the roads to France, the danger of Savoyard expansion into Lombardy, and the need to prevent an alliance of the enemies of Milan with Savoy, who could turn the flank of Milanese defence —the first was the least pressing. The other two interests were not easily reconciled with one another, and the intricate politics of Piedmont created many awkward situations for Giangaleazzo in the ten years after Armagnac's invasion.

---

[1] Saraceno, "Regesto", *MSI* XX 189, no. 120; Gabotto, "Documenti Inediti", *MSI* XXXIV 139–40, nos. 49, 51–3; "Eporediensia", 457, no. 62, and 508, no. 218 (dated 1390). La Salle was expected in Turin by the middle of May, Armagnac not until 22 June: Gabotto, *Ultimi Principi d' Acaia*, 153; Saraceno, *op. cit.* 189, no. 120.

Amadeus VII died suddenly in November 1391, leaving an eight-year-old son as his heir. The young Count succeeded his father in an atmosphere troubled by suspicions and jealousy among those closest to him; and the enemies of Savoy did not miss the opportunity to create additional embarrassments. The most active of these enemies was Teodoro of Montferrat, who fomented riots in the Valais, instigated the predatory activities of the Condottiere Facino Cane, and encouraged the Marquis of Saluzzo to renounce his allegiance to Savoy.[1]

Amadeus of Achaia was now the most influential person at the Savoyard court; but the royal princes of France also took an interest in the affairs of the young Count, whose mother was a daughter of the Duke of Berri, and whose grandmother was a Bourbon. Giangaleazzo, anxious for the success of his proposals of alliance with France, could not afford to antagonize the French princes, by making difficulties for Amadeus VIII. He could never be sorry at heart to see the power of Savoy weakened in Piedmont; but he restrained Teodoro from disturbing the peace, as far as he could do so without forfeiting his friendship; he denied all responsibility for the actions of Facino Cane, over whom neither he nor Teodoro had any real control; and he offered his services as mediator between Teodoro and the Prince of Achaia, in a dispute which nominally arose over the claims of Savoy to the homage of the lords of Azeglio.[2]

While these problems were being discussed in Pavia, and while the Duke of Burgundy was winning extensive influence in Savoy, where his daughter was betrothed to Amadeus VIII, Amadeus of Achaia gathered an army to enforce the suzerainty of Savoy over the Marquis of Saluzzo. Teodoro joined forces with the Marquis early in 1394. Meanwhile, fresh revolts broke out in the Valais; and Facino Cane's exploits against Savoy brought constant protests to Pavia. Giangaleazzo could not escape responsibility for the actions of the Condottiere, to whom he had rendered financial aid in order to have a claim upon his services;[3] but he could not exercise any effective control over Cane's movements. He himself confessed as much, and offered to place lands, goods and persons under ban for the satisfaction of Savoy.[4]

[1] Gabotto, *Ultimi Principi d' Acaia*, 161–70.   [2] *Ibid.* 171–84.
[3] Giangaleazzo advanced a loan to Cane on 20 November 1393: Romano, "Regesto", *ASL* xxi, 2, 52, nos. 139–40. These documents probably have no particular political significance.
[4] Giangaleazzo's letter of 24 March 1394: Gabotto, "Documenti Inediti", *MSI* xxxiv 131, no. 77.

When, however, the Prince of Achaia gained a crushing victory over the forces of Saluzzo at Monasterolo, Giangaleazzo decided to intervene. In May 1394, a month after the battle of Monasterolo, the Prince was negotiating to enter the service of the League of Bologna together with Bernard of Armagnac. This did not imply any personal hostility towards the ruler of Milan, for Amadeus was at the same time helping Louis of Orleans in a campaign directed from Asti.[1] But it was an ominous sign, and Giangaleazzo decided that he must once again play the part of a peacemaker. Hitherto he had restrained, without seriously discouraging, Montferrat and Saluzzo in their attacks on Savoy; but the victory of Achaia threatened to upset the balance of power in Piedmont. Moreover, Coucy was expected to arrive at Asti within the course of a few months, to launch the Orleanist campaign against Genoa; in the hope of straightening out the complexities of the intricate situation in Piedmont before he arrived, Giangaleazzo arranged a truce between Achaia and Saluzzo in August 1394.[2] Two months later, when Coucy, in the name of the Duke of Orleans, signed an offensive and defensive alliance with Teodoro of Montferrat, Amadeus of Achaia agreed to join, on condition that he retained a free hand against Saluzzo.[3]

The peace lasted, albeit uneasily, for a little over a year. Coucy's campaign against Genoa was in full swing; the Prince of Achaia was supporting him; Facino Cane was engaged, first in Orleanist, then in Genoese service; and the power of Saluzzo was crippled. But early in 1396, when Louis of Orleans had transferred his claims on Genoa to Charles VI, and Giangaleazzo was no longer so eager to be of service to Coucy, Teodoro of Montferrat began again to harry the Piedmontese lands of Savoy; Cane returned to create new disturbances, and the forces of Montferrat and Achaia came to blows in May 1396. Two months later, the Prince of Achaia captured from his enemy the important city of Mondovì.[4] Giangaleazzo offered his mediation once

---

[1] Letter of 18 May 1394: Martène et Durand, *Amplissima collectio*, I 1542. Florence decided on 8 August to refer the offer to her allies: Jarry, *Origines*, 73 note 3.

[2] Cognasso, *Amedeo VIII*, II 79–81, implies that Giangaleazzo secretly supported Saluzzo and Montferrat; cf. Gabotto, *Ultimi Principi d' Acaia*, 215–17. For Giangaleazzo's part in the negotiations for peace: *ibid.* 218–30; Jarry, *Origines*, 53–4.

[3] The alliance of 16 October 1394: Benvenuto di San Giorgio, "Historia Montisferrati", *RIS* xxiii 632–7.

[4] Gabotto, *Ultimi Principi d' Acaia*, 268–78.

more, in full accord with Amadeus VIII and the Duke of Burgundy; but Teodoro obstinately refused to accept any conditions which did not guarantee to him the restoration of Mondovì.[1]

Meanwhile, Giangaleazzo's position underwent a change. The Franco-Florentine alliance of September 1396 drew his serious attention to the problem of Piedmont as a potential road for a French invading army. The Florentines hoped to bring Savoy into the alliance against Milan; and Buonaccorso Pitti, on his mission to Paris in July 1396, was instructed to approach the young Count and his advisers.[2] The answer was polite and non-committal. Amadeus VIII "answered me, expressing much joy at my message, that when the time came, he would do that which would be welcome to the Commune, and of which the Commune would be content". Oddo de Villars and Iblet de Challant, two of his principal advisers, were definitely favourable to the Florentine cause: "they answered me, rejoicing, that they would so work it that the Count of Savoy would make alliance with our Commune".[3] The negotiations, however, advanced no further; and when Bologna, at the beginning of the Mantuan war, proposed to seek the help of Savoy, the Florentine government declared that no help could be expected from that quarter.[4]

Nevertheless, Giangaleazzo recognized the danger that French pressure, exercised through the powerful medium of Philip of Burgundy, might compel Savoy to favour his enemies. His interests now lay more than ever in strengthening the power of Montferrat and Saluzzo against Savoy; and it was probably through his offices that Wenceslaus confirmed Teodoro's claims on Turin and other lands of the Prince of Achaia in November 1396.[5] But Giangaleazzo did not wish any party in Piedmont to have grievances against him. He could at least make sure that Savoy would remain neutral until the French were ready to act; while the disaster of Nicopolis brought preparations in France to a standstill, the Duke of Milan induced Teodoro, in July 1397,

---

[1] *Ibid.* 280–4.

[2] Commission of 18 July 1396: *ASF*, Dieci di Balìa, Legazioni 2, 36 & t.

[3] Pitti's report, 27 December 1396: Paris, Bibliothèque Nationale, *Fonds italiens* 1682, p. 39.

[4] "Se dicesseno di quello di savoia, pare abbino per condotto, dite loro che noi non veggiamo nè quando mai nè donde lo possino avere." Commission of 23 March 1396/7: *ASF*, Signoria, Legazioni 1 75 t.

[5] For this confirmation: Gabotto, *Ultimi Principi d' Acaia*, 292.

to accept his arbitration of the outstanding differences between Montferrat and Achaia.[1]

While the appointed arbitrators conducted their investigations at Pavia, the truce was constantly violated by both parties;[2] and when Bernard of Armagnac's preparations against Milan were nearly completed, what Giangaleazzo had feared came to pass. Amadeus VIII sent messengers to Venice, in March 1398, to offer his services to the League, in return for any conquests that he might make between the Po and the Ticino.[3]

Giangaleazzo circumvented the danger by concluding the truce of Pavia. Meanwhile, the peace between Montferrat and Achaia continued to function uncertainly, while constant messages reached Pavia bearing on the process of arbitration, or reporting breaches of the truce between the two parties.[4] Giangaleazzo was in a difficult position; he did not wish to offend Savoy, but there was only one course open to him as arbitrator. His award, which was pronounced in January 1399, admitted the claims of Montferrat to Turin and the other disputed lands in Piedmont.[5] Not only was Teodoro his friend, but he claimed these lands with the approval and authority of Wenceslaus, to whom Giangaleazzo owed his own Ducal title.

The Prince of Achaia rejected the award, and both parties took up arms. Amadeus VIII supported his cousin, without becoming personally involved in the quarrel; and Facino Cane, after serving in Giangaleazzo's army from September 1397 to July 1398, returned to Piedmont and began to lay the foundations of his own territorial dominions in the district.[6]

Giangaleazzo offered his services once more in the cause of peace. Amadeus VIII also made efforts to pacify the feud, but the growing menace of Cane's depredations compelled him to support the Prince of Achaia with all the forces at his disposal.[7] The Prince and Teodoro accepted the arbitration of the Duke of Burgundy in February 1400; but Philip was unable or unwilling to give an award, the period of the compromise elapsed, and both sides prepared to fight again.[8]

---

[1] On 31 July: Benvenuto di San Giorgio, *op. cit. RIS* xxiii 647–57. Giangaleazzo had worked hard during the winter, to prevent a union of the League with Savoy: Gabotto, *Ultimi Principi d' Acaia*, 287–94.
[2] *Ibid.* 323–40.   [3] Lucca, *Regesti*, 436–8, nos. 1974–9.
[4] Gabotto, *Ultimi Principi d' Acaia*, 340–57.
[5] *Ibid.* 359–60 (on 20 January).
[6] *Ibid.* 360–5; Galli, "Facino Cane", *ASL* xxiv, 2, 229–40.
[7] Gabotto, *Ultimi Principi d' Acaia*, 366–73.   [8] *Ibid.* 387–96.

Finally, Amadeus VIII, impressed by the need to drive Facino Cane out of Piedmont at all costs, accepted the office of arbitrator in November 1400; Teodoro, in return for a sealed promise that certain of his rights would not be violated, consented, at Giangaleazzo's instance, to dismiss Cane from his service.[1]

Giangaleazzo had good cause to seek the favour of Savoy, for the danger of a German invasion was already threatening him. Amadeus VIII, who had been confirmed by Wenceslaus in the office of Imperial Vicar in 1399, hesitated to abandon his titular lord in favour of Rupert;[2] but he awaited the result of the Bavarian's expedition to Italy, before he proclaimed an award between Montferrat and Achaia. Meanwhile, the disputants came to blows again, and Cane fought for Teodoro until Giangaleazzo called him away to join the Milanese army which was assembling against Rupert. It has been suggested that Cane's activities in Piedmont were instigated by the Duke, in order to demonstrate his power to Amadeus;[3] but the two princes apparently worked in close accord to preserve the peace of Piedmont. A truce of four years was finally proclaimed between Montferrat and Achaia at the end of November 1401.[4]

A new enemy, even more closely connected with Milan, immediately arose to harass the Savoyards. This was Antonio Porro, the Duke's counsellor, and Count of Pollenzo and Santa Vittoria in Piedmont. Porro declared war on the Prince of Achaia on 26 December 1401. The cause of the quarrel is not known. Giangaleazzo may have deliberately set him to make difficulties for Savoy, in view of the Duke of Burgundy's activities at Paris in favour of Rupert;[5] but it seems at least equally probable that Porro was engaged on some private dispute of his own. His attack on the lands of Achaia went on even after the death of Prince Amadeus in May 1402. Amadeus VIII, on the other hand, was bent on preserving peace with Milan, after Rupert's ignominious withdrawal.[6]

Amadeus VIII sent an ambassador to discuss "important and secret business" with the Duke in the middle of August 1402.[7] But, in spite of the apparently excellent relations existing between them, the interests of the two states were too diametrically opposed for their friendship to be genuine. When Amadeus learnt that negotiations were in progress for an alliance against Milan, he offered his services to Venice against the Duke.

[1] *Ibid.* 406–14.   [2] *Ibid.* 432–3.   [3] By Gabotto: *ibid.* 425.
[4] *Ibid.* 415.   [5] This was suggested by Gabotto: *ibid.* 447.
[6] *Ibid.* 450–5.   [7] *Ibid.* 462.

This renewal of the offer of 1398 came too late; by the time
that it was received in Venice, the Duke was dead.[1] But it
illustrates the difficulties which still faced Giangaleazzo in his
struggle for predominance in Italy; and it strengthens the sup-
position that he proposed, at the time of his death, to remove
the threat of an overwhelming coalition of powers against him,
by concluding a peace which, recognizing the conquests he had
already made, would leave an opening for him to renew his
intrigues.

Giangaleazzo was generally successful in averting the hostility
of Savoy, which would have exposed him to the danger of flank
attacks from the west; but he had to pay a price for this immunity.
His policy in Piedmont was based on expediency, and not on the
best interests of his state. He had to submit to the pacific encroachments of Savoy on his Piedmontese border, because he
could not afford to divert his attention from other spheres; the
forces, which would have enabled him to resist these encroachments, were all devoted to other struggles. An obscure but unremitting conflict was engaged in the lands of Vercelli, in which
the power of Savoy was gradually establishing its superiority.
The lords of the district were persuaded one by one to transfer
their allegiance to Savoy, and, in spite of every precaution, the
Milanese government was unable to put a stop to these desertions.[2]
The boundaries of Savoy advanced steadily towards the Sesia;
and the heavy taxation of Giangaleazzo's last years drove many
of his subjects to seek refuge under the milder Savoyard government.[3] The Piedmontese policy, which Giangaleazzo pursued
with all his customary skill after the union of the Visconti
dominions in 1385, was dictated by other considerations than
those which governed the situation in Piedmont itself. It was one
of the drawbacks which accompanied that union, that pressure
from the west could not effectively be answered, until the bitter
struggle engaged in other regions had been successfully concluded.

---

[1] Copialettere Carrarese, 396–7, note 4 to no. 734.

[2] "Però il movimento principale designavasi non già verso Milano ma verso
Savoia, ed i Visconti medesimi per altri interessi lasciavano fare": Gabotto,
"Età del Conte Verde", *MSI* xxxiii 241; and *v. Id.*, *Ultimi Principi d' Acaia*,
77 and 96; Seregni, "Documenti Viscontei", *ASL* xxx, 1, 233. The Dolpazzi
petitioned Giangaleazzo in 1396 for compensation, on account of losses
sustained in the defence of his interests in the *Vercellese* against Savoy:
Gabotto, "Documenti Inediti", *MSI* xxxiv 160–1, no. 97. A disputed
border-line was under discussion in 1398: "Eporediensia", 513, no. 242.

[3] Gabotto, *Ultimi Principi d' Acaia*, 396; Cibrario, *Memorie Storiche*, 275.

THE EARLY PROPOSALS FOR THE MARRIAGE
OF VALENTINA VISCONTI (1379–1385)

The betrothal of Valentina to her cousin, Carlo Visconti, in 1379, forms an episode full of obscurities. Professor Romano, in his article on the first marriage of Lucia Visconti (*ASL* xx, 604 note 1), accepted the story of this betrothal; but later ("Valentina Visconti e il suo matrimonio", *ASL* xxv, 2, 11) he implied that it was a piece of bad fiction. (The implication may have been unintentional, for it arises from an answer to M. Camus, who quotes as his authority for the betrothal what is certainly "un cattivo romanzo"; but the impression conveyed by Romano's reference is that he dismissed the whole story as a product of the imagination.)

It was undoubtedly something more than that. A promise of Giangaleazzo relating to it, on 26 August 1379 (*Repertorio Visconteo*, ii 294, no. 2495), and a fragment of the actual contract of betrothal, dated 10 May 1380 (published by Seregni, "Primo Fidanzamento di Valentina Visconti", in *Rivista delle Scienze Storiche*, i, 2 162–5), have survived. According to the account given by Giangaleazzo himself in the "Processus" which he drew up against Bernabò in 1385, the project fell through because it was found impossible to secure the necessary Papal dispensation (*RIS* xvi 798 A; Romano accepted this reason for the non-fulfilment of the marriage, in the earlier of his articles quoted above). But a manuscript volume in the *Bibliothèque St Geneviève* at Paris contains, not only a complete copy of the deed of betrothal (MS. 2068, p. 46t), but, immediately following it, a bull of dispensation granted by Urban VI on 2 June 1380. It was in June, too, that Lodovico Gonzaga of Mantua, in a "Memoria in eundo Mediolanum .xx. Junii Mccclxxx", instructed his envoy to enquire "de auditis circa parentelam domini Karoli cum filia Comitis Virtutum" (*ASMa*, E. xlix. 1).

It is impossible to determine exactly the reasons for the abandonment of the project. Giangaleazzo can never have regarded it as more than an unpleasant necessity forced upon him by his uncle; and Bernabò, as he grew convinced of the Count's harmlessness, may have decided to make better use of his son's eligibility. Carlo was married, in 1382, to Beatrice of Armagnac, whose family was to be consistently hostile to Giangaleazzo in later years.

The proposal for the betrothal of Valentina to Louis II, Duke of Anjou, was made in July 1385. M. Camus ("Venue en France", *MSI* xxxvi 10), following Ferrai ("Politica di Giangaleazzo", *ASI* 5, xxii 39 and note 1), maintained that the proposal originated at the Angevin court; but Professor Romano's version (*Matrimonio di Valentina Visconti*, 20), in which he corrected his earlier and garbled account ("Valentina Visconti", *ASL* xxv, 2, 18–19), is the more probable one. Pierre de Craon, an Angevin knight, arrived in Paris from Milan on 11 June 1385. On the 14th, "Monseigneur de Berri visita Madame [Marie de Berri, the widowed Duchess of Anjou] et li parla de marier le Roy [Louis II] à la fille du conte de Vertus" (le Fèvre, *Journal*, 142); and it is probable that proposals were brought by Craon from the Count.

The project, however, was not pleasing to the Angevins, and nothing further is heard of it. Envoys of Wenceslaus were in Lombardy in August 1385, possibly to confer the Imperial Vicariat of his new dominions on Giangaleazzo (Lindner, "Geschichte des deutschen Reiches", ii 312 note 2); and the proposal to marry Valentina to John of Görlitz, the half-brother of Wenceslaus, may well have arisen in the course of their visit.

The prospect of Louis of Valois as a bridegroom for his daughter was, however, too brilliant for Giangaleazzo to ignore. M. Camus ("Maison de Savoie", *BSBS* iv 117–23) constructed an elaborate theory that Amadeus VII himself proposed the match, in order to alienate Wenceslaus from Giangaleazzo and so promote his own designs on Asti. His arguments do not survive the criticisms of Professor Romano (*Matrimonio di Valentina Visconti*, 14–17); but Romano's own contention, that the Count of Savoy had no share at all in the negotiations, does not seem to me acceptable. Amadeus would not have gone to Piacenza in November 1385, as Romano suggested (*ibid.* 11–13), merely to sign in person a mistrustful truce. It seems certain, from subsequent events, that an understanding of some sort was reached at that meeting; and the support of Amadeus, intimately connected with the French crown, promised to be of value in future negotiations. This was the opinion expressed by Dr Gabotto (*Ultimi Principi d' Acaia*, 47): "non sembra sia estraneo il viaggio del Conte Rosso a Piacenza." It does not in any way affect the main contention of

Professor Romano ("Giangaleazzo Visconti", *ASL* xviii 15), that "le prime proposte dovettero senza dubbio partire da Giangaleazzo"—a verdict that was sustained by Jarry ("Actes additionnels au contrat de mariage de Louis d'Orléans", *BEC* lxii 25).

THE "LEAGUE OF NORTHERN AND CENTRAL ITALY" IN THE SUMMER OF 1385

The discovery by Dr Collino of what appeared to be an alliance between the Count of Vertus, the Communes of Florence, Bologna, Lucca, Pisa, Siena and Perugia, the lords of Mantua and Ferrara, the Malatesta and other princes of Romagna, and various cities and rulers of the Mark of Ancona, the Duchy of Spoleto and the Papal Patrimony, has given rise to some confusion over the diplomacy of Giangaleazzo in the summer of 1385. This League, according to a copy found in the Archives of Florence, was signed at·Pisa on 9 October 1385;[1] its terms, according to Collino, demonstrated the wise foresight of Florence, and the responsibility of Giangaleazzo for the difficulties which were to arise between him and the Republic over his relations with the other Communes of Tuscany.[2] It is perhaps worth while to discover the truth of this story, as it has been accepted by Silva ("Governo di Pietro Gambacorta", 224–5), by Landogna (*Politica dei Visconti*, 57), by Valeri ("Stato Visconteo", *NRS* xix 463), and very recently by Professor Visconti (*Storia di Milano*, 276–7), and has passed into the history of the period, as evidence either of the unreliability of Giangaleazzo's word, or of the tendency towards closer union among the Italian states at the end of the Trecento, under the auspices of Giangaleazzo.

The Count of Vertus did, in fact, form two alliances in August 1385. The first was concluded at Pavia with Francesco Gonzaga, Niccolò d'Este, and Francesco Carrara (*v. supra*, Chapter VII): the second, at Legnano, with the Republics of Florence, Bologna, Lucca and Pisa (*v. supra*, Chapter VIII). They were both designed to secure Giangaleazzo's position after the overthrow of Bernabò in May; the negotiations which led up to them have been illustrated, in the one case by Miss Pastorello, in the other by Collino. They were not followed by any of the preliminaries which would have been necessary to prepare the ground for a League as extensive and important as that which Collino described. More-

[1] Collino, "Politica Fiorentino-Bolognese", *MAT* 2, LIV 166–7, Doc. 69.
[2] *Ibid.* 133–4.

over, it is strange to find that Carrara, who was already an ally of Giangaleazzo, was excluded from the wider agreement. Not only is there no evidence of negotiations for this League, but there is no reference to it in any of the Chronicles, or in the subsequent correspondence of the powers involved.

This is the negative evidence. On the concrete side, there is the evidence of the date. It can only be a copy of the alliance signed at Pisa on 9 October, four years later. The members of the League, and its terms, in so far as they are quoted by Collino, correspond exactly with those of the Pact of Pisa in 1389, the abortive product of Pietro Gambacorta's diplomacy; and the interpretations which have been placed upon the League of 1385 cannot be applied to what was recognized on both sides to be a temporary agreement between two powers hastily preparing for war.

APPENDIX IV

GIANGALEAZZO AND THE BOLOGNESE
CONSPIRACY OF 1389

Palmieri, in his study of the plot discovered in 1389 to overthrow
the existing government of Bologna,[1] showed that the conspiracy
did not originate with Giangaleazzo; the conspirators, needing
the support of an outside power, appealed to the Count of Vertus
for help, and offered to place Bologna under his rule. Palmieri
dealt exhaustively with the conspiracy as an episode in the
domestic affairs of Bologna; I propose to give here a brief account
of the connection between Giangaleazzo and the conspirators, in
relation to the Count's general policy during the year 1389.

The original proposal of the conspirators was that Giangaleazzo
should enter Bologna by force of arms; but a new plan was quickly
substituted. The General Council of the city, faced by the im-
posing military preparations of Milan, was to be stampeded into
voting for the surrender of authority to the Count, rather than
incur the heavy expenses and dangers of a threatened invasion.
Giangaleazzo eventually agreed to this plan in principle; nevertheless, he remained an accessory. Although the conspirators
could not act without his support, he never took direct charge of
the plot, but left the work and the details to them.

The conspirators represented the alliance of juridical and
feudal elements, which had formed the backbone of the Ghibelline
cause since the days of Frederick Barbarossa. The lawyers were
represented by Bartolomeo Saliceto, a renowned teacher of law,
on whom fell the task of winning over the Council and securing
the votes which would transfer the dominion of the city to Giangaleazzo. Ugolino da Panico, a great landowner with extensive
domains in the Bolognese Contado, was at the head of the feudal
nobility involved in the plot; his part was to ensure, by force of
arms if necessary, that the district followed the example of the
city, and opposed no resistance when the new lord of Bologna was
proclaimed. Both parties, the juridical and the feudal, discontented with the existing Communal régime, turned naturally to

[1] Palmieri, "Congiura per sottomettere Bologna al Conte di Vertù",
AMR 4, VI 169–218.

Giangaleazzo, whom they regarded as the leading Ghibelline in
Italy, and—with perhaps greater justification—as the only
prince powerful enough to help them.

The conspirators approached the Count through Francesco
Gonzaga in December 1388, and met with a refusal.[1] Giangaleazzo was on the point of beginning negotiations with the legitimate government of Bologna; he did not wish to jeopardize the
chances of a settlement by treating at the same time with seditious
elements. That this was the reason for Giangaleazzo's refusal is
confirmed by his eventual acceptance in principle of the offer of
the conspirators in May 1389, at the moment when the conference of Pavia was breaking down.

The Florentines were not slow to get wind of their enemy's
intentions. They had for some time been conscious that Bologna
was singularly ill-placed to resist a sudden blow struck from
Milan; and urgent warnings were sent to the Bolognese as early
as January 1388, when the troops of Giovanni degli Ubaldini
were wandering across Romagna and Emilia.[2] Rumours that
Giangaleazzo intended to launch an attack on Bologna were
prevalent in July 1389; the Florentines protested indignantly to
Pietro Gambacorta, the would-be pacifier of Italy, and sent 200
lances to sustain the Bolognese in the defence of their liberty.[3]
Palmieri, however, has found no evidence that Giangaleazzo
had planned any move against the Republic at this time. The
conference of Pisa was about to open at last, under the auspices
of Gambacorta; and the temper of the Florentines was not such
that the Count could afford to provoke them by a sudden assault
on Bologna, while the conference was in progress.

The discussions at Pisa, however, seemed destined to repeat
the failure at Pavia earlier in the year. Giangaleazzo would not
modify his proposals, to which Florence answered neither yes
nor no; both sides were rapidly enlisting troops; and for the first
time the Count gave his serious attention to the Bolognese plot.
Giovanni degli Ubaldini was sent, at the end of August, to Parma,
where he nominally enlisted troops and secretly negotiated with
Ugolino da Panico and the other conspirators. It was proposed
that, with the help of a small force supplied by Ubaldini, the

[1] *Ibid.* 187–92.
[2] Collino, "Preparazione della Guerra", *ASL* xxxiv, 2, 225–32.
[3] "Confortandogli al mantenimento di loro stato e libertà": Commission
of 15 July 1389: *ASF*, Dieci di Balìa, Legazioni i 199. And v. Silva, "Governo",
250; Pastorello, *Nuove Ricerche*, 68 note 3.

possession of the valleys towards the Florentine border should be secured simultaneously with the revolt in the city.[1]

Ubaldini's presence in Parma, and the gathering of a large body of troops around him, had not passed unnoticed. From Siena came the report that "pare vogla fare la 'mpresa di Bologna".[2] The Bolognese were aware of the danger, and sent a protest to Giangaleazzo against the mobilization of his army on their border.[3] The Count replied that there was no cause for alarm, but that he alone could not remain undefended, while all his neighbours were feverishly enlisting troops. "Si nobis de armigeris ultra solitum providemus gentibus, nullam debetis in admirationem deduci; cum nullus sit, qui nostrum honorem et statum diligat, quem meditemur nobis consulure [*sic*], ut rebus sic dispositis, et fortificantibus se aliis, nos stemus penitus improvisi."[4]

The attack on Bologna was never made. The Florentines accepted Giangaleazzo's terms at the last moment, and the Pact of Pisa was signed on 9 October 1389. Giangaleazzo declared that he immediately dissolved the army gathered at Parma.[5] The Florentines doubted his word; but if the army was not dissolved, we may assume that it was at least recalled from the Bolognese frontier, for nothing more is heard of the threat against the Republic until the outbreak of the war, six months later.

The first arrest of the Bolognese conspirators occurred in the middle of November, and the whole plot came to light; but none of the confessions published by Palmieri implicates Giangaleazzo in the proceedings of the conspirators after the Pact of Pisa. Although the conspirators kept in touch with one another, there is no evidence that there were any further developments of the plot after the crisis of September 1389. Giangaleazzo, having postponed a danger that he was not yet fully prepared to meet, was no longer immediately interested in the propositions of discontented Bolognese citizens. To pursue the plans made for a revolution in Bologna would have been contrary to the very practical purpose which prompted him to accept Gambacorta's proposals.

---

[1] Palmieri, *op. cit.* 193–5.

[2] Despatch of 22 September 1389: Lucca, *Regesti*, 282, no. 1417.

[3] Undated letter: Zambeccari, "Epistolario", 102 no. 85.

[4] Giangaleazzo to Bologna, 25 September 1389: from a copy in Bologna, indexed in Frati, "Raccolta di lettere politiche", *ASI* 5, xi 143, no. 22 = 19.

[5] Corio, *Storia di Milano*, ii 348.

The acquisition of Bologna was one of the ultimate aims of Giangaleazzo's policy; but it involved more than the danger of an open challenge from Florence. Venice and the Pope were closely interested in the fate of Bologna. Whatever hopes the Count may have placed in an apparently legal submission of the Republic to his authority, he could not be sure that a superficial respect for legal forms would allay the suspicions of Venice or mitigate the resentment of the Pope. He was not yet prepared even for a war with Florence; the possibility of a joint attack by the three powers interested in preserving the independence of Bologna was a risk that he dared not run. Giangaleazzo was prepared, when war seemed inevitable, to contemplate a desperate bid for the possession of a Republic which would otherwise be ranged on the side of his enemies. When peace was ensured, if only for a brief interlude, he wisely withdrew from so dangerous an undertaking; he was not strong enough to meet the consequences. It was not until twelve years later, when his power had begun to seem invincible, that he finally felt ready to defy all opposition and take Bologna for his own.

DOCUMENTS

No. 1

Despatch of Galeazzo Busoni to Francesco Gonzaga: Pavia, 17 October [1387][1]

ASMa: E. xlix 3

Magnifice et excelse domine domine mi singularissime. Que autem super tractatu huius pacis hactenus occurrerunt dominationi vestre notifico per presentibus....[2] ...diebus continuis postquam ipsi vestre dominationi scripsi, Omnes de conscilio huius domini continuatis vicibus et dietis fuerunt in colloquio cum Ambaxiatoribus Serenissimi domini Imperatoris et domini Verone de verbis siquidem dictis et prolatis hinc inde diebus predictis. Hodie hora tarda super sala...[2] conveneramus franciscus turchetus et Ego propter adiscere que fiebant quia ibidem venerant ad dominum Comitem dicti Ambaxiatores Imperatoris. Pasquinus nos Ambos vocavit et traxit a parte dicendo que acta fuerunt et Incipiendo a principio et prosequendo particulariter usque ad finem Narravit hoc modo videlicet quod predicti Ambaxiatores domini Verone huic domino exponi fecerant, qualiter dominus eorum se recomendabat huic domino, et quod de eo habebat unum filium et servitorem, et sic dignaretur eum admittere et sibi conservare quia ipsum reperiret sibi fore bonum filium et bonum servitorem cum proposito bene mentis ad obsequendum voluntatem suam. Et quod quia iste dominus preter ius et nulla precedente causa legittima occupaverat aliquas terras suas, dignaretur illas non velle tenere, sed ipsas sibi totaliter restituire. Cui per conscilium responsum fuit, quod nichil preter Justiciam occupatum fuerat per istum dominum illo domino, neque spem ullam fieri aliquo, quod que tenebat vellet aliqualiter restituire neque dare. Et quod nisi aliud mandatum vel aliam commissionem haberent, poterant recedere et ire pro factis suis quocumque vellent. Ex quo heri aliter aperuerunt se dicentes quod dominus suus contentabatur dimittere isti domino vallem de lieder cum Rocha, vallem tigniani cum Rocha, Ripam tridenti cum Rochis suis et Sermionum et esse filius et servitor suus, isto domino relaxante sibi alias terras et fortilicias quas in gardexana sibi occupaverat nulla alia mencione facta per eos de aliis terris et pecunia per istum dominum postulatas. Quo dicto isti domino per suos valde turbatus misit respondendo

---

[1] This letter was erroneously dated 1401, and placed under that year in the files.

[2] The letter is torn at the top and bottom corners on the right-hand side.

eis videlicet quod satis clare fecerat eis patefieri Intencionem suam, quod sua Intencio non Indigebat in...aliqua et propterea quando ad id se disponerent et mandatum haberent, bene quidem; et quando autem non, non erat tempus altercationis, poteram ire pro factis suis. Ex quo hodie ampliaverunt oblationes suas, addentes ultra terras predictas primo oblatas Castellarium Laguselli Monzabanum et pontum; quod relatum fuit isti domino, qui declaravit ultimam voluntatem et intencionem suam, et super qua imponerat, ut nisi sic fieret amplius nichil sibi dicatur, que fuit isto modo limitata videlicet quod vult totam gardexanam cum omnibus iuribus et pertinenciis suis quocumque sibi spettantibus, totam riperiam Mincii cum fortiliciis et pertinenciis suis, et ob reverenciam domini sui domini Imperatoris, alia castra que petierat contentabatur non petere, videlicet hostiliam et lomachum et portum; sed quod volebat Rocham de ripolis includeri debere et esse in Iure suo gardexane, ac etiam quod si que roche vel fortilicie dictarum parcium Gardesane et Riperii mincii non essent sufficientes ad possendum se custodire de Introytibus suis quod dominus Verone assignet tot Introytus de terris vel villis suis circavicinis qui sufficient ad faciendum dictas expensas dictarum custodiarum que per se custodiri non possent. Et quod ubi quesiverat v^cM ducatos, contentatur remittere sibi .cc.M et esse contentus recipere in terminis iuste limitatis, tantum .ccc.M ducatos. Cui tali declarationi, dicti Ambaxiatores domini Verone responderunt quod gardexana erat maius factum quam crederetur et quod in ea includebantur villa Francha et multe alie terre, et quod iste dominus vellet avertere quod dignum foret, et est quod dominus Episcopus bambergensis habuit dicere ad unum quod illi de conscilio huius domini responderunt et addiderunt peticionibus antedictis quod fuit et est Intencionis huius domini velle suas fore quascumque terras domini Verone quas eum habere contingeret, usque ad conclusionem pacis videlicet quod non erat nisi occupare bona unius, et sine alia conscientia dicere sua fore, et velle ipsa retinere per se. Sed quia Mandatum tam plenum ad talia promittendum vel faciendum, non habebant dicti Ambaxiatores quesiverunt velle retrocedere Veronam. Et rogaverunt quod sibi prorogaretur Salvus conductus suus parte ipsius domini, ut possent retrocedere. Quibus responsum fuit, ut quoniam Intencio domini sui sit velle effectualiter facere predicta, et quod concedat eis potestatem opportunam, tam super predictis quam super factis domini Padue, et domini Mantue, videlicet quod quicquid ipse dominus Comes fecerit et declaraverit pro ipsis dominis Mantue et Padue ratum erit, nam licet dicti domini se posuerint de factis eorum in manibus suis, tamen vult si debeat concludi in pace, quod habeant quod iustum sit et decens pro parte sua, nec aliter posset pax ista effectum habere. Et eis respondentibus quod bene intelligebant verba domini Comitis et quod accipiebant salvum conductum, tenentes quod regressus eorum si huc retrocedant, non erit nisi ad bonum finem conclusionis pacis. Et sic factus est eis salvus conductus. Et isto sero hora xxiiia Ambaxiatores domini Imperatoris venerunt acceptum comeatum a domino Comite antedicto cras mane hinc recessuri et unaa cum eis Ambaxiatoribus predictis domini Verone, Ituri directe Veronam. Ex quo contentarer multum, quod nisi Ludovicus motus sit de Mantua aut alius, retardaretur usque ad octo dies, adhuc veniendum, si autem est in itinere, duo sunt principalia, que iusta sunt ipsum adhuc conducendum...domini Marchionis de quo Ludovicus habuit informationem. Et inconveniencia gencium domini Padue que iuste poterit recordari, quia a recessu domini Jacobi citra bene deberet venisse responsio; si autem non recessit de Mantua adhuc potest differre per spatium predictum octo dierum vel plus adhuc veniendum, quia ego interim alia incumbencia possetenus solicitabo. Addidit etiam dictus Pasquinus quod propter tempestatem que viguit in lacu, dominus Guillelmus et dominus Spineta non potuerunt ire acceptum Ripam. Et quod propter brevitatem temporis ad obsequenda alia que habebant pre manibus in Verona, dimittebant ire Ripam, que haberent ad omnem voluntatem suam, quia stabat ad postulationem et mandatum suum. Ista propria nocte cum toto exercitu, et omni suo exforcio equitabant Veronam, qualia forent predicta vel qualis tractatus esset non expressit. Sed dominacio vester habet stare multum attenta et tenere gentes suas unitas quantum potest, ut casu occurrente prout inopinati multi casus occurunt persepe, possit ad negocia sua quoad decet intendere. Comunis opinio familancium isti domino extra Concilium est, quod si persequatur ad guerram infra breve spacium temporis subjugabitur Verona. Et inter consciliarios maior pars declinat ad pacem, prout ex ore Nicoleti de diversis habui qui est unus ex adversariis pacis, qui dixit hodie michi, istum suum dominum multum placatum fore et refrigidatum, et... opinione huius domini non colligebat posse sequi preter pacem, nisi mutaret opinionem, bene quod istud fuit ante parlamentum predictum, ...et ante dicta verba mihi dicta per dictum Pasquinum, et quod multi erant qui de pace tantum consulebant ipso domino....Omissis...

    Papie .xvii. octobris de sero, tamen expeditus
est nuncius .xviii. hora xiiia.
Per familiarem dominacionis vestre Galeacium de
buzone cum recomendatione.
Magnifico et Excelso domino domino meo singularissimo
domino Mantue &c.

No. 2

Minute of the Council of Siena: 5 June 1388

ASS: Concistoro, Deliberazioni, vol. cxxxiv = 143, pp. 26–7

(.v. Junii 1388).

In nomine domini amen. Certi savi huomini electi per li magnifici 26 t.
Signori signori Priori governatori del comune e popolo de la Città
di Siena a provedere e provisioni fare per buono e pacifico stato de
la Città contado e distretto di Siena col magnifico et excelso Signore
misser lo Conte di Vertù e intorno a le imbasciate a lui mandate e
risposte per lui fatte ad esse ambasciate e sue proferte &c. providdoro
e ordinaro in questo modo cioè:

In prima providdoro e ordinaro e' savi predetti che per Signori
priori e ufficiali de la Balìa si mandi e mandare si debba Ambasciadori
uno o più come piacerà a essi Signori al sopradetto magnifico Signore
con certa ambasciata, el tenore de la quale è questo.

Prima doppo le dovute Reverentie da fare a tanto Signore Raco-
mandino tutta la comunità di Siena sì come suoi devoti figliuoli e servidori con quelli Savi modi che credarranno convenirsi a la magnifica
sua signoria.

Apresso expongano a la magnifica sua signoria come avendo Inteso
da l' ultimo Ambasciadore a lui mandato la proferta sua cioè se e la
nostra Comunità piacesse esso magnifico Signore mandarebbe qua
suoi Ambasciadori uno o vero più e' quali si dovessero pienamente
informare de le Ingiurie a noi facte e da cui e le cagioni e poi così informati come piacesse a noi andassero una volta o più come facesse per
bisogno ne' luoghi necessarii acciò che le cose mal fatte tornassoro a
loro dovere &c. E' priori e tutta la comunità di questo à ricevuta
grande allegreza e grande conforto e di questo ringratino la sua Signoria per quello modo che a la prudentia d' essi savi Ambasciadori
parrà convenirsi, supplicando e chiedendo di gratia a la sua magnifica
signoria che li piaccia la detta ambasciata mandare avendo grande
speranza che essa ambasciata gittarà buon frutto a la Comunità di
Siena suoi figliuoli e servidori.

Apresso spongano a la magnifica sua signoria conciò sia cosa che ne
li Animi e chuori unitamente di tutta la cittadinanza di Siena suoi
devoti figliuoli e servidori sia fermo tenere la magnifica sua Signoria per
nostro singularissimo padre e signore protectore e difensore e ad essa
sua Signoria   à piacuto per sua benignità e gratia ricevarci e tenerci 27.
per suoi figliuoli e servidori che per amplificare la sua magnifica signoria e per buono effetto e pace de la cittadinanza di Siena suoi figliuoli,

piaccia a la Signoria sua questo con manifesto Segno dimostrare e che come piace a la sua signoria o là o vero qua, come a lui piace si pratichi de' modi che sieno da tenere e per lui e per noi e componare e fermare quello che piacca a lui acciò che la signoria sua sia certificata e secura de la nostra filiatione e noi de la signoria sua siamo aiutati e difesi da ogne Signore comunità o vero compagne che volessoro per alcuno modo oppressare la comunità nostra e suo contado terre e distretto.

Ultimamente dicano che le proferte non somettono però che non è onesto che figliuoli e servidori profferischano al padre e signore le cose che sono sue e Intorno a le dette materie parlino saviamente e con quella reverentia e vocaboli che a la loro prudentia parrà convenire ad accendare ad amore quello signore verso de la comunità nostra.

Anco providoro e ordinaro e' savi predetti che in quanto il magnifico miser lo conte di vertù dimandasse a' detti nostri ambasciadori se avessoro el mandato a poter alcuna cosa componare che per li detti Ambasciadori si risponda di no ma quando quelli vostri figliuoli priori di Siena e la comunità tutta sapremo che la magnifica signoria vostra voglia attendere a praticare e componare che' l mandato subito mandaramo. Dicendo intorno a questa materia come credaranno convenirsi.

No. 3

Commission of the Florentine envoys going to Pavia, and letter to the same: 20 and 28 January 1388/9

ASF: Dieci di Balìa, Legazioni i, pp. 164–5 and 167

(*a*) Nota e informatione a voi Messer Luigi guicciardini e Messer Giovanni de' Ricci di quello che avete a fare in Lombardia fatta per gli dieci della balìa del comune di Firenze nel Mccclxxxviii adì xx di gennaio.

Andrete a Bologna E visiterete gli antiani per parte de' nostri Signori e nostra dicendo come andate al conte E pregandoli che facciano che loro ambasciadori sieno presti sì che andiate insieme.

Poi sarete co' dieci della balìa E dopo le saluti direte come noi mandiamo al Conte pregandogli che ordinino che gli ambasciadori loro insieme con voi muovano. E che tutti insieme andiate e spogniate l' ambasciata. E mosterrete a' detti dieci la informatione che vi diamo dicendo che si paresse loro aggiungere o scemare a quella, che possono. E se eglino facessono che fosse d' importanza scrivereteci Il che, E noi subito vi risponderemo Sì che se ne elegga Il migliore che tutti desideriamo uno fine.

Di poi andrete insieme con gli ambasciadori di bologna a Messer lo conte di Virtù. E lui saluterete affectuosamente per parte de' nostri Signori e nostra.

Poi gli direte come qua furono del mese passato Messer Guillelmo bevilacqua e Messer Bartolomeo de' benzoni suoi ambasciadori. E tra l' altre cose exposono come da poich' era finita la guerra di padova, era tolta via la cagione altre volte allegata per lo nostro comune e per lo comune di bologna, del non fare lega colla Magnificentia sua. E che egli offereva fare la detta lega. E se altra via si vedesse migliore per la sicurtà nostra e de' bolognesi, ch' egli era presto a seguirla. E che a questa parte noi dicemmo a' detti ambasciadori che noi non possavamo rispondere sanza conferire co' nostri collegati e maxime co' bolognesi. E che alla magnificentia sua si risponderebbe per voce viva. E che per questo noi vi mandiamo là.

E prima commenderete Il suo pensiere e il suo motivo in volere dare sicurtà pace e riposo al paese. E che a noi pare da far lega. E aspettate vedere da lui come la Intende. E se dice a difesa degli stati, sta bene. Se dicesse pure a non offendere l' uno l' altro, mosterretegli che migliore e di più substantia e effecto, è far   la lega a difesa degli stati come **165** altra volta proferse con patti e modi ragionevoli. Nella quale lega egli procacci e noi procacceremo di farvi venire I signori di lombardia E le comunità di Vinegia e di Genova. E noi e' bolognesi anche procacce- remo quanto possibile ci sarà che le comunità e' Signori di toscana e della Marca e di Romagna vi vengano. E che voi sete presti a ogni suo piacere entrare nella pratica della lega.

E così Siamo contenti che voi pratichiate la detta lega. E nella pratica verrete a mettere e ragionare I capitoli usati e ragionevoli. E tra gli altri che qualunque de' collegati offendesse l' uno l' altro, tutti gl altri collegati debbino essere contro a quello tale offendente. E quando la lega procedesse essendo a questo capitolo, si vorrà venire a ordinare di chi abbia a dichiarare qual sia l' offendente e l' offeso. E sopra ciò ci scriverete.

E che la lega non si extenda avere difendere l' uno collegato l' altro contro alla chiesa o contro alla casa de' reali di Francia.

E che' l detto Signore non si debbi in alcuno atto impacciare ne' fatti di toscana nè in alcuno luogo di qua dal fiume della Secchia.

E che noi e' bolognesi non ci possiamo in alcuno atto impacciare ne' fatti di lombardia nè in alcuno luogo di là dal detto fiume della Secchia.

E che le sicurtà per lui offerte in genere aspettiamo procedano da lui di darci quelle che vede che sieno sufficienti a levare I suspetti nati. E udirete quello ch' egli vorrà dire, E ove riuscirà.

E se pur dicesse chiedete voi le sicurtà che voi volete, allora in

ultimo verrete a dire che tra l' altre sicurtà che ci piacerebbono si è che' l
Re di Francia promettesse per lui l' observantia della lega e de' patti che
si facessono. E ancora dell' altre sicurtà che si vedessono essere utile
a torre I sospetti.

Se' l Conte vi dicesse ch' egli vorrebbe che s' attendesse al disfare le
compagne di Messer Johanni aguto e degli altri che sono di qua, direte
che come egli dee sapere a noi non sta Il potere disfare le compagne
però che sono gente libera e non ci sono obligati Se non ad alcuno certo
patto e in certo caso di venire a' nostri servigi, e per gli nostri danari,
quando n' avessimo bisogno, Richiedendogli .xv. dì innanzi. E per
questo e a ciò che non offendano noi nè nostri collegati ànno ricevuto
alcuno denaio da noi. Nondimeno, quando voi fossi con lui in concordia
de' capitoli della lega, e procedendo essa lega noi faremo nostra diligentia e potere intorno a levare via le dette compagne insieme con lui
e con gli altri che pur de' modi si dovranno vedere per lui e per degli
altri.

Informeretevi d' ogni novella che potrete sentire E de' fatti di Francia
e d' asti E d' ogni altro luogo. E di tutto ciò che potrete sapere, e delle
pratiche che terrete spesso ci aviserete.

Non vi legate di non potere fare lega con altrui nè così lui non chiedete
si leghi a noi.

E non parlate seperati l' uno da l' altro ma sempre insieme siate a
ogni ragionamento e pratica e parlanza, E insieme ancora con gli
Ambasiadori bolognesi. E sanza loro non parlate.

(b) Domino Loisio et domino Johanni de Ricciis.

Questa mattina ricevemmo vostra lettera e quella che scrivesti a'
Signori nostri. E alle parti che sono rimase dubbie noi respondiamo.
Alla prima ove dite che pare a cotesti Signori dieci che nello sporre Si
dicesse al conte che per suoi ambasciadori e de' bolognesi e nostri si
richiedessono I Vinitiani e' genovesi alla lega &c., vi diciamo che questo
non ci pare utile. Ma di seguire come sta nella commissione, perchè fa
per noi che noi e' bolognesi cerchiamo da noi riducere I Vinitiani e'
Genovesi alla lega con Firenze e bologna. E poi tutti insieme da una
parte far lega col conte. E pure hieri avemmo lettera dal duca di
genova che a questo si contenta, E che subito manderà suo ambasciadore al Conte di Virtù. E ove pur questo non si potesse obtenere
sarebbe da seguire che ciascuno per se medesimo intervenisse nella
lega. Alla seconda parte ove dicono che si excepti lo Imperadore come
la Chiesa e' Reali di Francia Siamo contenti. Alla terza parte ove dite
che a ciò che la chiesa della sicurtà del Re di Francia fosse più giusta
pareva loro che la sicurtà del detto Re fosse comune, rispondiamo che

questo non ci pare, perchè 'l Conte non à bisogno di sicurtà da noi nè
mai la chiese. Ma àlla proferta a noi e Pasquino de' capelli suo cancelliere altra volta offerse a' nostri ambasciadori questa sicurtà del Re di
Francia. Alla quarta parte ove dicono parrebbe loro utile chiedere che
in questa lega venisse il Conte di Savoia, diciamo che questo non è
utile anzi dannoso. E noi scriveremo a' dieci Il perchè e faremgliene
stare contenti. Alla quinta parte del non parlare l' uno sanza l' altro,
Seguite quello vi commettemmo. E se gli ambasciadori bolognesi
vogliono potere parlare per loro seperatamente possono fare il piacere
loro. Ma voi due non parlate l' uno sanza l' altro perchè nel parlare
separato non è utile alcuno. Alla sexta parte, ove dite par loro da
chiedere che 'l conte non si possa impacciare da Modona in qua, vi
diciamo ci pareva utile dire dalla secchia in qua, perchè egli da indi in
qua non à a fare alcuna cosa. E facciavamlo in favore de' bolognesi.
E parci si chiegga del non s' impacciare dalla Secchia in qua. E se ne
dicesse niente, venire allora a dire da Modona in qua. Altro non bisogna
rispondervi se non che sollicitate Il vostro cammino seguitando in ogni
altra parte la vostra commissione. E di quella non uscite. Datum in
Firenze adì xxviii di gennaio Mccclxxxviii a hore xxiii.

No. 4

A letter of some Sienese merchants to the government of Siena:
Venice, 29 June [1390][1]

ASS: Concistoro 1821, no. 19

Magnifici et potentes domini. Credentes dominacionem vestram
audivisse quod Illustris princeps dominus Comes Virtutum Mediolani
Imperialis Vicarius generalis perdiderat civitates suas Padue Verone
et Vincencie, que dominio suo rebelaverant, de qua adversitate
Florentini qui hic sunt multa signa gaudiorum ostendebant et multa
scripserunt ad diversas partes italie semper addentes mendacia,
Reverenter ad gaudium significamus eidem dominacioni vestre quod
prefatus Illustris dominus Comes die lune proxime preterita reaqui-
sivit dominium Civitatis Verone. Nam Spectabilis miles dominus
Ugolotus de blanchardis Intravit per vim civitatem predictam Verone
et interfectis capitaneo populi et mille vel duobus millibus popularibus
dicte Civitatis de minutis, Nam populus grassus semper stetit ad
amorem prelibati domini Comitis, obtinuit dominium libere Civitatis
predicte. Civitas vero Vincencie steterat continue et hodie est ad

---

[1] This letter is placed in the files of the year 1387.

obedienciam et subiectionem domini Comitis prelibati. Speramus quoque dictum dominum Ugolotum hodie applicare debere Paduam cum gentibus prefati domini Comitis, Et statim cum ibi erunt, dictam civitatem habiturum, quia non sunt in ea cum domino Francisco de carraria gentes alique de quibus possit fieri capitale, cum sint omnes quasi rustici Inermes et non assueti in factis armorum, ac multum timidi de adventu dicti domini Ugoloti, a quibus non speratur haberi resistencia. Et iam sentimus quod multi ex notabilioribus civibus Padue se et bona sua reducunt Venecias properanter. Quid autem sequetur vestre dominacioni curabimus intimare. Sed non speramus quod sequi debeat nisi bonum. Quoddam breve quod mittebant rectores Vincentie Capitaneis et rectoribus Padue qui sunt in castro et cittadella Padue, Et quod breve non potuit portari dictis Capitaneis et Rectoribus propter campum domini Francisci predicti de cararia portatum Spectabili Militi domino Bertrando de rubeis in Veneciis et per ipsum dominum Bertrandum datum Mariano Socini, ad vestri evidenciam et declaracionem veritatis mittimus vestre Magnificentie his inclusum.

Dat. Veneciis die .xxviiii. Junii.

Vestri fideles et devoti Servitores universitas mercatorum Civitatis Senarum.

(A tergo) Magnificis et potentibus Dominis dominis Prioribus et gubernatoribus populi et comunis Senarum.

No. 5

Giangaleazzo to Siena, 13 October 1390

ASS: Concistoro 1828, no. 7

Magnifici filii carissimi. Non processerunt hucusque comunia negotia contra statum Inimicorum nostrorum communium Arciguelforum Florentie in illis partibus prout sperabamus et rationabiliter debuisset, Nec, ut sentimus, de presenti procedunt, quia non fecerunt nec faciunt gentes nostre, quod verisimiliter facere debuissent. Et si procedere debent melius quam hucusque processerint, expediens et necessarium esse videmus quod aliter provideatur et melius quam provisum fuit usque nunc. Ad quod plus quam unquam dispositi sumus, non intendentes quod quicquam omnino pro nostra parte defficiat. Et quia non videmus huiusmodi efficaces provisiones fieri posse, nisi primo cum Spectabile Capitaneo nostro Paulo de Sabellis, late super omnibus conferemus, deliberavimus tandem, et dicto Capitaneo nostro mandavimus, quod cum illis quos secum venire voluerit de sola familia sua statim ad nos veniat, ut secum expedienter super omnibus loqui et oportunos pro finali exterminio Arciguelforum Florentie ordines capere valeamus. Nunquam enim Magnifici filii ad hoc aptius tempus fuit, cum ipsi Arciguelfi sue subversores patrie, expensas guerre quas hucusque taliter qualiter substinuerunt, non possint amplius tolerare. Ne autem propter suam absentiam gentes nostre frustrentur, vel interim aliquod proveniat Inconveniens, Ordinavimus quod Egregius vir Johannestodeschus de petramala a kalendis novembris in antea ob hanc causam exerceat Capitaneatus officium, Et quod loco Johannistodeschi elligatur alius marescallus qui nostris gentibus inter ceteros gratus sit. Dat. Mediolani die .xiii. octubris Mccclxxxx⁰.

Galeaz Vicecomes Comes Virtutum
Mediolani &c. Imperialis Vicarius Generalis.

Pasquinus.

(A tergo) Magnificis filiis nostris carissimis Prioribus gubernatoribus Comunis Senarum.

No. 6

Despatch of Busoni to Gonzaga: Pavia, 23 October 1391

ASMa: E. xlix. 3

Magnifice excelse domine domine mi singularissime. Heri reversus fui Belzoiosum ut dominationi vestre scripsi propter esse cum Ambaxiatoribus eiusdem dominationis vestre ad expeditionem suam. Et stetimus usque ad xxiiᵃᵐ horam et tandem per Ambroxium moreglam ex relatione Franceschini [Barbavara] de novaria responsum fuit ut reverteremur hodie in xviᵃ hora, quia illa hora expeditionem haberemus. Et sic fecimus et hodie in ascensu suo ad equum, dum Iret ad nemora, audienciam dedit; Et aliqua dixit premordiando ipse presens verba, super proditione sibi facta per Petrum de corigia. Et postea in conclusione dicendo dum licenciaret ipsos Ambaxiatores, quod cito me remitteret ad dominationem vestram cum his que grata forent dominationi vestre secundum quod dominus Johannes et dominus Anthonius de omnibus dictis et peractis sunt plenissime informati. Et quod parte sua salutarent dominationem vestram.

Ex revolutione facta per dictum Petrum, Et ex retornacionem factam per exercitum huius domini de tuscia inter petram sanctam et lucham, remanent valde stupefacti omnes curiales huius domini. Et ex dictis duabus causis michi dictum fuit ipsum dominum non dedisse audienciam vestris Ambaxiatoribus nec aliquibus aliis, quia omnes curialiter expelli fecit de castro. Et ex alia tercia causa, de qua quodam modo informatus est dictus dominus Johannes videlicet quod inter istum dominum et conscilium suum muliebrem dum simul esset cum domina comittisa, Franceschino de novaria et Mengino satis disputatum fuit inter eos si debebatis interpellari de accipiendo unam ex sororibus dicte domine comitisse in coniugem, et tandem fuisse per eos inter se conclusum quod sic; Et quod cause alegate fuerunt per eos adinvicem, hoc esse fiendum maxime ad tollendas omnes suspiciones que alegari unquam possent per aliquos emules suos et vestros quod haberetis dubitare de ipso ne vos deciperet vel violaret, quia ex tali parentela roboraretur vinculum dilectionis inter vos et ipsum, et toleretur omnis suspicio, ubi pur per vos dubitari antea posset. Et quod postquam dicebat et reputabat se ita vestrum, et vos ita suum, sicut dicebat et aparebat, melius erat pro ipso et vobis ad sic faciendum; Et breviter quod dominus iste assensit ad hoc, Et restavit conclusio quis deberet esse mediator in facto. Et isto medio, videlicet non heri sed die Sabati, quia hic tractatus videtur transivisse ad aures dictarum dominarum, Et quod ipse domine dixerint aliqua verba videlicet quomodo dominatio vestra remaneret bene contenta, si acciperet aliquam earum, videndo eam et recordaretur de errore comisso per sororem suam, et quomodo ipsa posset remanere contenta et secure stare sine dubio, quando essetis turbatus recordando de dicto errore, et quod de talibus verbis domina comitissa ipsas valde redarguit. Que verba pervenerunt ad aures domini comitis et ex ipsis stetit valde turbatissimus. Et dixit quod ex verbis earum comprendebat eas non velle maritari, et postquam nolebant quod unquam se amplius non impediret, Et quod ulterius de hoc sibi sermo non fieret. Et quod hec fuit causa quia ita heri steterat turbatus.

...... Omissis......

Dat. Papie xxiii octobris 1391.

Per Excelse dominationis vestre familiarem et servitorem

Galeazium de buzone cum recommendatione sua.

Magnifico et Excelso domino domino Francisco de Gonzaga Mantue &c. Imperiali vicario et domino generali domino meo singularissimo.

No. 7

Extract from another report of Galeazzo Busoni: Pavia, 28 October 1391

ASMa: E. xlix. 3

Magnifice excelse domine domine mi singularissime.

......Omissis......

Ut autem omnium que didici dominacio vester noticiam habeat, ecce eidem significo me perquisivisse a dicto Pasquino de casu adventus dicti Rugerii et quid credebat de pace, qui respondit, quod causa adventus dicti Rugerii huc, erat quia Ambaxiatores partium fuerant et se abocaverant insimul, et quod coram duce et eius conscilio ac magno magistro Rodiorum, quelibet parcium alegaverat rationes suas et iustificaverat factum suum. Et deventum esse tandem ad istud, quia per partes nunquam reduceretur negocium ad terminationem aliquam quia quelibet earum staret super se, quod compromittant se in dictis duce et magno magistro et stent contente de omni terminatione quam faciant, ex quo dictus Rugerius venerat pro habenda Intencione istius domini si de hoc contentabatur. Et similiter principalior Ambaxiator Florencie vocatus Guido Stefani, a fide Iverat Florenciam ad accipiendam Intencionem Florentinorum super dicto compromisso fiendo, in cuius redditu habebitur evidens noticia quid sequi debeat. Et quod iste dominus deliberavit in conscilio suo ad finem ut toti mundo pateat quod per eum non stat, quin pax sit, et quod ipse non sit causa destructionis huius patrie sed adversa pars, sic quod Rugerius revertatur de presenti Januam ad faciendum quod Guilelmus et alii eius Ambaxiatores consenciant huic compromisso et illud faciant, et pronuncient compromissarii quicquid velint, quoniam dominus iste sperat fovere tam bonum Jus, et causam suam ita Justam fore, quod ipsi honorabiliter senciabunt pro eo. Nescitur adhuc quid faciet adversa pars, Sed dicit Pasquinus se bene sperare quoniam stricta Civitate pisana ut mercancie et victualia non curant, sicut stricta est, quia ab extra erit exercitus et per mare obsidio Galearum, nam in portu pisano sunt due galee huius domini bene armate et tres bragentini et illuc conducta sunt lignaria cum quibus palsicatur et clauditur ille portus, ut nulla omnino victualia vel mercancie intrare ibi possint, Expediet quod ipsi Pisani capiant partitum, vel de adherendo huic domino, vel contra eum. Et exinde expediet quod Florentini eficiantur magis molles quam hactenus fuerint. De exercitu dicit quod Est ad Massam super Lucano, ut scribit dominus Le[?] et hoc propter convencionem .xv. dierum habitam cum Pisanis ut allias scripsi; quesivi si idem exercitus erat rediturus ad has partes vel non, dixit quod non. Et quod iste dominus quando pax non sequatur, omnino dispositus est fortificare exercitum suum in tuscia ubique melius stare possit, sive placeat sive displiceat cuicumque velit. Et quod penitus vult tenere guerram ad domum alterius, et non revocare ipsam ad has partes, et hic contra Bononienses etiam providere ut fuerit expediens.

Quesivi de adventu domini Jacobi de plano hodie, qui mihi respondit, quod eius adventus est ad querelandum de damno dato per gentes exercitus huius domini super pisano territorio, Et de clausura portus pisani per Galeas huius domini, Et pro senciendo ad quid finaliter intendat iste dominus super hoc. Super quibus dicit Pasquinus istum dominum consuluisse conscilium suum, Et tandem deliberasse respondere dicto domino Jacobo et expedire eum hoc modo videlicet quod intencio sua est, pace non sequente, non removere exercitum suum de tuscia, et illum tenere inter pisas et Florenciam et omnino prohibere quod mercancie vel victualia non transeant de Pisis Florenciam, sive in placere domini Petri de gambacurtis sive in displacere eius cedat. Et quoniam ipse dominus Petrus promittat expresse servare modum et servet de non promittendo [sic] merces vel victualia conduci Florenciam, Prorogabitur terminus antedictorum .xv. dierum ad maiorem terminum, de non intrando nec dampnificando territorium pisanum, secundum quod conventum fuerit inter partes, et quod iste dominus non querit aliud nisi quod pisani claudant viam Florentinis in non permittendo victualia vel merces aliquas Florenciam conduci, qui actus est reducendi Florentinos ad pacem, velint vel non. Et quod super hoc revertitur Pisas dictus dominus jacobus, et credit Pasquinus quod dominus Petrus non tantum amore quantum timore hoc faciet. Et si non faciet, exercitus se ponet super pisano inter Pisas et Florenciam nisi non tantum lucrabitur dominus Petrus quantum forte crederet.

Venit dominus Guido de Sano huc, qui nititur non amplius reverti Senas pro sua mansione, et affirmat omnino tantam caritudinem esse quod ibi nemo bene potest vivere. Et Biordus venit, a Campo, qui similiter alegat non esse modum quod gentes illius exercitus possint supportare tantam incomoditatem et indigenciam nisi aliter provideatur. Quibus dantur bona verba, Et dicitur eis quod bona provisio adhibita est et melius adhibebitur, Et omnino intencionis huius domini esse, quod exercitus stet super terris Inimicorum in tuscia.

[In a postscript] Sencio insuper quod dominus Petrus tantum animo et opere adheret Florentinis, et quod convencio quam fecit cum domino jacobo del Verme pro .xv. diebus fuit pro possendo seminare et pro melius capiendo partitum cum Florentinis. Et quod a paucis diebus citra apud Pisas ad unum miliare, duo corerii huius domini interfecti fuerunt. Et circa xxx^{ta} forensiti et Rebelles Comunis Florencie qui tractabant contra Florenciam Capti fuerunt, Et misi vinculati Florenciam per dictum dominum Petrum.

No. 8

Despatch of Sienese envoys: Milan, 26 October 1392

ASS: Concistoro 1832, no. 4

Magnifici singniori nostri. Giugnemo qui a milano domenica adì xx di questo mese et subito facemo sentire a Pasquino la venuta nostra. Risposeci che 'l farebe sentire al singnore et che quando fusse tempo di poterli parlare ce lo farebe sentire, perchè el singnore cavalcò lunedì seguente a cusaco per fare sue caccie et co lui andò la contessa con tutte le donne sue, a noi fece dire che andassimo là martedì, et che ci darebe audientia, et così facemo. Volse che Pasquino et misser Giovanni da rapolano ci facessero conpangnia, giunti a cusaco, volse el singnore che andassemo alla caccia co lui. scavalcato che fu messo giù a sedere subito ci die audientia, perchè l' ambaxiata vostra con quella riverentia che sapemo tucta et interamente disponemo. el singnore ci vidde molto volentieri et veramente esso intese bene l' effetto di nostra imbaxiata, et parveci che bene notasse le parole usate per missere piero gambacorti. Et Ritratto in sè con un sospiro ci disse, che in tucto era disposto aitare e' suoi figliuoli di Siena et che noi tenessemo per certo che quello che aveva fatto a' sanesi non era disposto a perd[on]arlo; et che sapeva bene quello chella conpangna de' fiorentini veniva a dire, ultimo ci pregò non ci fusse fadigha atendere infine a giovedì seguente et che allora per lo consiglio suo farebe fare risposta. Giovedì in sulla terza el consiglio mandò per noi et in effetto essi riplicaro et affermaro tucto ciò che 'l Signore ci disse, cioè di provedere et aitare e' suoi figliuoli di siena ma che al singnore pareva et così pregava noi che fussemo contenti, che s' atendesse la venuta dell' imbaxiadori fiorentini e de li altri collegati et che sentivano erano a Ferara et che fra otto dì nel più lungo sarebero qua, allora el singnore più utilmente udito et inteso della loro intentione pigliarebe modo all' aiuto nostro. Anco da capo affermandoci esso Singnore provederebe sì in aitarci noi saremo contenti. Allora rispondemo come lo 'ndugio era pericoloso et da capo replicamo tucti e' modi che' Fiorentini tengano con noi, et la generatione della guerra che tacitamente continuo ci fanno et de' trattati et delle conditioni che' Ribelli nostri nostri [sic] fanno contra 'l Regimento somossi e penti dalloro et delle genti de l' armi le quali erano ne' confini nostri, et pensavamo avessero discorso per tutto el nostro contado et con tucte altre ragioni che potemo et sapemo lo demo ad intendare quanto la lungheza del tempo a noi portava pericolo e danno importabile. udito le parole nostre el consiglio si ristrinse insieme et poi ci resposero, chelle parole nostre singnifarebero al Singnore a cusaco et venardì ci farebero risposta. ieri che fu venardì non ci fecero alcuna risposta. sentimo iersera da misser g. da rapolano che 'l singnore aveva diliberato aspettare e' detti imbaxiadori ma che per certo noi tenessimo esso ci aitarebe e per quello che comprendiamo da lui saremo aitati et crediamo l' aiuto sarà di denari. Noi non vediamo che parendo al singnore che attendiamo l' enbaxiate scritte, altro potiamo fare, massimamente comprendendo la sua buona intentione; nondimeno non restaremo a ffare con solicitudine quello che vederemo bisognare intorno alla comessione per voi fatta, et acciò che none abiate amiratione et perchè di tucte delle cose occorenti siate avisati diliberamo mandare questo fante proprio.

Iersera al tardi adì xxv di questo mese, sentimo dal consiglio del Singnore le novità di Pisa, delle quali al parere nostro il consiglio ne mostrò grande allegreza, et in pertanto non sapiamo se questa cagione facesse mutare proposito al singnore, Nè se' fiorentini et gli altri collegati facessero mutare proposito et pensiero, nondimeno noi cercaremo come detto è lo spaccio quanto più ci sarà possibile.

Anco singnori nostri voi sapete e' denari e' quali ci desti e vedete le conditioni che possano essere cagione di soprastare qui più che non pensavate et pertanto vi preghiamo quanto più si può voi diate modo abiamo almeno cento fiorini però che qui non è huomo che ci credesse d' uno quatrino et voi non dovete volere che abiamo vergognia nè pensiamo al comune nostro fusse onore.

Noi pensiamo che doviate sentire che 'l Signore fa fare ora nuovamente una cittadella a milano la quale gira più d' uno miglio et fàlla presso al castello suo di porta giovia et viene nella detta cittadella tucto el borgo di porta vercelina, ongni altro avanzo viene di fuore della città di milano, et ongni giorno vi lavorano più di tremilia persone, e pensa el singnore averlla fatta a pasqua di natale. saràlli di grave spesa.

Quello da mantova sentiamo à messo in ordine rifare il ponte da borgoforte, el signore à fatto providere di fare uno ponte presso a quello a sei miglia pure in sul po et oltre a questo à ordinato di fare uno ponte in sul' olio per lo quale possa colle genti sue intrare in sul mantovano. Ma come detto è le novità di pisa potranno essere cagioni mutare gli animi del uno e del altro. Dat. in milano adì xxvi d' ottobre a vespero.

> Veri d' anbruogio et
> Niccolò piccoluomini vostri ambaxiadori Ivi.

In questa matina adì xxvi del presente mese venne a noi messere g. da Rapolano el quale iersera al tardi tornò dal Singnore da cusaco et disseci come el singnore, misser antonio poro et lui mandava a Pisa per suoi imbaxiadori et che esso misser G. facesse avisato la vostra sengnoria che giunti là fussero due vostre imbaxiatori co le quali delle conditioni occorenti ora di presente a Pisa potessero conferire. Ancho da capo ci disse come el Signore per le conditioni acadute a Pisa diliberava per bene del fatto noi soprastessemo alcuno poccho, confortandoci sempre che in tucto aveva diliberato d' aitarci.

Singnori nostri, noi semo qui et per aventura per la novità detta e' pensieri si mutaranno et pertanto avisateci di quello che volete che noi facciamo per questo fante proprio. Piacciavi far dare a questo fante cinque fiorini d' oro. Dat. a milano adì xxvi d' ottobre a nona per li vostri servidori Veri d' anbruogio et Niccolò piccoluomini vostri imbasciadori Ivi.

Magnifici et potenti singnori nostri singnori priori governatori del comune e popolo della città di siena.

No. 9

Despatch of a Sienese envoy: Pavia, 21 February 1392/3

ASS: Concistoro 1833, no. 106

Magnifici Signori Miei. Da Pisa Scrissi a la magnificienzia vostra quanto alora fu neciesario e per la detta avisai la signoria vostra come ambasciadori del signore misere lo Conte erano andati a Firenze e dissi chi erano, Salvo che scrissi era el vescovo di Pavia e per erore canbiai el nome però che esso vescovo è di Novara, e gli altri so' come scrissi. Somi ingiegnato sapere la cagione di loro andata e domandatone strettamente di vostri cari amici che so' qua, non è honesto domandarne chi sa; e' l tutto quello ne sento è per fare vista di voler fare legha gienerale co' fiorentini e' bolognesi e' loro colegati e sento poichè furo' a Firenze so' andati a bologna, più inanzi non si può nè no si dè scrivare.

A dì .x. del presente per la grazia di dio mi so' ritrovato qua non oste [sic] e' camini pesimi di nevi e d' altre cose asai pure salvi siamo condotti e subito fui con misere G. da rapolano, poi con Pasquino e de la comesione per la signoria vostra a me fatta, da loro presi consiglio essi per loro grazia e per contemplazione di voi Signori e de la vostra comunità mi videro graziosamente e a fede comprendo, mi consigliasero; pol del sicondo dì la sera fatto notte fui a la presenzia del signore e a la sua ecielsitudine sposi quello che per voi enposto mi fu. esso grazioso e benigno padre e Signore per rispetto vostro e de la comunità vostra mi vide volentieri e la risposta sua è graziosa come a bocha per la grazia di dio referirò.

Da poi so' ristato qui alchuno giorno perchè da Pasquino fui consigliato aspettarsi poche però che misere nicolao de' diversi e milano malabarba doveano partire da milano e essere qua e che qua del fatto nostro potrei meglio co loro conferire, essi venoro dopo tre dì. so' poi co loro stato e del fatto de le paghe per la brigata costà condutto n'ò detto a loro quello ch' è stato di bisogno e sollicitatoli Io e fatto altri per me n' à parlato, per infino a qui quelo che da lo' s' è auto si è che per ancho nè noi nè la brigata à ragione domandare denari conciò sia cosa che costà so' venuti le paghe per due mesi e esi ànno voluto sapere quando fu condotta la brigata e come se la signoria vostra a .xx. di gienaio si condusse di che essi dicono che essi so' pagati per infino adì .xx. di marzo e che per ora denari non si dien pagare per questa cagione, e oltre a questo l' usanza del signore come sapete è che' soldati forniti di servire la paga fano canova xx dì e poi ànno l' altra paga e fano che per infino adì xx d' aprile non dovere mandare costà denari, e alegano el signore fa così a tutti e' suoi soldati e dicono el vero apreso che in altre parti non si paga se non a questa usanza o simile ma che niente meno el signore vole che cotesta brigata oltre a l' altre sia ben pagata e così è la verità e ancho essi dicono el simile. e che senza falo nessuno a' tenpi douti come detto è o prima costà sarano le paghe di mese in mese come tocha. ànomi voluto far fare lettere del signore e' l simile da lor parte a la signoria vostra come siate certi al modo detto le paghe veranno ed io per ciercare meglio se possibile fusse che vorei denari o lettere di denari, non ò per anco volute le dette lettere, se si potrà si farà meglio e dove no converà si facci come si potrà. co riverenzia parlando Io so' venuto dal canto vostro di denari sì mal fornito che non si può sofferire el sudore. faràssi per me quelo sare possibile e ingiongnaròmi subito el più che si potrà essere da la vostra signoria.

Di nuovo qua non è alchuna cosa Salvo che a dì due o veramente tre di questo mese si conchiuse legha gienerale da questo Magnifico Signore al comune e dugio di gienova libera a ghuerra e pacie. e' l dugio vechio di gienova cioè misere antoniotto adorno è andato ed è a vinegia però che per la detta lega qui nè ne le terre del signore più stare nè esse nè nesuno loro ribelo e simile ne le terre loro e' ribeli del signore. e questo è ciertissimo e fermo.

Altro al presente no vegho bisogni scrivare se no che Io mi racomando a la signoria vostra, e che vi piaccia fare el salario mio prima che fornisca lo ser[v]izio vostro e di ciò carisimamente vi prego venendo ad altro tempo arei la fadiga e' l dano, non si dè volere per voi, che sete discreti e benigni.

Per lo vostro Servidore Vanni di Ghinuccio
Azoni per la signoria vostra ambasciadore
in Pavia adì xxi di febraio 1392.

Magnifici e potenti Signori Signori priori
governatori del comune e popolo de la
città di Siena Signori Suoi.

No. 10

Despatch of a Sienese envoy: Pavia, 25 May 1393

ASS: Concistoro 1833, no. 13

Magnifici signiori miei. adì xvi di questo mese vi scrissi per lo vostro choriere chome el signore missere lo Conte à mandato Ambrogio da viguardo suo fameglio ben savio e ben sperto in chosì fatti servigi a le genti d' arme che sonno nel [sic] marcha e ne' paesi. E dà stretta comesione a tutti e' chapitani e molti altri e in singularità al Conte d' urbino strengniendoli quanto si può che per amore e gratia di lui non vogliano venire in su vostri terreni e intorno a ciò oporre ultimo de potentia. E pure in quanto questo non si potesse otenere, À in chomesione di cerchare acordo per denari però che ben pare al signiore che venendo si ricevarebe infiniti danni e' quali si voglia per ongni modo cessare se si può. ben credo che loro pensieri non sieno di pagare essi. E pertanto vi ricordo con reverentia che sarebe da mandare uno o più a Perogia o a Urbino o dove a voi paresse più vicino a loro a ciò che' l comesario del signiore avesse con chui conferire senza avere a venire a siena però che in chosì fatte chose el tempo è molto charo.

E chome vi scrissi à mandato a misere Jachomo d' apiano che deba fare a la sua stanzia E de' suoi denari dugento balestrieri a ciò che li posiate avere a' vostri bisogni.

L' inbaxiadori da fiorenza si sonno partiti, misere Filipo corsini se ne va ad avignione, E misere pazino a Fiorenza. ànno parlato per quello ch' io senta de' fatti di questo mencio. El signiore Manda sua imbasciata a fiorenza misere piero da corte e Rugieri chane, a mostrare chome quello che fa el può fare di ragione e no è contra e' chapitoli de la pacie, partiranno domani da qui.

Per l' altra vi scrissi chome e' denari sarebone presti e per questa cagione andai a milano a solicitarli e in efetto non potei ancho fare che venisero. chostoro al vero sonno asai gravati però che ànno

mandato ora di questo dì sesanta milia fiorini in Francia, per la dote
di sua figliuola. Nientedimeno Io so' tornato qua con misere nicholaio
de' diversi e dò fede che tosto li mandaranno. Farònne mio potere
senza indugio.

Qui è una inbasciata de re di Francia ed è un grande signiore e
mostra sia per grandi fatti. Credo partirà domane e alora avarò più
tempo a parlare de' vostri bisongni che in buona fè esso è stato qui
sette dì che continuo sonno stati tutti el consiglio e misere paschuino
in estretti parlamenti.

El signiore scrive a gianni tedossche che li piaccia di lasarvi per
infino fatta stata la sua brigata, La quale avete a' vostri soldi. so' certo
avete auta la letera e ben si vede che vi sarebe malagevole a trovare
ora de l' altre e ancho di qui sarebe tropo duro a trare e' denari per la
prestanza.

A me fu dato a 'ntendere che la cosa sarebe breve da' vostri anti-
cesori, E quanto al fatto de' balestrieri E anco del mandare le page,
E chosa pure da sspacciarsi in corto termine. Ma pensate se io ò aten-
dare qui la rissposta de la marcha, a che ora io ne verò a fine. E pertanto
per dio provedete ch' io ne possa venire senza vostra riprensione. de
l' altre vostre chomesioni v' informarò al mio tornare.

Èmi achaduto a riprichare a la signoria vostra per questi vostri
cittadini che vengono da santo antonio. in Pavia adì xxv di magio.

Per lo vostro servitore Monaldo di mino
umilmente vi si rechomenda.

    [A tergo] Magnifici e Potenti Signiori
    signiori Priori Governatori del chomune e
    Popolo de la città di siena signiori suoi.

No. 11

A Despatch of Sienese envoys: Pavia, 7 June 1395

ASS: Concistoro 1836, no. 43

Magnifici et potentes domini nostri. Giognemo in Pavia adì iiii° del
presente mese di Giugno e subito facemmo sentire a Francesco Barbavara di nostra venuta per pregarlo che quando tempo fusse gli
piacesse adoperare che fussemo a la presentia del nostro Signore. Poi
adì .vi. di questo mandò per noi il Signore Guilielmino D' alesandria
e uno cavaliere honorato e da bene, e subito andammo al castello
d' esso Signore, e come fummo a la camera del Signore uscì fuore Fr.
barbavara e presici per la mano amenò dentro dove il Signore era. el
quale ci vidde gratiosamente e con buono volto e levatosi ritto ci si

fecie a riscontra due passi dimandandoci che è di quelli miey figliuoli
da Siena? per noi gli fu risposto che bene. Et da poi gli sponnemo
l' ambasciata che per la vostra signoria ci fu imposta, la quale intesa
ci rispose prima a la parte de le racomandigie che aveva rachomandata
cotesta città e tutt' i cittadini come propriamente Milano e pavia e
di questo rendessemo ben certi. A l' altre parti ci respose che Noi ne
conferissemo con Pasquino e esso ci darebbe expeditione a' fatti nostri.
E perchè l' ora era tardi non potemmo adì parlare con altri, da poi
questo dì .vii. di Giugno fummo con Pasquino nel castello del Signore
ne la camera del consiglio segreto, e lui per parte de la vostra Signoria
salutammo et gli dicemmo come ci avavate comandato per vostra
parte l' andassemo a visitare e apresso come fu di comandamento del
Signore gli sponemmo tutta l' ambasciata che al dicto Signore avavamo
exposta. esso ci vidde letamente et le visitationi e saluti riceve gratiosamente. a l' altre parti rispose che ne sarebbe col Signore et che prestamente ci farebbe dare spaccio sì che saremmo ben contenti. come le
chose seguiranno più oltre afforzaremo significare a la vostra Signoria.
Qua oltre sono gli ambasciadori da Fiorenza e da bologna con più di
settanta cavalli. credesi vogliano fare legha col Signore. noi per anco
non aviamo sentito altro. Ècci qua il sire di chosi e il gran conestabile
con assai brigate e ogni dì ci s' aspetta imbasciata dello 'mperadore e
già è proveduto...[1] stanze. Altre novelle non ci so' al presente. noi
c' ingiegnaremo prendere spaccio ne le commissioni nostre et tornare
a la presentia de la Signoria vostra. Dat. in Pavia adì vii di giugno iii
Indictione Mccclxxxxv.

Servitores dominationis vestre Cinus Vannis

et Jacobus Bartholomei.

No. 12

Commission of Florentine Ambassadors to Pavia, 13 June 1396

ASF: Dieci di Balìa, Legazioni 2, pp. 25–6

Nota e informatione a voi Messer Palmieri altoviti e Messer Lodovico
degli albergotti di quello che avete a fare col Duca di Milano fatta per
gli dieci della balìa del comune di Firenze adì xiii di giugno Mccclxxxxvi.

Imprima Andrete al detto Duca dove sia. E saluteretelo per parte
del nostro comune affectuosamente. E con lui vi rallegrerete pienamente delle conventioni fatte tra lui e noi e' collegati suoi e nostri

---

[1] A flaw in the paper prevents the figure from being legible.

narrandogli quanto bene utile e sicurtà a lui e a noi e a tutto el paese seguiterà se le dette conventioni e i capitoli di quelle saranno dirittamente come si conviene e come speriamo observate. Confortandolo che faccia che' suoi collegati e adherenti le observino Interamente che di lui ci rendiamo certi. Et noi dalla nostra parte siamo pienissimamente disposti a observarle e così faranno I nostri collegati della qual cosa veggiamo che ne seguirà utilissimo frutto e grande bene del quale Il detto Duca e noi dovremo essere molto contenti.

Di poi gli ridurrete a memoria come Messer Broia e Brandolino del mese d' aprile passato passarono più volte per lo nostro terreno. Et prima combatterono la forteza di Tegoleto del contado d' arezo e rubarono la villa di bestiame e di masserizie e non possendo vincere la forteza fedirono più huomini che la difendeano. Di poi andarono alla pieve a puglia di là da arezo la quale era in forteza. E quella vinsono per forza e tutta la rubarono che era piena di bestiame e di grano e d' altre cose Ivi rifuggite e fedirono e uccisono degli huomini ch' erano nella detta pieve. Di poi andarono in quello d' anghiari e fecion qui zuffa e ruberie, sperando torre per trattato Il nostro castello della pieve a santo Stefano. Ma non venne loro fatto perchè n' avemmo sentimento. E I trattatori furono presi e fattane Justitia. E stati alquanti dì nel paese valicarono poi per la valle di Chio dove fecion molto danno e uccisonvi huomini xvi e molti ne fedirono. E apresso del mese

25 t. di Maggio proximo passato le brigate de' detti Messer broya e Brandolino come che non vi fosse Messer Broia partendosi del terreno d' orvieto cavalcarono furtivamente nel nostro terreno di Montepulciano dove fecion grandissimo danno di bestiame grosso e minuto che predarono e presono ventidue prigioni oltre a molti altri che fedirono. E questo è intervenuto perchè non temavamo tali cose considerando la lettera della sua Magnificentia della quale porterete la copia continente come I detti Messer broia e brandolino erano a' suoi servigi per tutto ottobre proximo e Biordo michelotti per tutto Aprile proximo. E che di loro non bisognava dubitare. E di queste offese vi dorrete con lui non obstante che pensiamo I suoi Ambasciadori co' quali ne facemmo ramarichio gliene debbono avere fatta relatione pregandolo che gli piaccia intorno a ciò provedere con effecto o per lettera o ambasciata che' detti prigioni sieno rilasciati e le cose tolte restituite. Subgiugnendo che di Biordo e sua brigata infino a qui non possiamo altro che lodarci.

Apresso gli direte fraternevolmente I modi che sono stati tenuti per quelli gentili huomini Castellani del Modonese in ribellarsi contro al Marchese loro Signore. E tutto col favore avuto da sua gente sotto nome di cassa o per altro modo e con aiuto di suoi subditi e accomandati, con victuaglia e recepti delle sue terre. Per la qual cosa Il pregherete che si degni provedere per modo che per suoi subditi accomandati o gente o sotto nome di sbanditi o cassi o per altra via non faccino contro al Marchese nè dieno aiuto o favore nè victuaglia a' detti Castellani non obstante che al presente sieno in certo compromesso col Marchese predetto.

Oltre a ciò gli direte che per levare ogni scontentamento al nostro popolo e che ragionevolmente dolere non si possa, gli piaccia provedere con effecto che al nostro comune sia restituito Il Castello di Marciano e di Toppole e Il palazo contro a Lucignano la qual cosa si dee fare perchè ne' capitoli della pace fatta a Genova chiaramente si contiene la detta restitutione doversi fare. E noi sappiamo che se egli vorrà che' l crediamo cele farà restitutione. E anche noi come che ragionevole non sia Ma per amore e piacere e per buona vicinanza faremo tornare a' Sanesi alcune forteze e Jurisditioni le quali per certi de' malavolti si tengono, e con Justitia, faccendo realmente restituire agli usciti di Siena I loro beni come si dee per gli Capitoli della pace. Et in questo adoperate per ogni modo e via che noi riabbiamo le dette castella.

Ancora gli direte che quella cosa che è più utile per observatione delle conventioni e per pace e riposo del paese è di provedere prestamente e con effecto di trarre la gente dell' arme del paese e dissolverla, sì la gente cassa e che si cassasse, E quella che è in Aspetto e suo e nostro per modo e forma convenevole e honesta sì che la detta gente no triboli e guasti Il paese e' suoi e' nostri Amici e vicini. Offerendo che noi dalla nostra parte insieme con lui siamo disposti realmente e dirittamente in questo procedere e così pensiamo che farà egli. E perchè questo porta assai a suo e nostro honore e bene del paese, Il pregherete che gli piaccia in questo dirvi di suo parere e darvi Il modo che gli pare da tenere in tale materia perchè voi avete in commissione, udito il suo parere, di subito significarcelo, e noi anzi che da lui vi partiate vi riscriveremo subitamente per modo che con lui rimarrete d' accordo. E questa non è cosa da guidare con lungheza nè da averne a mandare qua altra ambasciata nè tenerne altra via se non di dirvi Il suo parere e aspettare la nostra risposta la qual pensiamo accordare con lui per vostro mezo saputa la sua Intentione.

Ultimamente Il conforterete e pregherete affectuosamente e con **26.** fraternale carità che gli piaccia le dette cose per voi domandate e dette volere fare e consentire. E disporsi realmente a vivere con noi e co' nostri in pace e sanza alcun velamento per modo che suspetto alcuno non ci abbia a essere. Mostrandogli che noi veramente e sanza fictitione siamo di questa medesima dispositione proferendo la nostra comunità al suo suo [sic] stato e grandeza essere apparecchiata e pronta.

Ancora perchè 'l duca ci à scripto dolendosi che Messer Bartolomeo da prato e Antonio degli Opizi e loro brigate ànno predato Il suo territorio di Reggio e di suoi accomandati dalla Mirandola direte che questa è cosa quando udimmo che ci dispiacque infino al cuore, e fu contra alla expressa volontà de' nostri Magnifici fratelli bolognesi e nostra, e fatto s' è ogni cosa perchè le bestie tolte si restituissono. E tutti I prigioni furono lasciati. E chiaretelo che' detti Capitani non ànno con noi a fare alcuna cosa Se non solamente se noi avessimo bisogno di loro che sieno tenuti venire a' nostri soldi conducendoli e dando loro I nostri danari. E questo ci fu forza a fare perchè 'l conte Giovanni ragunava e avea ragunata molta gente per offenderci. E ànno promesso in modo di compagna non offendere nè cavalcare Il terreno del detto duca. Di che ànno fatto contro alla loro promessa e sacramento di che ci duole quanto più può. Ma questi sono de' modi della gente d' arme la qual non cerca se non d' acceder fuoco e far male. E questo s' è veduto per Messer Broia e Brandolino nelle offese che ci ànno fatte de' mesi passati, e anche nell' anno passato essendo a suo aspetto. E siamo certi ogni cosa essere stata contro alla volontà del detto Duca. E di questa materia v' informate bene a bologna.

Se vi dicesse de' fatti di Jacopo da Montepulciano di farlo lasciare, risponderete che come a' suoi Ambasciadori fu detto, noi di ciò siamo bene disposti. Ma di fatto non si può fare per più cagioni. Ma noi speriamo e rendiamci certi che crescendo l' amore e la carità tra lui e noi, come crediamo, di questo e dell' altre cose si faranno I suoi piaceri a luogo e a tempo.

Informatevi bene dello stato del detto duca e delle sue terre e de' suoi subditi e de' suoi modi e conditioni, E d' ogni novella che potete sentire, e aviseretecene.

Farete la via da bologna. E sarete con gli antiani e co' dieci I quali manderanno insieme con voi loro ambasciadori. E mosterrete loro la vostra commissione sì che insieme vi conformiate in quello che avrete a dire e fare.

Ancora direte loro come sentiamo di certo secondo che abbiamo fatto loro significare che' l conte Giovanni da barbiano con sua brigata à ricevuto danari e dee Ire subito a' danni de' lucchesi a petitione de' loro usciti per trattato che ànno in terre de' lucchesi. E dee passare il detto Conte giovanni per le terre de' nobili da Foglano. E pertanto gli pregherete che a questo provegghino per modo che' l detto conte giovanni non sia lasciato passare nè altri che andasse a' danni de' lucchesi.

Oltre acciò per[chè] noi sentiamo che a reggio si raguna brigata di gente cassa del duca di Milano, vogliamo che vene informiate a bologna e per lo camino sì che se bisogna parlarne col duca, il facciate.

A mantova raccomanderete al Signore I fatti del fratello e nipote d' arrigo di ser filippo di ser piero musani.

Abbia a mente che il dì che tornerete &c.

No. 13

Paris, *Bibliothèque nationale: nouvelles additions latines,*
vol. 1152, pp. 45t–46t

Magnifico Francisco de Barbavariis

Omnis actio Magnifice domine que a ratione suscipitur a definitione proficisci debet, Tullius inquit. Quis enim finis dabitur paucis pauperibus Civibus et Comitativis Papie vestris servitoribus, qui solverunt quousque facultas eis suppetere potuit, qui rerum et bobum robarias innumeras et lectorum sub asta venditione et carceris penam tulerunt, nonnullis Civibus et incollis dicte Civitatis, in fantium sinu ridentibus; qui ditiores, et numero plures, nichil solvunt, nichil voluerunt inter tantum guerrarum pondus et belli strepitum, non pulsati pro subsidio subvenire? Hii totiens cruciati Cives cogentur hanc patriam deserere, quo fiet ut insueti ad onera substinenda ponere colla jugo, stimulis pongentibus assuescent posse tantis presentibus et futuris dispendiis providere, nullo huius Civitatis maiorem quam nunc publice impense sarcinam supportante. Quis non honestius, Quis non utilius judicabitur? Lucida res et ultima vestris occulis preposita est, et omnes dicere musant, hoc sepius contingit, rem nulli obscuram, honestam et utillem pro statu Clarissimi principis nostri Ducis Mediolani &c. Papie ac Virtutum Comittis, et huius Civitatis aut omnino negligunt exequi aut pede claudo retardant. Ait Virgilius: Scinditur incertum studia in contraria vulgus. Ordo fochum iam precogitatus est, iam Magnificentie vestre prepositus, sanctum et venerandum opus, videntur maiori focho floreni xxv et minori florenus unus, ex hac serie alma contingere. Sic omnes velle deberent huic saluberrime dispositione, ex qua intentum suum princeps noster Inclitus obtinebit, ex qua tota hec Civitas letabitur, et eius melior fiet condicio non expectata prece, non requisitione, sua sponte mentem deflectere. Credendum est hanc Inventionem rerum potissimam partem, gratiam divini spiritus in illum tam salutiferi facti Inventorem mirabiliter influxisse. Quanta fuerit Civium letitia, dum noverint comunis impense laborem iustis partibus coequatum! Tanto maior dolor est, cum vident ex una eadem vicinia Alterum tueri, alterum cruciari, Sedicio pariter et discordia, que hac in patria nunc ex ordine infando vigent ex sancta fochum dispositione tollentur, Inclita si quidem fama tante rei vires, hinc et illinc acquirens liquidumque per aera volans, perpetibus penis, sic Regiis tectis et casurum eluminibus, nunciabit, Illustrissimus princeps dux Mediolani Papie ac Virtutum Comes, Civitatem et Comittatum suum papie, omissis infandi usibus Regio ritu fochum institutione gubernat. Hec urbs nobilis et antiquissima, de fletibus in risum, de merere in gaudium, de formidine in securitatem, his modis beatissimis convertetur, predo civilis de urbano luco diffugiet, nec amplius satelites de pauperibus manus quot horis pegionum violentia suggent, quem opportebat miserrimam feminellam, tot lacrimis, tot ab amicis hostiis querere ne lectuli termina robarentur. Ex quo civitas hec, ex procelosis fluctibus in tranquillum portum, ex tanto ventorum turbine in gratiosum reductum, curru fochum levissimo deducetur finaliter, ab ethne monte longius collocabitur. Non est vir, sed agros ubera admoverunt, qui prohibet contradicit, et obstat, nec hec totius huius populi Papiensis divina exequatur opinio, in tantum nostri principis usum perventura. Non est amicus nec diligit statum dominationis qui his ceptis non annuit, qui mecum non est, contra me est. Agrediamini vos o cara dei soboles, magnum nostris horis incrementum, et amplectemini hos eternorum fochum sanctissimos fasces harum rerum exordia literis aureis ad gloriam vestri devotissimi nominis effingentur. Nunc vestro auxilio consiliove cernetur, nobis parta quies. Nunc vestigia mala dissolvent! Nunc pavore pulso sperare salutem incipiemus, hoc rectum et laudabile fuerit ingens emolumentum, decus et ornamentum principi nostro, natisque suis Illustribus et natis natorum et qui nascentur ab illis, et Intrate ordinarie huius civitatis incredibiliter ex his annalia augmenta succedent. Excellentiam igitur vestram in qua plene confidimus, et spes tota nostra consistit, piis precibus cogimur exorare ut vices vestras apud gloriosum principem nostrum dignemini oportunis maturatis aditibus experiri, quod huiusmodi almus ordo fochum omnium salus debitum sortiri effectum vestris bonis operibus cognoscatur hec principi nostro non est meta sed ordo. Nam quotiens vigentibus necessitudinibus pro deffensione patrie totiens in manibus suis Imperium est, et nos sumus et erimus semper parati Iussa capescere semper avere et personas et filios proculdubio exposituri. Quod enim in decus et utile principi nostro et toti Civitati sequetur, quod omnis Nobilitas urbis et plebis optat, non sine numine dei putamus debere quadam felicitate concedi.

Compillata per Sabastianium de Georgiis de Papia,
Anno domini Mccclxxxx°viii. die penultimo mensis Martii.

No. 14

Commission of an embassy from Florence to Venice, 5 July 1398

ASF: Signoria, Legazioni ɪ, pp. 115–17

Brieve ricordo a voi Messer Bartholomeo popoleschi e Filippo di Gucciozo ambasciadori a Vinegia fatta &c. adì .v. di luglo Mccclxxxxviii.

El vostro fine è conducervi a Vinegia e quando serete là salutarete quella signoria e ringratiaretela di quanto n'à facto sì della triegua nella quale siamo certi sono stati di puro buono e sincero animo e simile del grande servigio di pagare tanta pecunia per noi. E che non si turbino nè meraviglino se nel rendere come siamo tenuti s'è avuta alcuna tardità. Imperò che per levarci le genti da dosso e contentare e' nostri caporali ci è convenuto e conviene pagare tanta somma di denari che serebbe uno stupore a dirlo e che noi abbiamo fatto chon la loro amicicia confidentemente e che piaccia loro sopportarci un poco e averci per scusati. E che noi daremo ordine averanno loro dovere.

Poi direte come possono comprendere che 'l duca di Melano è venuto su questa triegua chon molta malicia e chon occulto suo vantaggio, selle cose rimanesseno così. Imperò che aquistando chon segreto modo e pacto tanto e di terreno e di potentia quanta è quella degl' ubertini e di quelli conti li quali sono tutti nostri cittadini e racchomandati lunghissimo tempo fa, troppi ci getterebbe mala ragione. E veramente nè triegua nè pacie nè altra concordia potrebbe mai esser buona se noi non riavessemo nostro honore e nostra ragione. E ch' elli è pure una cosa fuori d' ogni ragione che nel far della triegua e sotto questa coverta elli ci vogla torre tanto di paese e di gente non essendovi mai dato uno colpo della spada. E che si costoro si fussono scoperti per sua parte come dice in secreto avere convenuto e patteggiato, noi abbiamo sì loro le mani in capo che in meno d' uno mese, avesse soccorso quanto volesse, gl' averemmo sì gastigati che si seriено pentiti di loro follia. E qui direte loro voglino averci sì l' occhio che si conservi nostro honore. Et per giustificatione di ciò direte che volendo egli la triegua non si intendesse per coloro non ratificasseno imperò che si poteva lasciare da alcuna delle parti uno o più le quali non essendo nella triegua avrebbe potuto fare guerra, tutto si levò via. Quanto maggiormente serebbe posto rimedio che niuno potesse dare per suo seguace o racchomandato se non coloro che pubblicamente fossono nella guerra e usati essere dalla sua parte? Sì che si vuole avere a questo fatto tale e sì fatto consiglio non ne segua nostro mancamento o vergogna. E di questa materia debba loro ricordare che' nostri ambasciadori ne parlarono specialmente e chiaramente dicendo non si consentirebbe mai che 'l duca desse per suoi adherenti alcuno de' nostri maxime perchè tutti costoro sono suti dalla nostra parte contra 'l duca, e mai non sono stati contra noi come è detto. E quando serete a Bologna fate ne facciate doglienza chon loro in forma sia nostro honore.

115t. Poi venite a quelli capitoli esso à mandati de' quali portate la copia sopra ci fatti delle compagne, e direte che 'l primo capitolo che parla di non tenere gente in aspetto serebbe di troppo grande pericolo a tutta la lega, considerato che 'l duca tiene sempre grandissima quantità di gente a soldo e puote in uno punto assalire qual vuole. E se noi non avessimo presto ricorso e certo d' avere giente per resistere a sue malicie serebbe uno poter perdere di leggiere in uno punto nostro stato. E che questo tener in aspetto non è provisione gente d' arme si potesse mantenere a campo nè cagione di fare o di mantenere compagne; e oltra ciò, è uno sicurarsi da loro, che venendo alle redemptioni che schifar non si possono si spende molto più. Sì che torre via questo non è se non farsi preda delle compagne. Et avere gente in aspetto è sicurtà contra 'l nimico, e levare via le redemptioni. Imperò che chi sta in aspetto non puote nè debba offendere e chi non è in aspetto non rimane potente da offendere nè da fare rimedire. Sì che conchiudete a questo ch' eglino ci prendano buon partito. E pare a noi che poichè 'l duca dice è disposto a pacie, e noi, nè crediamo alcuno collegato, non siamo per dinegarla, ma per volerla largamente, pure ch' ella sia honesta sicura e ragionevole, che si possa al presente porre silentio su questa parte. E venire a dare ordine e principio d' attendere alla pacie e allora, e di questo e d' ogni altra cosa, si potrà seguitando pacie, o rimanendo pure nella triegua, ragionare e chon gl' ambasciadori del duca e di tutti gl' altri collegati si potrà di ciò e d' ogni altra cosa prendere buon partito. E però avisi la signoria quando s' abbi a mandare per questa cagione e noi siamo presti per la nostra [parte] mandare e praticarla pure in conspetto della loro signoria e non altrove. Dicendo che adunando per la pacie s' ella non seguisse serebbe una meza rottura. Et che almeno si potrà in confermatione della triegua conchiudere e praticare di questo e non parrà la cosa così rotta, ma più tosto confermata.

El secondo capitolo di non lasciar fare compagne è buono sancto e giusto. E lo quale noi siamo sempre presti non solo consentire per scrittura ma observare senza obligatione se extrema necessità non cene costrignesse, com' alcuna volta facciendo el nimico compagna ci è suto necessità di farne. Et elli alcune volte chon noi à tenuto trattato di rischiere le compagne e come noi l' abbiamo fatto dalla nostra parte sempre egli fattosi beffe di noi e non fattolo egli.

El terzo capitolo è di natura, che volendolo noi observare non 116.
troveremmo mai gente a soldo e serebbe impossibile observarlo e ben
lo cognosce egli, ma sì nel primo e sì nel terzo capitolo astutamente
cerca o di legarci a cose impossibili o che siano di nostro disfaccimento
e singular pregiudicio.

......Omissis......

Sopra' fatti di quelli conti potete dire come conviene che 'l duca si
rechi o a ragione o fondisi sulla guerra. A ragione non ànno potuto
quagli antichi nostri racchomandati essendo obbligati al comune,
liberarsi a loro posta. Sì che a ragione non potendosi costoro essersi
racchomandati a lui in nostro preiudicio non gl'à potuti ricevere. Della
guerra non à potuto nè puote far fondamento, con ciò sia cosa che mai
non si sieno scoperti a guerra se non per la nostra parte. Et non è
convenevole la triegua s' intenda se non per coloro che sono in guerra
o notoriamente seguaci di chi à avuta la guerra.

......Omissis......

A vinegia farete in singularità querimonia della novità fatta al 117.
Conte Anthonio da Montegranelli come verrete per la copia della
lettera avuta sopra ciò la quale sia qui soscritta. E mostrarete come
chiaro si puote dire la triegua esserci rota se 'l duca di melano vuole
ostenere che quelli conticelli sieno suoi seguaci o racchomandati.
Conchiudendo che piaccia loro significarlo e volere o che el duca gli
lasci stare e non s' impacci de' fatti loro, o stare contento ch' eglino
s' intendano nostri come di ragione sono, che sappiamo bene non
intende rompere triegua.

No. 15

Commission of Florentine envoys to Venice: 7 April 1400

ASF: Signoria, Legazioni 2, pp. 30t–33

Nota et Informatione a voi Messer Filippo magalotti e Nicholò di
G. da uzano Ambasciadori a Vinegia, facta &c. Adì vii d' aprile
M.iiiiC.

Quando sarete a Vinegia insieme con messer Bartolomeo e chon
andrea visitarete la signoria, e facto le salutationi verrete dolcemente
e chon amichevoli parole a dire quanto di confidentia sempre abbiamo
avuta e abbiamo in quella inclita Signoria, Sì perchè la conversatione
de' nostri mercatanti n' è cagione e molti servigi facti hinc inde, Sì
perchè al temporale che occorre ci pare necessario qualunque in italia
attende a vivere libero s' intendano insieme, e che l' uno abbi cura, e

gelosia dello stato e conservatione dell' altro. Et come che questo
tocchi a molti pure ci pare singolarmente, riguardi la loro Signoria, e
la nostra. Imperò che qualunche di noi mancasse di suo stato, non è
vero l' altro possa difendere Il suo, dicendo che vivere pure a speranza
di dio ed aspectare dio provegha, ci pare sia cagione di grandissimo
pericolo. E che ben sappiamo lo nimico della libertà non puote sempre
vivere ma che chi in questo mezzo la perdesse starebbe inforsi di
raquistarla, Et non sarebbe senza singulare et inextimabile danno e
disfacimento di chi la perdesse.

Di poi verrete a narrare come la nostra signoria venne in lega chon
loro solo per questa difesa. E che tutto per honore della loro signoria,
come si conviene fusse per strictura consentito, potesseno fare pacie
triegua e ogni altra concordia paresse loro, pure fu detto per loro a
parole che fra gli amici debbono essere più che carta, e così speravamo,
che per la loro signoria niente si farebbe senza consentimento de'
collegati e in singularità della nostra signoria. Et come queste per
guido di messer tommaso e altri ci fu detto, lo credemmo e rendemmoci
certi così dovesse seguire. Ora come ne' facti della triegua e ultimamente della pacie si vede, non che noi siamo suti contenti, o cosa
di che potessimo e dovessimo essere consolati, ma pure el formare de'
capitoli ci è suto occulto ne' quali come si vede e in facto e in ragione
sono commessi non piccoli errori, e tutto intervenuto per non essere noi
alla pratica. Et ben à sempre potuto vedere la signoria, che noi
vogliamo e desideriamo pace e che la guerra n' è grave, ma pure la
vorremmo tale fusse pacie, la più vera e migliore si potesse e che 'l
31. nostro popolo avesse a sperare observantia   e fede, e ancora, che non
ci fusse vergogna nè mancamento di nostre ragioni, e tale pacie mai
non fu che si denegasse. E qui venite a dire quanto è di mancamento di
nostro honore che del castello di castiglione tolto a tradimento al conte
Antonio e disfacto nel tempo della triegua non si sia facta alcuna
restitutione, o mentione di ristituire, avendo el loro ambasciadore
factone larghe promesse che tutto si ristorrebbe. Simile che nostro
castello di collelungo non s' abbi a rendere come noi abbiamo a rendere
ad altrui. E se si volesse dire, che 'l duca si scusa chon allegare abbi
promesso a' pisani di mantenerli in tutto quello possedevano questo
non è vero nè ragionevole. Imperò che collelungo non è loro, nè fu
mai. Et che nè piombino nè l' elba nè parecchie altre terre de' pisani,
elli non à mantenute loro E che del nostro nè puote nè debba fare promessa. duolci ancora che avendo noi a riavere secondo la pacie di
gienova Marciano e toppole, eglino ce n' abbino sospesi diecie anni. Et
oltra ciò la Forteza del calcione che' sanesi tolsono al nostro accom-
mandato Dego talomei e che si richiese nominatamente, non ne sia

fatta mentione come di berignone. Et quello abbiamo a rendere infino a una bertesca sia suto nominato.   E che tutti rianno el loro, e guadagnano di questa pacie, noi soli ne vegnamo a perdere e honore e ragione.

Duolci ancora cordialmente, e di questo tutto 'l nostro popolo ne mormora gravissimamente, che nel facto di quelli Conti e gentiliuomini di casentino si sia facto giudice el duca di melano lo quale è parte, e cosa toccha a lui et che contra ogni ragione di facto furo messi nella triegua et ora nella pacie inchiusi chon tanto nostro mancamento e di nostre ragioni. Et dicono tutti, la lega cho' Vinitiani si fecie a difesa e mantenimento de' collegati, ora è questo della difesa e mantenere nostre ragioni? Che dove sono tenuti mettere la spada, non ànno voluto mettere le parole quanto bisognava. Et dal picciolo al grande tutti sanno dire, che non era bisogno strigner così questa pacie essendo in triegua, la quale non era meno sicura che la pacie. Sì che ben si poteva questa cosa indugiare e chon buon modo ridurre le cose al dovere, e maxime in quello non si poteva ragionevolmente negare. Ora siamo messi in pacie chon quegli traditori e ribelli nostri, e lo richiedere nostre ragioni,   e conviene fare al nostro nimicho, questo   31 t. è sì grave cordoglio che niuno ne puote rimanere nell' animo suo contento.

Dolgonsi ancora che nel prohemio della pacie apparisca, chella loro excellentia sono capo della lega, di questa pacie abbino gravato e pregato el duca di melano, Et ch' ella si sia tractata nella camera sua. Questo suona sì male nell' orecchie di tutti quanto dire si puote. E pare a ciascuno grande abbassamento e mancamento d' onore di quella signoria e di tutta la lega, conchiudendo che per queste cose tutte e per molt' altre si potrebbeno dire, publicamente si dicie noi siamo vituperati. Et ècci tolta ogni riputatione, a dire che noi abbiamo a rendere infino a una bertesca ciò ch' abbiamo guadagnato, e noi perdiamo collelungo, le ragioni nostre contra quelli Conti e' Ubertini e debbiamo aspettare a quello per la pacie di genova ci debbe essere renduto .x. anni. Et che per questa ragione e perchè qua non si può credere sia suto chon proposito di torci le nostre ragioni piaccia loro procurare queste cose s' acconcino. E lievisi via le cagioni delle murmurationi e scontentamenti, che non crediamo se 'l vorranno adoperare da dovero non ottengano molto maggior facto; e che buona è la pacie, ma non è nulla se non ve ne puote essere buona volontà. Ora tutte queste cose oltra quello che messer Bartolomeo e andrea ebbeno in nota, dirte, parlandone non obstante quanto detto n' abbiamo, e dolcie, e pugniente come vederete la materia richiega a ben del facto e a nostro honore. E questo rimettiamo in voi.

Se vengono a muoversi ad alcuna cosa, sollecitatelo e sforzatevi trarlo innanzi quanto più si potete.

Se rimanesseno pure in lloro usata durezza, provato ch' averete ogni cosa: Et anchora se pure dicesseno di fare quanto potesseno, in ogni caso dopo queste doglenze e ogni loro risposta, venite chon loro a dire com' eglino veggiono el nimico sotto la triegua quanto s' è facto grande in toscana. E che elli à messo e facto di qua questa compagna di messer Ottobuono terzo e di ceccolino. E che eglino ànno cavalcato, facto ricomperare e oppressato el signore di Fuligno nostro accomandato, e tutto dì oppressano. Et che simile fanno a città di castello dove abbiamo cinquanta lancie, e ingegnansi di tirarli dalla parte del duca, e torci ogni nostro amico e accomandato, Et in singularità el signore di cortona. Et tutto dì ladroncelli vengono sul nostro terreno di nocte, e rubano e anco uccidono, e poi si riducono sul loro terreno, e quando le

32. cose se richeggiono niuno nostro sottoposto per loro ingiuste ripresaglie vi puote usare, nè ricoverare el suo. Et è tanta questa noia e persecutione che fanno disperare tutti nostri sudditi. E se su per lo terreno loro, alcuno nostro è trovato si è preso; e veggiamo di largo, che di giorno in giorno crescerà questa lebbra in forma che porta pericolo che nostri sudditi per straccha e come disperati non si mettano ad abbandonare le terre, o forsi a fare peggio per non potere fare altro. Et che per niuno modo veggiamo di potere stare così. E per questa cagione piaccia loro volere provedere, per forma che questo non sia, e che questa pacie la quale per loro rispetto siamo acconci ad observare ci sia pacie. E perchè considerato che questo tiranno mai non observa alcuna cosa se non quanto ben gli mette, e non si cura di rompere sua fede, e che tutto dì essendo la triegua à tenuti trattati nelle nostre terre, e grandi e piccioli e mette in questo tanto spendio e sollecitudine, che come che per la gratia di dio infino a qui abbiamo ritrovato trattato in saminiato, in arezo, in Montepulciano, in Volterra e in Pietrabuona pure potrebbe essere una volta loro facto cosa, che serebbe troppo nociva come intervenne di monteluco la bernardenga, che costò più di fiorini .xxx. M a raquistare. E trovòssi chiaro per quelli furono presi, tutto e donde ebbe principio, che fu nel suo luogotenente in siena. Non pensorono noi ci mettessimo a riaverlo. Et perchè sempre ci à rotto ogni accordo e pacie e lega c' è rotto la triegua in mille modi, e offesoci gravamente come averete in nota. E poichè noi veggiamo questi segni ci pare essere certi ch' elli un dì a sua posta e maxime potendo fare qualche gran tracto, ci rompa la pacie. E che voglino aver el pensiere ci provedere a questo, e mettere un poco sè nello stato e luogo nostro e fare conto s' elli avesse tolto Mantova Ferrara e Padova, quello ne parebbe loro e quanto vorrebbeno e serebbe ragione noi facessimo per

loro. Et considerare che tutto suo studio e pensiero è direto in toscana e contra noi, che se ci si potesse levare dinanzi, si vede venire signore del tutto senza resistenza. E che se ci vedesse e uniti e in concordia insieno chon loro e chon gl' altri collegati, da dovero, e proveduti e anco forti, esso per paura di sè, si ritirerà adietro. E che non pensino mai nell' animo suo sia contento, che la loro signoria gli tolse di mano Mantova, e che facessino liga contra lui, tutto ch' esso simili e facci vista di 32 t. non vedere. E per questa cagione serebbe necessario acciò che la pacie stia ferma e observisi, noi fortificassimo la lega di tal compagnia ch' elli avessi materia di stare a' termini suoi e venire a quanto bisogna per lo presente e per lo futuro. Et se mosso fusse per messer Bartolomeo e per Andrea, entrate sul ragionamento d' ostericchi e di savoia. E se mosse non fusse, fate d' indurgli a pratica de' rimedi. E se non si movessono egli, movetelo voi, o fate muovere a quello di Padova che sempre n' è suto di buono animo e intorno acciò adoperate quanto possibile sia.

Et perchè questo è solo per lo futuro, per lo presente a riparare a' fatti e circamenti suoi di qua, e acciò che come è decto la pacie ci sia attenuta, vogliamo introduchiate questa materia meglio che saprete in modo voglino in nome della lega e a comune spesa di tutti, mettere in toscana solo per guardia e difesa e non per altro quella giente fusse abastanza, sì che elli vedesse avere a fare chon tutta la lega e non pure chon noi. E se venisseno a voler sapere quanta giente bisognerebbe direte loro ch' elli à in questi paesi fra di soldo e in compagna più di .M. lancie e infinita gente da piè. Et che vegghino quello bisogna mettere contra questo. E nella fine venite a dire non possa essere meno di .v. C lancie e .v. C balestrieri non tanto per riparo quanto per dimostratione e non per difesa [sic] d' alcuno ma solo per sicurtà e difesa. Et in queste leghe e provedimento di gente, vi fermate e stringetevi quanto n' è possibile rescrivendone ciò che seguita di questa materia. Et se da queste cose si dilungasseno, direte come la nostra signoria e tutto 'l nostro popolo non sperava questo anzi ci rendiamo certi che a questi provedimenti sarebbeno più pronti e voluntarosi di noi considerato così ne sono tenuti per fede, e ancho perchè la nostra difesa è la loro medesima dicendo come voi ne scriverete loro risposta, E che questo sia uno mectere in disperatione el nostro popolo, e riputarsi in tutto abbandonato, e essere dato in preda al tiranno. E questo e ogni altra parola sia utile al facto direte. Venendo a chiedere uno grande numero di pregati nel quale tutto ordinamente direte. Scrivendoci ogni cosa come detto n' abbiamo.

Ora conchiudendo voi siete savii vedete quanto ne dichiamo, e sapete quello ne bisogna, sì che fate e adoperate ogni cosa vedete sia bene e utile e honore della nostra signoria.

33.   L' altre cose ebbeno in commissione messer Bartholomeo e Andrea anco sollecitate insieme con lloro come vedete ben sia; e ogni cosa sempre abbiate con lloro chon voi e tutti e' quactro seguite la pratica e questi facti quanto vedete ben sia.

Scriveteci spesso quanto fate e ogni cosa che occorre, anchora per fante proprio se fusse cosa lo meritasse.

A bologna e a Ferrara visiterete quelle signorie e Salutarete per nostra parte facciendo loro le profferte si convengono e di vostra andata e della ragione perchè siete mandati, parlatene come vederete che sia bene.

Simile se 'l Signore di Padova o di Mantova fussono o venissono a Vinegia, parlate colloro, visitateli e salutategli come parrà alla prudentia vostra sia nostro debito e honore.

Abbiate a mente &c.

No. 16

Extracts from a despatch of the Florentine envoys in Rome: 9 August 1402

ASF: Legazioni e Commissarie, 7 bis, p. 2 & t

E non maravigliate Signori se' l Papa e questi suoi fratelli furono tanto caldi al principio e ora sono così raffredati, imperò che come vi dicemmo per altro, il veschovo di Cervia venne qua ambasciadore di Carlo malatesti. E diceva venire a proferire lui e' fratelli al servigio del Papa. E poi sentiamo chiaro è venuto a petitione del ducha a trattare accordo col Papa. E che l' acordo è per fermo, cioè che 'l ducha non renda, ma lasci libera Perugia e 'l papa gli conceda non vicariato ma in titolo di marchionato, o di ducato, Bologna. E questo trattato cominciò più mesi fa, e soprasedette alla nostra mandata. E allora già è uno mese fu eletto ambasciadore el quale sappiamo per andare a concludere questo. E di ciò crediamo dire vero perchè l' abbiamo da più fidedegnissimi. ora veduto non avere darci quello vuole, sentiamo domane o l' altro parte questo ambasciadore col vescovo di cervia, e vanno a carlo, e carlo debba andare al ducha a fermare questo. Apresso sentiamo di certo che 'l duca à mandato qua lettere a certi mercatanti melanesi per le quali comanda loro che parlino al Papa, dolendosi della legha cercha con noi, e che allui serà di necessità cerchare de' rimedii e in effetto minatoria contro al Papa. ...da altra parte pensiamo per segni veggiamo che tutto questo sia fatto ad arte, il fine ce 'l mosterrà, ma è tanta la incostantia loro che non si possiamo fermare a nulla. Gl' ambasciadori dello re ànno sentito tutto da altri che da noi. E pare loro udite le difficultà che noi ragionevolmente spicciamo, e pur veggendo la pertinacia di costoro, E considerando il frutto debba riuscire di questo, dicono che se 'l papa non volesse   venire a questa lega che lo 2t. re è disposto farla egli e in persona venire e per la libertà fare quello ànno fatto i suoi passati. E che questo facciate noto alla signoria vostra, e che ci abbiate buona diliberatione, e rispondiatene, sì che tornando allo Re, venuta la vostra risposta che l' attendono, possiano referire quanto ne risponderete. Rendendosi certi che venendo lo re in legha con voi, di necessità il papa converrà venire. Apresso si sono cordialmente doluti con noi, che della rotta e perdita di bologna niente per lo nostro comune fu mai scritto alla maestà reale, quasi accennando che voi non abbiate quella confidentia e speranza in lui che siamo certi avete...due sono le difficultà, il perchè questo fatto rimane. L' una perchè 'l Papa vuole abbiate di tassa più 500 lance di lui, l' altra che conduciate le Mille lance, delle quali di sopra diciamo. non sappiamo come gente è condotta o resta a condurre....Piaccia...rispondere... E non consentendo costoro a quello scriverete, quello abbiamo a fare. ...lo stare qua a essere tenuti a parole non ci pare honore della signoria vostra....questi ragionamenti sono tutti menati senza notitia de' Cardinali,...ed essendo il fatto della importanza che è, l' ànno avuto a male forte, e la maggiore parte di loro ànno proferto a noi venire nella presenza del papa e nostra, e a parole dire e con scrittura confermare questa lega essere necessaria a tuto e salute di santa chiesa. Apresso messer G. [Giovanni Tomacelli, the Pope's brother] s' aveva messo d' animo venire capitano generale come v' abbiamo detto, ora questi ambasciadori dichono tutto fuori che lo re dice vuole venire in persona, e non vuole essere sotto altri....Lo Veschovo di Firenze ricevute le vostre lettere à in questi fatti operato con somma diligentia, e simile il cardinale de' gaietani e Guasparre coscia e maestro Antonio predetti. ...E perchè la cosa è tanto necessaria, ne siamo confortati da messer conte di carrara, e da tutti gl' amici vostri sì che per dio come per altri n' abbiamo detto abbiate l' ochio a prendere tale partito che il pentire non segua....

BIBLIOGRAPHY[1]

(a) CHRONICLES, AND OTHER HISTORIES OF THE PRE-MURATORIAN PERIOD

AMMIRATO, SCIPIONE. *Istorie Fiorentine;* parte prima, tomo secondo, con l' aggiunte di Scipione Ammirato il Giovane (Firenze, 1647).

"Annales Forolivienses": a cura di Giuseppe Mazzatinti, in *RIS* NS XXII, 2.

"Annales Mediolanenses", in *RIS* XVI.

"Annales Sanenses", in *RIS* XIX.

BENVENUTO DI SAN GIORGIO, Conte di Biandrate. "Historia Montisferrati", in *RIS* XXIII.

BRUNI ARETINO, LEONARDO. "Historiarum Florentini Populi, Libri XII", a cura di Emilio Santini, in *RIS* NS XIX, 3.

"Chronicon Bergomense Guelpho-Ghibellinum", auctore Castello de Castello, in *RIS* XVI.

"Chronicon Estense", in *RIS* XV.

"Chronicon Placentinum", auctore Johanne de Musso, in *RIS* XVI.

"Chronicon Siculum Incerti Authoris", ed. Giuseppe de Blasiis, and published by the Società Napolitana di Storia Patria: *Monumenti Storici,* serie I, Cronache (Napoli, 1887).

"Chronicon Tarvisinum", auctore Andrea de Redusiis de Quero, in *RIS* XIX.

"Chronique du religieux de St Denys, contenant le règne de Charles VI": publiée par M. L. Bellaquet, in the *Collection de documents inédits sur l'histoire de France* (Paris, 1840 sqq.).

CONFORTO DA COSTOZA. "Frammenti di Storia Vicentina", a cura di Carlo Steiner, in *RIS* NS XIII, 1.

CORIO, BERNARDINO. *Storia di Milano,* riveduta e annotata da Butti e Ferrario, vol. II (Milano, 1856).

"Corpus Chronicorum Bononiensium", a cura di Albano Sorbelli, in *RIS* NS XVIII, 1, vol. 3.

DATI, GREGORIO. "*Istoria di Firenze*" dal 1380 al 1405, ed. Luigi Pratesi (Norcia, 1904).

DELAYTO, JACOBO. "Annales Estenses", in *RIS* XVIII.

[1] This is not intended to be an exhaustive bibliography of Visconti history. I have included in it only the works to which I have had occasion to refer in the footnotes to this book.

374   *BIBLIOGRAPHY*

DELLA CHIESA, GIOFFREDO. "Cronaca di Saluzzo", in *Monumenta Historie Patrie: Scriptorum*, tomus III (Torino, 1848).

"De Rebus Estensium", edito per cura di Carlo Antolini, in *Monumenta Ferrariensis Historie: Scriptores*, fasc. 2. Estratto dagli Atti della Deputazione Ferrarese di Storia Patria (Ferrara, 1901).

"Diario d' Anonimo Fiorentino dall' anno 1358 al 1389", ed. Alessandro Gherardi, in *Documenti di Storia Italiana*, VI: Cronache dei Secoli XIII e XIV (Firenze, 1876).

"Diurnali detti del Duca di Monteleone", a cura di Federigo Faraglia, published by the Società Napolitana di Storia Patria: *Monumenti Storici*, serie I, Cronache (Napoli, 1895).

FROISSART, JEAN. *Les Chroniques*, ed. Kervyn de Lettenhove, tomes X–XVI (Bruxelles, 1871–2).

GATARI, GALEAZZO E BARTOLOMEO. "Cronaca Carrarese, confrontata con la redazione di Andrea Gatari", a cura di Antonio Medin e Guido Tolomei, in *RIS* NS XVII, 1.

GHIRARDACCI, CHERUBINO. *Della Historia di Bologna*, parte seconda (Bologna, 1657).

GIOVIO, PAOLO. *Vite duodecim Vicecomitum Mediolani Principum* (Lutetie, 1549).

GOBELINUS. *Cosmodromion, in lucem editum studio et opere Heinrici Meibomii* (Francoforti, 1599).

GRAZIANI. "Cronaca detto Diario", in *ASI* XVI, 1 (1851).

GRIFFONI, MATTEO. "Memoriale historicum de rebus Bononiensibus", a cura di Lodovico Frati e Albano Sorbelli, in *RIS* NS XVIII, 2.

LE FÈVRE ÉVÊQUE DE CHARTRES, JEAN. *Journal*, publié par Henri Moranvillé (Paris, 1887).

LIBERATI, A. "Frammento di una Cronica Sanese del 1390", in *BSSP* XVII (1910).

MALAVOLTI, ORLANDO. *Historia de' fatti e guerre de' Sanesi;* la seconda parte (Venetia, 1599).

MATTIOLO, PIETRO DI. *Cronaca*, pubblicata da Corrado Ricci (Bologna, 1885).

"Memorie Storiche della Città e dell' antico Ducato della Mirandola", pubblicate per cura della Commissione Municipale di Storia Patria della Mirandola: vol. I, *Cronaca delle Mirandola* (Mirandola, 1872).

MINERBETTI. "Cronica volgare di Anonimo Fiorentino dall' anno 1385 al 1409 già attribuita a Piero di Giovanni Minerbetti", a cura di Elina Bellondi, in *RIS* NS XXVII, 2.

MORELLI, GIOVANNI. *Cronica*, published with the *Istoria Fiorentina di Ricordano Malespini* (Firenze, 1718).

MORELLI, GIOVANNI. "Ricordi fatti in Firenze", in *DET* XIX (Firenze, 1785).

PELLINI, POMPEO. *Dell' Historia di Perugia*, 2 vols. (Venetia, 1664).

PITTI, BUONACCORSO. "Cronica, con annotazioni, ristampata da Alberto Bacchi della Lega", in the *Collezione di Opere inedite e rare* (Bologna, 1905).

PLATINA (BARTHOLOMEO SACCHI CREMONESE). "Historia Urbis Mantue", in *RIS* xx.

POGGIO BRACCIOLINI. "Historia Florentina", in *RIS* xx.

PORCACCHI, TOMMASO. *Historia dell' origine et successione dell' Illustrissima famiglia Malaspina* (Verona, 1585).

POSSEVINUS, ANTONIUS. *Gonzaga* (Mantue, 1628).

RONCIONI, RAFFAELLO. "Delle Istorie Pisane Libri XVI", in *ASI* VI, 1 (1844).

SALVIATI, JACOPO. "Cronica, o Memorie", in *DET* XVIII (Firenze, 1784).

SARDO, RANIERI. "Cronaca Pisana", in *ASI* VI, 2 (1845).

SERCAMBI, GIOVANNI. "Le Cronache", a cura di Salvatore Bongi, published by the Istituto Storico Italiano, in the *Fonti per la Storia d' Italia*, vols. XIX–XXI (Roma, 1892).

SOZOMENO PISTOIESE. "Specimen Historie", in *RIS* XVI.

STELLA, GIORGIO. "Annales Genuenses", in *RIS* XVII.

"Vita Caroli Zeni", in *RIS* XIX.

(b) COLLECTIONS AND INDICES OF LETTERS AND DOCUMENTS

ACHERY, LUC D'. *Spicilegium*, vol. III (Parisiis, 1723).

Antiqua Ducum Mediolani Decreta (Mediolani, 1654).

L'Archivio Gonzaga di Mantova (Pubblicazioni della R. Accademia Virgiliana di Mantova: series I, Monumenta):
Vol. I: a cura di Pietro Torelli (Ostiglia, 1920).
Vol. II: a cura di Alessandro Luzio (Verona, 1922).

AZZI VITELLESCHI, G. degli: "Le Relazioni tra la Repubblica di Firenze e l' Umbria nel secolo XIV, secondo i documenti del R. Archivio di Stato di Firenze" (Appendix to vol. x of the *Bollettino della R. Deputazione di Storia Patria per l' Umbria*).
Vol. I: *Dai Carteggi* (Perugia, 1904).
Vol. II: *Dai Registri* (Perugia, 1909).

BIGAZZI, PIETRO. *Firenze e Milano; Saggio di lettere diplomatiche del secolo XIV e XV* (Nozze Arese-Serristori. Firenze, 1869).

Capitoli del Comune di Firenze: Inventario e Regesto, tomo primo, ed. Cesare Guasti (Firenze, 1866); tomo secondo, ed. Alessandro Gherardi (Firenze, 1893).

Carteggio di Paolo Guinigi, a cura di L. Fumi e Eugenio Lazzareschi. This forms vol. XVI, pt. 1 of the *Memorie e Documenti della Storia in Lucca*, and vol. III of the *Regesti del R. Archivio di Stato in Lucca* (Lucca, 1925).

"Commissioni di Rinaldo degli Albizzi", vol. I: ed. Cesare Guasti, in *Documenti di Storia Italiana*, I (Firenze, 1867).

"Il Copialettere Marciano della Cancellaria Carrarese, 1402–3", a cura di Ester Pastorello, published by the Deputazione Veneta di Storia Patria: *Monumenti Storici*, serie I (Documenti), vol. XIX (Venezia, 1915).

CORDERO DE PAMPERATO, S. "La dernière campagne d'Amédée VI, comte de Savoie, 1382–3", in *Revue Savoisienne*, XLIII (Annecy, 1902).

DOUËT D'ARCQ, L. *Choix de pièces inédites relatives au règne de Charles VI*, publiées pour la Société de l'Histoire de France, tome I (Paris, 1863).

DUMONT, JEAN. *Corps universel diplomatique du droit des gens*, tome II, partie 1 (Amsterdam and la Haye, 1726).

"Eporediensia. Documenti e Studi sulla Storia d' Ivrea", in the *Bibliotheca della Società Storica Subalpina*, vol. IV (Pinerolo, 1900).

GABOTTO, FERDINANDO. "Documenti Inediti della Storia di Piemonte al tempo degli ultimi Principi di Acaia (1383–1418)", in *MSI* XXXIV (3, III, 1896–7).

GUASTI, CESARE. *Ser Lapo Mazzei; Lettere di un Notaro a un Mercante del Secolo XIV*, 2 vols. (Firenze, 1880).

Inventari e Regesti del R. Archivio di Stato in Milano.

Vol. I: *I Registri Viscontei*, ed. Cesare Manaresi (Milano, 1915).

Vol. II: *Gli Atti Cancellereschi Viscontei*; parte seconda, Carteggio extra Dominium, ed. Giovanni Vittani (Milano, 1929).

Vol. III: *I Registri dell' Ufficio degli Statuti in Milano*, ed. Nicola Ferorelli (Milano, 1920).

LA TRÉMOILLE, GUY DE. *Livre des Comptes*, 1395–1406, publié d'après l'original par Louis de la Trémoille (Nantes, 1887).

LUCCA. *Inventari del R. Archivio di Stato*, pubblicati per cura della R. Sopraintendenza Generale agli Archivi Toscani, vol. I (Lucca, 1872).

—— *Regesti del R. Archivio di Stato*, vol. II (Carteggio degli Anziani) parte 2 (dall' anno 1369 all' anno 1400), raccolto e ordinato da L. Fumi (Lucca, 1903).

LÜNIG, JOANNES CHRISTIANUS. *Codex Italie Diplomaticus*, 4 vols. (Francofurti et Lipsie, 1725–1735).

MAIOCCHI, RIDOLFO. *Codice Diplomatico dell' Università di Pavia*, published by the Società Pavese di Storia Patria, vol. I (Pavia, 1905).

MARTÈNE ET DURAND. *Veterum Scriptorum et Monumentorum... amplissima collectio*, tomus I (Parisus, 1724).

MORBIO, CARLO. *Codice Visconteo-Sforzesco, ossia Raccolta di Leggi, Decreti e Lettere famigliari dei Duchi di Milano* (Milano, 1846).

MOTTA, EMILIO. "Documenti Visconteo-Sforzeschi per la Storia della Zecca di Milano", in *Rivista Italiana di Numismatica*, VI (1893).

MUGNIER, FRANÇOIS. "Lettres des Visconti de Milan et de divers autres personnages aux Comtes de Savoie, 1360–1415", in *Mémoires et Documents* publiés par la Société Savoisienne d'Histoire et d'Archéologie, XXXIV (2ème série, IX, Chambéry, 1895).

OSIO, LUIGI. *Documenti diplomatici tratti dagli Archivi Milanesi*, vol. I (Milano, 1864–5).

PALACKY, FRANZ. "Über Formelbücher, zunächst in Bezug auf böhmische Geschichte, nebst Beilagen", Zweite Lieferung, in *Abhandlungen der Königlich-Böhmischen Gesellschaft der Wissenschaften*, 5, V, for 1847 (Prag, 1848).

"Parlamento Friuliano, parte seconda", per cura di Pietro Silverio Leicht, in the *Atti delle Assemblee Costituzionali Italiane* (published by the R. Accademia dei Lincei), serie prima, sezione 6 (Bologna, 1925).

PELLEGRINI, D. FRANCESCO DE. "Documenti Inediti relativi al Dominio dei Visconti sopra Belluno e Feltre dal 1388 al 1404", in *AIV* 3 XIII and XIV (1867–8).

PREDELLI, RICCARDO. "I Libri Commemoriali della Republica di Venezia; Regesti, tomo III", published by the Deputazione Veneta di Storia Patria: *Monumenti Storici*, serie I (Documenti), vol. VII (Venezia, 1883).

Repertorio Diplomatico Visconteo: Documenti raccolti e pubblicati in forma di regesto dalla Società Storica Lombarda, 1263–1385, 2 vols. (Milano, 1911–8).

ROMANO, GIACINTO. "Regesto degli Atti Notarili di C. Cristiani, dal 1391 al 1399", in *ASL* XXI, 2 (1894).

ROUSSET DE MISSY, JEAN. *Supplément au corps universel diplomatique du droit des gens*, tome I, partie 2 (Amsterdam and la Haye, 1739).

RTA. Deutsche Reichstagsakten, ed. J. Weizsäcker, published by the Königlich-Bayerische Akademie der Wissenschaften, vols. III–V (Munich and Gotha, 1867–85).

SALUTATI, COLUCCIO. "Epistolario", a cura di Francesco Novati, published by the Istituto Storico Italiano, in the *Fonti per la Storia d' Italia*, vols. XV–XVIII (Roma, 1891–1911).

SANTORO, CATERINA. "I Registri dell' Ufficio di Provvisione e dell' Ufficio dei Sindaci sotto la dominazione Viscontea"; vol. I of *Inventari e Regesti dell' Archivio Civico del Comune di Milano* (Milano, 1932).

—— "Il Registro di Giovannolo Besozzi, Cancelliere di Giovanni Maria Visconti, con appendice di altri atti Viscontei", published as *Analecta Trivultiana*, I (Milano, 1937).

SARACENO, FILIPPO. "Regesto dei Principi di Casa d' Acaia, 1295–1418", in *MSI* XX (2, V, 1882).

SAUERLAND, H. J. "Aktenstücke zur Geschichte des Papstes Urban VI", in *Historisches Jahrbuch*, XIV (München, 1893).

SEGRE, ARTURO. "I Dispacci di Cristoforo da Piacenza Procuratore Mantovano alla Corte Pontificale", in *ASI* 5 XLIV (1909).

THEINER, AUGUSTIN. *Codex diplomaticus Dominii temporalis Sancti Sedis*, vol. III (Roma, 1862).

VERGERIO, PIER PAOLO. "Epistolario", a cura di Leonardo Smith, published by the Istituto Storico Italiano, in the *Fonti per la Storia d' Italia*, vol. LXXIV (Roma, 1934).

ZAMBECCARI, PELLEGRINO. "Epistolario", a cura di Lodovico Frati, published by the Istituto Storico Italiano, in the *Fonti per la Storia d' Italia*, vol. XL (Roma, 1929).

(c) OTHER WORKS

ANSELMI, GASPARE. *Della Vera Origine del Duomo di Milano, finora attribuita a Gian Galeazzo Visconti; Rivendicazione al Popolo Milanese* (Milano, 1881).

ANZILOTTI, ANTONIO. "Per la Storia delle Signorie nel Diritto pubblico Italiano del Rinascimento", in *SS* XXII (1914).

ARGELATI, FILIPPO. *De Monetis Italie*, pars tertia (Milano, 1750).

BARBIERI, GINO. *Economia e politica nel ducato di Milano, 1386–1535* (Milano, 1938).

BATTISTELLA, ANTONIO. "I Lombardi in Friuli", in *ASL* XXXVII, 2 (1910).

BELTRAMI, LUCA. "Storia documentata della Certosa di Pavia". Vol. I: *La fondazione e i lavori sino alla morte di Giangaleazzo Visconti, 1389–1402* (Milano, 1896).

BESTA, ENRICO. "La Scuola giuridica Pavese nel primo secolo dopo la istituzione dello studio generale", in *Contributi alla Storia dell' Università di Pavia pubblicati nel XI Centenario dell' Ateneo* (Pavia, 1925).

BETTONI, COUNT F. *Storia della Riviera di Salò*, vol. III (Brescia, 1880).

BIANCHETTI, ENRICO. *L' Ossola Inferiore*, 2 vols. (Torino, 1878).

BISCARO, GEROLAMO. "Il Banco Filippo Borromei e Compagni di Londra, 1436–9", in *ASL* XL, 1 (1913).

BOITO, CAMILLO. *Il Duomo di Milano e i disegni per la facciata* (Milano, 1889).

BOLOGNINI, GIORGIO. "Le Relazioni tra la Repubblica di Firenze e la Reppublica di Venezia nell' ultimo ventennio del secolo XIV", in *NAV* IX (1895).

BORSA, MARIO. *La Caccia nel Milanese dalle origini ai giorni nostri* (Milano, 1924).

—— "Un Umanista Vigevanesco del secolo XIV (Uberto Decembrio)", in *Giornale Ligustico*, XX (1893).

BORSIERI, GIROLAMO. *Il Supplimento della Nobiltà di Milano* (Milano, 1619).

BOSDARI, FILIPPO. "Il Comune di Bologna alla fine del secolo XIV", in *AMR* 4, IV (1914).

—— "Giovanni I Bentivoglio, Signore di Bologna, 1401–2", in *AMR* 4, V (1915).

BOSELLI, GIOVANNI VINCENZO. *Delle Storie Piacentine*, tomo II (Piacenza, 1804).

BOUCHOT, HENRI. "I Primitivi Francesi, 'l'ouvraige de Lombardie'", in *l'Arte*, VIII (1905).

BRUNETTI, MARIO. "Nuovi Documenti tratti dall' Archivio di Stato di Venezia; figli e nipoti di Bernabò Visconti", in *ASL* XXXVI, 2 (1909).

CAGGESE, ROMOLO. *Classi e Comuni Rurali nel Medio Evo Italiano*, vol. II (Firenze, 1909).

CALVI, GIROLAMO L. *Notizie sulla vita e sulle opere dei principali Architetti, Scultori e Pittori che fiorirono in Milano durante il governo dei Visconti e degli Sforza*, parte I (Milano, 1859).

CAMUS, JULES. "La Maison de Savoie et le mariage de Valentine Visconti", in *BSBS* IV (1899).

—— "La Venue en France de Valentine Visconti Duchesse d'Orléans", in *MSI* XXXVI (3, V, 1900).

CAVALCABÒ, AGOSTINO. "Un Cremonese Consigliere Ducale di Milano", in *BSCr* II (1932).

CENA, ERNESTA GEROLA. "Il Ponte Visconteo presso Bassano", in *Bollettino del Museo Civico di Bassano*, V (1908).

CERUTI, ANTONIO. *I Principi del Duomo di Milano sino alla morte del Duca Gian Galeazzo Visconti* (Milano, 1879),

CESSI, BENVENUTO. *Venezia e Padova e il Polesine di Rovigo* (Città di Castello, 1904).

CESSI, ROBERTO. "La Politica Veneziana di terra firma dalla caduta dei Carraresi al lodo di Genova", in *MSF* v (1909).

—— "I Problemi monetari Veneziani fino a tutto il secolo XIV", published in *Documenti Finanziari della Repubblica di Venezia*, serie 4, vol. I (Padova, 1937).

—— "La Regolazione delle entrate e delle spese", in the same publications, serie 1, vol. I, parte 1 (Padova, 1925).

—— "Venezia e la prima caduta dei Carraresi", in *NAV* NS XVII (1909).

—— "Venezia neutrale nella seconda Lega anti-Viscontea (1392–1397)", in *NAV* NS XXVIII (1914).

CHAMPION, PIERRE. *Vie de Charles d'Orléans* (1394–1465), in the *Bibliothèque du xve siècle, XIII* (Paris, 1911).

CIAPESSONI, P. "Per la Storia della Economia e della Finanza Pubblica Pavesi sotto Filippo Maria Visconti", in *BSP* VI (1906).

CIBRARIO, GIOVANNI ANTONIO LUIGI. *Della Economia Politica del Medio Evo*, Libri III (Torino, 1839).

—— *Memorie Storiche, opere minori* (Torino, 1868).

—— *Operette e Frammenti Storici; il Conte Rosso* (Firenze, 1856).

—— *Opusculi Storici e Letterarii* (Milano, 1835).

CIRCOURT, ALBERT DE. "Le Duc Louis d'Orléans, frère du roi Charles VI", in *RQH* XLII–XLVI (1887–1889).

CLEMENTINI, CESARE. *Raccolto Istorico della fondatione di Rimino, e dell' origine e vite de' Malatesti*, vol. II (Rimino, 1627).

COCHIN, HENRI. "Jean Galéaz Visconti et le Comté de Vertus", in *ASL* XXXII, 1 (1905).

COGNASSO, FRANCESCO. *Amedeo VIII* (1383–1451), 2 vols. Collana Storica Sabauda (Torino, s.d.).

—— "Aneddoti di Storia Viscontea", in *BSP* XXV (1926).

—— *Il Conte Rosso* (1360–1391). Collana Storica Sabauda (Torino, s.d.).

—— "Note e Documenti sulla formazione dello Stato Visconteo", in *BSP* XXIII (1923–4).

—— "Ricerche per la Storia dello Stato Visconteo", in *BSP* XXII (1922).

COGO, G. "Il Patriarcato d' Aquileia e le aspirazioni de' Carraresi al possesso del Friuli, 1381–1389", in *NAV* XVI (1898).

COLLAS, ÉMILE. *Valentine de Milan, Duchesse d'Orléans* (Paris, 1911).

COLLINO, GIOVANNI. "La Guerra Veneto-Viscontea contro i Carraresi nelle relazioni di Firenze e di Bologna col Conte di Virtù", in *ASL* XXXVI, 1 (1909).

COLLINO, GIOVANNI. "La Guerra Viscontea contro gli Scaligeri nelle relazioni ", &c. in *ASL* xxxiv, 1 (1907).

—— "La Politica Fiorentino-Bolognese dall' Avvento al Principato del Conte di Virtù alle sue prime guerre di conquista ", in *MAT* 2, liv (1904).

—— "La preparazione della Guerra Veneto-Viscontea contro i Carraresi nelle relazioni ", &c. in *ASL* xxxiv, 2 (1907).

COMANI, F. E. "Sui dominî di Regina della Scala e dei suoi figli; indagini critiche ", in *ASL* xxix, 2 (1902).

—— "I Denari per la dote di Valentina Visconti ", in *ASL* xxviii, 1 (1901).

—— "Usi Cancellereschi Viscontei ", in *ASL* xxvii, 1 and 2 (1900).

CORBELLINI, ALBERTO. "Appunti sull' Umanesimo in Lombardia ", in *BSP* xv–xvii (1915–1917).

CUSIN, FABIO. *Il Confine Orientale d' Italia nei secoli XIV e XV*, vol. i (Milano, 1937).

—— "L' Impero e la successione degli Sforza ai Visconti ", in *ASL* NS i (1936).

CUTOLO, ALESSANDRO. *Re Ladislao d' Angiò-Durazzo*, 2 vols. (Milano, 1936).

DE BOÜARD, MICHEL. "L'Empereur Robert et le grand Schisme d'Occident, 1400–3 ", in *MAH* xlviii (1931).

—— *La France et l'Italie au temps du grand Schisme d'Occident; les origines des guerres d'Italie* (Paris, 1936).

DELAVILLE LE ROULX, J. "Un anti Grand-Maître de l'Ordre de St Jean de Jérusalem, arbitre de la paix conclue entre Jean Galéas Visconti et la République de Florence, 1391–2 ", in *BEC* xl (1879).

—— *La France en Orient au XIVe Siècle; Expéditions du Maréchal Boucicault*, vol. i, in the *Bibliothèque des Écoles françaises d'Athènes et de Rome*, fasc. 44 (Paris, 1886).

DEL GIUDICE, PASQUALE. *Nuovi studi di Storia e Diritto* (Milano, 1913).

DE MARCO, E. "Crepuscolo degli Scaligeri: la Signoria di Antonio della Scala, 1381–1387 ", in *Archivio Veneto* 5, xxii and xxiv (1938–9).

DE NOLHAC, PIERRE. *Pétrarque et l'humanisme, d'après un essai de restitution de sa Bibliothèque*, published in the *Bibliothèque de l'École pratique des hautes études: Sciences philologiques et historiques*, fasc. 91 (Paris, 1892).

DURRIEU, PAUL. *Les Gascons en Italie* (Auch, 1885).

382   *BIBLIOGRAPHY*

DURRIEU, PAUL. "Michelino da Besozzo et les relations entre l'Art italien et l'Art français à l'époque du règne de Charles VI", in *Mémoires de l'Institut national de France: Académie des Inscriptions et Belles-Lettres*, XXXVIII, 2 (Paris, 1911).

—— "La prise d'Arezzo par Enguerrand VII Sire de Coucy", in *BEC* XLI (1880).

—— *Le Royaume d'Adria* (Paris, 1880, and in *RQH* for that year).

EGGER, JOSEF. *Geschichte Tirols von der ältesten Zeiten bis in die Neuzeit*, Band I (Innsbruck, 1872).

ERCOLE, FRANCESCO. "Comuni e Signori nel Veneto", in *NAV* NS XIX (1910), also republished in:

—— *Dal Comune al Principato; Collana Storica* (Firenze, 1929).

FABRETTI, ARIODANTE. *Biografie dei Capitanei venturieri dell' Umbria*, vol. I (Montepulciano, 1842).

FAVALE, SARAH. "Siena nel quadro della Politica Viscontea nell' Italia Centrale", in *BSSP* XLIII (NS VII, 1936).

FERRAI, L. A. "La Politica di Giangaleazzo Visconti nei rapporti diplomatici coi Valois nei primi anni del suo Principato", in *ASI* 5, XXII (1898).

FORMENTINI, MARCO. *Il Ducato di Milano* (Milano, 1877).

FRANCESCHINI, GINO. "Giangaleazzo Visconti arbitro di pace fra Montefeltro e Malatesti, 1384–8", in *ASL* NS III (1938).

—— "La Politica di Giangaleazzo Visconti, le milizie italiane e i rapporti Visconti-Montefeltro", in *Atti del Primo Congresso Storico Lombardo in 1936* (Milano, 1937).

FRATI, LODOVICO. "La Guerra di Giangaleazzo Visconti contro Mantova nel 1397", in *ASL* XIV (1887).

—— "La Lega dei Bolognesi e dei Fiorentini contro Giangaleazzo Visconti, 1389–1390", in *ASL* XVI (1889).

—— "Una Raccolta di lettere politiche del secolo XIV nella Biblioteca Municipale di Bologna", in *ASI* 5, XI (1893).

GABOTTO, FERDINANDO. "L' Età del Conte Verde in Piemonte secondo nuovi documenti", in *MSI* XXXIII (3 II, 1895).

—— *Gli Ultimi Principi d' Acaia e la politica Subalpina dal 1383 al 1407* (Torino, 1898).

GALANTINO, FRANCESCO. *Storia di Soncino, con documenti*, vols. I and III (Milano, 1869–70).

GALLI, E. "Facino Cane e le guerre Guelfo-Ghibellini nell' Italia Settentrionale, 1360–1400", in *ASL* XXIV, 1 and 2 (1897).

GALLI, GIUSEPPE. "La Dominazione Viscontea a Verona, 1387–1404", in *ASL* LIV (1927).

BIBLIOGRAPHY 383

GIORGI, FRANCESCO. "Alberico e Giovanni da Barbiano nel Bolognese; Ricerche e documenti", in *AMR* 3, XII (1895).

GIULINI, GIORGIO. *Memorie spettanti alla Storia, al governo, ed alla descrizione della Città e della Campagna di Milano*, vols. XI–XII (Milano, 1771). (Vols. II–III of the *Continuazione delle Memorie*.)

GOZZADINI, GIOVANNI. *Nanne Gozzadini e Baldassare Cossa* (Bologna, 1880).

GREGOROVIUS, FERDINAND. *History of the City of Rome in the Middle Ages*, translated from the fourth German edition by Annie Hamilton, vol. VI, pt. 2 (London, 1898).

GRIMALDI, NATALE. *La Signoria di Barnabò Visconti e di Regina della Scala in Reggio*, 1371–1385 (Reggio, 1921); and a review by Alessandro Visconti, in *ASL* XLIX (1922).

GUICHENON, SAMUEL. *Histoire généalogique de la royale Maison de Savoye; nouvelle édition*, 4 vols. (Turin, 1778–80).

HELMOLT, HANS FERDINAND. *König Ruprechts Zug nach Italien* (Jena, 1892).

HUBER, ALFONS. *Geschichte Oesterreichs*, Band II (Gotha, 1885).

JARRY, EUGÈNE. "Actes additionnels au contrat de mariage de Louis d'Orléans et de Valentine Visconti", in *BEC* LXII (1901).

—— *Les Origines de la domination française à Gênes*, 1392–1402; *documents diplomatiques et politiques* (Paris, 1896); and a review by Romano in *ASL* XXIV, 1 (1897).

—— *La Vie politique de Louis de France, Duc d'Orléans*, 1372–1407 (Paris, 1889).

—— "La Voie de Fait et l'alliance Franco-Milanaise", in *BEC* LIII (1892).

KURZ, ALBRECHT. *Oesterreich unter Herzog Albrecht IV*, Band I (Linz, 1830).

LABANDE, EDMOND-RENÉ. "Le rôle de Rinaldo Orsini dans la lutte entre les Papes de Rome et d'Avignon, 1378–1390", in *MAH* XLIX (1932).

LANDOGNA, FRANCESCO. "Maestro Marsiglio di Santa Sofia e Giangaleazzo Visconti", in *BSP* XXXIII (1933).

—— *La Politica dei Visconti in Toscana* (Città di Castello, 1929).

LATTÈS, ALESSANDRO. "Degli antichi Statuti di Milano che si credono perduti", in *Rendiconti del R. Istituto Lombardo di Scienze e Lettere*, 2, XXIX (1896).

—— *Il Diritto Consuetudinario delle città lombarde* (Milano, 1889).

—— *Studii di Diritto Statutario* (Milano, 1886).

LEADER, G. TEMPLE and GIOVANNI MARCOTTI. *Giovanni Acuto (Sir John Hawkwood); Storia d'un Condottiere* (Firenze, 1889).

LEROUX, ALFRED. *Nouvelles recherches critiques sur les relations politiques de la France avec l'Allemagne de 1378 à 1461* (Paris, 1892).

LEVI, EZIO. "Francesco di Vannozzo e la lirica nelle corti Lombarde durante la seconda metà del secolo XIV", in *Pubblicazioni del R. Istituto di Studi Superiori in Firenze*, vol. XXXIV (Firenze, 1908).

—— "Medesina da Desio cortigiano di Bernabò Visconti", in *ASL* XXXIV, 2 (1907).

LICHNOWSKY, FELIX. *Geschichte des Hauses Habsburg*, vols. IV and V (Wien, 1839–1841).

LINDNER, THEODOR. "Geschichte des deutschen Reiches unter König Wenzel" (being the first part of *Geschichte des deutschen Reiches vom Ende des vierzehnten Jahrhunderts bis zur Reformation*), 2 vols. (Braunschweig, 1875–1880).

—— "Die Schlacht bei Brescia in October, 1401 (zur deutschen Geschichte in fünfzehnten Jahrhundert)", in *Mittheilungen des Instituts für Oesterreichische Geschichtsforschung*, Band XIII, Heft 3 (Innsbruck, 1892).

LONATI, GUIDO. *Stato Totalitario alla fine del secolo XIV; illustrazione storica di un Codice Bresciano di Decreti Viscontei.* Supplemento ai Commentari dell' Ateneo di Brescia per il 1935 (Toscolano, 1936).

LUZIO, ALESSANDRO. "I Corradi di Gonzaga, Signori di Mantova", in *ASL* XL, 1 and 2 (1913).

LUZZATTO, GINO. "Il Debito Pubblico nel sistema finanziario Veneziano dei secoli XIII–XV", in *NRS* XIII (1929).

MAGENTA, CARLO. *I Visconti e gli Sforza nel Castello di Pavia, e loro attinenze con la Certosa e la Storia Cittadina*, 2 vols. (Milano, 1883).

MAIOCCHI, RIDOLFO. "Francesco Barbavara durante la Reggenza di Caterina Visconti", in *MSI* XXXV (3, IV, 1899).

—— "Lo Scisma d' Occidente e Giangaleazzo Visconti", in *Rivista di Scienze Storiche*, II (Pavia, 1905).

MANCARELLA, ANDREA. "Firenze, la Chiesa, e l' avvento di Ladislao di Durazzo al trono di Napoli", in *ASN* XLIV–XLVI (NS V–VII, 1919–21).

MANFREDI, GIUSEPPE. *Storia di Voghera*, ristampata (Voghera, 1908).

MANFRONI, CAMILLO. *Colonizzatori Italiani*, vol. II (*Dal secolo XIV al XVI*), published in the collection l' *Opera del Genio Italiano all' Estero*, serie dodicesimo (Libreria dello Stato, 1933).

—— "La Crisi della Marina Militare di Venezia dopo la guerra di Chioggia", in *AIV* 8, XII, 2 (1909–10).

MEDIN, ANTONIO. "Le Rime di Bruscaccio da Rovezzano", in *Giornale Storico della Letteratura Italiana*, XXV (1895).

—— "I Visconti nella poesia contemporanea", in *ASL* XVIII (1891).

MEYER, ALFRED GOTTHOLD. *Lombardische Denkmäler des vierzehnten Jahrhunderts* (Stuttgart, 1893).

—— *Oberitalienische Frührenaissance; Bauten und Bildwerke der Lombardei*, 2 vols. (Berlin, 1897–1900).

MIRA, GIUSEPPE. "Provvedimenti viscontei e sforzeschi sull' arte della lana in Como, 1335–1535", in *ASL* NS II (1937).

MIROT, LÉON. "Un Document inédit sur la rencontre de Valentine Visconti et des Seigneurs de Milan avec Louis d'Anjou, en juillet 1382", in *BSBS* XVII (1912).

—— *La Politique française en Italie de 1380 à 1422*; pt. 1, les préliminaires de l'alliance florentine (Paris, 1934).

MONE, FRANZ JOSEPH. "Zur Handelsgeschichte der Städte am Bodensee vom 13 bis 16 Jahrhundert", in *Zeitschrift für die Geschichte des Oberrheins*, IV (Karlsruhe, 1853).

MOTTA, EMILIO. "Le Relazioni dei Conti di Werdenberg-Sargans coi Duchi di Milano", in *Bollettino Storico della Svizzera Italiana*, IX (Bellinzona, 1887).

MUIR, DOROTHY. *A History of Milan under the Visconti* (London, 1924).

MULAZZANI, CONTE GIOVANNI. "Studii economici sulle Monete di Milano", in *Rivista Italiana di Numismatica*, I (Milano, 1888).

MURATORE, DINO. "Bianca di Savoia e le sue nozze con Galeazzo II Visconti", in *ASL* XXXIV, 1 (1907).

—— "La Nascita e il Battesimo del Primogenito di Giangaleazzo Visconti, e la Politica Viscontea nella primavera del 1366", in *ASL* XXXII, 2 (1905).

MURATORI, LODOVICO ANTONIO. *Delle Antichità Estensi Continuazione, ossia seconda parte* (Modena, 1740).

NASALLI ROCCA DI CORNELIANO, EMILIO. "I Decreti Signorili Viscontei e Sforzeschi e il Diritto agrario", in *Atti del Primo Congresso Storico Lombardo in 1936* (Milano, 1937).

NAVA, AMBROGIO. *Memorie e documenti Storici intorno all' origine, alle vicende ed ai riti del Duomo di Milano* (Milano, 1854).

NOVATI, FRANCESCO. "Aneddoti Viscontei", in *ASL* XXXV, 2 (1908).

—— "Per la Cattura di Bernabò Visconti", in *ASL* XXXIII, 1 (1906).

—— "Un Frammento di Zibaldone Cancelleresco Lombardo del primissimo Quattrocento" (in collaboration with Attilio Antonielli), in *ASL* XL, 2 (1913).

—— "Le Querele di Genova a Giangaleazzo Visconti", in *Giornale Ligustico*, XIII (1886).

NOVATI, FRANCESCO. "Trattative di Giangaleazzo Visconti con Condottieri di Ventura durante la guerra contro Antonio della Scala", in *ASL* XXXIX, 2 (1912).

OLIVI, L. "Del Matrimonio del Marchese Niccolò III d'Este con Gigliola figlia di Francesco Novello da Carrara", in *AMM* 3, V (1888).

PAGNINI DELLA VENTURA, GIOVANNI FRANCESCO. *Della Decima e delle altre Gravezze della Moneta, e della Mercatura de' Fiorentini, al secolo XVI*, tomo secondo (Lisbona e Lucca, 1765).

PALMIERI, ARTURO. "La Congiura per sottomettere Bologna al Conte di Vertù", in *AMR* 4, VI (1916).

PANCOTTI, VINCENZO. *I Paratici Piacentini e i loro Statuti*, 2 vols., in the *Biblioteca Storica Piacentina*, vols. XIV and XV (Piacenza, 1925–1927).

PASCHINI, PIO. *Storia di Friuli*, vol. III, 1381–1797, in the *Collezione "Forum Julii"* (Udine, 1936).

PASTORELLO, ESTER. *Nuove Ricerche sulla storia di Padova e dei Principi da Carrara al tempo di Giangaleazzo Visconti* (Padova, 1908).

—— "I Preliminari della pace fra Milano e i Carraresi nel 1402", in *NAV* NS XXII (1911).

PEZZANA, ANGELO. *Storia della Città di Parma, continuata*, vols. I and II (Parma, 1837).

PIATTOLI, RENATO. "Di un Ignoto Tentativo di Giangaleazzo Visconti per far ribellare la terra di Prato nel 1402", in *Archivio Storico Pratese*, X (Prato, 1931–2).

—— "Il Problema Portuale di Firenze dall' ultima lotta con Giangaleazzo Visconti alle prime trattative per l' acquisto di Pisa, 1402–5", in *RSAT* II (Firenze, 1930).

PICOTTI, G. B. "Qualche Osservazione sui caratteri delle Signorie Italiane", in *RSI* XLIII (NS IV, 1926).

PIERI, PIERO. *La Crisi militare italiana nel Rinascimento nelle sue relazioni con la crisi politica ed economica* (Napoli, 1934).

POGGIALI, CRISTOFORO. *Memorie storiche di Piacenza*, vols. VI and VII (Piacenza, 1759).

POSTINGER, C. T. "Documenti in Volgare Trentino della fine del Trecento relativi alla Cronaca delle Giudicarie; Lotte fra gli Arco, i Lodroni, i Campo ed il Vescovo di Trento", in *AAA* 3, VII (Rovereto, 1901).

PROFESSIONE, ALFONSO. *Siena e le Compagne di Ventura nella seconda metà del secolo XIV* (Civitanova Marche, 1898).

RADO, ANTONIO. *Maso degli Albizi e il partito oligarchico in Firenze dal* 1382 *al* 1393; *dalla Repubblica Fiorentina alla Signoria Medicea* (Firenze, 1926).

RAMBALDI, P. L. "Stefano III, Duca di Baviera, al servizio della Lega contro Giangaleazzo Visconti, 1390", in *ASL* xxviii, 1 (1901).

RAYNALDO, ODORICO. *Annales Ecclesiastici*, vol. viii (Lucae, 1752).

RIBOLDI, EZIO, E GIOVANNI SEREGNI. "I Documenti Viscontei nel Museo Civico di Pavia", in *ASL* xxxiii, 1 (1906).

RIEZLER, SIGMUND. *Geschichte Baierns*, Band iii (Gotha, 1889).

RIGHI, ALESSANDRO. "L' Amnistia del 1392 concessa ai Veronesi da Giangaleazzo Visconti", in *ASL* xxxiv, 1 (1907).

RIVA, GIUSEPPE. "I Documenti Viscontei dal 1279 al 1402 nei Regi Archivi di Stato in Pisa, Siena e Firenze &c.", in *ASL* xxvii, 1 (1900).

ROMANELLI, PIER BARTOLO. *La Calata di Giovanni III d'Armagnac in Italia e la disfatta di Alessandria* (Alessandria, 1924, and in the *Rivista di Alessandria* for that year).

ROMANO, GIACINTO. "Una Bolla dell' Antipapa Clemente VII relativa alla fondazione della Certosa di Pavia", in *BSP* ii (1902).

—— "Giangaleazzo Visconti Avvelenatore; un Episodio della spedizione Italiana di Ruperto di Baviera", in *ASL* xxi, 1 (1894).

—— "Giangaleazzo Visconti e gli Eredi di Bernabò", in *ASL* xviii (1891).

—— "Un Giudizio di A. Biglia sulla formazione storica dei Visconti e del Ducato di Milano", in *BSP* xv (1915).

—— "La Guerra tra i Visconti e la Chiesa, 1360–1376", in *BSP* iii (1903).

—— "Un Matrimonio alla corte de' Visconti", in *ASL* xviii (1891).

—— *Il Matrimonio di Valentina Visconti e la Casa di Savoia; risposta a J. Camus* (Messina, 1899).

—— "Niccolò Spinelli da Giovinazzo; diplomatico del secolo XIV", in *ASN* xxvi (1901).

—— "Di una Nuova Ipotesi sulla morte e sulla sepultura di Giangaleazzo Visconti", in *ASI* 5, xx (1897).

—— "Nuovi Documenti Viscontei tratti dall' Archivio Notarile di Pavia", and "La Cartella del Notaio C. Cristiano nell' Archivio di Pavia", in *ASL* xvi (1889).

—— "Intorno all' Origine della Contea di Vertus", in *Rendiconti del R. Istituto Lombardo*, 2, xxx (1897).

—— "Il Primo Matrimonio di Lucia Visconti e la rovina di Bernabò", in *ASL* xx (1893).

—— "Sussidio di guerra per l' invasione di Giacomo d'Armagnac nel 1391", in *BSP* ii (1902).

ROMANO, GIACINTO. "A proposito di un Testamento di Giangaleazzo Visconti", in *BSP* XVII (1917).

—— "Tornandoci sopra; a proposito di alcuni recenti studi sul matrimonio di Valentina Visconti col Duca di Touraine", in *ASL* XXIX, 1 (1902).

—— "Valentina Visconti e il suo matrimonio con Luigi di Turaine", in *ASL* XXV, 2 (1898).

—— "I Visconti e la Sicilia", in *ASL* XXIII, 1 (1896).

ROSSI, LUIGI. "Gli Eustachi di Pavia e la flotta Viscontea e Sforzesca nel secolo XV", in *BSP* XIV (1914).

ROSSI, VITTORIO. "Un Grammatico Cremonese a Pavia sulla prima età del Rinascimento", in *BSP* I (1901).

ROVELLI, GIUSEPPE. *Storia di Como*, parte III, tomo 1 (Como, 1802).

SABBADINI, REMIGIO. *Giovanni da Ravenna*, 1343–1408; being *Studi Umanistici*, no. 1 (Como, 1924).

ST PIERRE, E. DE. "Cenno storico intorno ad Amedeo VI", in *AAT* XXXVI (1900–1).

SALVEMINI, STEFANO. *I Balestrieri nel Comune di Firenze* (Firenze, 1905).

SALZER, ERNST. "Über die Anfänge der Signorie in Oberitalien", published by Ebering in *Historische Studien*, Heft 14 (Berlin, 1900).

SANDRI, GINO. "Domenico da Firenze, il ponte di Valleggio e la deviazione del Mincio, 1393–4", in *Atti dell' Accademia di agricoltura, scienze e lettere di Verona*, 5 XVI (1938).

SANGIULIANI, ANTONIO CAVAGNA. *L' Agro Vogherese; Memorie sparse di Storia Patria*, vol. I (Casorate Primo, 1890).

SANT' AMBROGIO, DIEGO. "Colonna votiva con tabernacoletto", in *ASL* XIX (1892).

SCARABELLI, LUCIANO. "Paralipomeni di Storia Piemontese dall' anno 1285 al 1617", in *ASI* XIII (1847).

SCARAMELLA, GINO. "La Dominazione Viscontea in Pisa, 1399–1405", in *SS* III (1894).

—— "Nuove Ricerche sulla Dominazione Viscontea in Pisa", in *BSP* XIV (1914).

—— *I Visconti nella guerra di Chioggia* (Catania, 1898).

SCHMIDT, OTTO. "Die Visconti und ihre Bibliothek zu Pavia", in *Zeitschrift für Geschichte und Politik*, V (1888).

SCHULTE, ALOYS. *Geschichte des mittelalterlichen Handels und Verkehrs zwischen Westdeutschland und Italien mit Ausschluss von Venedig*, 2 vols. (Leipzig, 1900).

SEGRE, ARTURO. "I Conti di Savoia e lo Scisma d' Occidente", in *AAT* 2, XLII (1906).

SEREGNI, GIOVANNI. "Un Disegno federale di Bernabò Visconti, 1380–1", in *ASL* XXXVIII, 2 (1911).

—— "I Documenti Viscontei dal 1279 al 1402 nel R. Archivio di Stato in Lucca", in *ASL* XXVI, 1 (1899).

—— "Documenti Viscontei negli Archivi di Vercelli", in *ASL* XXX, 1 (1903).

—— "Il Primo Fidanzamento di Valentina Visconti", in *Rivista delle Scienze Storiche*, I, 2 (1903).

SFORZA, GIOVANNI. *Storia di Pontremoli dalle Origini al* 1500 (Firenze, 1904).

SICKEL, THEODOR. "Das Vicariat der Visconti", in *Sitzungsberichte der Kaiserlichen Akademie der Wissenschaften, Philosophisch-Historische Classe*, XXX Band, Heft 1 (Wien, 1859).

SILVA, PIETRO. "Il Governo di Pietro Gambacorta in Pisa e le sue relazioni col resto di Toscana e coi Visconti", published in the *Annali della R. Scuola Normale Superiore di Pisa; Filosofia e Filologia*, vol. XXIII (Pisa, 1912).

—— "Ordinamento interno e contrasti politici e sociali in Pisa sotto il Dominio Visconteo", in *SS* XXI (NS III, 1913).

SIMEONI, LUIGI. "Due Documenti sul sacco di Verona del 1390", in *ASL* XXXIII, 2 (1906).

SIMONSFELD, H. "Beiträge zur Bayerischen und Münchener Geschichte", in *Sitzungsberichte der Königlich-Bayerischen Akademie der Wissenschaften, Philosophisch-philologische und historische Classe* (München, 1896).

TAGLIABUE, M. "La Politica finanziaria nel governo di Giangaleazzo Visconti", in *BSP* XV (1915).

THALLOCZY, LAJOS. *Mantovai Követjárás Budán*, 1395, published by the Magyar Tudományos Akadémia, in *Ertekezések a Történeti Tudományok Köréböl*, Köt. 20, sz. 4 (Budapest, 1905).

TOESCA, PIETRO. "Ancora della Pittura e della Miniatura in Lombardia nei secoli XIV e XV", in *l' Arte* XVI (1913).

—— "Michelino da Besozzo e Giovannino de' Grassi; ricerche sull' antica Pittura Lombarda", in *l' Arte*, VIII (1905).

—— *La Pittura e la Miniatura nella Lombardia dai più antichi monumenti alla metà del Quattrocento* (Milano, 1912).

TONINI, LUIGI. *La Storia civile e sacra Riminese*, vol. IV (Rimini, 1880).

VALENTINI, ANDREA. "Gli Statuti di Brescia dei secoli XII al XV", in *NAV* XV (1898).

VALERI, NINO. "L'Eredità di Giangaleazzo Visconti", in the *Sèguito alla Biblioteca della Società Storica Subalpina*, vol. CLXVIII (Torino, 1938).

VALERI, NINO. *Guelfi e Ghibellini in Val Padana all' inizio del Ducato di Giovanni Maria Visconti* (Torino, 1935, and in *BSBS* XXXVII, of the same year).

—— "L' Insegnamento di Giangaleazzo e i consigli al Principe di Carlo Malatesta", in *BSBS* XXXVI (1934).

—— "Lo Stato Visconteo alla morte di Giangaleazzo", in *NRS* XIX (1935).

VALOIS, NOËL. *La France et le grand Schisme d'Occident*, 4 vols. (Paris, 1896–1902).

VALSECCHI, FRANCO. *L' Assolutismo illuminato in Austria e in Lombardia;* vol. II, Lombardia; parte 1, politica interna (Bologna, 1934).

VERCI, GIAMBATTISTA. *Storia della Marca Trivigiana e Veronese*, vols. XVI–XVIII (Venezia, 1790).

VERGA, ETTORE. "Un Condanna a morte contro Carlo Visconti figlio di Bernabò", in *ASL* XXIX, 1 (1902).

—— "Le Sentenze criminali dei Podestà Milanesi, 1385–1419", in *ASL* XXVIII, 2 (1901).

VISCONTI, ALESSANDRO. "La Politica Unitaria Italiana dei Visconti nei secoli XIV e XV", in the *Atti del Primo Congresso Storico Lombardo in* 1936 (Milano, 1937).

—— *Storia di Milano* (Milano, 1937).

VOINOVITCH, LOUIS DE. "Les Angevins à Raguse", in *RQH* XCIII–XCIV (1913).

VOLTA, ZANINO. "L' Età, l' emancipazione e la patria di Giangaleazzo Visconti", in *ASL* XVI (1889).

WENCK, KARL. "Eine Mailändisch-thüringische Heiratsgeschichte aus der Zeit König Wenzels", in *Neues Archiv für sächsische Geschichte und Alterthumskunde*, XVI (Dresden, 1895).

WINCKELMANN, ALFRED. *Der Romzug Ruprechts von der Pfalz* (Innsbruck, 1892).

ZANETTI, GINEVRA. "La 'Mediolanum' medioevale nella difesa delle 'italice libertates'", in *Atti del Primo Congresso Storico Lombardo in* 1936 (Milano, 1937).

ZERBI, LUIGI. *I Visconti di Milano e la Signoria di Lucca* (Como, 1894).

INDEX

The references under each heading have been arranged as far as possible in chronological order

("GG" stands for Giangaleazzo throughout)

Abbiategrasso, 177

Adda, R., 2, 7, 34, 126

Adige, R., 143, 165, 169

Administration, Chapter v; of the Visconti, 311–13; of GG, 313–15, 316–19; 1378–85, 25–6; in the Mark of Treviso, 82; 1390–2, 137–42; 1392–6, 177–9; during the Mantuan war, 226–9; 1401–2, 296; and v. Finance

Adorno, Antoniotto, Doge of Genoa, 62 note, 97; and the war of 1390–2, 128–9, 133; buys Serravalle, 133; and the conference of Genoa, 135–6, 349; driven from Genoa, 1392, 148–9, 354, 150; Doge, 1394–6, 157

"Adria, Kingdom of", 155–9, 315

Adriatic Sea, 69, 72–3, 304

Aegean Sea, 72–3

Agnelli, Pisan family, at GG's court, 182

Agriculture, GG's encouragement of, 53, 228

Albania, 72

Albergotti, Lodovico, Florentine envoy to GG, 1389, 102–4; 1394, 166 note; instructions of, 1396, 357–61

Albert III, Duke of Austria, 74, 76, 80–1

Alberti, Florentine family, 84

Albizzi, Maso degli, party leader in Florence, 84; and fall of Gambacorta, 1392, 152; power in Florence, 1393, 162; in Paris, 1396, 204; position in Florence, 1397–8, 230

Albornoz, Cardinal Egidio, 7

Aldighieri, Gherardo, 213 note

Alençon, Cardinal Philip of, Patriarch of Aquileia, 69

Alessandria, 13; revolt of, 1392, 140; battle of, 1391, 131–2, 135, 138, 141, 203

— Guglielmino da, 356

Alidosi, lords of Imola, 88; allies of Florence, 97, 144

— Lodovico, 233, 291

Alpi di Podere, 289

Alps, the, 2, 6, 45, 61, 69, 74, 80–1, 169, 170–1, 262, 281, 307, 319, 322

Altoviti, Palmieri, Florentine envoy to GG, 1396, instructions of, 357–61

Amadeus VI, Count of Savoy, and Galeazzo Visconti, 8–9, 13; and GG, 15–16, 17, 18–19; death, 1383, 20

Amadeus VII, Count of Savoy, and GG, 20–1, 34, 61–3, 67; and Valentina's betrothal, 330–1; and Florence, 1389, 345; and the war of 1390–1, 118–19, 129, 322–3

Amadeus VIII, Count of Savoy, 323, 325–7; and GG, 1398, 214, 220; and Rupert of Bavaria, 1401, 266

Amadeus, titular Prince of Achaia and Morea, lord of Piedmont, 67–8, 322–7; and GG, 1389–90, 105, 119; and Montferrat, 1397, 212

"Amigo", the, observer at GG's court, 127, 128–9, 145

Anagni, election of, 1378, 15

Ancona, Mark of, 86, 343, 113, 332, 355

Angera, County of, bestowed on GG, 176, 190, 267

Angevins, v. Anjou

Anguissola, family of Piacenza, 300

Anjou, House of, the Angevins (and v. Louis I and II, Dukes of Anjou), and Naples, 1–2; lands in Piedmont and Provence, 17, 19–20, 62; Visconti marriage proposals, 20, 24–5, 27, 30–1, 63, 330; claims on Naples, 64, 72, 87–8, 117, 154, 188, 191; driven from the *Regno*, 260

406 *INDEX*

Stradella, 24
Suabia, 170
Superba, the, *v.* Genoa
Switzerland, the Swiss, 26, 300; and
    v. Chur, Sargans

Talomei, Dego, 366
Taxation, *v.* Camera
Teodoro II, Marquis of Montferrat,
    18, 21, 62, 75, 119; in Pied-
    montese politics, 1391–1402,
    323–7, 212; after GG's death,
    300
Terzo, Ottobuon, of Parma, Con-
    dottiere, 199; in Umbria, 1399–
    1400, 251–2, 368, 257; in 1401,
    264, 269, 274 note; after GG's
    death, 300
Thuringia, House of, 262
Ticino, R., 2, 220, 326
Tivoli, 106 note
Todi, 250
Tomacelli, Giovanni, 371
Toppole, 359, 366
Tornielli, family of Novara, 300
— Antoniolo, agent of GG, 148
Torre, 76
Tortona, 13
Touraine, Duke of, *v.* Louis of
    Valois
Treasury, *v.* Camera
Trent, the *Trentino*, Riviera di
    Trento, Val di Trento, 74; and
    GG, 119, 170; and the Mantuan
    war, 213, 220; Rupert of Bavaria
    at, 270; after GG's death, 300;
    and *v.* George, Bishop of
Treviso, 69, 79, 81, 82
— Mark of, 6; and GG, 125, 157,
    160, 172; after GG's death, 299
Trezzo, 34
Trinità, 67
Turchetto, Francesco, 338
Turin, 19, 62, 129 note, 322, 325–6
— Peace of, 1381, 18, 20, 28, 35, 72
Turks, the, in the Balkans, 72–3, 117;
    and battle of Nicopolis, 212, 232;
    and Byzantine Empire, 183 note
Tuscany (and *v.* Florence, Perugia,
    Pisa, Siena), 1, 6, 27–30, 59,
    61, 66, 68; politics of, 1385–90,

84–7, 89–97, 99–103, 343, 105–6,
    108–12, 115, 116; and the War
    of 1390–2, 121–2, 123, 132–4,
    347, 349–50, 136; in 1392, 142,
    147–8, 150, 152–3; GG and,
    1392–6, 159–61, 163–5, 170,
    192, 194, 202, 207; and the
    Mantuan war, 209–10, 216, 217–
    19, 229, 231, 223, 232; and GG,
    1398–1400, 234, 238, 239, 244–6,
    251–2, 253, 255; and Peace of
    Venice, 256–7, 258, 368–9; and
    GG, 1402, 281–2, 285, 287, 290,
    293; after GG's death, 299; in
    GG's policy, 303, 304–5, 307,
    310, 314
Tyrol, 170, 294

Ubaldi, Ubaldo, of Perugia, jurist,
    183
Ubaldini, family of Tuscany, 289
— Giovanni d' Azzo degli, Con-
    dottiere, 74, 75; in Romagna,
    1387–8, 93, 335; in GG's service,
    1389–90, 106, 335–6, 112–13,
    121–2, 123
Ubertini, Counts of, 244, 361, 367
Udine, 69, 71, 147; and *v.* Friuli
Ufficio delle bollette, in GG's
    dominions, 52
Umbria, 85; and GG, 30, 88, 89,
    93–4, 106, 112, 142, 147, 160–1,
    207–8, 234, 251–2, 257; and
    Boniface IX, 259, 261, 265, 282;
    after GG's death, 300; in GG's
    policy, 305; and *v.* Perugia
Unterwalden, Canton of, 300
Urban VI, Pope, 15, 16, 20; and
    GG's marriage, 24, 329; and
    GG, 1386, 64–6; and Naples,
    88; in Tuscany, 89–90; and GG,
    1387–8, 93–4, 97; death of, 116;
    and GG's title, 171
Urbino, 355; and *v.* Montefeltro
Uri, Canton of, 300
Uzzano, Niccolò, Florentine envoy
    to Venice, 1400, instructions
    of, 365–70

Valais, the, 20, 118, 323
Valcamonica, the, 295

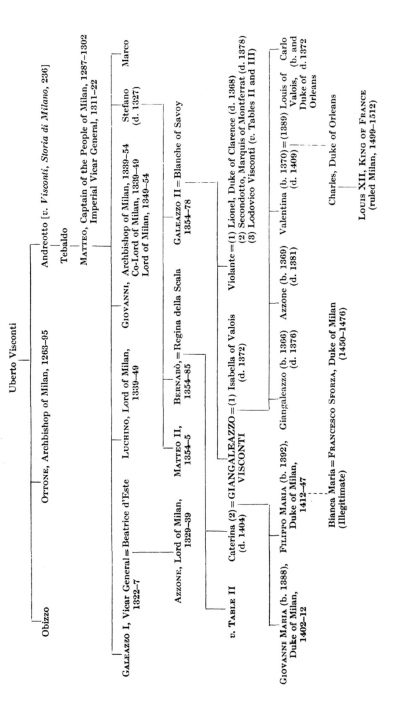

TABLE I. THE VISCONTI

Uberto Visconti

Obizzo

Ottone, Archbishop of Milan, 1263–95

Andreotto [v. Visconti, Storia di Milano, 236]

Tebaldo

Matteo, Captain of the People of Milan, 1287–1302
Imperial Vicar General, 1311–22

Galeazzo I, Vicar General = Beatrice d'Este
1822–7

Azzone, Lord of Milan,
1329–39

Luchino, Lord of Milan,
1339–49

Matteo II,
1354–5

Giovanni, Archbishop of Milan, 1339–54
Co-Lord of Milan, 1339–49
Lord of Milan, 1349–54

Stefano
(d. 1327)

Marco

Bernabò, = Regina della Scala
1354–85

Galeazzo II = Blanche of Savoy
1354–78

v. Table II

Caterina (2) = Giangaleazzo = (1) Isabella of Valois
(d. 1404)   Visconti   (d. 1372)

Violante = (1) Lionel, Duke of Clarence (d. 1368)
            (2) Secondotto, Marquis of Montferrat (d. 1378)
            (3) Lodovico Visconti (v. Tables II and III)

Giangaleazzo (b. 1366)
(d. 1876)

Azzone (b. 1369)
(d. 1881)

Valentina (b. 1370) = (1389) Louis of   Carlo
(d. 1409)   Valois,   (b. and
                               Duke of   d. 1872
                               Orleans

Giovanni Maria (b. 1388),
Duke of Milan,
1402–12

Filippo Maria (b. 1892),
Duke of Milan,
1412–47

Bianca Maria = Francesco Sforza, Duke of Milan
(Illegitimate)   (1450–1476)

Charles, Duke of Orleans

Louis XII, King of France
(ruled Milan, 1499–1512)

TABLE II. THE DESCENDANTS OF BERNABÒ VISCONTI

BERNABÒ VISCONTI = Regina della Scala

- Marco = Elizabeth of Bavaria, m. 1367, d. 1382
  - Anna
- Lodovico = Violante Visconti, his cousin (v. Tables I and III), m. 1380, d. 1404 (in prison)
  - Giovanni
- Carlo = Beatrice of Armagnac, m. 1382, d. 1404
  - Gianpiccinino
  - Carlo
- Taddea = Stephen III, Duke of Bavaria, m. 1369, d. 1381
  - Lewis of Bavaria
  - Isabella = Charles VI, King of France
- Verde = Leopold III, Duke of Austria, m. 1366
  - Ernest I, Duke of Austria
  - Emperor Frederick III
  - The Hapsburgs
- Caterina = Giangaleazzo Visconti (v. Table I)

- Antonia = Everard, Count of Wurtemberg, m. 1380
- Valentina = Peter, King of Cyprus, m. 1378, d. 1393
- Agnese = Francesco Gonzaga, Lord of Mantua, m. 1375, d. 1390
- Mastino, d. 1405
- Rodolfo, d. 1389 (in prison)
- Anglesia

- Maddalena = Frederick, Duke of Bavaria, m. 1382, d. 1404
- Elisabetta = Ernest, Duke of Bavaria, m. 1396, d. 1432
- Lucia = Edmund Holland, Duke of Kent, m. 1407

TABLE III. THE MARRIAGE PROPOSALS OF 1380–82

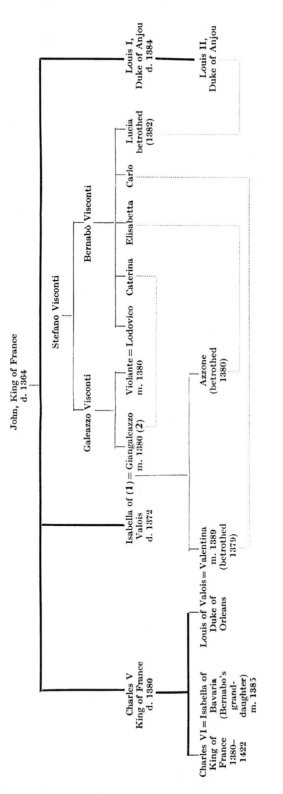